Teaching
Modern Latin
American Poetries

Teaching Modern Latin American Poetries

Edited by
Jill S. Kuhnheim
and Melanie Nicholson

Modern Language Association of America
New York   2019

MLA and the MODERN LANGUAGE ASSOCIATION are trademarks owned
by the Modern Language Association of America. For information about obtain-
ing permission to reprint material from MLA book publications, send your request
by mail (see address below) or e-mail (permissions@mla.org).

Library of Congress Cataloging-in-Publication Data

Names: Kuhnheim, Jill S., editor. | Nicholson, Melanie, 1955– editor.
Title: Teaching modern Latin American poetries / edited by Jill S. Kuhnheim,
    Melanie Nicholson.
Description: New York : Modern Language Association of America, 2019. | Series:
    Options for teaching, 10792562 ; 48 | Includes bibliographical references. |
    Summary: "Offers techniques for teaching modern Latin American poetry in
    college courses, including considerations of teaching the *silva*, human rights,
    poetry in indigenous languages, community-based learning, lesser-known
    contemporary poetry, Afro-descendant poetry, performance, the long poem,
    and queer theory. Provides classroom exercises and assignments"—Provided
    by publisher.
Identifiers: LCCN 2019026078 (print) | LCCN 2019026079 (ebook) | ISBN
    9781603294669 (cloth) | ISBN 9781603294096 (paperback) | ISBN
    9781603294102 (EPUB) | ISBN 9781603294119 (Kindle edition)
Subjects: LCSH: Latin American poetry—20th century—Study and teaching
    (Higher)—United States. | Latin American poetry—21st century—Study and
    teaching (Higher)—United States.
Classification: LCC PQ7082.P7 T43 2019 (print) | LCC PQ7082.P7 (ebook) |
    DDC 861.09/98071—dc23
LC record available at https://lccn.loc.gov/2019026078
LC ebook record available at https://lccn.loc.gov/2019026079

Options for Teaching 48
ISSN 1079-2562

Cover illustration of the print and electronic editions: *Maracaiola* © Beatriz
Milhazes. Image courtesy of James Cohan, New York.

Published by The Modern Language Association of America
85 Broad Street, suite 500, New York, New York 10004-2434
www.mla.org

Contents

Part III: Poetic Contexts and
     the Idea of Latin America

Jill S. Kuhnheim

Introduction:
Teaching the Language of Poetry

Poetry offers exciting pedagogical possibilities in the early twenty-first century. A language-based genre that sets in motion alternative ways of producing meaning, poetry enters into dialogue with literary traditions formed around the myriad relations of sound and sense. In its written forms, poetry requires its audience to slow down and utilize specific reading and analytic skills that may not be developed in students who live in contemporary environments that are increasingly dominated by the visual and that privilege the speed of information exchange. Teaching poetry offers these students the opportunity to hone their reading and listening skills. Textual experiences that may begin with close readings may also expand through the alternative modes of circulation for poetry available today—electronic media and performance reawaken links to orality and the visual arts, and may initiate interartistic dialogues. In response to the notion that poetry is too literary, too difficult, or too unfamiliar to teach in a variety of contexts, this book offers college-level instructors strategies and new approaches to the genre that will reinvigorate and expand their teaching repertoires. The essays in this volume remind us, furthermore, that poetry may startle readers into illuminations about a range of topics, combining social and aesthetic perspectives. Rather than serving as a basic guide

1

to teaching poetry in a Latin American context, this collection of essays presents fresh possibilities for including a range of Latin American authors, artists, works, and topics in literature and language courses as well as in other disciplines. Many of these essays demonstrate how poetry from Latin America might be incorporated into and expand the scope of classes in African American Studies or Indigenous Studies (broadening a conventional definition of the Americas in both cases), in Latin American Studies, and even in history or anthropology in some cases.

This is the first pedagogically focused book on poetry that uses Latin American poetry as its corpus. In the past, instructors compiling readings for survey classes turned frequently to critical essays by Octavio Paz and others on the canonical authors and movements of the early twentieth century, and to texts that deal with theoretical issues in the genre (Roman Jakobson, Yuri Lotman, Julia Kristeva, Isabel Paraíso, Carlos Bousoño, et al.). Rather than adapt materials from a North American context and apply them to examples from the South, this book features essays with a pedagogical emphasis on poetry written by scholars who are well versed in Latin American literary and cultural contexts.[1] (Its pedagogical approach also seeks to address an absence of creative writing courses as laboratories for developing poetic literacy in Spanish and romance language departments.) The essays can be read and used independently of one another, depending on the focus of the course or the interests of the instructor. Each chapter provides insights and suggestions for instructors who may be experienced in the field as well as for new teachers approaching some of this poetry for the first time.

Since "Latin America" is a heterogeneous region where perceptions of unity are most often produced from outside, it is inherently comparative and therefore invites comparative teaching approaches. While sharing certain social and cultural practices and historical roots, the region comprises very different countries whose residents may have little in common with others in the region, aside from elements of a common colonial past. By collecting essays under this broadly regional rubric, then, we are consciously constructing an academic object of study.[2] The linguistic, cultural, and economic legacies of the conquest have produced various Latin Americas and a growing number of discursive communities with ethnic, cultural, and linguistic differences (Campo 126). There has been much recent discussion about the term "Latin America," which does not usually include the three Guineas, Belize, or parts of the Caribbean not colonized by Spain or Portugal (Holloway 2–3). Brazilian historian Moniz Bandeira notes that the term "gained force when multilateral institutions adopted it after the Second World War" (qtd. in Perrone, *Brazil* 29), and Charles Perrone has also explored Brazil's changing relation to the concept of Latin America (139–41). In fact, Brazil has often been excluded or marginalized in the idea of Latin America and, as Walter Mignolo has recognized, there are others who do not identify in regional terms: "indigenous people are not necessarily 'Latin' and perhaps not entirely 'Americans' either" (*Idea* 115). Michel Gobat notes that the concept of Latin America has long been associated with whiteness and his historical perspective draws attention to "the transnational mobilization of an imperial concept—the Latin race" against the threat of external intervention (1348). The essays here address some of the area's breadth as they consider works from Mexico, Chile, Peru, Ecuador, Colombia, Cuba, Brazil, Argentina, Guatemala, Nicaragua, and Uruguay; furthermore, they take into account distinct indigenous linguistic groups within these national communities, such as the Kaqchikel Maya and Zapotec. Of course, there are many other national and cultural communities that are not represented here (Venezuela, Costa Rica, and Paraguay among them, along with myriad autochthonous voices). However, the topics in many of the essays—for example, Bridget Franco's contribution on experiential learning through poetry or Fernando Rosenberg's essay on teaching poetry and human rights—cross national and regional boundaries and can be applied to examples from other countries and communities.

The majority of the essays in this volume are geared toward courses taught in the language of poetic production, that is, Spanish or Portuguese. In fact, a great deal of the quality poetry produced in Latin America over the twentieth century has yet to appear in English translation. (Two relatively recent anthologies that do offer students a broad sampling of works in translation are Stephen Tapscott's *Twentieth-Century Latin American Poetry* and Cecilia Vicuña and Ernesto Livon-Grosman's and *Oxford Book of Latin American Poetry*). In the present volume, Melanie Nicholson's second essay discusses strategies for teaching Latin American poetry in translation to a primarily English-speaking group of undergraduates. Tiffany Creegan Miller and Clare Sullivan also confront the issue of reading indigenous poetries with students who are unfamiliar with the original languages. In these cases, the poetry in question is presented in translation into Spanish (typically by the poets themselves); in some cases, English versions are also available. Sullivan discusses strategies for a bilingual English-Spanish classroom in which the art of translation itself is both interrogated and practiced; in the process, students become increasingly aware of the phonic and formal qualities of poetry in Nahuatl or Quechua and problems inherent in cultural "translation" broadly defined.

Essays that consider poetry and film, music, or performance, whose topics also may extend to diverse societies, form another conversation within the volume. Pushing beyond the conventional parameters of Spanish American poetry, the essays here that deal with Brazilian and indigenous poetries extend bridges that will allow teachers to include more of these works in a variety of courses. While the idea of Latin America has undoubtedly moved beyond its physical boundaries through migration northward, for reasons of practicality we have limited the geographical and cultural range of this volume by not including Latino poetry from the United States or border literatures as possible topics. We encourage colleagues to develop another volume to explore this rich terrain.

While *Teaching Modern Latin American Poetries* is primarily concerned with works from the second half of the twentieth century and the first part of the twenty-first, it is important to recognize that this contemporary corpus has developed out of much older poetic traditions. Although numerous literary histories provide detailed accounts of the broad sweep of Latin American poetry (we refer the reader to the list of works cited), there is relatively little available material that brings us into the twenty-first century and that traces the connections between earlier manifestations and contemporary poetry. The present volume is dedicated to that task. Many teachers who cover Latin American poetry are most familiar with works and movements from the first half of the century. Our intent is to link new material to canonical authors and movements as one way of developing a fresh approach to the canon. Readers who wish to become familiar with the key moments and figures of Latin American poetry prior to the 1980s may begin with Melanie Nicholson's overview of Latin American poetry and Gwen Kirkpatrick's essay highlighting some of the aesthetic issues that will resonate throughout the twentieth century and into the twenty-first.

Poetry is an expansive genre. Many works from the second half of the twentieth century and from the early twenty-first demonstrate that the genre is not just the realm of a lettered elite, not a remote aesthetic; rather, in Alice Fulton's words, "poetry is about what happens now" (7). Defining a creation as a poem puts it in dialogue with literary tradition, but poetry may also tell us something new, in new ways. Our understanding of tradition may shift when we look back from recent practices, and this collection offers multiple ways for teachers to do this. Contemporary poetry often engages public culture and issues that affect students' lives now: it may communicate about experiences of racial, national, or gendered identities; immigration and exile; or it may offer auto-ethnographic self-portraits and form collective subjects or plural cultural identities. It may bring the past alive by addressing a history of colonization, imperialism, and racism through complex aesthetics that join European and autochthonous formal patterns and traditions of communication. Poets express these themes in beautiful, sonorous, rhythmic, colloquial, shocking, hallucinatory, or exploratory language. Each of these essays demonstrates that poetry does not live only in the classroom—it is an ongoing practice and a popular art form. Teaching more recent manifestations of poetry that often circulate in multimedia forms that include voice, music, and visual elements will create new readers, new audiences for the genre.

These essays also express the literary diversity of a region that extends from Mexico and the Caribbean through Central America's seven nations to the twelve South American countries.[3] Within this diversity it is possible to describe some trends, many with roots in earlier twentieth-century movements and styles, as Melanie Nicholson outlines in her overview in the first section of this book. While Jacobo Sefamí has noted the legacy of Octavio Paz in the craft and balance of recent Mexican poetry (882), there is a general turn away from poetry as a meditative and intellectual discourse, toward the recognition of a plurality of practices, themes, techniques, and poetics. Linked, perhaps, to the influence of the mid-century antipoetry of Nicanor Parra and to a desire to respond to societies marked by authoritarian regimes, some poets employ colloquialism, objectivism, direct speech, and frank observation in work that has been called new realism, hyperrealism, or "unadorned poetry," such as that of Bolivian Oscar Cerruto (García Pabón 154). In marked contrast to this is the artifice, metalinguistic complication, and radically altered syntax of the neobaroque, which highlights the discontinuity between things and their representations. In this style of poetry, which garnered attention in the 1980s, words are not transparent conveyors of meaning but elements of composition. Language is central to these poets who employ sound, images, and ideas to "question the logic of inherited European paradigms, effecting a cultural resignification that affirms the periphery as the center of this writing" (Kuhnheim, *Beyond the Page* 118). The neobaroque may be connected to a broader struggle to communicate, within and without artifice, locally and globally, at the start of the twenty-first century.

The availability of new spaces and means of circulation for poetry has resulted in the proliferation of multiartistic, genre-crossing approaches to poetry. Found in installations, recordings, and performance poetry (live and on the Web), this poetry draws on visuality and music, film and popular culture. Growing out of concrete poetry in Brazil and the ongoing interchange between the lyric and music, this poetry takes advantage of mass mediatization, cyber environments, and the ability to add sound and image to written work. An example of this, which could be linked to precursors such as Nicolás Guillén, is Argentine Washington Cucurto's use of cumbia rhythms to express the experience of a peripheral world that is denigrated by the dominant culture.

There has been increased attention to indigenous languages, pan-indigenous identities and themes, and poetry as a means of autochthonous expression and the preservation of minority languages. Contemporary poets often use classical themes (such as love and desire) and forms (such as the sonnet or the *silva*) to resist gender binaries and express erotic, non-normative sexual identities. Other traditional subjects, such as the natural world, appear reformulated in terms of ecology and environmental justice. All these developments offer teachers inventive ways of approaching the range of poetries circulating today in essays that dialogue with the literary traditions from which they arise.

The essays that follow are distributed among three sections: "Poetic Literacy and the Latin American Canon," "Orality, Multimedia, and Comparative Arts," and "Poetic Contexts and the Idea of Latin America." The first section, along with this introduction, creates a context for teaching Latin American poetry relative to issues of form and canon from the twentieth century, while the following sections develop approaches to more recent work that has grown out of these issues. The essays' appendixes include recommended online resources, supplementary materials, and sample course syllabi.

The first section of the book, "Poetic Literacy and the Latin American Canon," begins with Melanie Nicholson's aforementioned overview of Latin American poetry, "Looking Back to Look Beyond." Jonathan Mayhew's discussion of the basics of poetic literacy focuses on the familiar question of how to develop a critical apparatus or metalanguage to approach the genre while cultivating familiarity with how poetry works. Which comes first in teaching, technical detail and generic history, or poetry itself? Traditional pedagogical approaches have often overemphasized the formal characteristics of poetry; the essays in this collection both highlight the excitement that poetry can generate and articulate formal characteristics (such as metrics and figurative devices) within a broader understanding of the power of poetic language. The balance among these issues is teased out or elaborated in several later chapters—by Justin Read in his presentation of the *silva*, by Tamara Williams in her pedagogical fore-grounding of the long poem, and by Jacobo Sefamí in his staging of the neobaroque compared to the historical avant-gardes. Bringing the first section to a close, Melanie Nicholson addresses the broad question of how to teach poetry in a general education context, pointing to Latin American poetry as a particularly dynamic area of inquiry for students from diverse fields. She also points toward the next section of the book with methods that involve translation, creative responses, and performance to enhance students' engagement with the process of reading and responding to po-etry. While a comprehensive history of Latin American poetry is beyond the scope of this book, each of these essays positions contemporary poetry and practices with respect to the literary and social histories from which they arose.

Like these teachers, who situate contemporary Spanish American po-etry relative to its historical contexts, in the second section Charles Per-rone reads Brazilian poetry in terms of a number of national, cultural, and aesthetic imperatives linked to this section's topic, "Orality, Multimedia, and Comparative Arts." Gwen Kirkpatrick's essay, "Simultaneous Senses and Vital Dialogues in Latin American Poetry," extends some of the liter-ary history Nicholson presents through an examination of poetry as public practice at critical social and political moments in the twentieth century. These essays employ new angles to illuminate the legacies of avant-garde experimentation and to put poetry in dialogue with other arts such as mu-sic, painting, or theater. Bruce Dean Willis updates the classic link between oral poetry and song when he teaches colonial Spanish and Nahua com-positions to show their re-elaborations in contemporary music in Mexico. Historical relationships to sound and the visual have been transformed by access to digital media, which offers new possibilities for the circula-tion of poetry. When Eduardo Ledesma presents poetry as a "fully mul-tisensorial experience" created with vastly different media, he challenges students' understanding of the genre. Every essay in this section includes elements that situate poetry as a social form, for the genre is increasingly read and taught in terms of its presentation context, as the voice of a people or a record of a mind in action, rather than as a form or an object. One of the ways poetry and society may be approached is by positioning poetry in performance, and Jill Kuhnheim describes how performance alters conventional definitions of the poetic and embeds a piece in a particular context. While poetry may interact with multiple art forms, it is still created through reading, and Teresa Longo demonstrates interpretation as a creative practice through a series of exercises that invite students to cocreate, riffing on Neruda and diagnosing the cultural dissidence that translation entails. She and her students approach poetry's "work in the world" through creative interactions with local/global issues. All these essays demonstrate how divergent views of art and language and multiple aesthetics coexist in postmodern poetic contexts.

In the third section, "Poetic Contexts and the Idea of Latin America," Juan G. Ramos studies the idea of comparative arts to explore the specific production of Afro-Hispanic communities in Colombia and Ecuador. Ramos illuminates how these Afro-diasporic poets connect with contemporary musicians and how their work participates in contemporary discussions of coloniality/decoloniality and of racialized subjugation. María Olivera Williams discusses how readings of early-twentieth-century canonical female poets, namely Delmira Agustini, of Uruguay, and Gabriela Mistral, of Chile, have shifted when readers adopt concepts from gender, culture, and sexuality studies of the late twentieth and early twenty-first centuries, and uses specific examples of how these frameworks have changed her classroom. She also demonstrates how to incorporate visual and historical material to link changing roles for women with modernity. Fernando Rosenberg situates poetry in society by examining the relation between poetry and human rights, particularly in conjunction with the global rise in attention to human rights in the 1980s and '90s. He proposes that modern and contemporary poetry rejects the strict separation between interior and exterior, which makes the genre an effective means of deepening, localizing, and historicizing the idea of human rights relative to Latin American intellectual history. Some of the authors he teaches—such as José Emilio Pacheco, Raúl Zurita, Enrique Lihn, Néstor Perlongher, and Diana Bellesi—are well-known figures who investigate the relationship between the politics of resistance and the poetic word. In a similar vein, Silvia Tandeciarz's essay details the strategies she uses to combine students' skills in cultural criticism and translation with their capacity for invention, linguistic experimentation, and performance. Over the course of the semester students create an original body of work while at the same time deepening their understanding of Latin American poetic traditions, contexts of production, and modes of expression. The common point of departure derives from a simple question: Why write poetry? The class then considers how poets in Latin America have answered this question in the context of activism (*militancia*) and human rights. Tandeciarz argues that the risk, self-discipline, collaboration, openness, and sensitivity this type of creative work requires could make it transformative for students and instructors alike. With transnational and multigenerational audiences, poetry can reveal intriguing information about different cultural contexts in the process of interpretation. Bridget Franco integrates a community-based learning project in her Introduction to Textual Analysis course taught in Spanish at the undergraduate level. Franco proposes that this type of engagement alters the learners' academic and personal experience with poetry and enhances student participation so that the benefits of the additional time commitment outweigh the costs to the instructor (and to the students). These essays that trace the connections between poetry and late-twentieth-century Latin American political and intellectual practices, particularly in the arena of human rights, will be of interest to teachers in Latin American Studies programs whose primary focus is not literary.

This final section of the book expands the idea of Latin America in multiple ways. John Burns's essay departs from the work of Octavio Paz to reconsider the Mexican canon when he teaches Mexico's infrarrealist poets (who include Roberto Bolaño, better known now for his narrative). As an interactive pedagogic strategy, Burns asks his students to develop wikis on contemporary Mexican culture and history and connects them with living members of the infrarrealist movement. Drawing from Brazilian works, Steven Butterman proposes that the genre of poetry, much like queer theory itself, remains in motion, in process. He uses queer theory to argue that undefining or unlearning can at times be a far more productive pedagogical process than giving a name or a solution. Butterman's teaching practice foments productive tension and simultaneous liberation by embracing ambiguity while challenging his students to engage and analyze poetic texts with queer eyes.

Poetry is central to the expression of the autochthonous Americas, yet earlier poetic movements have often been approached critically through ethnopoetics rather than in aesthetic terms. Tiffany Creegan Miller observes that indigenous poetry is often situated as a precolonial forerunner of contemporary poetry. In response to this limited approach, she teaches recent Maya poets in order to demonstrate how these cultures are not stuck in the past but are transforming themselves and taking advantage of electronic media to build community and extend their audiences. The work of lesser-known poets such as Guatemala's Humberto Ak'abal (in Miller's essay) represents a fascinating intersection between Maya cultural expression and the defense of indigenous rights. Clare Sullivan also uses online resources to teach Zapotec poetry; she offers us ways to incorporate indigenous poetries into translation classes or to examine lyrical expression through the lens of the poets' self-translation into Spanish. Both these authors underscore how teaching indigenous literatures expands students' familiarity with diverse cultures, creating a window into radical cultural difference. Each author presents possibilities for teaching indigenous literatures if we do not know the native language, and offers ideas about how and where such literature might fit into diverse curricula. These essays may allow readers who do not have access to a regional indigenous language to broaden their perspectives in classes on literatures, cultures, poetry, and translation.

The essays in *Teaching Modern Latin American Poetries* highlight approaches that introduce students to the pleasures and challenges of contemporary poetries produced in the "other" America. Reading them will affirm what Joan Retallack and Juliana Spahr have proposed about teaching contemporary North American works:

> The most vital and intelligent contemporary poetries should not wait for decades to enter the consciousness of literature students. If, as we have claimed, poetry is the linguistic laboratory of the times in which one lives; if it is the live culture of our language practices as they are being pressured to acknowledge and articulate the constantly shifting residue of ongoing history; if to experience the poetries of one's times is to experience language on the edge of new reckonings—then students should have access to this work now. (6)

All these essays bear witness to the adaptability of poetry and to the variety of roles this genre plays in contemporary Latin American cultures. Bringing together multiple perspectives on poetry's myriad forms illuminates literature's ability to shift frameworks and to connect us to each other, as it connects interior life to exterior events.

Notes

1. Some recent books that deal with current approaches to the genre in a North American context are *Poetry and Pedagogy: The Challenge of the Contemporary* (Retallack and Spahr) and *Poetry and Cultural Studies: A Reader* (Damon and Livingston).

2. While no title is completely descriptive, "Latin American" has been most inclusive in its usage. "Iberoamerican" excludes the Mesoamerican, "Spanish American" does not include Brazil, and so on. The term is evidence of persistent coloniality in the region since it comes from Michel Chevalier's travel to Mexico in the nineteenth century and his desire to ally members of the Spanish and Portuguese colonies with the French (Holloway 4–5). Two recent works that further complicate the idea of Latin America are Gobat's "The Invention of Latin America: A Transnational History of Anti-Imperialism, Democracy, and Race" and Mauricio Tenorio-Trillo's *Latin America: The Allure and Power of an Idea*.

3. The 2012 edition of the *Princeton Encyclopedia of Poetry and Poetics* (Greene et al.) is the first to include distinct Latin American national (rather than regional) entries and an entry titled "Indigenous Poetries of the Americas," an indication of the ongoing recognition of diversity in the region.

Part I

Poetic Literacy and the Latin American Canon

Melanie Nicholson

Looking Back to Look Beyond: Latin American Poetry from Its Origins to the Present

Many instructors in the humanities and literary-minded students will have some acquaintance with the works of José Martí, Pablo Neruda, and Octavio Paz; they may even have studied other Latin American writers, such as Rubén Darío, César Vallejo, or Gabriela Mistral. We recognize, however, that some readers of this volume may be considering teaching Latin American poetry for the first time and so may benefit from a broad overview. Those with experience teaching Latin American poetry, on the other hand, may want to refamiliarize themselves with the history of the genre in this region, or to present an encapsulated version of it to their students in preparation for a unit on contemporary poetry. For all these readers we offer the following pages, which survey certain key moments and figures in the evolution of Latin American poetry from the colonial period to the late twentieth century. In most cases, we present poets, works, and aesthetic movements that form part of the Latin American literary canon; in other cases, however, we suggest additions to the canon based on recent scholarship. In contrast to the other essays in this volume, "Looking Back to Look Beyond" does not propose new readings of Latin American literary history or recommend innovative pedagogical practices; its purpose, rather, is to provide a roughly chronological overview in order to create a

15

context for the essays that follow, most of which question or expand the canon. The reader already conversant with this history may disregard the present essay and proceed with a clear conscience to explore the subsequent contributions. For those who desire more detail or in-depth analysis, we recommend the essays and monographs in Works Cited.

Foundations: Colonial- and Romantic-Era Poetry

As citizens of nations that were once colonies of Spain or Portugal, Latin American poets have sought modes of expression that correspond to their position as both insiders and outsiders vis-à-vis the tradition of the Western canon. This is why Gordon Brotherston observes that, "[i]n Latin American poetry, the metropolitan, or inherited European, tradition has persistently found itself in conflict with others distinct from it," in particular, the oral or written traditions of the indigenous cultures (7). Colonial poets writing in Spanish or Portuguese tended to adhere to a criollo paradigm; that is, they followed the formal and thematic models of the European Renaissance or baroque periods. There are certain notable exceptions, such as the heroic portrayal of the indigenous Araucanian enemy in Alonso de Ercilla's sixteenth-century Chilean epic *La araucana* (*The Araucaniad*); the inclusion of Nahuatl words and phrases, indigenous names, and Mexican flora and fauna in the popular verses of the seventeenth-century nun Sor Juana Inés de la Cruz; or the incorporation of indigenous and African elements in the work of the Brazilian baroque poet Gregório de Matos. But it was not until the early nineteenth century that poets began to integrate significant autochthonous elements into their verse. A prime example is Andrés Bello's "Silva a la agricultura de la Zona Tórrida" ("*Silva* to the Agriculture of the Torrid Zone"), which praises the yucca, the potato, and the *nopal* ("prickly pear cactus") as markers of a utopian South American landscape.

The wars of independence sparked a patriotic sentiment that coincided with the fervor of literary Romanticism, with its emphasis on subjectivity, autonomy, and the historical particularities of place. In the words of Stephen Tapscott, "As a set of tropes and forms and themes, Romanticism in Latin America introduced poets to the power of the local and to the vagaries of articulate public selfhood" (5). The Cuban-born writer José María Heredia, for example, in his 1820 poem "En el Teocalli de Cholula" ("On the Teocalli of Cholula") grapples with Mexico's complex and often violent past as he imagines its future, ripe with natural and human potential. Poets responding to the American landscape or to indigenous cultures remained faithful to the classical tradition, often pressing Spanish and Portuguese into Latinate syntax. But these poets stand at the threshold of a true literary appreciation of the potential of the New World, seen on its own terms.

For many inhabitants of the former Spanish and Portuguese colonies, the nineteenth century ushered in a mood of optimism regarding political sovereignty and even—as Simón Bolívar once dreamed—the possibility of a harmonious confederation of nation-states. José Joaquín de Olmedo's nine-hundred-line poem "La victoria de Junín: Canto a Bolívar" ("The Victory at Junín: Song for Bolívar,"), written in 1826 to commemorate the battle of Junín and Ayacucho, encapsulates this spirit of patriotic zeal and forward-looking continental vision. But, within a framework of gradual economic and political development, the nineteenth century played itself out in internal conflicts, petty but brutal dictatorships, and the consolidation of rigid social structures with the indigenous and mestizo (racially mixed) populations at the bottom.

Romantic values remained dominant across the arc of the century. National and regional literatures began to take shape, forming around ideologies of nationhood and cultural identity as distinct from European colonial models. These literatures feature the costumbrista (local color) verses written in countries such as Peru and Colombia, or the gaucho ballads from the pampas of the Southern Cone, the epitome of which is the epic poem *Martín Fierro* (1872 and 1879) by the Argentine José Hernández. With poetry and essays extolling the American landscape and native peoples, Antônio Gonçalves Dias led the first generation of Brazilian romantics, giving rise in his *Poemas americanos* ("American Poems") to an Indianist trend that would develop throughout the nineteenth century. This trend, known as *indigenismo* in Spanish, was characterized by sympathetic descriptions of the lifeways of the indigenous peoples from an exteriorized point of view. In sum, as Ernesto Livon-Grosman observes, the political struggle set in motion by the wars of independence from Spain and Brazil was "mirrored by a literary struggle to formulate a uniquely Latin American poetics" (xxxiv).

A Change in the Air: *Modernismo* and *Postmodernismo*

In Spanish America, a truly unique poetics would finally emerge in the last decade of the nineteenth century.[1] *Modernismo* (as distinct from both Brazilian *modernismo*, associated with the avant-garde, and Anglo-American modernism) provides a context for the present volume because it represents the first pancontinental movement, one that allowed readers and writers from Mexico to Argentina to share a common aesthetic. Furthermore, *modernismo* marks the first occurrence of reverse influence, as poets in Spain modeled their work after poets from Spanish America. With the Nicaraguan writer and cultural ambassador Rubén Darío as its leader, this movement drew initial inspiration from French fin-de-siècle Parnassianism (emphasizing the beauty of form) and Symbolism (emphasizing melodic sounds, a sense of mystery, and a thematics of decadence). The worn-out forms of late Romantic versification gave way to a new musicality, a flexibility of meter and rhyme, and a cosmopolitan flavor. In response to the pseudoscientific attitudes shaped by positivism and to the increasing industrialization and urbanization of the republics, early *modernista* poetry and prose presented an aesthetic vision that removed the poet—and by extension the reader—from the hard realities of everyday life.

The writers generally associated with the first phase of Spanish American *modernismo*—including, in addition to Darío, José Martí, and Julián del Casal in Cuba, Ricardo Jaimes Freyre in Bolivia, and Salvador Díaz Mirón in Mexico, among others—placed a high value on lyrical beauty, sometimes lapsing into preciosity. It was in the second phase, which was roughly coincident with the turn of the twentieth century, that the underlying tensions of Latin American political and cultural realities emerged, changing the tenor of much *modernista* poetry. Darío's often anthologized poem "Lo fatal" ("Fatality"), from his 1905 collection *Cantos de vida y esperanza* (*Songs of Life and Hope* 230), presents the reader with a melancholic reflection on the pain of living as a conscious self. In contrast, his free-verse oratorical poem "A Roosevelt" ("To Roosevelt"; 84–87), from the same collection, pronounces a forthright critique of North American imperialism alongside an affirmation of the enduring spiritual and cultural values of Latin America. Taken together, these poems point to the breadth and versatility of the second phase of Spanish American modernism.

Accompanying Darío on the uncertain road out of *modernismo* were two iconoclastic figures who, in the words of Gwen Kirkpatrick, prefigured "the dissonant trend in Spanish American poetry" of the twentieth century: Leopoldo Lugones, of Argentina, and Julio Herrera y Reissig, of Uruguay (*Dissonant Legacy* 1). Both poets, argues Kirkpatrick, "exaggerate and then naturalize the inherited conventions of European writing, and by doing so they change the very linguistic and ideological support base of its transmission" (2). By giving primacy of place to the urban middle class, by introducing ruptures with conventional logic and syntax, and by shifting and fragmenting the position of the lyrical speaker, Lugones and Herrera y Reissig point toward the even greater ruptures that will characterize the avant-garde. The end of Spanish American *modernismo* as a recognizable movement coincides with the death of Darío in 1916 and the advent of the First World War.

Chronologically parallel to the sui generis work of Lugones and Herrera y Reissig, a number of poetic trends generalized under the rubric of *postmodernismo* marked a turn toward personal conscience and questions of gender, race, and class. Perhaps the most significant trend of this poetry of transition, as Mike González and David Treece observe, was a voice that "struggled to make itself heard from within a double oppression," that of women in a peripheral society (34). Uruguay's Delmira Agustini, while she adhered to the rhetorical refinement of early *modernismo*, wrote frankly erotic verses that broke the barriers of bourgeois *buen gusto* ("good taste") and lyricized "the autonomous energy of female consciousness" (Tapscott 63). The Salvadoran poet Claudia Lars, whose work has been little studied or taught, contemplated her experiences as a woman with precise, limpid images and evocative understatement. The often anthologized Argentine poet Alfonsina Storni addressed issues of gender imbalance and bourgeois rigidity with a sharp intelligence and sometimes bitter irony, and her later writing moved stylistically into the territory of the avant-garde. The work of Gabriela Mistral, a Chilean poet, teacher, and diplomat who became Latin America's first winner of the Nobel Prize for Literature in 1945, is often reductively read through an autobiographical lens that focuses on her provincialism and her defense of the dispossessed; recently this picture has expanded to include her lesbian identity. In fact, Mistral's work is tonally complex, and the surface placidity of her poems often masks a sense of rage or despair. In short, these and other women writers grouped amorphously in the *postmodernista* period introduced a sense of poetic adventure within a generally conventional formalism, a verbal directness, a complex sense of irony, and a note of protest and defiance, all qualities that would inform Latin American poetry for years to come.

Further Openings: The Latin American Avant-Garde

In the third decade of the twentieth century, Latin American poetry underwent changes that critics often refer to as ruptures with tradition. Experimental modes took hold, poetry assumed a more transnational and cosmopolitan character, and individual voices from underrepresented groups—including women, Afro-descendants, and indigenous peoples—began to make themselves heard. Chronologically overlapping the *post-modernistas*, but vastly divergent in aesthetic principles and practices, the poets of the avant-garde in both Spanish America and Brazil attacked traditional poetry on numerous fronts. Rather than hold beauty as an ideal, they embraced aesthetic complexity. The sonorous syllabic verse was replaced with stammering, disquieting rhythms, and the communication of meaning gave way to the immediate linguistic or imagistic experience of the reader. Far more than a change in literary sensibilities, however, the avant-garde in Latin America also represented cultural responses to paradigm shifts in Western thought and lived experience, taking account of Freud and Einstein, the devastation of the First World War, and the rapid modernization and consequent displacement of people and ways of life, particularly in the case of marginalized populations.

The Colombian poet and critic Juan Gustavo Cobo Borda has referred to the *vanguardia* as "ese desorden saludable que nos liberó de tantas constricciones" 'that healthy disorder that freed us from so many constrictions' (39). As numerous critics have noted, it is impossible to treat the Latin American avant-garde as a single cohesive movement. Nor can we conflate the European avant-garde with the Spanish American *vanguardia* or the Brazilian form of vanguardism known as *modernismo* (discussed below). And, while we are primarily concerned here with poets and poetry, we duly note Vicky Unruh's observation that the Latin American avant-garde "may best be understood . . . as a multifaceted cultural activity, manifested in a variety of creative endeavors and events and seeking to challenge and redefine the nature and purpose of art" (*Latin American Vanguards* 2). Unruh makes the additional point that the Latin American avant-gardes were simultaneously international and autochthonous, absorbing influences from abroad but orienting them toward their own cultural realities and needs (10).

Reflecting the increasing ubiquity of film, as well as the influence of the surrealist notion of illogical juxtapositions, avant-garde poets placed a high value on the unusual or striking image. For Spanish American letters, this image-laden poetry first took the form of *ultraísmo* ("Ultraism"), a movement that was born in Spain but flourished—briefly—in Argentina, thanks largely to the efforts of Jorge Luis Borges. As Unruh, Beret Strong, and others have convincingly shown, the Latin American *vanguardias*, emerging under historical circumstances quite distinct from those of the European avant-gardes, adhered to relatively conservative modes of expres-

sion. If Borges's metaphors do not strike the modern reader as revolutionary it is because, rather than shaking off centuries of accumulated culture,
the Latin American *vanguardistas* often directed their energies toward establishing a sense of shared national culture.

As one of the founding fathers of *vanguardismo*, Oliverio Girondo
spent time in Europe and returned to his native Argentina anxious to generate a new literary language. Girondo broke ground with his collection
Veinte poemas para ser leídos en el tranvía (1922; "Twenty Poems to Be
Read on the Streetcar") and for decades acted as an important transmitter
of new energies to younger generations of poets. Chile's Vicente Huidobro, clearly inspired by his collaborations with the French poet Pierre
Reverdy as well as by cubism in the plastic arts, initiated as early as 1917 a
movement he called *creacionismo*. In poems and manifestos such as "Arte
poética" ("Ars Poetica") and "Non serviam," Huidobro promoted the
idea that poetry should not merely reflect reality but also *create* it (*Obra
poética* 391, 1294).

In roughly the same moment in which the Argentine *ultraístas* pasted
their broadsides in the streets of Buenos Aires, the Mexican *estridentistas* ("stridentists") of the early 1920s applied the ideals of the Mexican
Revolution to the intellectual and artistic life of the country while simultaneously supporting international leftist causes. In the late 1920s and
throughout the 1930s, the Contemporáneos—a group organized around
a journal of the same name—produced poetry, prose, literary criticism,
and theatrical works of high quality, generally avoiding the public polem-
ics of the *estridentistas* in favor of a more interiorized spirit of intellectual
and artistic renovation. Several members of this group, including Jaime
Torres Bodet, Salvador Novo, Xavier Villaurrutia, Carlos Pellicer, and
José Gorostiza, enjoyed extended poetic careers and served as mentors
for the young Octavio Paz, who would become Mexico's most important
twentieth-century writer.

In Peru the *vanguardia* never developed into a cohesive movement.
But, through the efforts of one man, José Carlos Mariátegui, key ideas and
works both from abroad and from within Peru's own intelligentsia were
brought into circulation. From 1926 until his premature death in 1930,
Mariátegui edited the journal *Amauta*, which embodied *vanguardismo*
as it combined new modes of cultural expression with an embrace of autochthonous Andean values. In an eclectic mix reflecting the new trends
in Latin American poetry, *Amauta* presented the early work of several of
the standard-bearers of Peruvian avant-garde literature, including Carlos

Oquendo de Amat, Martín Adán, Gamaliel Churata, Alberto Hidalgo, Alejandro Peralta, César Moro, and Emilio Adolfo Westphalen. The influence of Moro and Westphalen, who embraced the tenets of surrealism, extends to important later poets such as Blanca Varela, Javier Sologuren, and Jorge Eduardo Eielson. In a development that paralleled the avant-garde but took poetry in a more popular direction, Nicomedes Santa Cruz revived Afro-Peruvian oral verse traditions such as the ten-verse *décima* form. Adopting the *décima* in performances, recordings, radio broadcasts, and books, Santa Cruz "paradoxically moves a marginalized element of Peruvian culture (the Afro-Peruvian) to the center" (Kuhnheim, *Beyond the Page* 12).

Among the nations of the Caribbean, Cuba manifested the richest and most prolonged avant-garde activity. In response to the United States' interventionism and to repressive local governments, protest movements sprang up that held both political reform and artistic innovation as their goals. Several of the most notable writers of the Grupo Minorista, including Jorge Mañach, Juan Marinello, and Alejo Carpentier, went on to found the eclectic *Revista de avance* (1927–1930), whose influence spread across Latin America. In another significant development, Nicolás Guillén popularized Afro-Cuban poetry, or *poesía negra*. Differentiating itself from the French *négritude* movement and the Harlem Renaissance, with which it shared a vindication of Afro-diasporic cultural values, Guillén's work celebrated the realities of daily life for mixed-race people in Cuba, including African-inflected speech rhythms. Lines of influence from Guillén and other poets of the *negrista* movement, such as his compatriots Emilio Ballagas and Ramón Guirao, Luis Palés Matos of Puerto Rico, and Manuel del Cabral of the Dominican Republic, would extend to prominent later-twentieth-century poets such as Excilia Saldaña, Nancy Morejón, and Víctor Fowler Calzada.

In Brazil, as in Spanish America, the late nineteenth century was marked by a turn toward the erudite refinement of the French Parnassian style, of which Olavo Bilac was the outstanding figure. In the wake of the abolition of slavery in 1888, the melancholy musicality of symbolism was skillfully adopted to a Brazilian context by João da Cruz e Sousa, the son of freed slaves. The conservative formal elegance of Parnassian-symbolist poetics, however, proved inadequate for the expression of the cultural values of the twentieth century, and a seismic shift began to occur around 1920.

The initiation of Brazil's avant-garde movements can be traced to a single historical moment: the celebration of the Semana de Arte Moderna

("Week of Modern Art") in São Paulo in February 1922. Organized to coincide with the centennial of Brazil's independence from Portugal, this multifaceted festival energized the country's intellectual and artistic community around new forms of expression that would coalesce under the term *modernismo*. Out of the Semana de Arte Moderna arose numerous writers and artists of importance to this movement and its long afterlife, including Manuel Bandeira, Mário de Andrade, Oswald de Andrade, Raul Bopp, Carlos Drummond de Andrade, and Cecília Meireles. These poets insisted on formal innovations and on thematic concerns that emphasized the American social and historical context. Furthermore, they championed the Brazilian vernacular as the only language suitable for their expression of these concerns.

Modernism in Brazil is generally characterized by a greater emphasis on nationalism than that of Spanish American *modernismo*. Ronald de Carvalho experienced futurism in Europe and subsequently adapted that aesthetic to the exigencies of his home country. Guilherme de Almeida wrote poetry celebrating Brazil's racial and ethnic mixture, an approach similar to that of Nicolás Guillén in Cuba. Mário de Andrade's famous *Paulicéia desvairada* (1922; *Hallucinated City*) examined the intertwined cultures of his native city, São Paulo, while his later poetry explores and celebrates elements of the Brazilian hinterlands. Cecília Mereiles represents a notable departure from the experimental and nationalist tendency, as she turned in her mature work toward a more contemplative mode and incorporated Asian mysticism into her unique poetics.

Of the myriad attempts at theorizing the Latin American avant-garde that proliferated in manifestos and proclamations across the continent, Oswald de Andrade's "Manifesto antropófago" (1928; "Cannibalist Manifesto") deserves special attention for its linguistic brilliance and synthetic presentation of complex ideas, as well as for its widespread influence in Latin America and beyond. Encapsulated in the manifesto's most famous phrase— "Tupy, or not tupy, that is the question" (173)—we hear in parodic terms the tension between the native (the Tupi Indians) and the cosmopolitan (Shakespeare's *Hamlet*). Turning the European commonplace view of South American cannibalism back on itself, Oswald proposes that this tension be resolved by means of "anthropophagy"; that is, European culture should be ingested, digested, and then regurgitated in new and uniquely Latin American cultural forms.

On the perimeters of the group activity that marked much of the *vanguardia*, including the publication of numerous journals and manifestos, two poets of now undisputed stature—César Vallejo and Pablo Neruda—emerged in what René de Costa calls "the other avant-garde" (360). Selections from Vallejo's first book, *Los heraldos negros* (1919; *The Black Heralds*), in particular the title poem of the collection, can be useful in showing the transition from *modernismo* to the *vanguardia*.[2] His second collection, *Trilce*, published in 1922, is generally considered the most radical achievement of the Spanish American poetic avant-garde. In *Trilce* Vallejo molds meanings through neologisms, broken syntax, unconventional typography, the strategic use of repetition, and the mixing of verbal registers. The result is a poetry that requires much vigilance on the part of the reader and renders the act of translation particularly challenging.

The linguistic and poetic transformations that characterize *Trilce*, in combination with the seriousness of its themes—guilt, sacrifice, death, memory, the crisis of faith, sexuality in its dark or violent aspects, and the incomprehensibility of time—brought Spanish American poetry into an entirely new sphere. Although Vallejo's posthumous publication, *Poemas humanos* ("Human Poems"), reveals a generally more accessible, message-driven poetics than *Trilce*, the sense that conventional language is inadequate to express the exigencies of modern existence remains. Vallejo's work as a whole, which eventually reached a wide readership across the Americas and in Europe, gave later poets the liberty to practice an intensely subjective and sometimes hermetic lyricism while addressing universal humanist themes.

Unlike Vallejo, who remained largely on the margins of the literary movements of his day, Neruda enjoyed recognition as a poet from an early age. One of the challenges in teaching Neruda is incorporating the numerous transformations of this protean poet while acknowledging certain defining characteristics. In a 1935 essay called "On a Poetry without Purity," Neruda advocates for "Una poesía impura como un traje, como un cuerpo, con manchas de nutrición y actitudes vergonzosas, con arrugas, observaciones, sueños, vigilia, profecías, declaraciones de amor y de odio, bestias, sacudidas, idilios, creencias políticas, negaciones, dudas, afirmaciones, impuestos" 'A poetry impure like a suit, like a body, with food stains and shameful attitudes, with wrinkles, observations, dreams, wakefulness, prophecies, declarations of love and hate, beasts, shudders, romance, political beliefs, negations, doubts, affirmations, taxes' ("Sobre una poesía" 522). This notion of "impurity"—of poetry as a multifarious, ever-evolving cultural space, one that insists on embracing the materiality of everyday existence—can help students make sense of Neruda's vast (and uneven) corpus as well as his influence over subsequent generations.

The confident privileging of the poetic "I," so absent or problematized in Vallejo, proved to be both one of Neruda's enduring strengths as a poet and a source of ongoing disparagement by his critics. The universalizing prophetic stance, with the whole of Latin American history as its theme, is developed on an epic scale in *Canto general* (1950; "General Song"), particularly in *The Heights of Macchu Picchu*. The voice of Neruda's odes (published in successive volumes beginning with *Odas elementales* ["Elemental Odes"] in 1954) seems to signal a radical shift from the anguished, lyrically convoluted voice that characterizes the poems of the *Residencia en la tierra* ("Residence on Earth") cycle (1933, 1935, 1947) or the sweeping political concerns of *Canto general*. In spite of these shifts, readers see in the odes, as well as in Neruda's later love poetry and even the conversational poetry of *Estravagario* (1958), an element that links all his works, that is, a concern for the vagaries of ordinary experience, particularly in relation to the natural and material world.

After the *Vanguardia*: The Poetry of Contemporary Latin America

In *The Gathering of Voices*, their comprehensive study of the poetry of twentieth-century Latin America, González and Treece observe a post-avant-garde split between formalist, Platonic poetry evincing "an elevation of thought toward universal categories" and social poetry that incorporated the poet and history into the public realm (192–195). While these two positions are apparent throughout the late twentieth century and indeed prove useful for the purposes of rough classification, it may be more accurate to envision two intertwining, rather than oppositional, threads. William Rowe, in *Poets of Contemporary Latin America*, suggests that we treat contemplative subjectivity and historical groundedness as two parts of the same whole—an approach captured by the book's subtitle, *History and the Inner Life*.[3] In this spirit of dynamic interplay, the following pages present a brief overview of some of the more recent tendencies in the field of Latin American poetry, whose pedagogical value is explored in this volume.

If we imagine one overarching category as that of Platonic, formalist, metaphysical, or intellectual poetry, we observe in many contemporary poets a preoccupation with abstractions or universals that supersedes a concern for social or historical realities. In Rowe's terms, the "inner life" is given precedence over "history." This poetics implies a meditative attitude on the part of the poet who turns toward the age-old themes of love, time, and death, and simultaneously toward the twentieth-century search for meaning in a world whose structures no longer seem stable. Following perhaps the example of the French symbolist poet Stéphane Mallarmé, the notion of critical poetry becomes crucial for many writers who interrogate the power of poetic language.

An early pivotal figure in this context is José Lezama Lima of Cuba, who edited the influential review *Orígenes: Revista de Arte y Literatura* (1944–56; "Origins: Review of Art and Literature"). Lezama's elegant and erudite poetry (notably influenced by the Spanish baroque master Luis de Góngora) is considered foundational for younger poets of the neobaroque, one of the dominant trends of the late twentieth and early twenty-first centuries. The term *neobaroque* was first coined by the Brazilian writer Haroldo de Campos and was later theorized by the Cuban Severo Sarduy. Neobaroque poets emphasize artifice, intertextuality (including allusions to other art forms), and the play of language on the surface of the poem. "Choosing a neobaroque style at the end of the twentieth century may seem anachronistic," observes Kuhnheim, "but these writers return to the mode of the conquest period and the *madre patria* to rewrite and redefine relationships between center and periphery. In doing so, they invoke a specifically Spanish cultural legacy and simultaneously demonstrate the impossibility of cultural translation" (*Spanish American Poetry* 11). The term has been invoked to describe poets such as Néstor Perlongher, Arturo Carrera, Tamara Kamenszain, and Diana Bellessi, of Argentina; Marosa di Giorgio, Eduardo Espina, and Eduardo Milán, of Uruguay; David Huerta and Coral Bracho, of Mexico; Mirko Lauer and Reynaldo Jiménez, of Peru; Raúl Zurita, of Chile; and José Kozer, of Cuba.[4]

The metaphysical strain in poetry was particularly prominent in twentieth-century Argentina, beginning with the neo-Romantic Generation of 1940, which was heavily influenced by surrealism. Olga Orozco, whose work also shows clear influence from Rainer Maria Rilke's poetry and from Neruda's *Residencia* cycle, wrote incantatory verse that lyricizes the poet's search for the absolute. Her younger compatriot Alejandra Pizarnik retreated from the historical moment to create intensely subjective lyrical interrogations of language, silence, madness, and death. Roberto Juarroz, constructing successive volumes collected under the title *Poesía vertical* (*Vertical Poetry*), employed a sparse, reiterative lexicon to consider, in sometimes startling ways, the logical paradoxes of existence.

João Cabral de Melo Neto, arguably the most important Brazilian poet of the second half of the twentieth century, employed a self-critical, austere language comparable to that of the North American poet Marianne Moore. Cabral's poetry is constructed with a formal rigor that explores the power of certain words, which are examined both as material objects and as concepts or abstractions. His attempt to produce poetry that obliterates the distance between form and content made Cabral a precursor of concrete poetry. In spite of this concern for the formal properties of language, Cabral distinguished himself from his contemporaries of the neo-Parnassian strain by rejecting an elitist stance and connecting his lyric sensibility to material and social realities. He identified his work, in fact, with the notion of antipoetry, discussed below.

Concrete poetry, which emphasized to an extreme degree the formal patterns of language on the page, emerged in various parts of Latin America in the 1950s, but primarily in Brazil. There its major proponents were the members of the Noigandres group, including Décio Pignatari, Haroldo de Campos, and Augusto de Campos. In Spanish America, the Swiss-born Bolivian poet Eugen Gomringer was also an early experimenter with concrete poetry, and in the late 1960s Octavio Paz developed a version of concretism that he called *topoemas*. By the manipulation of typography, color, and the distribution of words and empty space on the page, concrete poets attempted a total merger of form and content. Linking poetic expression to artistic minimalism, scientific formulas, and the language of advertising and mass media, these poets divested the lyric of any association with narrative or sentiment.

The intellectual or formalist strain of poetry that constantly interrogates the power of poetic language itself is probably best exemplified in the work of Octavio Paz. Paz's work resists classification: even his seemingly abstract philosophical inquiries remain tethered to the social and political realities of his day. Much of Paz's poetry moves beyond the historical concerns of *mexicanidad* ("Mexicanness") to address the relationship of art to political power, the transcendent potential of erotic union, and the role of the individual consciousness in a world dominated by dehumanizing forces. If his philosophy is grounded in daily existence, his poetry can also ascend into a rarefied atmosphere. Most poems, in fact, move (sometimes seamlessly, sometimes awkwardly) between the two realms. Beyond his vast body of lyrical work, Paz wrote theoretical texts that left a strong mark on his own and subsequent generations in Latin America and abroad.

Two volumes worthy of note in the context of the present collection are *El arco y la lira* (1956; *The Bow and the Lyre*) and *Los hijos del limo: Del romanticismo a la vanguardia* (1974; "Children of the Mire: From Romanticism to the Avant-Garde").

If—with the proper caveats—we can consider Lezama Lima, Paz, Cabral, and others mentioned above as tending toward meditations on universal themes and a preoccupation with poetic language as such, we can imagine another overarching category of post-avant-garde work that has been called social or conversational poetry. These poets incorporate the lyric "I" into the public and historical realm, often employing colloquial diction meant to capture so-called ordinary speech. Building on the formal experiments of the *vanguardia*, they reject syllabic meter, rhyme, and other traditional techniques and thus open poetic language not only to conversational diction but also to slogans, clichés, and other linguistic fragments culled from popular culture. The themes and concerns generally associated with this trend relate to the here and now of contemporary life, whether domestic, social, spiritual, or political. In another shift initiated by certain *modernista* and avant-garde poets in both Spanish America and Brazil, the urban space becomes the undisputed territory of poetic inquiry and expression. Certain strains of this social poetry can be seen as a continuation of the Marxist-oriented work of Neruda, Vallejo, and others, in which the poet acts as spokesperson for the dispossessed.

A number of outstanding poets writing from the middle of the century on have found in social poetry a fitting modality for examining the place of women in Latin American society, among other concerns; a partial list might include Rosario Castellanos, of Mexico; Julia de Burgos, of Puerto Rico; Ana Istarú, of Costa Rica; Daisy Zamora, of Nicaragua; María Mercedes Carranza, of Colombia; Carmen Ollé, of Peru; Marjorie Agosín, of Chile and the United States; and Adélia Prado, of Brazil. Early classifications of these poets sometimes termed them confessional, assuming an identity between the intimate poetic voice and a straightforward expression of personal sentiment. Later criticism has recognized an ironic, ludic, self-questioning, or self-deprecating tone, as the poet weighs the realities of her quotidian existence (or that of other women) against inherited ideals of femininity. In the words of María Mercedes Carranza, "Creí en la verdad: / dos y dos son cuatro, / María Mercedes debe nacer, / crecer, reproducirse y morir / y en esas estoy" 'I believed in the truth: / two and two are four, / María Mercedes should be born, / grow, reproduce and die / and that's what I'm doing' (472). In his chapter on

Carmen Ollé, William Rowe observes that readers and critics often pay exclusive attention to the thematic material of contemporary women poets, overlooking their "concern with language as form and not just representation" (*Poets* 331). This is an important reminder that simple diction and the formal strategies that mimic discourse—regardless of the gender of the poet—should not lead us to equate this poetry with uncritical or unsophisticated exposition.

Not surprisingly, the historical realities of North American imperialism, civil wars, and repressive governments that marked much of mid- to late-twentieth-century Latin America gave rise to a vast body of political poetry, in which a straightforward tone is associated with a call for collective action, a vision of a new political utopia, or a desire for collective memory. Although the Republican cause in the Spanish Civil War inspired this type of poetry from the 1930s to the 1950s, it was the 1959 Cuban Revolution that provided a fresh context and a common cause that spanned the continent in the 1960s and 1970s. In Cuba itself, Nicolás Guillén's poetry assumes a new shape in poems such as "Tengo" ("I Have"), in which the poet enumerates the newfound freedoms of the common Cuban: "yo, Juan sin Nada no más ayer, / y hoy Juan con Todo . . ." 'I, Juan with Nothing only yesterday / and today Juan with Everything' (*Summa poética* 195). From the early 1960s to the 1980s, the work of other Cuban poets such as Heberto Padilla, Roberto Fernández Retamar, and Fayad Jamís often follows a trajectory of revolutionary euphoria, through disenchantment and even despair, to a renewed hope.

The violent conflicts that shook Central America in the 1970s and 1980s galvanized another group of influential poets. The Nicaraguan Ernesto Cardenal, whose production is too vast and varied to fit under any single rubric, combines Marxist and Christian ideals related to liberation theology. Referred to as exteriorism or documentary poetry, his style incorporates the concrete details of social, historical, and political realities into wide-ranging poems that balance the deliberately banal with high lyricism. Giaconda Belli, from Nicaragua, and Claribel Alegría and Roque Dalton, from El Salvador, are the outstanding representatives of an ideologically committed generation that wrote poetry bearing testimony to the leftist resistance to imperialism and repression. As a fighter in the People's Revolutionary Army (Ejército Revolucionario del Pueblo, or ERP), Dalton incarnated the very notion of the guerrilla poet.

A different poetic response marks the work of several Southern Cone poets living under the dictatorial regimes of the 1970s and 1980s or in exile from those regimes. When the conversational, message-driven style no longer served to express the experience of trauma, these poets experimented with techniques that built on those of the earlier *vanguardia*. The Chilean Raúl Zurita has produced a body of work that is alternately hermetic and shockingly direct. Zurita has also explored nontextual means of poetic expression, such as skywriting the verses of a poem or carving the phrase "ni pena ni miedo" 'neither pain nor fear' on the surface of the Atacama Desert. His compatriot Carmen Berenguer writes fragmentary, free-associative pieces that often incorporate marginalized voices, particularly those of urban areas such as Santiago, while highlighting the poetic qualities of everyday speech. Juan Gelman, directly involved in leftist guerrilla activity in Argentina and subsequently exiled, found in César Vallejo a model of sentimental humanism combined with a ferocious denunciation of injustice. These poets craft a simultaneous space of meditative subjectivity and impassioned collective discourse.

The propensity of social poetry to employ the language of everyday life is carried to an ironic extreme in a current called antipoetry, whose originator and undisputed master is Chile's Nicanor Parra. Rather than faithfully representing quotidian exchanges, or giving voice to common people in an attitude of sympathy or protest, Parra's poems parody both the speaker and the speech. In doing so, they cast a critical eye on virtually everything held sacred by virtually everyone. In the language of an ironic manifesto that serves as an ars poetica for antipoetry, Parra's "Montaña rusa" ("Rollercoaster") challenges the reader to reject any inherited notions of what poetry should be: "Durante medio siglo / La poesía fue / El paraíso del tonto solemne. / Hasta que vine yo / Y me instalé con mi montaña rusa. // Suban, si les parece. / Claro que yo no respondo si bajan / Echando sangre por boca y narices" 'For half a century / Poetry was / The paradise of the solemn fool. / Until I came / And settled in with my rollercoaster. // Get on board, if you like. / But don't blame me if you come down / Bleeding from the mouth and nose' (*Antipoems* 92). Parra's challenge, it seems, was accepted: as Federico Schopf observed in 2010, "More than fifty years after the appearance of *Poemas y antipoemas* (1954), it is now clear that antipoetry has inaugurated a new beginning in the arena of Spanish American poetry in the twentieth century" (172).

We began this overview by considering the tension between European and autochthonous elements in the evolution of Latin American poetry. The continent that Columbus "discovered" was of course not an empty one, and yet the indigenous peoples that inhabited it have, since the Con-

quest, struggled to be considered full participators in Latin American culture. As we have seen, criollo or mestizo writers of the nineteenth century
began to incorporate the concerns of native peoples through movements
known as Indianism (in Brazil) and indigenism or *mundonovismo* (in Spanish America). But, given the relative inaccessibility of indigenous languages
for Spanish or Portuguese speakers, as well as the cultural practice of oral
rather than written poetry, few original American voices have been heard or
widely disseminated. One exciting new development in this field is the recent publication of several anthologies and collections by indigenous poets
such as Natalia Toledo and Juan Gregorio Regino, of Mexico; Humberto
Ak'abal and Calixta Gabriel Xiquín, of Guatemala; and Elicura Chihuailaf,
of Chile. As Clare Sullivan explains in her essay in this volume, these bilingual poets typically translate their own work into the mainstream language
of their country. Although we cannot expect an individual poet to act as a
spokesperson for his or her indigenous community, these publications nevertheless represent a welcome advance from the silence or the exteriorized
hablar por ("speaking for") that until recently characterized most readers'
experience of indigenous Latin American poetry.

Notes

1. Critics have argued about the inclusive dates of *modernismo*, though most
agree on the period from 1885 to 1915 as an approximate framework. We refer
readers to the extensive bibliography on this subject, highlighting in particular the
work of Ricardo Gullón, José Olivio Jiménez, Cathy Jrade (*Modernism*), Gwen
Kirkpatrick (*Dissonant Legacy*), Gerard Aching, and Iván Schulman.

2. For teaching Vallejo's poetry in English or in Spanish, I recommend *The
Complete Poetry of César Vallejo: A Bilingual Edition*, edited and translated by
Clayton Eshleman. This 2007 anthology is widely available and contains useful essays by Mario Vargas Llosa and Efraín Kristal, as well as a chronology of Vallejo's
life and works by Stephen Hart.

3. Rowe, in fact, proposes a somewhat different dichotomy for characterizing
the poetry of twentieth-century Latin America: "the work of the avant-gardes and
the tradition of politicized poetry" (*Poets* 1).

4. For a thorough study and anthology of neobaroque Latin American poets,
see the critical anthology *Medusario*, as well as Kuhnheim's *Spanish American Poetry at the End of the Twentieth Century: Textual Disruptions*, pp. 115–44.

Jonathan Mayhew

Poetic Literacy:
Beyond Nervous Cluelessness
and the New Critical Residue

The resistance to poetry among students at all levels (and even some professorial colleagues) might be described as a "nervous cluelessness," to borrow a phrase from the linguist Geoffrey Pullum. According to Pullum, the haphazard and inaccurate teaching of English grammar tricks otherwise well-educated native speakers into doubting their instincts and misapplying shaky criteria derived from the prejudices of prescriptive grammar. In the same way, ill-informed and anxiety-producing preconceptions derived from past classroom experiences shape students' engagement with poetry. Even at the graduate level, students believe that poetry is hard, that they do not understand it (especially when it is not in their native language), and that it exists not to be read but to be analyzed—a sterile and specialized academic exercise unconnected to other kinds of reading. While some students assume that every aspect of the textual surface must be accounted for in excruciating detail, others labor under what the poet Kenneth Koch has called the "Hidden Meaning assumption, which directs one to more or less ignore the surface of the poem in a quest for some elusive and momentous idea that the poet has buried amid the words and music" (111). Often, a folk postmodernist belief that poetic meaning is almost completely indeterminate and subjective, and that the reader cre-

ates his or her own meaning freely, exists in tacit tension with the techno-
cratic view of analysis—and with the fear of not understanding anything
at all.

Once I made the mistake of assigning my graduate students a short
analysis of a poem of their own choice, explaining only that I wanted to
assess their skill at literary analysis and academic writing in Spanish. While
some of the papers were acceptable, I found evidence of what I call the
New Critical residue: the remnants of a poetic pedagogy inherited from
Anglo-American New Criticism. The introductory college textbooks that
attempt to carry on the legacy of Cleanth Brooks and Robert Penn Warren's 1960 *Understanding Poetry* often reduce this knowledge to mechan-
ical syllable-counting and the enumeration of tropes and figures; hence,
even some of the better papers conveyed through their rhetoric that poetic
analysis should aim for workmanlike dullness. A few students, for example,
covered their bases by promising to address both style and theme. Treatment of meter and rhyme was perfunctory at best, sometimes confused,
and, in the case of virtually every student, utterly disconnected from the
rest of the paper. A lack of regular meter left students at an impasse, while
metrical uniformity prompted the simple conclusion that the poem was
"musical." My students were also hesitant to come up with strong interpretations of the poems they were considering, perhaps in the belief that
interpretation had to be deferred until analysis was complete.

The failure of the assignment was my fault, as I had not explained
what a graduate version of this quintessentially undergraduate task might
entail. Nevertheless, I think my flawed pedagogy is instructional insofar as
it lays bare some of the pitfalls of the New Critical residue. The treatment
of a poem as an inert object of analysis, "of interest mainly as a mechanism
that has to be taken apart" (Koch 101), lends itself to plodding, wooden
prose, devoid of rhetorical flair. Decontextualized and divorced from other
significant dimensions of literary criticism, poetic analysis becomes cut off
from almost all of the problems of keenest interest to contemporary criticism. Indeed, I have found that even literary colleagues are uninterested in
reading monographs that are composed of poetic analyses.

In place of the context-free analysis proposed by the New Criticism, I
propose that poetry courses examine poems in the context of their concrete
history and their implicit theories of poetic language and genre. Though
few students may become scholars of poetry, many may end up teaching
poetry to undergraduates in introductory and survey courses, poised to
enable or prevent the transfer of *poesiphobia* to subsequent generations.

The Poetry Base

One problem with the New Critical residue is that it arbitrarily excludes a large part of the "poetry base," which Koch defines as the sum total of one's expertise in poetry (71). In other words, a great deal of conventional poetic analysis selects, out of all possible ways of understanding poetry, only a few pertinent facets related to versification and rhetorical terminology. A large part of what an instructor may know about poetry is excluded, not because it is unimportant, but because it does not appear to further any relevant pedagogical outcomes. The memorization of the names of rhetorical figures might be a legitimate classroom goal, but even a knowledgeable teacher with a substantial poetry base might have to look up a term like *anacoluthon* in the dictionary. In other words, mastery of terminology might not be as significant as we think it is.

In any given classroom situation, only a minuscule part of the instructor's base comes into play. The aim, after all, is not to transmit the entirety of one's knowledge to a group of students but to ensure that the students achieve basic competence in preparation for higher-level intellectual pursuits. This narrowing, however, comes at a cost. Because rudimentary analytical tools are so difficult to master, a pedagogy based primarily on them, at the expense of the larger context that makes literacy meaningful in the first place, often cannot achieve even the basic proficiency to which it aspires.

What elements, left out of traditional analysis, might we consider fundamental to teaching students poetic literacy? Ideally, a college instructor would have a strong historical sense and an awareness that poetry, and consequently the way we read poetry, changes from century to century and from place to place. My study of the sometimes obscene poetry of Catullus in an undergraduate Latin class, for example, showed me that the expectation that poetry represents an elevated discourse was a neoclassical precept, not a classical one. On my junior year abroad I encountered the post-Romantic perspective of the Spanish poet Claudio Rodríguez, who held that in the eighteenth century Spain had produced no poetry at all, only poem-like texts devoid of the spark of inspiration. An awareness of such shifting literary expectations can lead students to realize that our definitions of poetry are always contingent rather than absolute.

Ideally, the poetry base is also participatory. For me, the writing and translation of poetry has been as significant as my academic study of it. My friendship with poets in Spain and in the United States has created a strong sense of allegiance to poetry in particular traditions, so that poetry can never seem a merely academic pursuit, with no claim on my personal identity. It is also difficult for me to separate poetry from music and the visual arts, since my work on Federico García Lorca, a multimedia artist, has been such a formative part of my scholarly formation. Thus, exposing students whenever possible to real-life experiences involving poetry and poets is crucial to overcoming their reticence to study it.

The poetry base of every instructor will be unique. In every case, though, it will include a set of biases and exclusions that can be put to good use in pedagogical situations. A strong dislike for a particular tradition of poetry, or a strong investment in another, can take the form of anti-intellectualism or an equally facile and detrimental elitism; alternatively, it can provide a source of productive resistance. For example, a scholar (or a student) who strongly resists a certain author may produce a more interesting reading than someone who writes from a position of naïve admiration. Whatever one's personal preferences, the ability to respond aesthetically to poetry—whether positively or negatively—is crucial: if one cannot form a strong reaction to a poem, then one cannot use that reaction as the source of insights of other sorts. For example, students who cannot perceive how a poem fulfills or fails to fulfill certain generic expectations will be at a loss to develop meaningful ideas about it. The poetry course should teach students to recognize tensions within the poetry they are reading and to recognize—and work with—the tension between their own biases and those of other readers.

Genre and Language

Debates in contemporary poetics often bring into play conflicting ideas about the nature of poetry. Two major operative constructs conceive of poetry as a genre on the one hand and as a set of discursive practices on the other:

> Poetry (usually what is meant here is lyric poetry[1]) is a genre of
> literature, characterized by its concision or brevity, its aesthetic
> use of language, and its grounding in a poetic speaker, often taken
> to be the alter ego of the biographical author. To qualify as such,
> poetry also has to aspire to be *good* poetry. In other words, it
> has to fulfill conventional aesthetic norms for this genre, as
> understood in a particular time and place.
> Poetry is a wide range of discursive and performative practices that
> have as their common element some distinctive use of language.

It is not a genre, since it encompasses several genres, and it has a tangential relation to literature, since it also incorporates forms that are primarily oral rather than literary.

The narrow first view describes a substantial portion of what many habitually think of when they hear the word *poetry*. Eighty percent of the poetry on my office bookshelves might fall within this definition. The broader second view extends to nonlyric genres, such as satire, epic, visual and conceptual poetry, and opera libretti. The awarding of a Nobel Prize in literature to the singer-songwriter Bob Dylan in 2016 elicited many defensive reactions based on conventional notions of the literary. For some writers and journalists, this category can apparently exclude the most familiar archetype of the lyric poet: a person who sings to the accompaniment of a stringed instrument. One friend told me he felt "funny" about the awarding of the prize to Dylan because he thought of literature primarily as "reading material."

While it is difficult to imagine a serious, historically informed scholar holding to the narrow view of poetry as a genre, outdated pedagogical practices impart that same view to students. What sparks might fly when these two conceptions collide—when we try to read heterodox texts according to more narrowly defined canons of lyric excellence? The existence of variable and seemingly conflicting ideas about poetic genre and poetic language, along with the proliferation of poetic practices that do not fall within conventional definitions of the lyric, present both challenges and opportunities for a new poetic pedagogy. There are challenges because there are no consistent criteria that will work with all texts that might be analyzed as poetry. The opportunities arise from the conflict among contrasting views of what we are talking about when we talk about poetry.

In addition to these generic considerations, approaches to poetry differ in their conception of poetic language. It seems that almost everyone agrees that poetry is distinguished by its language, but what does this mean? A simple exercise, usable for both undergraduate and graduate classes, that will generate a set of theories of poetic language is to have students fill in the blank in the following sentence: "Poetic language is more _____ than ordinary language." Some might use words like *constrained, beautiful, precise, self-conscious, concentrated, musical, noninstrumental, metaphorical, emotive, elevated, pure,* or *refined.* There are no wrong answers here, since each of these words corresponds to a theory (or part of a theory) that has guided ideas about poetry at some historical juncture. (Some of these theories might also form part of the New Critical residue.) We might say that theories of constraint, for example, are operative in definitions that equate poetry with verse, which follows phonological rules that are stricter than those governing nonmetrical language. Theories that hold poetic language to be more elevated in register correspond to neoclassical norms of decorum. The idea that poetry should be refined, noninstrumental, and an end in itself is the legacy of symbolism.

Most contemporary theorists would reject the idea of an intrinsically poetic language, stating instead that all discourses and languages are already poetic, at least in potential. The poet works through a process of selection or generic framing rather than by using language that is actually *different* in any definable way. This position would appear to be more theoretically defensible than the claim that poetry must always deviate from linguistic norms or be written in a wholly different lexicon. David Antin ridicules the deviationist theory of poetic language, with its assumptions that "poetry is different because it has a funny sound, a funny way of talking, and a funny way of thinking" (206). Needless to say, the concept of "ordinary language" is itself theoretically indefensible in this context, insofar as it implies a language that is nonfigurative, arrhythmic, and otherwise devoid of intrinsic interest.

These ideas about genre and language are significant because they frame and structure the close reading of poetry along meaningful axes of debate — as an alternative to treating close reading as an essentially sterile exercise that will demonstrate elementary competence. There is a difference, for example, between being able to recognize simile as a rhetorical figure and the ability to talk about the function of such a device in relation to generic and linguistic expectations. The Spanish hendecasyllable might be metrically identical in two writers working centuries apart, but it is unlikely to be functionally identical. What we might call poetic literacy, then, is a historically informed view of poetic genre (what has counted as poetry or lyric poetry in various historical frameworks) as well as of poetic language (anything distinctive in the selection or treatment of language, along many possible axes of opposition).

The Uses of Bad Poetry:
Neruda's *Canción de Gesta*

Ironically, the teaching of bad poetry often provides more efficient insight into poetic conventions than the exclusive focus on canonical texts. By "bad poetry" I mean poetry that has an uneasy relation to the standards we might associate with a conventionally good poem. Needless to say, there is no absolute standard for the conventionally good, and individuals will disagree both about what the standard is, or ought to be, and about whether any particular poem achieves it. This absence of consensus, though, does not make the concept of "bad poetry" less useful. In fact, the uncertainty surrounding value judgments is itself of pedagogical value. What bad poetry exposes, on a very basic level, are mismatches between texts and the generic and linguistic expectations that we bring to bear on them.

One exercise I have used in both graduate and undergraduate courses is to bring in some poems I wrote as deliberately inept parodies, with lines like "I have wept on fishing boats / and on library steps, / and in the stacks." I included overt sentimentality, bathos, deliberate verbosity and prosiness, arbitrary line breaks, preciosity and pretentiousness, fake wisdom and overbearing sententiousness, and every other lyrical blunder that came to mind. The students are easily able to perceive the ineptness of my writing. Aside from its entertainment value, the exercise obliges students to articulate aesthetic criteria. This is not always easy to do. Why do they find "prosaic" language unacceptable in a poem, for example? What is a good line break as opposed to an arbitrary one? What happens when poets use clichés?

This exercise prepares the way for subsequent class discussions surrounding generic expectations. Some of Pablo Neruda's later political poetry, for example, challenges most of the implicit aesthetic criteria of poetry, or lyric poetry. Given Neruda's towering status as Spanish America's most decorated poet, his work lends itself particularly well to an examination of poetic values. In 1966, after Neruda had traveled to the United States at the invitation of the PEN Club, a group of about 150 Cuban intellectuals, among them Alejo Carpentier, Nicolás Guillén, and Roberto Fernández Retamar, signed an open letter accusing the Chilean poet of selling out to the American imperialists. In reply, Neruda appended a bitterly personal poem, "Juicio final," to a new edition of *Canción de gesta* ("Song of Deeds"), his poetic celebration of the Cuban revolution first published, in Cuba, in 1960. Deeply wounded by the insult from the Cubans, some of whom he had considered friends, Neruda responded by accusing them of cowardice, cynicism, and betrayal. Although the poem is perhaps an effective rhetorical performance, and might go part of the way toward satisfying aesthetic and generic expectations, it is, in my experience, a good example to use in the classroom as a test of exactly what those expectations might be.

Bad poetry often frustrates a basic tenet of the pedagogical residue: the belief that form is inseparable from content. This organicism, as preached by the New Critics, encourages us to see why the choice of a particular form or a particular device is appropriate for the expression of a particular message. What happens, though, when a poet seems uninterested in this aesthetic criterion? "Juicio final," like many other poems in *Canción de gesta*, is written in regular eleven-syllable lines, with a shift from consonant to assonant rhyme after the first section. Meter, among other things, is a framing device: the visual disposition of the poem on the page tells us that this is poetry, and also orients attention toward the sound and texture of the words—the suppleness or fluidity of the movement from one line to the next. Neruda's verse, however, arguably uses meter primarily as a generic marker:

> Este libro, primero entre los libros
> que propagaron la intención cubana,
> esta Canción de Gesta que no tuvo
> otro destino sino la esperanza
> fue agredido por tristes escritores
> que en Cuba nunca liberaron nada
> sino sus presupuestos defendidos
> por la chaqueta revolucionaria. (105)

> This book, first among the books
> that spread word of the Cuban intention,
> this *Song of Gesta* that had no other
> destiny but hope
> was attacked by miserable writers
> who in Cuba never liberated a thing
> but their budgets
> defended by the revolutionary jacket.[2]

Neruda's use of meter is paired jarringly with an apparent disdain for aesthetic effects. Lines like "fue agredido por tristes escritores" do not invite the sort of attention to the sound of the words that we might expect from a line from Garcilaso de la Vega or from Neruda's more canonical works.

Printed in paragraph form, this writing is not distinguished prose either:

> Este libro, primero entre los libros que propagaron la intención cubana,
> esta Canción de Gesta que no tuvo otro destino sino la esperanza, fue
> agredido por tristes escritores que en Cuba nunca liberaron nada . . .

Of course, it is doubtful that Neruda was attempting to write beautiful lines of poetry. In other poems from this book he makes his poetic intentions clear, directly anticipating the objections of those who might protest against his subject matter: "dicen que aquí murió la poesía, / dicen que no debo hacerlo" 'They say poetry died here / they say I shouldn't do it' (65). His seeming anti-aestheticism, on the other hand, does not preclude a rather conventional kind of poetic rhetoric elsewhere in the collection: "Tesoros del Caribe, espuma insigne / sobre ilustres azules derramada, / costas fragantes que de oro y plata / parecen, por la arena elaboradas" 'Treasures of the Caribbean, eminent foam / spilt on illustrious blues, / fragrant coasts that seem of gold and silver / forged by the sand' ("La libertad" 40). Neruda, even in his most politically utilitarian poetry, is not averse to quasi-baroque flourishes that might seem almost *too* poetic, and students can be encouraged to recognize and respond to these rhetorical choices.

Neruda's violation of aesthetic expectations, then, is more complicated than it first appears. Perhaps the norm that he calls into question the most resolutely is the ban on instrumentalism, the use of poetic rhetoric to further nonaesthetic aims. Of course, poems often mimic speech acts or express direct messages, but generic expectation characterizes these communications as secondary to genre and form. Neruda's attack on the Cuban intellectuals in "Juicio final" is not devoid of poetic devices, but it uses them in furtherance of an agenda that is not framed by the principle of aesthetic distance:

> A uno conocí, cínico negro,
> disfrazado hasta el fin de camarada;
> éste de cabaret en cabaret
> ganó en París las últimas batallas
> para llegar campante como siempre
> a cobrar sus laureles en La Habana.
>
> Y a otro conocí neutral eterno,
> que huyendo de los nazis como rata
> se portó silencioso como un héroe
> cuando era su voz más necesaria.
> Y otro tan retamar que despojado
> de su fernández ya no vale nada. . . . (106)
>
> I met one, a cynical black,
> disguised until the end as a comrade;
> this man won the last battles in Paris
> from cabaret to cabaret

to arrive as carefree as ever
to accept his laurels in Havana.

And another I met, eternally neutral,
who, fleeing like a rat from the Nazis
behaved silently like a hero
when his voice was most necessary.
And another, a broom plant who stripped
of his fernandez is worth nothing. . . .

The specificity of the charges against Nicolás Guillén, Alejo Carpentier, and Roberto Fernández Retamar leaves little room for the transcendence and identification we often expect from accomplished lyric poetry. Another topic for classroom discussion might be why the play on Fernández Retamar's name succeeds or fails as an example of verbal wit. Students should be able to see for themselves the unseemly aspects of the poem, including opportunistic racism ("cínico negro"), dehumanization, and outright dishonesty. (It is important to point out to students that the accusations against Neruda might also be ethically and politically questionable.) The idea that Alejo Carpentier's return to Cuba in 1939 was an act of cowardice ("huyendo como rata de los nazis") seems particularly questionable. The desire to investigate the factual basis of Neruda's accusations, though, shows the extent to which the poet is encouraging an unaccustomed response from his readers: normally we don't feel called upon to ask such questions of lyric poems. We might, for example, tell students not to be so literal-minded if they inquired too closely about the real-life circumstances behind a lyric occasion like William Carlos Williams eating his wife's plums (Williams 372).

"Juicio final" can be read as a historical document about a leftist public intellectual who fell out of favor with the Castro regime as strategies diverged in the Communist parties of different nations of Spanish America in the 1960s. Read as a rhetorical performance, though, it holds more than documentary interest. What is at stake, finally, is the viability of a poetics of direct public statement at the poem's particular historical juncture. The use of poetry as a directly communicative act of praise or denunciation might not have seemed strange to an ancient or medieval poet, but current norms militate against so frontal an approach. Neruda's unique stature as a major twentieth-century poet as well as a prominent public intellectual positioned him to employ whatever poetic means were at his disposal to settle a personal score in a way that was unusual for his time. The historical approach for classroom analysis I am proposing, then, involves a detailed account of a poem's enunciative situation, both in the context of shifting generic norms for poetry itself and in the role of the poet as public intellectual. Since we often think of lyric enunciation as an idealized or fictive kind of speech, the more literal-minded approach I am suggesting has the advantage of casting into relief some of these unexamined expectations.

By advocating teaching poetry that counters expectations for the lyric, I do not suggest that the goal is to lead a class of students to condemn "Juicio final" as a bad poem in a simplistic way. We might even ask students to defend it as an effective rhetorical performance. It would be equally limiting, though, to say that aesthetic criteria become irrelevant for political poetry, and that therefore we should read this poetry simply for its message. The goal, instead, is to shake loose some of the prejudicial residue of poetic analysis by showing the futility of simply pointing out the function of literary devices in a decontextualized and therefore meaningless manner. Fissures between generic expectations and actual poems are revelatory in sometimes unpredictable ways. Another benefit of reading works that flout conventional aesthetic values is that students can be empowered to develop their own judgments rather than adopting an overly reverential attitude toward the canon. The residue of organicism often leads students to assume that form and content always form a seamless whole, rather than looking for the more interesting fissures that lead to potentially richer and more nuanced insights.

When turning our attention to "good poems"—those that we might view as fulfilling conventional expectations about language and genre—we still need to take into account the historical principles that guided our explication of a "bad poem." Our criteria for analyzing poetry, after all, are always implicitly evaluative, so the foregrounding of questions of value—whether aesthetic or political—is a way of making poetic analysis into a vital intellectual practice rather than a perfunctory tool. Discussions about the rhetorical function of literary devices can enliven the classroom and empower students to develop their own insights. Students can learn that debating questions of aesthetic value is not a way of avoiding ideology. Rather, it shows us how to bridge the gap between our often stale pedagogical residue and our ultimate goal: to situate poetry historically in the context of meaningful controversies about the variable functions of literary language.

Notes

1. The lyric is one of four major genres, along with drama, narrative, and the essay—or creative nonfiction in contemporary parlance.

2. All translations are my own.

Justin Read

An Entrance to Dark Forests: The Spanish American *Silva* from Sor Juana to Bello and Storni

When it comes to teaching Sor Juana's "Primero sueño" ("First Dream"), we are all sinners. This is not a moral judgment against anyone reading this essay but a strictly pedagogical observation. I myself have been teaching Sor Juana's great *silva* for the better part of two decades now, and I cannot recall one instance in which students left the classroom with any more clarity regarding the poem than that with which they entered. Quite the opposite, in fact: though as an instructor I work to help my students clarify Sor Juana's images, elucidate the overall philosophical argument of her poem, locate her historical position within the grander course of the baroque and the Counter-Reformation, parse her inscrutably circular syntax, and so forth, no matter how much I strive over the course of a fifty-minute class, or weeks of fifty-minute classes, the enhancement of knowledge is always accompanied by the augmentation of confusion.

In other words, Sor Juana compels instructors of her work to fail. Whatever clarity a teacher may provide is only ever exceeded, doubly or even triply, by darkness. And, worse, all we who enter here must guide our students into the darkness of the "Primero sueño" by design. Thus a diabolical plan comes into focus: the teaching of "Primero sueño," and of the

43

silva form generally, must be strategically oriented to failure—to grasping, perhaps proudly, greedily, lustfully, enviously, at that which always exceeds one's reach—as a positive outcome. No pedagogical tactic or strategy will ever succeed in mitigating or eliminating poetic excess, since excess (that which eludes understanding, perpetually misapprehended) is constitutive of a poem like the "Primero sueño." Sor Juana's *silva* is a tightly composed work of art that constantly questions and resists the limits of its own composition. This fact becomes clear only when the poem is read in conjunction with other works that likewise compose, decompose, and recompose poetic and political norms: in this case, Andrés Bello's "Silva a la agricultura de la Zona Tórrida" (*"Silva* to the Agriculture of the Torrid Zone") and Alfonsina Storni's "Carta lírica a otra mujer" ("Lyrical Letter to the Other Woman").[1]

As a poetic form the *silva* provides minimal compositional structure and a great deal of decompositional poetic license, suggesting paths to recomposition—the creation of new poetic forms and perhaps even new social practices. As concerns upper-division literature courses, this tripartite structure (composition-decomposition-recomposition) proves significant in revealing the relevance of traditional-elite poetics to contemporary Spanish American poetry and society. The possibilities for misunderstanding traditional forms are numerous. Poets like Sor Juana or Bello, and even Storni now almost a century after her passing, often appear inaccessible to readers in a contemporary setting. They are conditioned by historical circumstances that may appear foreign to twenty-first-century Latin American readers, let alone most undergraduates at North American universities. Instructors may feel obliged to prove to students that these poets are responding to current configurations of identity, political ideology, and the discourses mobilized to convey them, when, in point of fact, they are not. Instead, one must recognize the poetic and ideological struggles that each poet faced and make them analogous to contemporary issues without radically decontextualizing the poetry. Sor Juana, Bello, and Storni all wrote *silvas*, a form whose excessive poetic license can border on moral and ethical license. All three wrote in highly politicized environments whose historical trajectories do, in a sense, continue into the present day, yet any revisionist approach to the poems through, say, contemporary gender or sexual politics must be a misreading. Indeed, one might say that we must take excessive care to find the most accurate means of misreading the *silva* among the numerous options for failure presented to us.

Sor Juana: Supernatural Excess

First published in 1692, merely three years before Sor Juana's death from yellow fever in the Convento de San Jerónimo in Mexico City, "Primero sueño" is emblematic of the baroque in its overbearing materiality and in its simultaneous negation of the material world. As the Mexican poet Xavier Villaurrutia stated in an undated lecture from the 1940s, "Primero sueño" is "a long poem in deliberate, conscious imitation of Góngora's *Soledades*, as [Sor Juana] herself confessed, only in an atmosphere and climate that is not Góngora at all, but rather particular to the poetess: night and dream" (774). The work of not only a practiced "poetess" but also a highly erudite theologian, Sor Juana's poem seeks to overwhelm the senses with materiality, to the point that one catches a glimpse of the soul in its *mise en abŷme*.

The pedagogical goal in working through the "Sueño" is not the illumination of Sor Juana's soul, or any soul for that matter, but rather a confrontation and deepening engagement with the poem's virtually impenetrable wall of words. The immediate problem facing the instructor is whether to assign the entire poem as homework (all 975 verses of it), or simply to utilize selections, as most anthologies do, typically with abundant annotation. I opt for the former, expecting that most students will understand very little. I do so because, as I constantly remind the students, one only ever rereads a poem. Even the first reading of a poem requires students to grasp for prior readings of other poems in order to make sense of things—efforts that will prove insufficient for "Primero sueño" and require them to read it again. The enormity of Sor Juana's *silva* needs to be confronted and misapprehended before smaller, more focused sections of it can be analyzed.

Once in class, we begin breaking the poem into smaller, more digestible pieces, beginning with the opening strophe:

Piramidal, funesta, de la tierra
nacida sombra, al Cielo encaminaba
de vanos obeliscos punta altiva,
escalar pretendiendo las Estrellas;
si bien sus luces bellas
—exentas siempre, siempre rutilantes—
la tenebrosa guerra
que con negros vapores le intimaba

la pavorosa sombra fugitiva
burlaban tan distantes. . . . (1–10)

Pyramidal, ill-fated, shadow from the earth
born, to the Heavens did direct
in vain obelisks' presumptuous point,
to scale claiming the Stars;
if well their beautiful lights
—freestanding always, always sparkling—
the tenebrous war
that with black fumes did intimate
the dreadful fugitive shadow
mocked from such distance. . . .

First, students work in groups of three or four to identify the poem's metrical patterns and rhyme scheme.[2] They determine that the strophe is composed of hendecasyllabic (11) and heptasyllabic (7) *versos llanos* (verses that stress the penultimate syllable) that do not seem to be rhymed beyond some assonant rhyme of *-o*, *-a*, and *-es*—precisely the most common endings of most words in the Spanish language. They also notice, with some prompting, that there does not appear to be any regular pattern to the distribution of hendecasyllabic and heptasyllabic verses—at which point I inform them that they have developed a basic definition of the *silva*.

The law of the *silva* form, which allows any admixture of rhymed (assonant or consonant) or unrhymed heptasyllabics and hendecasyllabics, compels poetic license and imposes few restraints. And it is this very tension between subjective license, objective (or objectifying) order, and legal order (both poetic and juridical) that will be at stake in this opening strophe and in the rest of the "Sueño." Before students can begin to comprehend this, their immediate task is to "straighten" the poetic diction that Sor Juana, like many pre-*modernista* poets, has ruthlessly coiled. The poetic effect of this *silva* derives in part from the unnecessarily ornate arrangements of syntax. We get the sense that something "pyramidal" and "dreadful" is rising to the heavens as the stars are glimmering. Yet the grammar seems to be twisted: there are multiple clauses that seem like full sentences until we realize that the entire strophe is but one grammatical sentence: "las Estrellas" 'the Stars' might be the subject of the opening clause, but this does not conform to the conjugation of the verb *encaminaba* ("directed"); likewise, the "pavorosa sombra fugitiva" 'dreadful fugitive shadow' is not the subject of the next clause but rather the direct object of *burla-*

ban ("mocked"). Students attempting to rewrite these verses in prosaic form typically produce ungrammatical sentences.

The first strophe introduces the major themes of the work as a whole: a confrontation between light and dark, which factors into tensions between objective order and subjective sensation. To wit, does celestial light exist regardless of human perception? Is human sensory perception even real? Objectively speaking, the sky may be empty, or perhaps it has an invisible architecture, rendered by Sor Juana as pyramids and obelisks. Subjectively speaking, perhaps humans cannot perceive this architecture directly (without mathematics, or poetry), or perhaps Sor Juana is making it all up, deceiving us poetically into believing there is order in the universe. These questions raise another: If Sor Juana sees the stars aloft on the tips of obelisks, in which direction is the light moving in this poem? Does the light of the stars shine down from heaven according to the mathematical laws of geometry? Or do the obelisks represent the movement of Sor Juana's gaze upward?

At this point I assume my students are completely lost, or at least I hope I have succeeded in disorienting them. Rather than describing the descent of night, and the rising of the stars and moon, the opening strophe depicts the *ascent* of darkness upon the earth. Sor Juana paints a "tenebrous war" between the light and the dark, in which the stars mock the "black fumes" of darkness for daring to rise (presumably to blot out the heavens). Darkness wins. Sor Juana does not give shape or architecture to the light but only to the dark. She allows us to visualize the "imperious silence" of the night as darkness seems to palpitate, pulse, respire around heavenly objects (20). It is darkness that comes in obelisks, funereal monuments. As a perceptive subject, how does Sor Juana see that which cannot be seen?

This is a metaphysical question of both theological and literary import. Sor Juana seeks to represent poetically that which cannot be represented, an impasse that appears to drive the poem itself into circular logic and extreme loquacity perfectly suited to the generous *silva* form. "Primero sueño" purports to represent a dream, and yet it takes roughly two hundred verses for anyone within it to fall asleep and start dreaming. When the dream ends, the dreaming mind encounters the bright burning light (of divinity? of the poet's vision?), and then Venus the fiery orb ascends in the East. In other words, the morning comes . . . for roughly one hundred verses.

The intervening 650 (or so) verses narrativize the soul's journey across the world and through time from the origin of civilization; "toda convertida / a su inmaterial ser y esencia bella" 'all converted / into its immaterial being and beautiful essence' (292–93), the poet's soul embarks upon "el vuelo intelectual con que ya mide / la cuantidad inmensa de la Esfera" 'an intellectual flight with which it already measures / the immense quantity of the Sphere' (301–02). In this context, "Esfera" is at once an abstract, immaterial shape (sphere) and the entirely material realm (or Sphere) of the universe. This duplicity is redoubled in Sor Juana's first stop on her flight, the pyramids of ancient Memphis (340–434). As is well noted in Sor Juana scholarship, the Egyptian pyramids in these long strophes make a cogent point of reference to the dark, "pyramidal" obelisks observed in the opening of the poem.[3] The passage then leads to several more mythological encounters that compel the instructor to trick students into forming false cognates, false associational chains, between the poem's immaterial shapes ("sphere," "orb," "pyramid") and generalized forms ("mountain," "tower") and an assortment of historical, or perhaps only mythical, people and places (Memphis, Ptolemy, Ulysses, Homer, Babel, Icarus).

These false cognates ultimately yield Sor Juana's real world lesson: Vain humans have harnessed God's natural laws (i.e., the invisible force holding the Sphere of the universe together) in order to ascend to the heavens and make themselves godlike in the material realm. For this, they are punished with destruction, confusion, and death. For example, the poet describes the Egyptian pyramids as overly material expressions of what should have been immaterial pursuits. According to Sor Juana's gloss of Homer, "las Pirámides fueron materiales / tipos solos, señales exteriores / de las que, dimensiones interiores, / especies son de alma intencionales" 'the Pyramids were only / material types, external signs / of that which, internal dimensions, / intentional classes are of the soul' (400–03). To climb to heaven and stare into the "Orb" (of God's light, of the sun) always results in blindness. If instead one closes one's eyes to pray or meditate (or dream), one has no need to build giant material pyramids in order to realize the perfect geometry of divine order. The abstract pyramids one can build in the mind's eye are far greater and more powerful than any human architecture (423–434), since pyramids of the mind can be infinite. Yet the realization of this prayer, meditation, or dream requires a certain degree of blindness, a descent into darkness. This darkness is implicitly evil in this section, compared to Galen's *mortífero veneno* ("lethal venom")—the poison the physician utilizes to make the cure (*pharmakon*). A duplicitous moral message arises: material light is vital but dangerous (one must not look into the sun too long), and in seeking immaterial light, one must close one's eyes and assume a just proportion of venomous darkness. The pursuit of either light directly involves an "excess" that the poem alternately creates and struggles to contain.

Students begin to grasp at this point that these moral arguments are specific to a historical setting. Who is a nun like Sor Juana to invite the reader to such excess? As a female intellectual of her time, Sor Juana was highly circumscribed in her activities. She had to commit herself to a convent in the center of Mexico City in order to pursue her intellectual life, and never left the building until she died. Indeed, she would eventually be silenced by the Inquisition there. Her dreams of flying were thus lines of metaphysical flight from her physical situation. Yet the Aztecs, like the ancient Egyptians, built their towers and pyramids to reach up to their sun gods, and as the poet dreamed of flying to the pyramids of Cairo, she was sleeping atop the ruined pyramids of Tenochtitlán. Sor Juana mobilizes her *silva* in order to exceed her historical lot as a woman, or, as Susan M. McKenna has stated, "Despite the limits imposed upon her as a woman in a religious vocation, she surpassed many of her male contemporaries in her enlightened perception of a changing world" (51). On some level too she mobilizes her *silva* in order to exceed her historical lot as a Mexican. As a devout Catholic criolla, Sor Juana did not identify as a member of an indigenous community in Nueva España, nor did she seek to speak for the other in her work as we now understand otherness. Nevertheless, "pyramidal" references cannot but bring these cultures to mind as suppressed absences. The mere mention of indigenous Mexican culture and religion in the "Sueño" would have constituted grounds for persecution as blasphemy. Yet Sor Juana found ways to avoid censure by the Inquisition, first, by overtly mentioning pagan pyramids on the other side of time and space (in order to covertly evoke the pyramids under her pillow); and, second, by sublimating those visible architectonic forms into invisible thoughts that could be held licitly and morally within the Catholic architecture of the Spanish Empire (through sublimation achieved by a kind of dark alchemy derived from ancient Greek thought).

To be clear, Sor Juana does not stray from her Catholic beliefs; rather, she mobilizes her orthodoxy in order to recompose a more evolved Catholic orthodoxy, for which she will be eventually be punished. She was not a radical feminist as we might now understand those terms. Rather, she composed a poetic and philosophical argument that adheres to the traditional law of the *silva* form even as it overruns the form's minimal compositional constraints. Through excessive philosophical and poetic erudition she promotes the decomposition of reality, or at least reality as it is perceived subjectively by the human mind. And she does so in a way that allows her to recompose a world in a more enlightened fashion as an intellectual, a woman, and a colonial Catholic subject, in spite of the repressive constraints of the Catholic Church itself.

Andrés Bello: Natural Excess

Andrés Bello wrote his "Silva a la agricultura de la Zona Tórrida" circa 1826, just after the Spanish American wars of independence.[4] I assign the poem in its entirety, without gloss or annotation, to be read prior to class time—but now the students have worked through at least one other *silva*, written in relatively close historical proximity to this one. Perhaps they will recall the "Primero sueño" as they scan the poem and discover that it is composed of heptasyllabic and hendecasyllabic verses in no particular order. They may recognize, in other words, that the "Silva a la agricultura de Zona Tórrida" is the same kind of poem as the "Primero sueño."

The long opening section of Bello's poem features not pyramids and obelisks but fruits and vegetables, a veritable cornucopia of tropical American agricultural goods. And so, instead of geometrical shapes or mythological names, we proceed to *granada* ("pomegranate"; 7), *uva* ("grape"; 9), *caña* ("cane"; 18), *almendra* ("almond"; 21), *nopales* ("nopal"; 23), *jazmín* ("jasmine"; 33), *palmas* ("palms"; 37), and *bananos* ("bananas"; 44), among many other fruits and vegetables. I point out that much of the produce mentioned may be used as intoxicants: the grape goes to the "scalding cask" (*hirviente cuba*) to be made into wine, a statement that leads into a delirious display of forest color and scents, "no de purpúrea fruta, o roja, o gualda / a tus florestas bellas / falta matiz alguno; y bebe en ellas / aromas mil el viento" 'not of purple, or red, or golden fruit / do your lovely forests / lack any hint; and drinks within them / a thousand aromas the wind' (9–12); the sugarcane's *miel* ("honey"; 19) will be extracted and refined into sugar; and then drink and smoke come into play:

> El vino es tuyo, que la herida agave
> para los hijos vierte
> del Anahuac feliz; y la hoja es tuya,
> que, cuando de suave
> humo en espiras vagarosas huya,
> solazará el fastidio al ocio inerte. (27–32)
>
> Wine is yours, that the injured agave
> To the sons pours
> Of joyous Anahuac; and the leaf is yours,

That, when in smooth
Smoke in idle puffs escapes,
Will ease restlessness into inert leisure.

These last verses usually take a good deal of time to unpack. Students understand *vino* ("wine") but do not usually register that this wine springs from the "injured agave" of "joyous Anahuac." Once they learn that Anahuac refers in Nahuatl to the area of Mesoamerica now occupied by Mexico, they will quickly realize that Anahuac is so happy because it has *pulque* (an alcoholic beverage made from fermented agave) or perhaps even tequila. The second clause about the *hoja* ("leaf") may take longer to uncoil because its words swirl around one another like the puffs of smoke they describe. The appearance of *hoja* here first seems to refer back to that of the agave but turns out to be, of course, tobacco, that which "will ease restlessness into inert leisure." Bello's poetic diction, in other words, seems to mimic that which the poem describes. His words curl like puffs of smoke or twist around one another as in a thicket or a bramble.

It is useful here to project on a screen or distribute to students the Real Academia Española (RAE)'s many definitions of *silva*. Before the familiar explanation of "[a] metrical, not strophic, combination in which heptasyllabic and hendecasyllabic verses alternate freely," the RAE defines *silva* as "[a] collection of diverse materials or themes, written with neither method nor order." The fourth, fifth, and sixth definitions are *zarza* ("bramble"), *selva* ("forest"), and *serba* ("fruit of the rowan tree"). Indeed, the etymological root of the Spanish *silva* is the Latin *silva*, which means "forest" as well as "type of poem." As perhaps Latin America's greatest philologist and grammarian, Bello surely understood that his *silva* was a kind of forest, and a wild one at that.[5] Yet his ode is also explicitly tied to farming, such that the poem, in addition to being a *silva*, also presents as a neoclassical georgic in the mode of Virgil (i.e., dedicated to agriculture above and beyond being merely pastoral). The excessive growth of the wild forest-*silva*, in other words, seems to coil into the georgic's ordered landscape, producing a poem that may fall into multiple forms and genres at once.

The intoxicant cornucopia with which the poem begins leads directly into a discussion of the corruption of urban life. "Providencia" 'Providence' (48) has graced the peoples of the equatorial torrid zone with a landscape of such fertility that it grows excessively:

No ya de humanas artes obligado
el premio rinde opimo;

> no es a la podadera, no al arado
> deudor de su racimo;
> escasa industria bástale, cual puede
> hurtar a sus fatigas mano esclava. . . . (56–61)

> No longer to human arts obligated
> Fertility yields its prize;
> It is not to the pruner, nor to the plow
> That its bouquet is a debtor;
> Scant industry suffices, which can take
> Fatigue away from a slave's hand. . . .

Natural abundance and an environment that fatigues the human body have encouraged, in Bello's estimation, a reliance on slave labor. Thus freed from the obligation of industry, nonslaves become a "blind tumult to imprison themselves / in miserable cities" 'y en el ciego tumulto se aprisionan / de míseras ciudades' (81–82), where the *ciudadano* (both "citizen" and "city dweller" in this case) suffers from "el ocio pestilente" 'pestilent leisure' (74). Such leisure in turn leaves ample time for moral decay:

> mas pasatiempo estima
> prender aleve en casto seno el fuego
> de ilícitos amores;
> o embebecido le hallará la aurora
> en mesa infame de ruinoso juego. (94–98)

> Yet pastimes esteem
> The treacherous lighting in chaste breasts of the fire
> Of illicit loves;
> Or drunken will the aurora find it
> At the infamous table of the ruinous game.

As a social and historical document, Bello's *silva* is directly addressed to excess. The lands of the newly independent Spanish America are too abundant, too fecund, for their own good. The excessive fertility of the natural realm translates directly into excesses in society—injustice, oppression, and licentiousness in all its forms, as "citizens" are reduced to "city-dwellers" in thrall to prostitutes, wine, and gambling tables. This excessive energy is also the source of warfare, violence that Bello fears will continue in the Spanish American nations after they have made the "león de España" 'lion of Spain' lie prostrate at their feet (373).

The natural and urban landscapes of Bello's *silva* are fundamentally composed of excessive energies that "naturally" result in decomposition (unruly brambles, rotting and fermenting fruit, sin, and a lack of industry). The poem is therefore a prescription for the recomposition of nations after more than a decade of war, an injunction to reclaim the territory by moving city folk back out to the countryside where they can "tame" the land through farming (presumably on geometrically ordered plots). This agricultural solution is likewise cultural, since by taking up ploughshares the city folk will also become true citizens. And they will also make this transformation by taking up another tool—poetry itself, epitomized by the very *silva* we have just been reading. Bello's poem is a *silva* seeking to become a georgic by pruning, containing, and managing the excesses of its own textual wilderness.

Yet Bello explicitly codes this wilderness as female—both the feminized fecundity of nature and the reproductive faculty of the female body. By contrast, soldiers, sovereigns, and tillers of the soil are always explicitly figured as male throughout the poem. Indeed, the poem ends by saying that the "vencedores" 'vanquishers' who have defeated Spain "pregonará a los hombres" 'will preach to men' of how they have honored the countryside and the simple life of the (male) who labors to harness the land (351–73). An overt goal of "Silva a la agricultura" is to frame feminine power as "excessive" so that it may be curtailed and contained by a (masculinized) nation-state and national culture.

Alfonsina Storni: Hysterical Excess

In the poetry of the twentieth century, not only were the traditional laws of poetic meter (including those of the *silva*) upended, but so too were established dynamics in Latin American nations of gender, race, class, and sexuality. Continued attention to the *silva* in the study of this period may show that poets did not respond to the characterization of femininity and nonreproductive sex as "excess" merely by resignifying it, much less by normalizing it. Indeed, they responded by making "excess" all the more excessive in order to push both poetic form and national or regional culture more generally into crisis.

A case in point is Alfonsina Storni's "Carta lírica a otra mujer" ("Lyrical Letter to Another Woman"), first published in the 1920 volume *Languidez* ("Languor"). Although my poetry courses do not always track to literary history or chronology of publication, I invariably teach Storni's poem in the wake of a unit on *modernista* poetry. Whereas the early core group of *modernistas*, exemplified by Rubén Darío, objectified women as types of "pure" beauty, a number of female poets of the late *modernista* (or *postmodernista*) and early *vanguardista* eras deliberately questioned the aestheticist-symbolist style of Darío and his adherents, especially as it pertained to gender. As Ignacio Ruíz Pérez has written with respect to Storni, Delmira Agustini, Gabriela Mistral, and Juana de Ibarbourou, "The objective of these women writers is the search for a space of their own on the margin of modernist tropes and topics; in other words, a space and a discourse from which to rethink and reconsider poetic language with the aim of expressing the experience of difference itself in new terms" (184; my trans.). Eulalia in Darío's "Era un aire suave" ("It Was a Gentle Air") may laugh, while Carolina from his "De invierno" ("Of Winter") may doze on her Oriental divan, but neither figure actually speaks. Agustini and Storni in particular frame their work self-consciously as a means of talking back to their male counterparts. As Jill Kuhnheim writes of Storni's explicatory introduction to her "antisonnets" of 1938's *Mascarilla y trébol*:

> Read against the background of other more avant-garde poets (who happen to be male), her words call attention to the fact that a female poet may be held to a different standard, for the explication implies that her lyric production is supposed to be more personal, more manageable. Simply calling her poems antisonnets may be part of her attempt to manage the possible accusation of obscurity, then, for with the term she follows the architecture of the sonnet, yet demonstrates her talent, her mastery of the form, while introducing possibilities for change, for flexibility. In this way she inserts herself into tradition, but alters it, maintaining her marginality in a move analogous to her general situation as woman writer within a patriarchal social structure. ("Politics" 392)

Accordingly, Storni and other female poets of her generation occupied a third space between *modernismo* and *vanguardismo* in which the articulation of female voices would subvert "patriarchal social structures," even if this space was—as both Ruíz Pérez and Kuhnheim call it—a space of "marginality."

The trap I have set for my students with the *silvas* of Sor Juana and Bello begins to close upon them with the "Carta lírica." As always they begin by scanning the poem in their small groups, and with a modicum of discussion they find that Storni's poem is composed entirely of hendecasyllabic verses—with the stunning exception of the final (pentasyllabic) verse, "Nada es posible" 'Nothing is possible' (83). We defer a reading of this last line until later. For the moment, the groups note that there is no identifiable rhyme scheme, though seemingly assonant rhymes abound. Finally, the groups are prompted to identify the poem's form, a question that usually elicits confusion and silence. I then remind them of "Primero sueño" and "Silva a la agricultura" so that the poems' formal similarities raise the question of whether Storni's work is, like the others, a *silva*. Technically, "Carta lírica" fulfills all the requirements of the *silva* form: an indeterminate number of unrhymed or assonantly rhymed heptasyllabic or hendecasyllabic verses—for, even though there are no heptasyllables, there is no firm rule that they are required. I suggest that the poem may be a *silva* in which Storni has taken the poetic license to exclude the heptasyllable entirely—a poem that is at once perfectly within the strictures of the *silva* form, being maximally composed of hendecasyllables, and yet somewhat in violation of the genre's rules. From the students, more confusion and silence, proof positive that *nada es posible*.

The next set of exercises is decidedly more interesting for students. After reading aloud the first few verses, which describe the "other woman's" face as "Pequeña, dulce . . . Ya ni sé . . . Divina" 'Small, sweet . . . What do I know . . . Divine' (4), students search sections of the poem in groups for further characterizations of the speaker's rival. The verses may describe the woman's body, as at the beginning of the poem: "Ah, ¿sois así? Decidme si en la boca / Tenéis un rumoroso colmenero, / Si las orejas vuestras son a modo / de pétalos de rosas ahuecados" 'Ah, is that how you are? Tell me if you have / A babbling beekeeper in your mouth, / If your ears are in the manner / of rose petal scoops' (12–15). Other groups may notice the presence of a man who brings the poetic voice into contact, so to speak, with the other woman: ". . . Ahora en vuestros brazos / Él se adormece y le decís palabras / Pequeñas y menudas que semejan / Pétalos volanderos y muy blancas" 'Now in your arms / He falls asleep and you utter small and / Light words to him that look like / Wisping and very white petals' (37–40). And still other groups may find—and even become disturbed to find—how the speaker begins to reach out and touch the woman, whether or not the woman wants it: "¡Oh, qué amargo deleite, este deleite / De buscar huellas suyas y seguirlas / Sobre las manos vuestras tan sedosas / Tan finas, con sus venas tan azules" 'Oh, what bitter delight, this delight / Of searching his tracks and following them / Over your hands so silken / So gossamer, with their veins so blue' (66–69). Once the groups have selected their verses, they are asked to reread them with the following question in mind: Who exactly is the other woman? Typical responses are that she has stolen the poet's man, or that there is some sort of love triangle involved; that she is white, with very fine white skin, almost transparent; and that she also seems to be an object of attraction (and repulsion) for the poet.

All of these answers are good, but they also fail utterly. This is not because the students are unintelligent (any more so than their professor, at least) but because Storni's "Carta lírica" is designed to fail. On an immediate level, much of the imagery fails to add up, even if it conveys meaningful content. Readers form false cognates. What, for instance, does it mean that the woman's mouth contains a "babbling beekeeper"? The words may evoke honey and buzzing beehives, but we are nevertheless asked to imagine a tiny, babbling person in a strange suit. Similarly, if there is some sort of love triangle, the poet does not seek to recover her man by pushing aside her competition; rather, she seeks at times to become either her ex-lover or the other woman. The poet imagines saying the words the man speaks to his new lover and the words the new lover speaks to him. She imagines her man kissing the other woman's hands and imagines kissing them herself, coming so close to the other woman's skin that she almost penetrates the surface of her body and enters her "veins so blue." Ultimately, it is the very imagination of these scenarios that is most problematic in the poem, for the simple reason that the poet never knows the other woman, never meets her, and therefore has no idea what she looks like or what she does with the male lover. The poet says so explicitly from the first verse: "Vuestro nombre no sé, ni vuestro rostro / Conozco yo" 'I know not your name, nor your face / Have I met' (1–2).

In other words, the poem is really an exercise in the *nada [que] es posible*. "Nothing is possible" does not mean that it is impossible, necessarily. Rather, the poem is an experiment in making the *nothing* into a reality in its own right. The title of the poem speaks to a direct communication — a letter — between two women. But in fact Storni's *silva* is composed of any number of failed communicative channels that compound one another's failure — that decompose each other. Any contact between the women is mediated not by a written text but rather by the man who has inserted himself between them. Because the poet has lost contact with the man, her poem is a dead letter that cannot be sent, much less received by a woman she will never meet or speak to. The poet's only mode of communication, therefore, is to objectify the woman just as (she imagines) the male lover objectifies her. There is no intersubjective communication, because, on the one hand, the imaginary woman, a fantasy, does not and cannot speak as a subject; and, on the other, because the poet herself constantly exceeds the limits of her own subjectivity, both by objectifying another woman and by objectifying her desire as written language. It is not the "otra mujer" of the poem who is truly the other woman; it is the poet who others herself by writing a "lyrical letter" that is, using the diagnostic terminology of the day, hysterical. Thus the poetic voice performs multiple voices at once her own and othered: the male lover, the female lover, the speaker, and perhaps the poet.[6] Notably, the title of the poem is itself double: the text is at once a *carta* and a *lírica*, missive and poem; on the latter account, the lyric is at once a *silva* and a poem that exceeds the rules governing the *silva* form. Storni, it seems, openly violated poetic law (at a time when this law was absolute and maximal under the rule of the *modernistas*) in order to critique the inherent violation that patriarchal order imposes upon women. The only way that women can converse in the "Carta lírica" is to become othered women—hysterics, excessive voices that cannot be contained within their own bodies or texts. "Carta lírica" is only a singular work to the extent that it opens onto a multiplicity of voices, a heteroglossia that cannot be controlled by a singular poetic form.

Pedagogical Excess

In the end, there is nothing to be learned from poems that are, in essence, both more and nothing more than they purport to be. There is nothing morally edifying about the study of a traditional form such as the *silva*. Reading *silvas* closely will not make students better people, or better citizens, or more civilized inhabitants of a world that is by all accounts ever more *bárbaro* ("barbaric, extraordinary, and morbidly funny"). Reading *silvas* teaches nothing, and nothing else matters. This is the point.

From *vanguardismo* into the contemporary age, Spanish American poetries become far more diversified and, in a certain sense, more personalized. Inherited (or, some might say, imposed) poetic forms like the *silva* often give way, especially among urban, educated writers, to free verse and concrete poetry. These forms demand absolute poetic license in order to establish resonance between the objective visual, syntactic, and semantic presentation of the text and the poet's own subjective motivations (or the reader's subjective reception, for that matter). On the other hand, reading them opens new dialogues with nonpatriarchal or non-Eurocentric traditions in order to establish historical resonance between the contemporary poet and people who have almost been lost to history (e.g., indigenous and black communities, women, or impoverished workers).

Contemporary Spanish American poetries, in other words, create new resonance between subject and object, to the point that difference between the one and the other, the now and the then, becomes confused. Resonance, of course, is not to be found within a word or a text, but only in what resides beyond these, between the objects we assign as homework and the intersubjective channels of communication between the students and instructors who read and discuss them. In the best of cases, students learn to forge (perhaps false) associational leaps in which these resonances occur. This is the excess to which the *silva* points, our entrance to dark forests. It is a way to make nothing matter.

Notes

1. English translations of all citations in this essay will be my own, made in consultation, in the case of Sor Juana, with Trueblood's version in *A Sor Juana Anthology*.

2. The first weeks of my poetry courses focus on the basics of versification (syllabics; meter; *agudo* [stress on the ultimate syllable of the verse], *llano* [stress on the penultimate syllable], *esdrújulo* [stress on the antepenultimate syllable]; *sinalefa* [combination of two consecutive vowels into a single syllable], etc.) before moving on to sonnets, including those of Sor Juana. The sonnet is almost the perfect vehicle for a course in Spanish American poetry: it is compact, rather austere in its adherence to compositional rules, abundant and prevalent in literary history up through the *modernistas* (and beyond), and readily analyzed thematically in terms of the break that typically occurs between the *cuartetos* ("quatrains") and the *tercetos* ("tercets"). In other words, the sonnet is the model of orderliness and concision that we seek to negate, obliterate, in the tenebrous excess of the *silva*.

3. As Carlos Vossler wrote in 1953, "Las pirámides . . . representan la aspiración del hombre por elevarse psíquica y espiritualmente; por consiguiente, se piensa en 'pirámides de luz' en oposición a la terrestre pirámide de sombra del comienzo del poema" 'The pyramids [from verse 383 onward] . . . represent humanity's aspiration to elevate itself psychically and spiritually; thus, one thinks of "pyramids of light" in opposition to the terrestrial pyramid of shadow from the beginning of the poem' (qtd. in Sabat de Rivers 106).

4. Bello intended "Silva a la agricultura de la Zona Tórrida," originally published in his London journal *Repertorio Americana* in 1826, to be the first part of a longer work, *América*. He also considered including it with an earlier *silva*, "Alocución a la poesía" ("Address to Poetry"), first published in his prior London-based journal, *Biblioteca Americana*, in 1823, in a work he planned to call *Silvas*

americanas. Neither *América* or *Silvas americanas* was ever completed, or ever appeared as such in print, although the two silvas and other unpublished fragments appear in Bello's *Obras completas* (*Complete Works*).

5. In the apostrophe of "Alocución a la poesía," Bello asks La Poesía ("Divine Poetry"), "¿Qué a ti, silvestre ninfa, con las pompas / de alcázares reales?" 'What to you, sylvan nymph, with pomp and splendor / of royal castles?' (44).

6. My mention of "performance" here is a nod not only to Judith Butler and Nelly Richard, but more directly to Vicky Unruh's definitive discussion of Latin American female writers in *Performing Women and Modern Literary Culture in Latin America.* Unruh's book speaks to the centrality of performance and declamation in Storni's dramatic works, but in a way that serves as direct commentary on Storni's poetry as well. Unruh connects "this process of reenactment and change to Storni's ongoing struggle, as Argentina's most renowned *poetisa* of her time, to refashion this public role and its prescribed expressive modes for women, not only into a more comfortable fit but also into a full-blown critique of its own terms" (31).

Jacobo Sefamí

Difficult Poetry:
Teaching the Avant-Garde
and the Neobaroque

How do we define "difficult poetry"? Is it the unfamiliar, incomprehensible, or weird? Some students consider all poetry difficult, convinced they will not grasp a poem's metaphors or a word's manifold meanings if they do not know the codes being represented. In general terms, that difficulty may be associated with lack of understanding. But difficulty should also be addressed as unfamiliarity or lack of practice. If I am asked to run a marathon, and I am not a runner, I face an impossible task. But if I establish a program of exercise and practice continuously, I will probably be able to run it after a while: what seemed difficult may become easy. With this analogy in mind, I would venture to say that students should be asked to read poetry often in order to familiarize themselves with different styles, historical periods, and approaches. After a while, what seemed odd and remote will become recognizable.

Some of the features that students may find difficult in poetry are

vocabulary (infrequent words, *cultismos* [highly academic or learned words], regional and local terms, archaisms, neologisms, technical or scientific references)
syntax (hyperbaton, missing elements)

60

tropes (indirect discourse, obscure metaphors, metonyms)
extraliterary references (historical, sociopolitical, mythological,
    personal)
illogical associations
wordplay, nonsense, or incomprehensibility

While these qualities, intrinsic to much poetry, may pose difficulties for readers, particular literary movements, styles, and poets have been identified by many critics as "difficult" (the historical baroque of the seventeenth century and Luis de Góngora, in particular, come to mind). In this essay, I concentrate on the Latin American avant-garde of the 1920s to the 1940s and the neobaroque in the latter part of the twentieth century. I will address the elements of difficulty mentioned above in trying to convey effective ways to teach this type of poetry to undergraduate students (some exercises may be too simplistic for graduate students).

Avant-Garde Aesthetics

Since the pictorial avant-garde in Europe precedes the literary one, it is useful to introduce this period to students with the famous Picasso painting *Les Demoiselles d'Avignon* ("The Young Ladies of Avignon"), explaining the use of geometric shapes and distortions of nudes. We must also point to the idea of returning to the basics in painting, the line and simple shapes. For poetry, the analogous basic elements are the verb and the noun.

A brief explanation of the poetic avant-garde, using the concepts elaborated by César Fernández Moreno in *Introducción a la poesía* ("Introduction to Poetry")—the rebellion against beauty, music, and the communicative function of language—also helps students understand the desire of avant-garde artists to challenge or to disregard traditional aesthetic values. This can be illustrated with Oliverio Girondo's poem "Es la baba" ("It's the Drool"; 144–45) and, in a later class, with the first poem from César Vallejo's *Trilce*. In both cases, the poets question—through the tropes of drool or excrement—the traditional view of poetry as portraying beauty. It is also important, in order to convey the spirit of the period, to read the manifestos of futurism by Filippo Marinetti, both the initial, general one, published in 1909, and the "Technical Manifesto of Futurist Literature," published in 1912. After reading these, students will clearly understand the belligerent, aggressive, destructive, and misogynist nature of the avant-garde (Marinetti's misogynist and fascist attitudes are well known), but in the technical manifesto they will also find the basic principles that correspond to the futurist style of poetry: the elimination of punctuation; a preference for nouns or verbs to the detriment of the adjective; the absence of conjunctions, prepositions, or relative pronouns; the use of other types of signs, such as mathematical signs; the search for new and original images; a break with traditional patterns of beauty; the exploration of meaninglessness; a sense of astonishment; and the annulment of logic.

Illogical Associations: New Images

From this grounding in the principles of the European avant-garde, a transition can be made to Vicente Huidobro's manifesto "El creacionismo" ("Creationism"; *Obra poética* 1338–42). There the Chilean poet shows how to create new images (as in cubism) by joining phrases that lack logical connection, using examples such as "The bird nests in the rainbow" and "The night is hat." Some exercises illustrating *creacionismo* can be elaborated with students: as one group prepares fifteen cards, each card bearing an incomplete sentence containing a subject and a verb, the other group prepares fifteen cards featuring different nouns preceded by prepositions. The instructor can then read sentences resulting from the random combination of a card from one group with a card from the other, such as "A man walks . . . into a sausage sandwich" or "The turtle moves . . . before a Beatles song." Thus students experience and enjoy one of the resources of the avant-garde: the generation of new, unusual images.

An examination of some of Huidobro's poems from his cubist-creationist period could complement this segment. For example, the poem "Teléfono" ("Telephone") from *Horizon carré* ("Squared Horizon"; *Obra poética* 446–47) can be very useful, since several elements of the avant-garde are present: the use of space (white spaces indicating distance or silence), capitalization (allowing a reading concentrated exclusively on uppercase letters, as a subpoem), fragmentation, and multiple perspectives, each unit expressing in various ways the experience of a phone call. In addition, the teacher can establish the relation between futurism and the technological inventions of the time (such as the telephone, the train, and the airplane) and can discuss in class how communication was affected by the telephone, the telegraph, photography, and film. Students can then be asked to consider how contemporary poetry might be affected by e-mail, text messages, *WhatsApp, Snapchat, FaceTime, Skype*, and so forth.

Altazor: Wordplay, Nonsense

Huidobro's *Altazor* is one of the most famous poems of the Latin American avant-garde. I concentrate on fragments that illustrate its main features (a review of the entire poem would take several classes to complete). The preface exemplifies Huidobro's playful tone, beginning with the parody of the biblical Genesis, and presents the ars poetica of the poem as impossibility: "Un poema es una cosa que sera. / Un poema es una cosa que nunca es, pero que debiera ser. / Un poema es una cosa que nunca ha sido, que nunca podrá ser." 'A poem is something that will be. / A poem is something that never is, but ought to be. / A poem is something that never has been, that never can be' (57; Weinberger 5). The last sentences of the preface can help formulate at least two readings of the poem: "Poeta, he ahí tu paracaídas, maravilloso como el imán del abismo. / Mago: he ahí tu paracaídas que una palabra tuya puede convertir en un parasubidas maravilloso como el relámpago que quisiera cegar al creador" 'Here's your parachute, Poet, wonderful as the charms of the chasm. / Here's your parachute, Magician, which one word of yours can transform into a parashoot, wonderful as the lightning bolt that tries to blind the creator' (60; Weinberger 11). The first reading, which is the more generally accepted one, concerns the fall into the abyss, a disintegration of language and the world; the other reading presents the poem as an ascent, a song that dispenses with words as it reaches a sublime, mystical state, one in which language is no longer necessary. In Weinberger's interpretation of the poem, "the new was sacred, space became the unexplored territory, and the future was the only mythical era" (Weinberger xi).

From the first canto, it is necessary to study the poem's harrowing vision of life, which presumably was influenced by the First World War (the poem was first published as a fragment, in French, in 1919). Above all, it is relevant to read the anti-Christian verses 91 to 108. The study of that fragment could be accompanied by the reading of excerpts from Octavio Paz's *Los hijos del limo* (*Children of the Mire*), in particular those related to the breakdown of religion, to the poetic traditions of German romanticism (as in the work of Jean Paul) and French symbolism (as in the work of Gérard de Nerval), and to the feelings of anguish and meaninglessness that attend the notion of the death of God (70–78).

With the third canto, Huidobro starts innovating and playing with language. The well-known fragments of the poem that begins, "Basta señora arpa de las bellas imágenes" 'Enough lady harp of the beautiful images' (95; Weinberger 71), can be used to explain a key pioneering mechanism for Huidobro and the avant-garde. This phrase creates images based on juxtapositions of disparate elements, from "Sabemos posar un beso como una mirada / Plantar miradas como árboles / Enjaular árboles como pájaros . . ." 'We already know how to dart a kiss like a glance / Plant glances like trees / Cage trees like birds . . .' (95; Weinberger 71). In each case, a logical phrase—"dart a glance," "plant trees," "cage birds"—is broken by a strange element in the middle. Students can make similar constructions, first writing simple verb-and-object phrases (such as "write books," "kick balls," "eat enchiladas," and "sing *rancheras*") and then combining them with illogical elements in *Altazor*'s style: "kick books as balls," "eat balls as enchiladas," "sing enchiladas as *rancheras*," and so forth. Completing this exercise, students will understand one of the strategies of the "cortacircuitos en las frases" 'circuit breakers in the sentences' (97; Weinberger 75).

Another important element of *Altazor* is the desire to erase the customary relationships between signified and signifiers (employing Ferdinand de Saussure's formula of the linguistic sign): "Y puesto que debemos vivir y no nos suicidamos / Mientras vivamos juguemos / El simple sport de los vocablos / De la pura palabra y nada más" 'And since we must live and not kill ourselves / As long as we live let us play / The simple sport of words / Of the pure word and nothing more' (97; Weinberger 75). Students can be asked to write words in as many languages as they know, without translating them. Then other students can try to guess the meaning by simply hearing the sound of the foreign words.

In canto 4 of *Altazor*, compound words that are initially unrecognizable and that play with morphology, creating neologisms, begin to appear. Special attention should be paid to the verses that begin, "A la horitaña de la montazonte / La violondrina y el goloncelo" 'The horslope of the hillizon / The violonswallow with a cellotail' (105; Weinberger 89). Having shown how Huidobro decomposes words, breaking them into two, instructors can then ask students to think of words containing four syllables in order to separate them into two syllables each and invent their own new words; for example, *testarudo* ("stubborn") and *sanguijuela* ("leech") become *testajuela* and *sanguirudo*. In addition to neologisms modeled on Huidobro's, created by breaking up and recompounding words, instructors can indicate at least three other types: neologisms created by Latino communities in the United States by mixing English and Spanish, such as *rufo* ("roof"), *aplicar* ("apply"), or *brecas* ("brakes"); neologisms modeled on those by Vallejo, using existing words but altering them (such as *tesórea*, an adjective created from *tesoro* ["treasure"]); and neologisms created by children, as well as by the act of speaking in tongues or glossolalia, where nonsense is the central feature. The class can consider such questions as, What meaning would a word like *horitaña* have, beyond the combination of "horizon" and "mountain"? How many speakers must use a neologism in order for it to become an effective form of communication? What happens to communication when words have no "meaning" at all?

Another interesting exercise derives from the fragment of *Altazor* that starts with "Pero el cielo prefiere el rodoñol" 'But the sky prefers the nighdongale' and ends with "rosiñol" 'nightingale' (106; Weinberger 91). Huidobro, who had used the word *rossignol* ("nightingale") in the original French version of the fragment, refrained from translating the word into Spanish (*ruiseñor*) in order to preserve the game of inserting solfège syllables in the middle of the word (ro*do*ñol, ror*re*ñol, ro*mi*ñol, ro*fa*ñol, ro*sol*ñol, ro*la*ñol, and ro*si*ñol); since *ruiseñor* does not contain *si* or any of the other syllables of the scale, it's not a logical starting word for the game. Huidobro could have used the name of another bird that contains one of the syllables, for example, *tórtola* ("turtledove"): tórto*do*, tórto*rre*, torto*mi*, tórto*fa*, tórto*sol*, tórto*la*, and torto*sí*. These lines invite students to play with language just as children do, for example, entering an extra syllable using the "f" sound after each syllable in a word: "La*fa* po*fo*-e*fe*-si*fi*-a*fa* no*fo* e*fes* di*fi*-fi*fi*-ci*fil* . . ." ("La poesía no es difícil" 'Poetry isn't difficult'). Students can also be encouraged to come up with other ways of playing with words.

The end of canto 4 anticipates the last lines of the poem, foreshadowing the appearance of the nonsensical vowels "Aia ai ai aaia i i." Interestingly, the construction of the word *eterfinifrete*, as it appears here—"El pájaro tralalí canta en las ramas de mi cerebro / Porque encontró la clave del eterfinifrete" 'The bird tralalee sings in the branches of my brain / For I've found the key to the infiniternity' (110; Weinberger 99)—is the sum of the words *éter* ("ether," also connoting emptiness), *fin* ("end," "goal"), *eternidad* ("eternity"), *infinito* ("infinity"), and the ending *-ete* (not a normal suffix), which evokes a musical instrument like the *clarinete* ("clarinet"). Thus the key paradox of the poem is revealed: nothingness, the volatile air, infinity, eternity, heavens, and music are what allow the singing of the vowels emanating from this epiphany or illumination. At the same time, *eterfinifrete* is a palindrome, which can be read from left to right and from right to left (not achievable in the English translation, "infiniternity"). At this point students can be asked to find palindromes on the Internet in order to see more examples of this type of wordplay. This is, after all, one of *Altazor*'s major achievements: the innovation in terms of language, the attention to the ludic aspect of writing.

From canto 7, one can highlight the residues of words that have been used throughout *Altazor*—such as *montaña* ("mountain"), *estrella* ("star"), *sol* ("sun"), *luna* ("moon"), *infinito* ("infinity"), *cielo* ("sky"), *golondrina* ("swallow"), and *firmamento* ("firmament")—as they appear in new combinations, such as *montresol* ("trierrasun"), *lunatando* ("moonaluning"), and so on, to analyze the final canto as a sum of the poem in terms of language, but one already stripped of meaning (137–38; Weinberger 149–51). Whether emphasizing the *caída* (the "fall" portrayed in canto 1) or the *subida* (the "rise" mentioned in the preface), a discussion of these two readings (failure or achievement) should take place in terms of language experimentation, and students should be given several opportunities, as I have suggested here, to carry out their own experiments with poetic language.

"Trilce I": Vocabulary, Obscure References

Another one of the high points of Latin American difficult poetry is César Vallejo's *Trilce*, a book that has generated many interpretations. I suggest using the critical edition by Julio Ortega because it contains summaries of key readings for each poem. It is necessary to point to the main features of the book as they pertain to biographical elements: Vallejo's imprisonment, his mother's death, and his tortured love life. The instructor should also note the ways in which Vallejo incorporates the poetics of the avant-garde: the technique of "crossing out" (*tachadura*; see Ortega's introduction, 13–14); the elimination of prepositions, conjunctions, and relative pronouns; the use of extraliterary codes and language; the propensity to resort to neologisms and archaisms; and cubist simultaneity, among other practices.

The often-anthologized first poem of *Trilce* (43; translated in *Complete Poetry* 167) is an effective place to begin tackling the juxtaposition of erudite language with the mundane that creates one of the initial barriers to understanding Vallejo's poetry. Students can be asked to look up difficult words or can be provided with definitions of terms such as

> *calabrina*: [palabra arcaica] hedor, intenso olor desagradable
> *hialóidea*: con calidades del vidrio
> *mantillo*: tierra abonada, humus; estiércol ya biológicamente
>   descompuesto

> *abozaleada*: posiblemente "abozalada"; tener puesto un bozal, un
> objeto que se les pone a los perros alrededor del hocico para que
> no muerdan

Then instructors may ask students to indicate the type of register that each word connotes. For example, *bemoles* ("B-flats") belongs to music but is also used as a colloquialism for difficulties; *testar* ("will") pertains to law, as it is linked to making a will; *guano* has a commercial use as a commodity; *calabrina* ("ponk") is an archaism that becomes a *cultismo*; *mantillo* ("muck"), like *guano*, relates to a fertilizer in agriculture; *abozaleada* ("muzzled") is linked to wild animals; the phrases "Quién hace tanta bulla" 'Who's making all that racket' and "un poco más de consideración" 'A little more consideration' are used in colloquial language. That is, by simply looking at the vocabulary, students can appreciate the strange lexical associations that increase *Trilce*'s hermetic nature.

After a first reading aloud, the instructor might offer Juan Espejo Asturrizaga's biographical anecdote explaining that the poem refers to the degrading jail routine of bringing the prisoners to the latrines four times during the day, in the morning and in the afternoon, with the guards shouting at the prisoners to defecate quickly (Vallejo, *Trilce* 43–44). The first reading of the poem, then, extrapolates on the metaphors or metonyms presented through some of the words or phrases, as Ricardo González Vigil explains: "[E]l *guano* puede valer por el excremento humano; el *mantillo* al calificarse de líquido, por la orina; y los vv. 14–16, por la postura en cuclillas de quien defeca en un hoyo o silo, sintiendo que no lo dejan evacuar tranquilo (lo que emergía como una 'península' queda como detenido por un bozal, en la 'línea mortal del equilibrio' de lograr despegarse del cuerpo y ser 'isla')" '[T]he *guano* could be read as human excrement; the *muck*, qualified as liquid, as urine; and the lines 14–16, by the crouching posture of those who defecate in a pit or silo, feeling that they don't let him evacuate calmly (what emerged as a "peninsula" is stopped by a muzzle "on the fatal balance line" to be able to detach from the body and become an "island")' (Vallejo, *Obras completas* 227; my trans.). As the first poem in the collection, "Trilce I" represents a challenge to traditional poetry (particularly Spanish American *modernismo*) that considers beauty (in language as well as theme) as a fundamental element. Students come to understand that writing a poem about defecating goes against traditional poetry.[1]

A second reading of the text could concentrate on poetry and its reception. The first two lines, "Quién hace tánta bulla, y ni deja / testar las islas que van quedando" 'Who's making all that racket, and not even letting / the islands that linger make a will,' can refer to the critics (or other authorities) who do not allow a poet's words to flow. It is suggested that the "guano," which can be read as the poem, will be better appreciated with time ("se aquilatará mejor"), which was exactly the case for *Trilce*. The line "la península párase . . . impertérrita / en la línea mortal del equilibrio" 'the peninsula raises up . . . imperturbable / on the fatal balance line' brings up the issue of poetic balance or equilibrium. *Trilce* plays with the notion of imperfection, as it is constantly referring to the impossibility of achieving beauty and harmony (see also poem 36).

Students could also produce a reading of the poem as a Latin American (Peruvian) appropriation of the European avant-garde, as can be seen with the reference to "guano" (as a commodity in the region), the jail experience, and the overall representation of marginalization, periphery (in the images of islands and peninsula), and injustice. The poem is written in an aggrieved tone. Without using the pronoun *I*, the speaker, as a subaltern subject, complains to someone with authority. The protest in the first two lines is followed by a plea to the interlocutor for mercy ("Un poco más de consideración" 'A little more consideration'), although, beyond the implicit jail experience, the exact situation that prompts the speaker's appeal is never described). Considering the poem's images linked to the idea of periphery—"islands," "insular heart," and "peninsula"—students come to understand that the experience of separation or *aislamiento* ("isolation") is significant to the speaker as a source of suffering, either emotional ("insular heart"), or physical ("DE LOS MÁS SOBERBIOS BEMOLES" 'OF THE MOST GRANDIOSE B-FLATS'). An observation on the economic aspects of the poem is also relevant to establishing elements of value: with time, the guano will become valuable; the invented adjective *tesórea* (translated in *Complete Poetry* as "fecapital") adds the positive view of the excrement, as it will become fertilizer (a treasure), and will make the land "produce" plants and life. From the lower strata and degrading nature of defecating the poem's language rises to the element of gold (the *oro* in *tesoro*) and the high culture that emanates from it. This trajectory in the poem could also be seen as rising from the most rudimentary organic function of the body and aspiring to the spiritual.

The Neobaroque

Another poetic mode often considered challenging to teach is the neobaroque. This is a style of poetry common in the late twentieth century in Latin America, in which artifice, figuration, and a consciousness of textuality are highly developed, often with explicit or covert reference to the baroque poetry of the early modern period. The term *neobarroco* as applied to Latin American literature was arguably coined by the Brazilian poet Haroldo de Campos, writing about Umberto Eco's *opera aperta* ("open work"), to refer to the unconventional nature of contemporary writing ("A obra"). As Campos was to insist on several occasions, Latin American cultures share a genealogy from the time of their cultural formations under the auspices of the European baroque; they contributed their own inflections to what came to be called the Barroco de Indias, or New World Baroque. Through the French symbolist poets Paul Verlaine and Stéphane Mallarmé, several of the poets of the *modernista* period (the late nineteenth and early twentieth centuries) revisited the poets of the seventeenth-century baroque, rereading Francisco de Quevedo, Luis de Góngora, and Lope de Vega in a spirit of appropriation and transformation. In twentieth-century Spain, the rebirth of the baroque pertains to the Spanish poets of the Generation of '27 (which refers to the tercentenary of Góngora's death), the Mexican poet and critic Alfonso Reyes, and the Cuban poet and novelist José Lezama Lima.[2]

In 1972, the seminal essay "El barroco y el neobarroco" ("The Baroque and the Neobaroque") by Severo Sarduy oriented the discussion of the baroque and its outcomes in Latin American literature to the French structuralist and poststructuralist poetics of the *Tel Quel* group. Pointing to writing strategies, Sarduy referred to intertextuality and intratextuality as signs of the heavily textual fabric of the neobaroque (which extends from literature to other media, such as film, the visual arts, music, and popular culture). By substitution, proliferation, or condensation of signs, this literature involves an unusual degree of artifice in language, especially the recirculation of metaphors from all epochs. Sarduy referred to various Latin American novels that had appeared a few years before his essay, but also pointed to Pablo Neruda and to a new type of poetry that Campos developed in *Galáxias* ("Galaxies"), a series of fifty texts published as individual poems starting in 1963, then collected in 1984 and 2004, that play on the border between prose and poetry, between semantics and sound. Using paronomasia as a major technical device, the book is a metonymic adventure in search of the materiality of language.

Lezama Lima's poetry, Sarduy's essays, the Poundian style of the Peruvian poet Rodolfo Hinostroza's *Contranatura* ("Against Nature"), the erudite new antipoetry of the Mexican Gerardo Deniz, and, in Brazil, the work of Campos and the *concretistas* ("concretists") served as the background for a new generation of poets that could be loosely linked to the neobaroque. The Argentine writer Néstor Perlongher coined the term *neobarroso*, evoking the dirt or mud (*el barro*) of the Rio de la Plata, and the Uruguayan poet and critic Eduardo Espina has spoken in the same playful tone of *barrococó* (a play on words incorporating both *baroque* and *rococo*). Since 1996, *Medusario*, a major compilation of neobaroque poetry, has circulated widely in Latin America, and this type of poetry became one of the dominant trends at the end of the twentieth century and the beginning of the twenty-first. I offer teaching strategies here on texts by José Kozer and Coral Bracho, two key neobaroque poets.

Syntax: Derivation and Metonym

When asked if his poetry was surrealist, Lezama Lima answered, "Claro que no es surrealismo, porque hay una metáfora que se desplaza, no conseguida por el choque fulminante de dos metáforas" 'Of course it is not surrealist, because there is a metaphor that derives, not obtained directly by the sudden shock of two metaphors' (qtd. in *Medusario* 26; my trans.). That is, while the avant-garde juxtaposes two very different elements in its aspiration to create a new, original image, the neobaroque works with a derivative form, based on dependent clauses, where in several cases the main phrase is left unfinished. The figure of the rhizome (theorized by Gilles Deleuze and Félix Guattari) has been used to illustrate this phenomenon, as there is no tree trunk, but only rootlets that grow independently, with no predictable direction. The marginalized elements (normally placed between parentheses) may constitute a large segment of the poem.

In "Gaudeamus" (from the Catholic hymn "Gaudeamus igitur" 'Let us rejoice'), José Kozer, a Cuban poet who emigrated to the United States in 1960, uses a complex syntax, with the same derivative technique described above, to construct one long sentence:

> En mi confusión
> no supe ripostar a mis detractores, aquellos
> que me tildan
> de postalita porque pronuncio la ce a la manera castellana o digo tío por
>   tipo (me privan) los mestizajes
> (peruanismos) (mexicanismos)
> de la dicción y los vocablos: ni soy uno (ni otro) ni soy recto ni ambiguo,
>   bárbaramente
> romo
> y narigudo (barbas) asirias (ojos) oblicuos y vengo del otro lado

del río: cubano
y postalita (judío) y tabernáculo (shofar y taled) violín de la Aragón o
      primer corneta de la Sonora Matancera. . . . (44)

In my confusion
I didn't know how to answer my detractors, those
who brand me
a poseur because I pronounce the c in the Castilian manner or I say fellow
      instead of guy (I love) miscegenations
(peruvianisms) (mexicanisms)
of diction and vocabulary: I am neither the one (nor the other) neither
      straight nor ambiguous, barbarously
flat-nosed
and big-nosed Assyrian (beards) oblique (eyes) and I come from the
      other side
of the river: Cuban
and vain (a Jew) and tabernacle (shofar and taled) violin of the Aragon or
      first trumpet
of the Sonora Matancera. . . . (Pérez Firmat 155–56)

The poem is a defense of plurality in response to attacks on those who don't fit into a single country and form of speech. It is a self-portrait, using at least three different approaches to identity: linguistic, physical, and spiritual. The experience of exile allows a pluralization of language: the speaker becomes all others. The poem is a self-portrait of a man who empties himself and fills himself with the features of others. Students might discuss the proper functions of punctuation marks, particularly the parenthesis, which in this poem serves a prosodic purpose (as a pause in the reading) rather than a syntactical one. They might also be led to observe that the link between language and image appears by contiguity. That is, the poem moves from differences in dialect to simultaneous and opposite physical appearances (at once flat- and big-nosed) to contrasting spiritual and cultural identities (as a Cuban Jew), and from the solemn and holy sound of the shofar in the Jewish liturgy to the popular rhythms of a trumpet in a salsa band. The colon functions as a sign that supports the metonymic effects; that is, the crossbreeding of languages has its equivalence, by way of contiguity, to the face. Interestingly, English, the primary language of the exiled poet's country of residence, is absent from the poem. But taking refuge in Spanish is a way to cope with exile, as the speaker realizes his condition later in the text: he is "nationless" (168). A class discussion about the nationalities of Latin American immigrants to the United States may be useful at this point since it is in the United States where the varieties of the Spanish language alluded to in the poem may be heard.

Kozer's "Gaudeamus" is an ideal text for conveying the peculiarities of the neobaroque in the proliferation of words, the unusual syntax, and the derivation of phrases. The complexity of the poem can be analyzed in class through the convergence of language varieties and Latino (Jewish) migrant identities. Its theme could not be more poignant in relation to current preoccupations with state language policy, diversity, and diaspora.

A Proliferation of Words

Finally, the Mexican poet Coral Bracho's "En la humedad cifrada" ("Coded in Moisture") offers students and instructors the opportunity to discuss the proliferation of signs (denoted in Severo Sarduy's essay) as a neobaroque feature. It begins:

> Oigo tu cuerpo con la avidez abrevada y tranquila
> de quien se impregna (de quien
> emerge,
> de quien se extiende saturado,
> recorrido
> de esperma)
> en la humedad
> cifrada (suave oráculo espeso; templo)
> en los limos,
> embalses tibios, deltas,
> de su origen; bebo
> (tus raíces abiertas y
> penetrables; en tus costas
> lascivas—cieno bullente—landas)
> los designios musgosos, tus savias densas
> (parva de lianas ebrias) Huelo
> en tus bordes profundos, expectantes, las brasas,
> en tus selvas untuosas,
> las vertientes.
> Oigo (tu semen táctil). . . . (35)

> I hear your body with the wet and calm eagerness
> of one who is impregnated (of who
> emerges,
> of who extends oneself saturated,
> overrun

with sperm) in the centered
dampness (soft oracle thick; temple)
in the slime, warm reservoirs, deltas,
of your origin; I drink
(your open and penetrable roots; in your lascivious
coasts—bubbling mud—plains)
the mossy plans, your dense sap
(heap of drunken lianas) I smell
in your deep, expectant shores, the embers,
in your oily forests,
the springs. I hear (your tactile semen). . . .
(Kuhnheim, *Spanish American Poetry* 133–34)

As in José Kozer's poem, the parentheses try to enclose elusive elements. The continuous overflow of various boundaries allows for the sensual spaces to be transgressed: "I hear (your tactile semen)." Swampy water coexists with fertile springs. Words accumulate in a rhizomatic fashion: "sperm," "warm reservoirs," "deltas," "bubbling mud," "plains," "semen," etc. Contrary to the erotic canon that refers to parts of the body, this poem presents a joy in the seminal fluid that runs through the body of the text (and the organs). Bracho's poem looks at the most tangible element of ejaculation or orgasm, that is, the semen, saliva, or the secretions produced during sex. Therefore, the poem celebrates the existence of these viscosities.

The apparent difficulty of this poem lies in the relentless accumulation of words and, as we have seen in other poets, in the unusual range of syntax contained in a single sentence. By studying the definitions of the words they may not know, and by establishing similarities and differences between them, students will realize that most of the unfamiliar words, which refer to viscosity in liquids, relate to one another and to an emblematic term (i.e., semen). Another useful exercise would be to write lists of words with similar features in reference to one of the senses. Students will note that the poem accumulates vocabulary with similar tactile or sensual properties, which offers them a key to the difficulty the accumulation appears to pose. Syntactical challenges can be addressed by testing whether the poem would make sense excluding all the words in parentheses. Then students can examine the use of the senses throughout the poem in verb phrases such as "I hear," "I drink" (taste), "I smell," and "I touch" (notably, sight is excluded), considering why these verbs are relevant to the text, particularly in the use of synesthesia. The class could end with a discussion comparing the poem's eroticism with that of, say, a selection from Pablo Neruda's *Veinte poemas de amor y una canción desesperada* (*Twenty Love Poems and a Song of Despair*). How would one characterize Bracho's perception of eroticism, or Neruda's?

In this essay I have tried to demonstrate that "difficult poetry" can become easy, once we familiarize ourselves—and our students—with certain poetic texts and their strategies. All the examples above concentrate on specific poems, but instructors can follow the strategies presented here while analyzing other difficult poems. I agree and reaffirm Lezama Lima's statement that "Solo lo difícil es estimulante" 'Only the difficult is stimulating' (9). If this idea is presented at the beginning of a unit on difficult poetry, and is reinforced throughout the unit, it can invigorate and empower students to overcome adversity and enjoy the richness of this type of poetry.

Notes

1. The use of scatological matters in poetry is not new. In the seventeenth century, Quevedo and even Sor Juana also combined feces and gold, high and low culture.

2. A useful comparison between the baroque and the avant-garde can be found in Octavio Paz's *Los hijos del limo* (*Children of the Mire*) and *Sor Juana Inés de la Cruz o las trampas de la fe* (*Sor Juana Inés de la Cruz, or the Traps of Faith*). At the level of the image, as Paz points out, there is an important coincidence between the ideas of the seventeenth-century writer Baltasar Gracián and those of the cubist poet Pierre Reverdy (in the latter case, they applied first to cubism and then were readapted by Breton for surrealism).

Tamara R. Williams

Minding the Gaps: Strategies for Teaching the Contemporary Spanish American Long Poem

Working with two contemporary book-length poems from Mexico—Sara Uribe's *Antígona González* and Luis Felipe Fabre's *La sodomía en la Nueva España* ("Sodomy in New Spain")—this essay explores strategies for teaching how to read the long poem, a poetic genre that has been a mainstay of Spanish American literary production over the course of centuries. The first strategy anticipates and engages students' resistance to the long poem, a resistance arising from misconceptions about the genre but also from marked shifts in the ways students born into the digital age access, select, read, and produce meaning. The others frame a renewed attention to literary genres and textual genealogies but also emphasize the formal and semantic mechanisms of citational poetry, that is, poetry that relies extensively on fragments from other texts, and explore the long poem as a generative source for theorizing on topics such as the nature of violence and the role of the state in contemporary Mexico; the history of gender construction; and metapoetical inquiries related to the inexhaustible capacity of poetry to engage and absorb readers, and to renew discourses in a continuous dialogue with distinct literary, historical, and social contexts. Though applied here to relatively recent texts, these strategies can be used effectively to examine long poems from the twentieth-century Latin American tradition such as

Ernesto Cardenal's *El estrecho dudoso* ("The Doubtful Strait"), Pablo Neruda's *Canto general* ("General Song"), and Nicolás Guillén's *El diario que a diario* ("The Daily Daily") (see Tamara Williams, "Ernesto Cardenal," "La historia," "Literatura"). Why and how to teach the long poem? Recent studies suggest that "Gen Z attention spans have shrunk to eight seconds," leaving young adults "unable to focus for extended amounts of time" (Finch). Moreover, "[a]lthough they are better educated, more techno-savvy, and quicker to adapt than those who have come before them," members of the postmillennial generation "refuse to blindly conform to traditional standards and time-honored institutions. Instead, they boldly ask, 'Why?'" (Chester 214). These developments, combined with a popular perception of poetry as "arguably neck-and-neck with mime as the most animus-attracting of art forms" (Gordinier), can't help but challenge the most seasoned instructors and long-poem enthusiasts. All is not lost, however, as research also suggests that, like the millennial generation, Generation Z students actually "have highly evolved 'eight-second filters'" and that, "once something has demonstrated attention-worthiness, Gen Z can become intensely committed and focused. They've come of age with an internet that's allowed them to go deep on any topic of their choosing and learn from like-minded fans" (Finch).

To anticipate and acknowledge this likely indifference or resistance to the material is the first step toward enhancing engagement and activating interest, curiosity, and dedicated focus. This in turn harnesses students' technical prowess and capacity to "go deeper" on the material at hand. To this end, I begin with four questions regarding my students' preexisting knowledge of, and experience with, the long poem: How would you characterize your experience of reading long poems compared with that of reading other literary texts? What long poems are you familiar with, within and outside the Spanish American tradition? What qualities do the long poems you are familiar with have in common? In what ways do the poems differ? The aim of the exercise is to explore and affirm what students already know while upending and complicating received notions and expectations about the long poem related to such qualities as point of view, theme, form, content, tone, language, rhythm, rhyme, and accessibility.

The first of these questions—"How would you characterize your experience of reading long poems compared with that of reading other literary texts?"—is designed to encourage students to explore and acknowledge any resistance they may have due to preconceptions about the genre as an impenetrable, outdated, and elitist cultural practice, or as a revulsive failure, as was famously the opinion of Edgar Allan Poe. The question also surfaces students' "affective filters"—emotional responses such as motivation, self-confidence, and anxiety that can impede or facilitate learning.[1] Invariably, only a few students respond to the question with enthusiasm; a good number will share that they find long poems challenging, and one or two admit to never having read a single one. When asked if they prefer other literary genres to the long poem, students answer with an overwhelming yes, volunteering a strong preference for novels, short stories, or nonfiction. They list the advantages of these genres as ease of reading, broad thematic range, narrative action, and character development. In sum, the responses confirm that most students see the long poem as less accessible than other genres and as comparatively limited in theme and structure, both perceptions that the two subsequent questions are designed to unsettle.

In order to affirm and redirect students' technological skills, I encourage them to consult Internet sources to retrieve details—for example, authors, titles, and places and dates of publication—of the long poems they've encountered. Their compiled responses generate a complex map that usually includes selected Greek and Roman epic poems, Dante's *Divine Comedy*, *El Cantar del Mío Cid* ("The Poem of the Cid"), Alonso de Ercilla's *La araucana* ("The Araucaniad"), Sor Juana Inés de la Cruz's "Primero sueño" ("First Dream"), Luis de Góngora's *Soledades* ("Solitudes"), José Hernández's *Martín Fierro*, Walt Whitman's *Leaves of Grass*, T. S. Eliot's *The Waste Land*, Ezra Pound's *Cantos*, Neruda's *Canto general*, Vicente Huidobro's *Altazor o el viaje en paracaídas* ("Altazor or a Voyage in a Parachute"), and possibly poems by Octavio Paz and Cardenal. (For the purposes of this essay, it should be noted that students rarely mention or question the role of poetry in drama, as in the works of the ancient Greeks, Shakespeare, Pedro Calderón de la Barca, or Lope de Vega.)

The ensuing discussion complicates the map with convergent and divergent observations regarding the long poem that help establish a framework for subsequent reading and the exploration of key debates and controversies in the genre's literary history. Reading Paz's essay "Contar y cantar (sobre el poema extenso)" ("Telling and Singing: On the Extensive Poem") provides a succinct historical overview of the genre that begins with the *Mahabharata* and concludes with a useful, albeit oversimplified identification of two dominant trends that persist until the 1970s. The first is represented by Mallarmé's *Un coup de dés jamais n'abolira le hasard* ("A Throw of the Dice Will Never Abolish Chance"), which Paz describes as "el canto del poeta solitario frente al universo" 'the song of the solitary poet before the universe.' The second, exemplified by Whitman's *Song of Myself*, Paz defines as "el canto de fundación de la comunidad libre de los iguales" 'the song to the foundation of a free community of equals' (30).[2]

In reading Poe's "The Poetic Principle," students who had expressed strong misgivings about the genre discover a notable accomplice, while in Poe's Argentine contemporary Esteban Echeverría, an accomplished author of the long poem, they find an adversary. Echeverría's Romantic vision of the genre, in particular his insistence on poetry that is "bella, grande, sublime y se manifieste bajo formas colosales" 'beautiful, grand, sublime and which should manifest itself under colossal forms,'[3] in turn invites a discussion about the thematic and structural limits of genre. Students can read for comparison Neruda's short metapoetical reflection "Sobre una poesía sin pureza" ("Toward an Impure Poetry"). Notions of purity and impurity are further and fruitfully explored by introducing selected *Cantos* by Pound and "La hora 0" ("Zero Hour") by Cardenal, whose radical innovations in poetry, mainly their intentional destabilization of the boundaries between poetry and prose, are articulated as a direct challenge to the popularity of the novel and the perception that it had eclipsed the epic genre. Indeed, both seek to beat the novelists at their own game, or, in the words of Cardenal, "En un poema caben datos estadísticos, fragmentos de cartas, editoriales de un periódico, noticias periodísticas, crónicas de historia, documentos, chistes, anécdotas, cosas que antes eran consideradas elementos propios de la prosa y no de la poesía" 'In a poem fit statistical facts, fragments of letters, newspaper editorials, news articles, historical chronicles, documents, jokes, anecdotes, things that before were considered elements of prose and not of poetry' (qtd. in Benedetti 129).

This call for radical inclusiveness broadens students' perceptions of poetry and invites them to rethink the contrast with the novel. The acknowledgment by the avowed Marxist Cardenal of the influence of the fascist Pound complicates narrow notions that prescribe or align certain literary forms with specific ideologies. It also invites a conversation regarding the paradoxical nature of these two poets' revival of poetry. For the North American and the Nicaraguan, the condition of possibility for this revival entailed both rigorous knowledge and enthusiastic embrace of past literary traditions (the Greco-Roman epic, the ode and the epigram, Italian troubadours, Petrarch and Dante, the Japanese haiku, Classical Chinese poetry, Spanish Golden Age literature and history, Latin American colonial history, etc.) as well as their use in new forms that spoke to a new age and a new sensibility. Their radical and sustained innovation, therefore, rested on centuries-old traditions transfigured and made new.

An exploration of the idea of the new in a literary work provides the foundation for the theoretical and aesthetic inquiries that will shape the reading of the poems by Uribe and Fabre. The breadth and depth of this exploration will depend on the students' abilities and the instructor's interests. A philosophical line of inquiry might consider Audrey Wasser's questions on the paradoxical nature of the concept of the new in literary history: "How is it that new works or new forms are possible within the determinate orders of history, language use, or the social? How are they in turn recognizable to already existing institutions? . . . Indeed, if we do not have a way of articulating the conceptual relationship between what is and what is not *new*, how can we hope to tackle the question of what is and what is not *literature*?" (3). Marjorie Perloff's *Unoriginal Genius* provides a framework for understanding how innovation in compositional processes and poetic form, including literary genres, has responded to the phenomenon of hyperinformation that defines our digital age. Linda Hutcheon's broad yet simple formulation of parody as "extended repetition with critical difference" (7) offers a supporting conceptual framework for naming and describing what is now a ubiquitous practice of creating the new through processes of appropriation, recontextualization, and recoding of "the rich and intimidating legacy of the past" (4) and, I would add, of the no less overwhelming complexity of the present. Students are then asked to consider how specific contexts—historical, cultural, aesthetic, technological, and scientific—might indwell in, and transform, a poetic text, and how it interpolates inherited aesthetic traditions and other forms of discourse.

The goal is to establish, from a variety of perspectives, that the condition of possibility for the new is the old. Acknowledging this condition sets up the imperative for a kind of reading—of inquiry—that takes both into account, that seeks therefore to produce meaning in the gaps wherein reside and emerge the critical differences between the new poem and its source texts. These gaps, in turn, provide the new text with definition, meaning and purpose.

Effacement and Visibility in Uribe's *Antígona González*

The reading of *Antígona González* is premised on assertions from the philosopher and art historian Georges Didi-Huberman and from the poet and professor Susan Stewart regarding issues of visibility and effacement, both matters of personal and political urgency as well as sources of considerable anxiety for those living in the digital age. In the era of mass media and increased democratization, argues Didi-Huberman, one might expect people and communities to be more visible to each other than ever before (12). However, precisely the opposite is the case. Indeed, people are *exposed* to—vulnerable to and unprotected from—political and aesthetic effacement and, in some cases, literal extinction, the consequence of being ensnared between the underexposure of neglect, censorship, and erasure, on the one hand, and the distorted overexposure of reiterative and stereotyping spectacle on the other (14). Didi-Huberman's understanding of the nature of erasure in the age of mass media may well describe the situation of Mexico and Mexicans since the intensification in 2006 of the drug war backed by the United States. From both sides of the United States–Mexico border, the official imaginary, projected incessantly by mainstream media and popular culture, overexposes the view of Mexico as a narcostate—a failed state that has lost its power and authority to the dark side of global capitalism, embodied in the figure of the drug lord. A former investigative reporter for *Proceso* ("Process"), and now a leading expert on narconarratives, argues that the blockbuster novels, prime-time news reports, *telenovelas*, and blockbuster television series that reinforce this representation, "while conceived as critical literary interventions, are in fact marketable commodities reproducing hegemonic discourses that frame the drug trade as a phenomenon operating outside of the state" while failing "to articulate an effective critique of the drug trade as a dimension located within state structures, historically determined by state power and subject to it" (Zavala). The civilian population, on the other hand, which has endured the horror and grief of the mounting death toll—estimated at 164,000 homicides and over 26,000 disappearances since 2007—receives relatively little attention in mainstream media beyond the occasional body count (see Breslow).

Echoing Susan Stewart's claim that "[t]he cultural, or form-giving, work of poetry is to counter the oblivion of darkness . . . a force against effacement—not merely for individuals but for communities as well" (1–2), I argue that poetry, a discourse less visible, less frequently circulated, and (arguably) less accessible than many news platforms can encode the experiences of persons and communities affected by the violence. Uribe's *Antígona González* supports this claim. A hauntingly oneiric reflection of "startling specificity" (Pluecker 191) that makes visible the violence that has gripped Mexico in the last decades, the book-length dramatic poem possesses the open-ended quality of an unfinished draft—part tentative personal diary, part detective notebook—out of which unfolds the story of a sister, Antígona González, in search of the body of her beloved and disappeared brother, Tadeo, in the state of Tamaulipas, where authorities remain unresponsive to the plight of those left behind to grieve.

Antígona González is masterfully composed of fragments of testimonials, interrogation transcripts, blogs, and newspaper reports related to the drug war, particularly to the two massacres that took place in the municipality of San Fernando, Tamaulipas, in 2010 and 2011. These fragments are combined with direct quotations and paraphrases from Sophocles's *Antigone*, as well as material from subsequent versions of her story (by Zambrano, Gambaro, Marechal, Yourcenar, and others) and by some of the Sophoclean heroine's most notable scholars, including Judith Butler, Rómulo Pianacci, and Joan Copjec. The text makes visible its reliance on sources through the creative use of punctuation, references, and citations. Uribe, moreover, transcends removal and graft—the dual operation of citational poetics as described by Antoine Compaignon (see Perloff, *Unoriginal Genius* 3)—to name works cited and consulted throughout the poem and in the section titled "Notas finales y referencias" ("Final Notes and References"), seven single-spaced pages of idiosyncratic endnotes and bibliographic entries that document the poem's sources. The poet, it should be added, also foregrounds her commitment to copyleft practices on the work's copyright page. That is, Uribe grants license for *Antígona González* to be copied, in part or in its entirety, using any medium (scan, photocopy, etc.), as long as her text is not modified in any way.

Guided by Perloff's admonition "to remember that the citational or appropriative text, however unoriginal its actual words and phrases, is always a product of choice" (*Unoriginal Genius* 169), the first assignment on *Antígona González* is designed to build students' knowledge of Uribe's selection of source texts and to draw their attention to how those texts are used and cited. Using familiar search engines and techniques to produce an inventory and classification of Uribe's sources builds a basic philological skill as well as confidence and capacity to explore the many ways the poem produces meaning through "a dialogue with earlier texts or texts in other media, with 'writings through' *ekphrases* that permit the poet to participate in a larger, more public discourse" (Perloff 11).

There are three possible axes of meaning production that emerge from this preliminary examination of the citational practices in *Antígona González*. The first is found in the dialogue between *Antígona* and her textual genealogy. This invitation is issued in a series of questions that appear within the first pages of the poem, the first of which is a direct quote from

El grito de Antígona, the Spanish translation of Judith Butler's *Antigone's Claim*: ": ¿Quién es Antígona en esta escena y qué / vamos a hacer con sus palabras? // : ¿Quién es Antígona y qué vamos a hacer con todas las demás Antígonas?" 'Who then is Antigone within such a scene, and what / are we to make of her words? // Who then is Antigone and what are we going to do with all the other Antigones?' (qtd. in Uribe 15; Butler 82).

Both questions encourage a comparative reading of *Antígona González* against other versions of the Sophoclean heroine's story. I therefore ask students to compare and contrast at least three works: Sophocles's *Antigone*, Uribe's *Antígona González*, and at least one other literary or visual retelling of the Antigone story. To frame the comparison, I draw on what George Steiner characterizes as the "Antigone and Creon syntax": "words, images, sinews of argument, synecdoches, tropes, metaphors" that evoke the story of "the confrontation of justice and the law, of the aura of the dead and the claims of the living," which Steiner views as "specific universals" associated with the myth of the Greek heroine throughout the ages (138). For the contrastive portion of the reading, I rely on Hutcheon's definition of modern parody as "repetition with critical difference" and ask students to pay close attention to narrative elements—character, action, space, time—as well as contextual referents, both sources for identifying the locus of the critical difference that defines the "new" in Uribe's text.

Three distinctions are worthy of note. While Sophocles's heroine seeks the right to bury the body of her deceased brother, Polynices, Uribe's Antígona is driven by a search for the body of her beloved and disappeared brother, Tadeo, a search that broadens to include an entire community's quest for those who have not been found in a shared hope for all those lost to appear. The action occurs in present-day Tamaulipas, mainly in the capital city of Tampico—described by one journalist as "one of Mexico's most violent cities in one of its most violent states" (Hollander)—and in the municipality of San Fernando, the site of two interrelated massacres in 2010 and 2011 in which more than 250 men, women, and children, mostly undocumented migrants from Central and South America, were killed. The most striking difference between Uribe's text and Sophocles's play, however, is the conspicuous absence of a Creon figure and hence of the "confrontation of justice and the law" (Steiner 138)—of kinship and the state, of the masculine and the feminine, of eros and reason—that has defined the Antigone myth and story over time.

Uribe's transformation of the core agon of the Sophoclean tragedy is the springboard for an inquiry into a second axis of meaning production, this time generated in the dialogue between *Antígona González* and the array of media sources quoted and recomposed throughout the text. The collective blog *Menos días aquí* ("Fewer Days Here"), which was started in September 2012 by Mexican activists calling for the end of the drug war, is a case in point. Run by a growing number of volunteers, the blog has a dual purpose. On the one hand, using information compiled from media sources countrywide, the collective seeks to establish a national count of all those who have died as a result of the violence in Mexico. On the other, they seek to keep alive the memory of all the dead: "Queremos ponerles nombres, rostros, dejar de banalizar la muerte" 'We want to give them names, faces, to stop banalizing death.' It is in fact the name of one of the volunteers or "counters" from this collective blog, the Mexican actress Antígona González, who provides Uribe with the title for her book and for its memorable protagonist.

Uribe not only acknowledges the blog in her "Final Notes and References" section but also echoes its core commitment to write against the grain of the spectacle of violence that has characterized the portrayal of the War on Drugs in popular culture and media. She achieves this by conveying the humanity of the dead, the disappeared, and those who grieve the loss, drawing readers in to accompany the isolated and bereaved Antígona in the search for Tadeo. As the search unfolds we are gradually exposed to a myriad of borrowed accounts that document, in painstaking detail, the names, primary relationships, addresses, and places last seen, of countless disappeared along with the stories of those left behind. Thus the reader witnesses, and participates in, a collective counting of and accounting for the tens of thousands disappeared in Mexico's drug war.

The related and final axis of meaning production is generated in the poem's explicit dialogue with Judith Butler (*Antigone's Claim*) and Cristina Rivera Garza (*Los muertos indóciles*) ("The Insurgent Dead"). In dialogue with Butler, *Antígona* can be read as a poem that examines the precarious ontological status of populations that, for all intents and purposes, are bereft of a state, living where "laws and norms that govern the accession to speech and speakability" are compromised or simply do not apply (Butler 3). Quoting Giorgio Agamben, Butler elaborates further: "Their ontological status as legal subjects is suspended. These are not lives being genocidally destroyed, but neither are they being entered into the life of the legitimate community in which standards of recognition permit for an attainment of humanness" (81).

The dialogue with Rivera Garza's *Muertos indóciles*, on the other hand, activates an alternative to the bleak outlook of effacement in a disemboweled state. Conditioned within this ontological circumstance, Antígona

González's quest to recover the body of her disappeared brother evolves into the need to re-member and reconstitute the body politic, the people of a society considered collectively as an organized group of citizens—in other words, community. As I have argued elsewhere, this process of re-constitution is made apparent in the poem's narrative unfolding of the city of San Fernando, which, initially devoid of human connection, is trans-formed into an intimate space of shared grief. As the story of the poem progresses, Antígona's search for Tadeo and her subsequent outreach to, and networking with, others who search and grieve, generate an affective scaffolding for the rekindling of compassion, of mutual recognition, of empathy, of moral sentiment and ethical action, and thus gradually restore the fabric of community (see Williams, "Wounded").

This narrative arc, finally, is supported metapoetically. The explicit reli-ance on, and generous acknowledgement of, other voices and texts, as well as Uribe's commitment to the poem's free distribution, are only two ways that *Antígona González* emplots a reflection on, and exercise in, the dispos-session of the authorial "I" to expose writing as a the communal practice it is and always has been. Rivera Garza describes this practice as a poetics of disappropriation that goes beyond a mere textual practice: "Ir más allá quiere decir aquí cuestionar el dominio que hace aparecer como individual una serie de trabajos comunales—y todo trabajo con y en el lenguaje es, de entrada, un trabajo de comunidad—que carecen de propiedad" 'Here to go beyond means to question the domain that makes appear as individual a series of communal works—and all work with and in language is, from the onset, a work in community—that lack property' (270).

Generic Perversion in Luis Felipe Fabre's
La sodomía en la Nueva España

I teach *Antígona González* with Luis Felipe Fabre's *La sodomía en la Nueva España*, another book-length dramatic poem, both haunting and refresh-ingly irreverent, that encodes the experience of the prosecution and death by burning of fourteen men and the flogging of a teenage boy on 6 No-vember 1658 by order of the Court of the Viceroyalty of New Spain as pun-ishment for sodomy. Drawing on histories of homosexuality in colonial Mexico, Fabre carefully reworks fragments of letters, diaries, chronicles, and legal proceedings into an *auto sacramental*, a dramatic form popularized by two indisputable masters of Spain's Golden and Imperial Ages, Lope

de Vega and Calderón de la Barca. That Fabre chooses to break the historical silence regarding the existence of gay and transsexual communities in
Colonial Mexico using the generic framework of the auto, a highly popular
didactic genre that sought to exalt the Catholic faith and to combat its
perceived enemies (which included alleged sodomites), yields a complex,
multilayered parody wherein the sacrifice and redemption of the transvestite
Cotita de la Encarnación, a thinly veiled Jesus character, gives way to a gay
version of the story of the life of Christ. Initially, students are daunted by
the poem's length, by its allegorical dramatic structure, and by its linguistic
and discursive hybridity. However, through a series of three scaffolded assignments (see appendix), each focused on one of the strategies outlined
above, they eventually are able to engage, understand, describe, analyze,
and theorize about *La sodomía* in remarkably sophisticated ways.

The first assignment focuses on identifying the generic affiliation of the
poem and its primary sources. Through a series of guided questions, students
are invited to explore the nature and purpose of the *La sodomía*'s affiliation
with the *auto sacramental*, an allegorical morality play traditionally written
in verse and performed for the Feast of Corpus Christi in celebration of the
Eucharist (the redemption of the body and blood of Christ). Additionally,
they are asked to consider Fabre's incorporation into the *auto sacramental* of
archival material related to the group execution of fourteen sodomites and the
flogging of a fourteen-year-old boy in Mexico City in 1658. Upon completion
of this assignment students are able to articulate the most notable difference
between *La sodomía* and the traditional *auto sacramental*, which is that Fabre's
sacrificed Christ figure is one of the fourteen men burned at the stake.

Following this comparative exercise, students are asked in the second
assignment to consider how and why the poem differs from its primary
sources—to identify the gaps—in order to home in on the poem's distinctive features. The second set of guided questions therefore asks students to explore the concept of parody generally, and then to work with
Judith Butler's understanding of parody as "a troubling return" and a
strategy of subversive repetition that exposes "the foundational categories
of sex, gender and desire as a specific formation of power" (*Gender Trouble*
xix). By the end of the second assignment students are visibly intrigued,
some even enthusiastic, about the poem's uniquely subversive queering of
the Golden Age genre as well as its exposure of relatively unknown historical events (see Williams, "Queering").

The third and final assignment asks students to produce a lengthier
integrative essay that considers *La sodomía* in light of Butler's theories on

parody, gender, and performance. The completed essays reveal that most students are able to read *La sodomía* as a complex, transgressive exploration of an antiheteronormative morality that both subverts and makes evident "reiterative power" (Butler, *Bodies* 3) of seventeenth-century Spanish imperial discourses—including the proliferation of the blockbuster genre that was the *auto sacramental*—in the production and regulation of compulsory heterosexuality. The text's emphasis on transvestite and transgender issues, finally, invites reflection on related topics in contemporary Mexico and in Latin America. More broadly, students will have developed a critical awareness of how a literary genre such as the *auto sacramental*, which was used extensively to promote a dominant ideology, promotes exclusionary and violent practices.

Used in teaching both undergraduate students in the United States and graduate students at the Universidad Nacional Autónoma de México, the strategies I have described above have proven successful in enhancing the ability of all students to better handle any long poem they encounter. I have employed them successfully in teaching texts from a corpus extraordinarily diverse in terms of size, form, and content that includes, but is not limited to, Aztec writers from the Conquest era such as Axayácatl and Nezahualpilli; works from the periods of independence, such as Pedro de Oña's *Arauco domado* ("Tamed Arauco"), Bernardo de Balbuena's *Grandeza mexicana* ("The Grandeur of Mexico"), Alonso de Ercilla's *La araucana*, Sor Juana Inés de la Cruz's "Primero sueño," and Luis de Góngora's *Soledades*; and nation-building texts from the eighteenth and nineteenth century such as Andrés Bello's "Silva a la Agricultura de la zona tórrida" ("*Silva* to the Agriculture of the Torrid Zone"), Esteban Echeverría's *La Cautiva* ("The Captive"), José Hernández's *Martín Fierro*, and Juan Zorrilla de San Martín's *Tabaré*. It also comprises works from the robust and extraordinarily eclectic revival of the long poem in the twentieth century, including historical narrative epics associated with social movements such as Pablo Neruda's *Canto general*, Nicolás Guillén's *El diario que a diario*, and Ernesto Cardenal's *Estrecho dudoso* and other poems. To these can be added poems considered more experimental in nature such as Huidobro's *Altazor*, José Gorostiza's *Muerte sin fin* ("Death Without End"), Octavio Paz's *Piedra de sol* (*Sunstone*), and Raúl Zurita's monumental trilogy. More recent additions include the works of Diego Maquieira, Gerardo Denis, Elicura Chihuailaf, and a growing number of performance artists such as the Zapotec rapper Mare Advertenica Lirika.

Most important, however, is the transformation of the experience of reading the long poem. What once seemed a disorienting, burdensome, or irrelevant exercise becomes a stimulus for intellectual curiosity and critical thinking and a source of the empowerment and excitement that inevitably accompany the ability to decipher and articulate a complex literary text's potential meanings. Ultimately, these strategies yield an enriched learning experience through meaningful comparative reading—both textual and contextual—across centuries, traditions, genres, and discourses while simultaneously inviting students to ethical reflections that consider the capacity and persistence of the poetic text to speak truth to power.

Notes

1. See Krashen pp. 31–32. While Krashen's work focuses on the role affective filters can play in impeding or facilitating acquisition in the second-language classroom, I have found that attention to these same filters has had a positive impact on overall learning in all courses, regardless of content.

2. All translations to English are mine unless otherwise attributed.

3. See Echeverría: "En poesía para mí, las composiciones cortas siempre han sido de muy poca importancia, cualquiera que sea su mérito. Para que la poesía pueda llenar su misión profética, para que pueda obrar sobre las masas y ser poderoso elemento social, y no como hasta aquí, entre nosotros y nuestros padres, un pasatiempo fútil y, cuando más, agradable, es necesario que la poesía sea bella, grande, sublime y se manifieste bajo formas colosales" 'In poetry for me, short compositions have always had little importance, whatever their merit. For poetry to fulfill its prophetic mission, to work on the masses and be a powerful force, and not, like until now, among us and our parents, an idle pastime, or at the most, pleasant, it is necessary for poetry to be beautiful, grand, sublime and be manifested in colossal forms' (qtd. in Mesa Gancedo 88).

Appendix: Assignments on
La sodomía en la Nueva España

The first assignment on Fabre's *La sodomía en la Nueva España* involves a series of questions that are designed to meet three objectives. The first is to engage students in the process of reading, describing, and contextualizing the text's primary sources: the auto sacramental as a genre, the November 6, 1658, entry in the diary of Fray Gregorio Martín de Guijo describing the burning at the stake of the fourteen men, and Serge Gruzinski's essay "Las cenizas de deseo: Homosexuales novohispanos a mediados del siglo XVII" ("The Ashes of Desire: Homosexuals in New Spain in the Mid-Seventeenth Century"). The second is to have students examine and describe the ways that Fabre transforms these sources into something new. The third is to have students begin to consider the implicit and explicit ways the text presents ideas related to gender, sexuality, community, repression, violence, etc.

The assignment, finally, requires students to read selections from Federico Garza Carvajal's *Vir: Perceptions of Manliness in Andalucía and México* as well as selections from Fabre's *Leyendo agujeros*. The guiding questions are:

1. Elaboren una investigación sobre lo que es un auto sacramental en la tradición literaria hispana. ¿Qué tipo de texto es? ¿Cuáles son sus características principales? ¿Y, ante todo, qué función ha desempeñado el género en la cultura hispana? ¿Cuándo tuvo el género su popularidad más alta y por qué?
2. Desarrollen un breve bosquejo en el que elaboran las maneras en que *La sodomía* es o no es un auto sacramental. Consideren, finalmente, hacia dónde empuja Fabre a sus lectores con su inovación del género.
3. El texto de Fabre se basa en documentos históricos (archivos, cartas, diarios, etc.) sobre el incidente de la quema a fuego de catorce sodomitas en noviembre de 1658. Lean una de estas fuentes—el fragmento del diario de Guijo—y consideren las maneras en las que Fabre utiliza las fuentes. ¿Qué pasa con Guijo en Fabre? ¿Qué pasa con el tono? ¿Qué dice/no dice Fabre? ¿Cómo opera la poesía—la repetición, el ritmo, la rima, el corte de línea, etc.—para dirigir al lector hacia una segunda lectura de los sucesos históricos? En la opinión de Uds., ¿en qué consiste esta lectura?
4. Lean el texto de Garza Carvajal. Comiencen a pensar en qué maneras la poética del silencio (o "de los agujeros") elaborado por Fabre logra una poesía que se acerca al silencio en torno a la experiencia real de la persona que ejerce una sexualidad alternativa. ¿En qué sentido refleja o coincide esta práctica poética con teorías de la sexualidad reciente (Lacan, Foucault, Butler, etc.)?

The second assignment on *La sodomía* is designed to develop students' ability to reflect critically on the nature and purpose of parody. To this end, they are required to read selections of Butler's *Gender Trouble* and consider the ways that Fabre's text unsettles the foundations of compulsory heteronormativity.

1. Lean los capítulos de *Gender Trouble* de Judith Butler. Elaboren un resumen de sus ideas centrales e intenten describir cómo desarrolla y construye su argumento.
2. Intenten explicar qué quiere decir Butler por el género como "performatividad." ¿En qué sentido podemos decir que "performamos" el género?
3. Busquen tres definiciones del término *parodia* y elaboren su propia definición. Piensen en ejemplos de parodia en la cultura popular a la altura de lo que hace Fabre. Es decir, parodia que sea política, incómoda, controversial, etc. Un argumento central de Butler (basándose en el trabajo de Lacan, Foucault, etc.) es que el discurso jurídico-teológico dicta un sistema de género heteronormativo que, además de ser binario, se considera "natural." En su capítulo "From Parody to Politics" sugiere que una de las maneras de subvertir el orden heteronormativo es por medio de la repetición que se manifiesta como un fantasma que ronda. ¿En qué sentido es el texto de Fabre una tentativa de este tipo de parodia?

4. Teniendo en cuenta el texto *Leyendo agujeros* de Fabre, elabore una lectura del *corpus* agujerado del sujeto homosexual colonial en *La sodomía.*

The third assignment related to *La sodomía* requires students to write a six- to eight-page critical essay on repetition as subversion of heteronormativity in the work of Luis Felipe Fabre.

Melanie Nicholson

A Course Model for the Liberal Arts Curriculum

At a recent retreat, a group of Bard College faculty members from an array of academic disciplines was given the following discussion prompt: "If you had only one chance—a single semester—to introduce your field of research and teaching to nonmajors, or even to students with little professed interest in your field, what would that course look like?" This question inspired me to develop a course called Engaging Latin American Poetry, whose rationale and design I discuss in this essay. The primary aim of this course is to reach liberal arts undergraduates who may not otherwise be involved in the study of Latin America or of poetry, including students with minimal familiarity with the Spanish language. At Bard I have offered this course to majors from biology, human rights, studio arts, music, literature, film, and art history, as well as Latin American studies; in fact, this mixture of backgrounds and interests has been key to the success of the course. The basic model I present in this essay corresponds to an undergraduate course conducted primarily in English; however, with the addition of critical and theoretical materials of the instructor's choosing, the same set of readings could be taught in Spanish to advanced language students and majors.

Current debates over the value of the humanities in higher education, often presenting the situation of the past two decades as a crisis for humanities departments and their faculty, have compelled us to give serious thought to what we teach, to whom, and to what ends. A 2013 article by Dan Berrett in the *Chronicle of Higher Education* describes the Humanities Project at Harvard University, in which the emphasis on counting majors has shifted toward an increased appeal to a broad spectrum of students. Speaking of general education requirements that include a course in "aesthetic and interpretive understanding," Berrett remarks that "[f]aculty members in the humanities effectively have one shot at firing up Harvard students' interest in their disciplines." This is exactly the challenge I have set for myself, taking Latin American poetry as my discipline and approaching the course as my one chance to ignite students' "aesthetic and interpretive understanding" of the field.

Considering this broad goal of inclusiveness, the objectives of Engaging Latin American Poetry are multilayered. First, students will gain a basic understanding of key historical events or processes that shaped Latin America and its poets in the twentieth century, such as the Spanish Civil War, the Cuban revolution, the military dictatorships of the 1970s and 1980s, and the ongoing struggles for indigenous rights. Second, students will grasp the broad outlines of the literary history of the region, beginning with *modernismo* and the avant-garde movements of the 1920s to the 1940s. Third, they will develop a reasonably complex notion of the myriad forms that poetry written in Spanish can take. Although they may not understand Spanish, they will spend time listening to the *sounds* of poetic Spanish, gaining an appreciation for rhythms and acoustic qualities that do not require a direct comprehension of meanings.[1] Finally, and perhaps most important, I hope students will gain both confidence and sophistication in their ability to speak and write about poetry. In short, I seek to foster a significant shift in students' notions about what it means to read, write, or otherwise engage with poetry in their own historical moment.

To achieve these multiple objectives, I divide the course into five units that reflect on Latin American poetry from distinct, though overlapping, perspectives: Backgrounds and Contexts; The Poet and the Polis; The Inward Gaze: Poetry of Metaphysics and Introspection; Indigenous Voices, Past and Present; and Unbinding the Text: Antipoetry and Poetry in Performance. In the following section I present the poets, texts, and pedagogical strategies for each unit in fuller detail. Finally, I describe the expectations for student work in the course, along with some of the exciting outcomes I have observed.

Course Content and Structure

Given the task of organizing a topic as broad and complex as Latin American poetry, I divide this course into specific sections that I consider the most efficacious and versatile, but instructors may substitute others as they see fit. Some alternative units might include The Poetics of Gender; Race, Class, and Gender through the Lens of Poetry; Poetry and the Visual Arts; or Poetry and Human Rights. Whatever the units of study chosen, students should be continually encouraged to look for points of interconnection and dialogue as they progress through the course readings. The five-part design allows the instructor to cover a representative range of Latin American poetry and also to address selected poets in depth.

The first unit, Backgrounds and Contexts, gives the course a chronological and conceptual underpinning, which is crucial in teaching students with little or no background in the field. In this section it is important to emphasize the interweaving of European and autochthonous American elements in Latin American poetry, considering both formal and thematic concerns. The first two chapters of Gordon Brotherston's *Latin American Poetry: Origins and Presence* (1–26), and Stephen Tapscott's introduction to *Twentieth Century Latin American Poetry* (1–20), as well as Cecilia Vicuña's and Ernesto Livon-Grosman's introductions to the *Oxford Book of Latin American Poetry* (xix–xxxviii), are excellent resources for this foundational material. After briefly framing the historical and aesthetic parameters of the course in the first class meeting, we spend the second day discussing *modernista* literature through the lens of Rubén Darío. Reading the poems aloud, students are asked to note the changes in imagery, structure, tone, and theme as we move from "El cisne" ("The Swan") and "Sonatina," which exemplify the image-rich, exoticizing, even decadent aesthetic of much early modernist poetry, to "Lo fatal" ("Fatality") and "A Roosevelt" ("To Roosevelt"), poems that encapsulate both the political concerns and the existential anguish that mark Darío's later poetry.

Week 2 of the course is dedicated to the Latin American *vanguardia* ("avant-garde") of the 1920s to the 1940s and touches on its complex relationship to the European avant-garde. We read and discuss a sampling of texts from Oswald de Andrade's *Manifesto antropófago* ("Cannibalist Manifesto") to poems by Vicente Huidobro, César Vallejo, Pablo Neruda, and others. As poets responded to the *esprit nouveau* ("new spirit") that was finding its way across the Atlantic, to a sense of the inadequacy of traditional forms for reflecting the demands of the new century, and to the need to establish a uniquely Latin American cultural identity, they transformed Spanish-language lyricism in ways that can still surprise us. In each of the four subsequent units, students are encouraged to read Latin American poetry across the arc of the twentieth century and into the twenty-first as a kind of dialogue between the historical avant-garde and later developments.[2]

In unit 2, The Poet and the Polis, we consider the different ways in which poets locate themselves within the larger communities they inhabit. From the Romantics to the Spanish American *modernistas*, poets often saw themselves as outsiders (*los raros*, in Darío's terms), criticizing the society around them from this marginalized but privileged position. In certain later works, the romantic notion of the alienated self sometimes leads to a figuration of the poet as spokesperson for a group that is considered voiceless. In order to investigate this notion, we read sections of Neruda's *Alturas de Macchu Picchu* (*The Heights of Macchu Picchu*), an epic poem in which the poet invites the long-dead builders of this sacred site to speak "por mis palabras y mi sangre" 'through my words and my blood' (213).[3] In other poems, such as "Explico algunas cosas" ("I'm Explaining a Few Things"), Neruda uses his subjective experiences as the basis for broad social and political commentary. In both of these works, the poet inhabits and speaks from the center of centrifugal social forces. A crucial poem by Vallejo, "Un hombre pasa con un pan al hombro" ("A Man Walks By with a Loaf of Bread on His Shoulder"), provides an important counterpoint to this privileged positioning of the poet. Here Vallejo's speaker questions his role as poet, intellectual, or consumer of high culture—in short, as anyone removed from the concrete world of the ordinary person or suffering citizen. By reading these three poems together, students begin to understand the contradictory roles a twentieth-century poet can assume, from prophet to witness to uneasy questioner, as well as the tensions these roles can produce within the larger society.

Foundational avant-garde poems such as those by Vallejo and Neruda may be read against mid- and late-twentieth-century poems that further complicate the poet's place in the "polis." To this end, the remainder of the second unit focuses on more contemporary works by Ernesto Cardenal, of Nicaragua; Juan Gelman, of Argentina; and Raúl Zurita, of Chile. William Rowe noted in 2000 that "the politically committed poet remains the most common image of Latin American poetry for European and American readers" (*Poets* 3). While acknowledging the committed character of much twentieth-century Latin American poetry, the instructor can effectively employ the work of these three poets to complicate students' often-simplistic impressions.[4] One basic pedagogical strategy is to call attention to differences—between poems, between poets, and even between the traditions of *littérature engagée* ("literature of commitment") in Latin America and the United States (Rowe, *Poets* 4). A thought-provoking conversation can emerge, for example, from a comparison between Neruda's *Alturas de Macchu Picchu* and Cardenal's *El secreto de Machu Picchu* ("The Secrets of Machu Picchu").[5] As they explore the contrasting perspectives of the poetic speakers in their responses to this ancient Incan site, students begin to formulate a healthy critique of Neruda's poet-centered redemptive approach, even while they weigh the sustained lyrical beauty of his poem against the more discursive quality of Cardenal's poem—a quality that Robert Pring-Mill terms "documentary" (ix).

We spend the two next class sessions on Gelman's bilingual compilation *Unthinkable Tenderness* and Zurita's *Purgatorio* (*Purgatory*). In both cases, students discover how responses to national trauma can be represented through an intense lyrical subjectivity that avoids both facile sentimentalism and overt propagandistic language, types of discourse that students might have associated with political poetry. With Zurita, we also have the chance to consider an ambiguously gendered poetic voice, as well as a poetics that draws on nontraditional and even nonlinguistic materials, such as the reproduction of an EEG, a psychiatrist's note, or skywriting.[6] These varied media help expand students' notions of what constitutes poetry, particularly political poetry. I have found that with minimal prompting students will generate their own complex questions of authenticity (for example, who can speak for the socially marginalized?) and complicity (for example, how does the poet address issues of blame and censure for the practices of repressive regimes?), as well as the overarching question of how poetry can respond to injustice. I end this unit on the poet's role in society by showing the 2011 film *Nostalgia de la luz* ("Nostalgia for the Light") by the Chilean director Patricio Guzmán. Juxtaposing the story of astronomers studying the cosmos through telescopes in the Atacama Desert with stories of those disappeared in the desert sands (from nineteenth-century miners to victims of the Pinochet regime), Guzmán's narrative and filmic techniques allow the class to establish points of contact with previous discussions of poetic responses to social and political concerns.

In order to counteract the impression that Latin American poetry is primarily concerned with sociopolitical issues, the third unit, The Inward Gaze: Poetry of Metaphysics and Introspection, focuses largely on the poet's preoccupation with the self and with the nature of language. Presenting the notion of the critical poem can help orient students toward the paradoxical use of poetry to question the very efficacy of poetry or of language more generally.[7] An obvious model for this current is Octavio Paz, and Eliot Weinberger's bilingual edition *The Collected Poems of Octavio Paz: 1957–1987* is an invaluable resource. While I ask students to read a fairly wide selection of Paz's poetry, class discussion centers on one short poem, "Entre lo que veo y digo" ("Between What I See and What I Say"; 484–87) and one longer poem, "Viento entero" ("Wind from All Compass Points"; 258–69).[8] Paz's tendency to craft the poetic line to convey the dialectical nature of thought provides opportunities for close readings that call students' attention to the inextricable nature of form and content.

After Paz, we consider two later poets from Argentina, a country whose philosophical-poetic tradition has remained strong. To introduce students to Roberto Juarroz's extensive body of work, I use *Vertical Poetry: Last Poems.* Lacking the reference points of autobiographical anecdote, historical moment, or sociopolitical commentary, Juarroz's poems demand a patient attention to the minute details of perception and reflection, as well as to the role of paradox. With this in mind, I divide the class into small groups and ask each group to read and respond freely to a poem of their choosing, then to work together to describe the particular uses of language at work in that poem. Another exercise on Juarroz grew out of a student's concern that the poet's use of repeated words, phrases, and simple images could be considered "aesthetic laziness." Following this student's cue, we worked as a group to create a thesis that criticized the use of repetition in Juarroz's poems; I then asked them individually to find one or more reasonable counterarguments to this thesis. The impromptu exercise proved very effective by allowing us to focus attention on the fundamentals of critical writing (argument, evidence, and counterevidence), while at the same time raising students' awareness of Juarroz's philosophical nuances, which are often conveyed in straightforward and reiterative language.

Although the third writer I choose for this unit, Alejandra Pizarnik, is not normally considered a metaphysical poet, her work evinces a way of poetic seeing that folds ever inward. An excellent source for Pizarnik's poetry is the bilingual collection *Extracting the Stone of Madness: Poems*

1962–1972. Like Juarroz, Pizarnik eschews external or historical concerns almost entirely, exploring instead psychic or existential tensions, as well as the power of poetry to organize or provide relief from these tensions. In contrast to Paz and Juarroz, however, Pizarnik relentlessly examines a pained subjectivity, providing a lens through which we can probe issues of gender. As they read any "poet of the inner life," students should be encouraged to consider how image and metaphor are used to embody abstract thought; in the case of Pizarnik, the metaphor of the body itself is a useful tool for comprehending the interplay between inner and outer experience.

Unit 4, Indigenous Voices, Past and Present, represents a major shift in focus as we take up issues of cultural identity and difference. Our earlier comparison of the Machu Picchu poems of Neruda and Cardenal introduced students to *indigenismo,* an approach reflecting sympathy with or comprehension of indigenous peoples, but from an exteriorized point of view. In order to further the class's understanding of *indigenismo* as a literary mode, we return to Cardenal, whose "Cantares mexicanos" ("Mexican Songs") and "Katúns" bring the indigenist perspective into contemporary focus (*Los ovnis de oro / Golden UFOs* 186–213, 352–65). As nuanced as it may be in Cardenal, however, this exteriorized perspective must be balanced with poetry written by indigenous authors. With this in mind, we look first at examples of pre-Conquest or immediately post-Conquest texts translated into Spanish from Nahuatl and Maya-K'iche'. This is a marvelous opportunity to introduce students to nonalphabetic forms of writing such as the Nahuatl and Maya codices—pictographic canvases that were ritually sung by trained elders—or the Incan quipu, a system of knotted cords. (Images of contemporary artistic quipus by the Peruvian poet and artist Jorge Eielson found on Web sites such as *MutualArt, Artnet, Pinterest,* and *Artsy* can provide a powerful visual complement to this material.) We discuss at this point certain problems inherent in the process of translation from the oral tradition to written indigenous languages, then into Spanish, and finally into English.

The remaining class meetings in this unit are dedicated to two contemporary poets: Humberto Ak'abal, a Maya-K'iche' poet from Guatemala (*Poems I Brought Down from the Mountain*), and Natalia Toledo, a Zapotec poet from the Oaxaca region of southern Mexico (*The Black Flower and Other Zapotec Poems*). Both Ak'abal and Toledo translate their own work into Spanish; Ak'abal's book is a bilingual Spanish-English edition, and Toledo's collection also includes the Zapotec original. Although digital recordings, widely available online, give students the chance to hear this poetry recited in its original language, most instructors do not have the expertise to consider the formal aspects of the untranslated poems.[9] Our discussions focus instead on images, metaphors, and internal structure, as well as on the cultural particularities that each poet foregrounds. Within this context, the class can reintegrate concerns that arose in the unit on The Poet and the Polis, considering the ways in which Toledo's and Ak'abal's speakers represent themselves both as individuals and as members of a community—in particular, a community that exists across generations, or, in the case of Toledo, a community of women.

Instructors can also take this opportunity to revisit issues that may have surfaced in previous discussions regarding the authenticity of the poetic voice. My students have rightly wondered, for instance, how to resist the tendency to read individual indigenous poets as spokespersons for an entire culture. They also confront the accuracy of poetic imagery, tone, and thematic concerns rendered in translation, here twice removed from the original. Instructors can encourage this type of questioning while cautioning students not to discard altogether the possibility of meaningful communication across languages. They can point out that poetry in fact has the power to maximize this communication through rhythm and other elements of sound that do not depend on verbal meanings.[10] To underscore this point, we listen to a recording of Ak'abal's "Cantos de pájaros" ("Bird Songs"), which consists solely of the poet's artful imitation of birds heard in the forests of Guatemala. The poem begins:

> Klis, klis, klis . . .
> Ch'ok, ch'ok, ch'ok . . .
> Tz'unum, tz'unum, tz'unum . . .
> B'uqpurix, b'uqpurix, b'uqpurix . . . (*Poems* 33)

In the fifth and final unit of this course, Unbinding the Text: Antipoetry and Poetry in Performance, we consider the experimental work of two contemporary Chileans, Nicanor Parra and Cecilia Vicuña. This unit functions well as a capstone precisely because it obliges students to interrogate every conventional notion of lyric poetry they might still retain. After reviewing briefly some of the radical directions we traced in earlier works, such as the fractured language of Vallejo's *Trilce* or the objective tone of Cardenal's "documentary poems," we find ourselves revisiting the fundamental questions "What is poetry?" and "How does poetry create meaning?" Using the bilingual edition of Nicanor Parra's *Antipoems: How to Look Better and Feel Great*, I ask students to identify the poetic speaker, his principal concerns, his attitudes, and his relationship to the reader. In this way we interrogate traditional constructions of the poetic speaker and conventions of poetic or lyrical language. To facilitate this discussion, I provide students with a passage from Rowe's chapter on Parra in *Poets of Contemporary Latin America*, in which he claims, "The speaker in Parra's poems is not privileged: the word 'I' is not used as a value . . . all enclosures of speaking, such as self, personality, confession, opinion, class, and knowledge, get blown apart" (22). We have not had the chance to laugh much before this point in the semester, so students welcome Parra's mordant irony and dark humor, his fresh use of cliché, and the very absurdity of his speaker, who can declare with impunity, "[M]y wife is buried / I killed her in a fit of rage / ages and ages ago" (*Antipoems* 31). In a second day dedicated to Parra's work, we look at several projected images of his *artefactos* ("artifacts").[11] These cartoon-like drawings with irreverent captions represent yet another attempt by Parra at dismantling readers' expectations of poetic expression. One particularly comical example consists of a crude representation of the Christian cross, accompanied by the caption "Voy y vuelvo" ("Be right back"). Students can enjoy spending the last few minutes of this class session sketching and sharing their own *artefactos*.

Cecilia Vicuña provides a rewarding conclusion to the semester, since she interweaves several of the strands we have followed, including not only the poet's alternately individual and communal voice, but also questions of gender, indigenous rights, the human relation to the land in Latin America, and poetic language itself. Vicuña's complex work has evolved from the text-based poetry of the 1970s into multivoiced, multilingual improvisatory performances.[12] She is also an internationally recognized multimedia visual artist. Her installation series *Quipu Menstrual* ("Menstrual Quipu") allows us to reconsider instances of nonalphabetic writing, in particular the Andean quipu that was mentioned with relation to Eielson's poetry (www.quipumenstrual.cl). But it also leads us to address questions of gendered art: Vicuña's visual representation of menstrual blood by means of thick strands of red yarn, installed in museum galleries but also in open public spaces or in the natural world, ties creative expression directly to the female body. The celebration of women's bodies and women's voices also resounds in Vicuña's textual poetry.

Since students at this point in the semester are busy working on their final papers and group projects, I ask them to read only one essay by Vicuña,

"An Introduction to Mestizo Poetics," and a small sampling of her lyric poetry taken from the 1992 collection *Unravelling Words and the Weaving of Water*. Class time can be used to explore the written poems but also to consider images or videos of Vicuña's visual artwork and performance pieces. Regardless of the materials the instructor chooses, students will enjoy investigating the myriad ways in which these genres and forms are interconnected. For Vicuña, the voicing of poetry is an integral part of its ability to communicate meaning. In her essay on mestizo poetics, she remarks, "In keeping with the mythical view of sound, intonation of specific tones became the key medium for spiritual communication. Through carefully modulated tones in speech and song, ritual participants enter a resonant state of consciousness where mutual creation and renewal occurs" (xxi). Taking all this into consideration, it is imperative that students hear Vicuña's own voice.[13] Experiencing her work in these varied ways, students are in a position to consider once again what poetry is, what the tasks of the poet are, how the poet belongs to a real or imagined community, and, finally, how the poetic word might actually effect change in the world.

Student Work, Critical and Creative

As its title suggests, the goal of this course is to foment students' overall engagement with Latin American poetry. Beyond class discussions, intellectual engagement is encouraged through short critical papers in which students are expected to present clear arguments and practice close textual analysis, which is modeled often in class. Students also have the opportunity to engage with the poetry on a less formal basis by writing short weekly responses in an online discussion forum. But, since poetry is after all a creative endeavor, it is crucial to give students numerous opportunities to engage creatively with the works we read. Thus, for any weekly response I invite them to substitute an original poem or a translation; they may also opt to memorize and recite a short poem or segment (in Spanish or English), or they may create and present to the class a work of visual art.

I have been pleased and surprised—and sometimes astonished—by the students' insightful online entries and formal essays, but even more so by their creative pieces. A creative writing major, for instance, wrote a complex poem titled "Like the Pulley Loose within Itself," using a line taken from Neruda's "Galope muerto" ("Dead Gallop") as her point of departure. An art major responded to Natalia Toledo's work with his own poem called "White Copal Resin, 4-oz. Bulk." A Spanish studies major memorized and recited Darío's "Lo fatal," then spoke to her classmates about the memorization process. She concluded with the insight that memorizing had taught her to pay close attention to the structure of the poem, noticing patterns she had not previously noticed, which led her to realize why the poem was pleasing to hear. The fact that this object lesson in memorizing and reciting poetry came from a student, and not from the instructor, made it all the more valuable for the group.

Some students chose to move beyond the limits of poetry as text. A biology major designed a surrealist collage featuring several images from Vallejo's poems. A literature major brought to class a small wooden box on which she had burned the phrase *ni pena ni miedo* ("neither pain nor fear")—the words of the two-mile-long "geoglyph" Zurita had carved into the Atacama Desert in 1993 (see Vicuña and Livon-Grosman 495). The box, like a tiny coffin, was empty. A student with a concentration in human rights constructed a pamphlet made of words and images that bore the title "Language is trauma is language destroying trauma." The beauty of these alternative responses—all of which were briefly presented to the group—was the communal sense they created in the classroom: students were visibly and audibly appreciative of each other's attempts at approaching the poetry in original ways.

For a final course project, I ask students to collaborate in groups of three to create an original work associated with Latin American poetry. Again, the results have been more than gratifying. One group built a complex mobile out of pieces of broken mirror, then embedded in the center of the sculpture a recording of their own voices, hauntingly reciting fragments of Pizarnik's poems. Another group created a fifteen-minute video based on Zurita's poem "El desierto de Atacama" ("The Desert of Atacama"; *Purgatory* 34–53). The film major in this group guided the other two students as they edited their segments, and each wrote a poetic narrative to accompany the others' images. A third group made a series of collages that mixed poetic text (lines from Juarroz's poetry), photographic images, and cartoon-like figures based on Parra's *artefactos*. Yet another group wrote and performed a guitar composition using lines from Zurita's *Purgatory*. These creations and presentations tend to be the high point of the course, as students demonstrate the learning about poetry that has taken place within the context of their own interests and talents.

The challenges of teaching a course like Engaging Latin American Poetry are considerable, beginning with the sheer extent of the subject matter it seeks to incorporate. I have found, however, that the goal of igniting students' interest in a field they know little about is best achieved through a wide array of poetic models and interpretive approaches. Crucial to the success of this method is the instructor's presentation of sufficient historical and literary context to help students comprehend those models as products of a national or regional culture, but also as explorations of individual poetic sensibilities. Even more important, in my experience, are the opportunities for creative responses that correspond to students' own circumstances and concerns, without abandoning the rigors of close reading and critical thinking. A delicate balancing act? Without a doubt—but one that can give students from a wide array of backgrounds a concrete knowledge of Latin America and its cultural practices, as well as the excitement arising from an informed and active engagement with contemporary poetry.

Notes

1. For ideas about teaching poetry "off the page," see Kuhnheim's essay in this volume; for an excellent discussion of emphasizing the sound values of poetry in the classroom, see Charles Bernstein's essay "Creative Wreading: A Primer" in Joan Retallack's *Poetry and Pedagogy*. As the phonic values of a poem may be very difficult to bring over into a different language, it is important to have the poems read aloud in their original language.

2. Advanced Spanish students may wish to examine in greater detail the formal and linguistic innovations of poets such as Jorge Luis Borges in his early *ultraista* period, Oliverio Girondo, Vallejo, or the Neruda of the first two *Residencias* (i.e., the first two collections in the series *Residencia en la tierra* [*Residence on Earth*]). A productive class period could also be dedicated to the *poesía negra* of Luis Palés Matos, Nicolás Guillén, and other Caribbean poets. In this case, the phonic values of the poems may be emphasized by means of recordings and by directing students to read aloud in a highly performative style.

3. Unless otherwise attributed, all translations from Spanish are my own.

4. Fernando Rosenberg's *After Human Rights* provides a nuanced discussion of the place of literature in contemporary discussions of human rights. See also Rosenberg's essay in this volume.

5. Kuhnheim's first chapter in *Spanish American Poetry* is an excellent resource for comparing Neruda's and Cardenal's poetic strategies.

6. In Zurita's *Purgatory*, the play of gender is constant and complex. In the opening section, for instance, an official identification picture of Zurita appears on the left side of the page, while the right side features the following handwritten note: "Me llamo Raquel / estoy en el oficio / desde hace varios años. Me encuentro /en la mitad de / mi vida. Perdí /el camino" 'My name is Rachel / I've been in the same / business for many / years. I'm in the / middle of my life. / I lost my way' (8–9, 11).

Across the bottom of the pages juxtaposing the ID photo with Rachel's note runs the line "EGO SUM QUI SUM." This serious play with gender can provide a touchstone for further gender-related questions as they arise during the semester.

7. In his pivotal essay "Los signos en rotación" ("Signs in Rotation") from *El arco y la lira* (*The Bow and the Lyre*), Octavio Paz provides the following definition, which I share with students: "A critical poem: . . . the union of these two contradictory words means: that poem that contains its own negation and that makes of that negation the point of departure for the song, equally distant from affirmation and negation. Poetry, conceived by Mallarmé as language's only possibility of identification with the absolute, of being the absolute, denies itself each time it is realized in a poem—unless the poem is simultaneously a criticism of that attempt" (250).

8. Other long poems by Paz that contemplate the problem of language include *Piedra de sol* (*Sunstone*; 1–35) and "Nocturno de San Ildefonso" ("San Ildefonso Nocturne"; 410–29); short poems might include "Escritura" ("Writing"; 252–53), "El otro" ("The Other"; 186–87), and "Epitafio sobre ninguna piedra" ("Epitaph for No Stone"; 550–51).

9. See the essays by Tiffany Creegan Miller and Clare Sullivan in this volume for a more extensive treatment of the challenges and rewards of teaching contemporary indigenous poetries.

10. Kuhnheim's essay in this collection provides a fuller exploration of the uses of sound in teaching Latin American poetry.

11. *Antipoems: How to Look Better and Feel Great* contains several examples of Parra's visual *artefactos*, and many others are available online.

12. A useful resource for helping students understand Vicuña's work as a performance poet-artist is *Spit Temple: The Selected Performances of Cecilia Vicuña*. *Cloud-Net*, an anthology of Vicuña's poems, also contains photographs of her performances and installations.

13. Audio clips of Vicuña's performances are available on audibleword.org, and numerous film clips can be found on *YouTube*.

Part II

Orality, Multimedia, and Comparative Arts

Gwen Kirkpatrick

Simultaneous Senses and Vital Dialogues in Latin American Poetry

Printed poetry's complex forms and verbal density can be bewildering even to sophisticated readers. Faced with a new poem, students often ask, "But what does it mean?" Many see poetry as a puzzle of symbols and metaphors that they cannot decipher on their own. Often for them poetry is only a dense thicket of signs and not part of their larger sonic and verbal surroundings. We need to help them move away from the printed page and begin to see the poetic elements in their everyday lives.

It can help to remember that poetry began in songs and chants and was transformed over generations before entering print culture. We can help students make contact with the oral tradition by asking them to recall nursery rhymes, rap music, or commercial jingles. When they recite or share examples with other students, they begin to build bridges to both written and oral poetry in Latin America. Quickly they can see and hear what these forms have in common—repetition, whether by rhyme, rhythm, choruses, or onomatopoeia. Once they recognize that many poetic forms originated as oral storytelling, entertainment, or marketing, they can grasp what meanings or purpose these forms carry. When they understand the use of repetition as a memory tool or a means of emphasis, they can begin to make sense of the formal structures that may have baffled them. Except in courses focused primarily on poetry, I don't insist that students learn more about form and meter than the following: to recognize a sonnet, an octosyllable, anaphora, and alliteration; and to distinguish partial and full rhyme. I realize this is a radical reduction, but as students master these things they gain enough confidence and interest to absorb much more along the way. They may still prefer free verse, but learning these simple tools unlocks centuries of tradition for them.

Why were poetic forms associated with orality neglected for so long? Why have many of them returned over time? These are questions that matter to all of us, not just in the study of poetry. To read and hear a selection of texts and music from different time periods can be like a journey through time that teaches us about different forms of community-making through the arts, and about the creation of both private and public literatures. It would take a vast interdisciplinary effort to trace the strands of influence in both popular and learned poetry and song in Latin America; this essay seeks to illuminate points of contact between languages, disciplines, and generations whereby modern Latin American poetry is continually created.

By making the effort to enter into poetry with all our senses, we can connect with a deep current of expression that binds us together, even across many languages. For example, students can listen on the Web to the Cuban poet Nicolás Guillén reciting "Sensemayá" ("Killing a Snake") and then share what they hear and understand ("Cuban Poet"). On seeing the written poem, they grasp that Guillén probably didn't expect his readers in Spanish to understand every word of the text—parts of which scholars have traced to African languages—but that he clearly counted on their sensing the frenzied speed and rising volume toward the poem's climax. The poem asserts the importance of repetition in rituals and evokes the African diaspora and centuries of slavery in Cuba. The poem never fails to arouse student interest: its mysterious words and repeated sounds and rhythms entrance them. Yet at the same time these sounds remind us that not all speakers of Spanish share a common history. Guillén's legacy from the Afro-Cuban community gives him words and songs that are unknown even to most of his contemporary Cuban readers. In approaching "Sensemayá" as a bridge to poetic orality, we learn that poetic language bears our histories in many different ways and that sometimes form itself is a central part of our histories.

Few nations or regions sharing one principal language incorporate the living presence of as many other languages, including indigenous languages as well as the languages brought by the African diaspora and by more recent immigrations, as does Spanish America. Today, after several centuries of Spanish-language contact, there are many forms of Spanish in the region: the Mexican lilt, African-influenced Spanish; the unmistakable Río de la Plata tonality and verb forms; Andean Spanish; and many other variants that are decidedly Spanish but also build on the vocabulary and syntax of indigenous, African, and other languages brought by immigration or, like English, primarily by commerce and media. Increasingly, countries like Paraguay, Bolivia, Peru, and Guatemala have officially recognized bilingualism or multilingualism, claiming languages in addition to Spanish—Guaraní, Aymara, Quechua, K'iche' Maya—as official national languages. Today we see writers in the United States asserting the legitimacy of literature in variants of English and Spanish or Spanglish. Within this mosaic in Spanish America, Spanish has been the dominant tradition, sometimes incorporating but more often excluding different literary traditions. In the period covered by this volume, however, the pace of incorporation has quickened. In the early decades of the twentieth century, just as the music and literature of the Harlem Renaissance began to transform culture in the United States, there were parallel changes in Spanish America, like the *negrista* movement and the influence of Caribbean music worldwide. This period also saw the growth of *indigenismo*, an aesthetic and political movement that focused, especially in the visual arts, on indigenous traditions and, in the social sphere, on the oppression experienced by indigenous peoples. (The *sikuri* musical groups that perform in many urban centers, even far from the Andean region, exemplify one such revival of traditional arts.[1]) Yet only more recently have we seen indigenous poets themselves forging new languages in Spanish to assert their identities, like the Chilean urban poetry that combines Spanish and Mapudungun, the language of the now primarily urban Mapuche community.[2]

Given the demographics of Spanish today, it is not clear that there is any longer a dominant tradition of Spanish; the continuing changes show the underlying dynamic of heterogeneous populations, their frequent geographic displacement, and their resulting literary production. And classrooms in the United States increasingly show the dynamics of these changes in our student populations. In the 1920s the Argentine poet Oliverio Girondo urged "faith in our phonetics, since it was us Americans who have put some oxygen into Spanish, making it a breathable language" (qtd. in Rowe, "Latin American Poetry" 147).[3] Girondo and Jorge Luis Borges were among the many writers of that time who believed that only the Americas could breathe new life into literature in Spanish. The Cuban writer José Lezama Lima stated in *La expresión americana* ("American Expression") that in the times of conquest Spanish on American shores needed to become porous and flexible, and to acquire a more popular tone (140). The Spanish conquerors of the Americas imposed their language as the only legitimate vehicle for state and legal functions and for nonlocal commerce. Ecclesiastical leaders, then as now, were more concerned with finding the right language for their message. The Roman Catholic Church imported European mass settings and Latin chant to the Americas, but it also incorporated local rhythms and tones. Some priests learned indigenous languages in order to preach and to convert, and the church continues to recruit indigenous speakers and musicians. Meanwhile, ordinary people in "contact zones" transformed language and its expressive forms to suit their everyday needs.[4] Language in action, despite attempts to establish normative grammars and "standard" usage, shifts its shape and tones in different linguistic and cultural environments. It follows then that poetry, a form of language in action, would possess the same fluidity, or porousness and oxygenation in the terms of Lezama Lima and Girondo.

The twenty-first century has witnessed an acceleration of linguistic and literary contact among Spanish speakers to a degree unknown before the spread of the Internet, social media, and electronic communication generally. As a result, many students have a head start on learning about poetry in Latin America, and using selections of poetry they may already know can help them understand the vitality and survival of popular and oral traditions. First, Pablo Neruda's *Veinte poemas de amor y una canción desesperada* ("Twenty Love Poems and a Desperate Song"), or his later *Cien sonetos de amor* ("One Hundred Love Sonnets"), are perennial favorites for gift-giving, even among infrequent poetry readers. Progressing from Neruda's poems to sonnets by other Latin American writers, students come to recognize learned written forms and to appreciate their expressive potential. Second, most students already know "Guantanamera," a song signifying popular solidarity adapted from the *Versos sencillos* ("Simple Verses") of the Cuban writer José Martí; its octosyllabic form and its full rhyme reach far back to the *romance* (narrative ballad) tradition from medieval Spain. And, third, students probably have heard the Mexican musical group Los Tigres del Norte, based in California, where the traditional form of the Mexican corrido,[5] and the recent narcocorrido[6] or new forms of the border corrido, are variants of the same oral verse tradition used by Martí. Of course, it is not just the Spanish oral tradition that has enriched Latin American poetry and song. Contemporary rap lyrics, salsa (a musical and dance form arising in New York City from Caribbean origins), and many musical forms in the Americas have roots in African traditions brought by the African diaspora. Chant forms and percussion from many indigenous traditions have also shaped particular forms of Spanish and of poetry. These examples from music can set the stage for revealing some of the multiple cultural and linguistic strands that weave together or stand apart to make up Latin American poetry.

Poetry in Latin America, like the language itself, combines both oral and written traditions. Neruda's sonnets and love poems arise from a learned but powerful tradition established by the early Italian Renaissance poet Petrarch. Still vital today, the sonnet carries with its form the legacies of many generations, cultures, and languages.[7] Neruda's twentieth-century sonnets are a gateway for students to other Latin American poets writing in the Petrarchan tradition. Sonnets are one of the most beautiful legacies of the brilliant seventeenth-century Mexican nun Sor Juana Inés de la Cruz. Sor Juana uses her own American context—the Nahuatl language, the African-inflected dialects of enslaved people, and a baroque style of Spanish (as in the stunning "Primero sueño" ["First Dream"]). Her writings illustrate the "oxygenation" of language and poetry as well as the convergence of powerful ethnic and cultural differences and the *mestizaje* (mixing in both the racial and cultural senses) in Spain's first viceroyalty, New Spain.[8] Her playful and sardonic poem "Hombres necios" ("Foolish Men") is an immediate favorite with contemporary students because they discover a woman writer from centuries ago who could subvert male hierarchy with both wit and logic.[9] The poem's alliterative and rhyming octosyllables that ask, "[L]a que peca por la paga / o el que paga por pecar?" 'Who is prostitution's real sinner?' (*Obras completas* 322) are unforgettable. Sor Juana is simply a magnificent figure: students will happily undertake more complex studies of poets they admire, so it is worth spending substantial time on their writings.

Although all structured poetic forms lose favor during the avant-garde experiments in modern Western poetry that lead to the dominance of free verse during most of the twentieth century, the sonnet never dies out. There are remarkable exceptions to the turn toward free verse, like the Chilean poet Gabriela Mistral, Latin America's first recipient of the Nobel Prize.[10] Mistral is undaunted by being out of step with her more avant-garde colleagues, for example, her compatriot Vicente Huidobro. She favors rural nature settings, while many of her contemporaries turn to urban environments for inspiration and new forms. But even poets who are the most pathbreaking in form or in theme at some point experiment with sonnets: Neruda in Chile, César Vallejo in Peru,[11] Alfonsina Storni in Argentina with her *antisonetos* ("antisonnets"), and many others stretch the limits of the sonnet during the age of avant-garde experimentation. At the turn of the nineteenth century, the Nicaraguan *modernista* Rubén Darío, one of the greatest poets in Spanish, had already experimented with the sonnet, using the Spanish fourteen-syllable alexandrine instead of the accustomed hendecasyllable (eleven-syllable line). But it is his truncated sonnet "Lo fatal" ("Fatality"; *Poesía* 311–12) that perhaps captures best the yearning and sense of defeat that mark much of his poetry and that of his generation. As the sonnet form breaks down in the first tercet, readers understand that not only form is breaking down: it is a soul in crisis. Students, especially young students, identify with this uncertainty and doubt about their life's direction. They see doubt and a sense of loss played out in the broken form. They also grasp the pathos of Darío's complex "Sonatina" (168–70), often parodied by subsequent poets for its excess and escapism. Although they may not understand some of its vocabulary or references, on listening to it they enter into its colorful and fantastic alternative universe with its quickly shifting rhythms. They understand that the *princesita* ("little princess") is trapped in a cage not of her own making and willingly suspend disbelief to enter into her world. Given their liking of "Sonatina," it might seem paradoxical that "A Roosevelt" ("To Roosevelt"; 258–59) is another favorite. Its thunderous negation of the United States' invasive power and its caricature of that nation's culture stir up student idealism and rebelliousness against authority. The poem also serves to illustrate the post-*Ariel*[12] moment of Latin American culture, when, faced with the growing dominance of the United States, the former colonies turned back to Spanish cultural roots, as in this poem that puts Cuauhtémoc and Columbus in the same camp. The poem also works as a sound study. When asked if it has any regular poetic form, students are confident that it is totally free of such restrictions. Demonstrating how it uses "o" vowels in *rima aguda* ("sharp rhyme") in alternate verses underlines how subtle written poetry can be. On reading it aloud again, students see clearly how the "o" ominously punctuates the poem's denunciations.

Unlike the later Petrarchan sonnet, the ancient Spanish *romance* depended on oral transmission for survival. The *romance* frequently combined expressions of love and sorrow with the record of historical events, like conquest and treason, often occurring in border areas. Set patterns of sound and rhythm—rhyme, meter, and stanza division—were memory aids for both singers and their audiences. (Students may recognize the English ballad, an analogue of the *romance*, from literary studies but are unlikely to have encountered it as public entertainment, where it once figured strongly.)[13] Martí's *Versos sencillos* have the octosyllabic structure and consonant rhyme (full rhyme) that show why verses like these could be recited, sung, and altered to suit the occasion over centuries by those who could not read. Though his "simple verses" are not at all simple, the poet strove to be unpretentious and used the recognizable structure of the *romance* in order to make his work accessible.[14] Today, students unfamiliar with the *romance* often take a different route to Martí, whom they revere after reading his essay "Nuestra América" ("Our America") and some of his poems. Those familiar with the song "Guantanamera" recognize Martí's brief verses and complete rhyme ("Yo soy un hombre sincero / De donde crece la palma / Y antes de morirme quiero / Echar los versos del alma . . ."; 'I am an honest man / from where the palm trees grow, / and before I die I want / to pour the verses from my soul' [Gonzalez and Treece 18]), and the knowledge that a crusading hero wrote poetry in strict form breaks down resistance to learning forms. Similarly, through songs by Los Tigres del Norte and other groups, students discover how the memory device of full rhyme in relatively short lines of eight syllables and fixed numbers of lines gives narrative or storytelling structure to regional forms like the corrido in Mexico or the *lira* in Chile, traditionally printed with striking illustrations. These written and visual forms traveled and served as newscasts; corridos read or sung from printed sheets, some illustrated by the artist Guadalupe Posadas, transmitted and celebrated news during the Mexican Revolution and offered cautionary tales of love, heroism, and social and political events.[15] There is a parallel phenomenon in Brazil of the traditional *cordel* form, still distributed in illustrated print versions (see Slater).

In traditions of poetic performance, improvisation has played an important role, particularly in the sung "duels" or *payadas* represented in *Martín Fierro*, José Hernández's two-volume gaucho poem of over two thousand verses, which Argentina has adopted as a kind of national epic. Like rap music today, which originated in call-and-response and improvised rhymed verbal dueling, these *payadas*, often accompanied by the guitar or a similar instrument, were usually narratives, telling the history of a success, a grievance, or a dream in poetic form. As many critics have noted, by the time *Martín Fierro* and *La vuelta de Martín Fierro* ("The Return of Martin Fierro") were published in the 1870s, the gaucho had become a marginal figure, losing his mobility and being exploited as a soldier drafted by the state. Thus the epic of *Martín Fierro* is one of displacement and nostalgia.

Until a few decades ago, recitation, especially dramatic recitation, was a vital form of entertainment in Latin America, from domestic parlors to campfires to governmental ceremonies. At public and private events, people recited poems, often lengthy ones meaningful to the particular group, and memory feats and dramatic delivery were held in high esteem. This practice culminated in the theatrical presentations of stars like Berta Singerman, who enraptured audiences of the Spanish-speaking world for decades in sold-out performances in large urban theaters (see Kuhnheim, *Beyond* 17–46). Declamation was regularly taught in most public and private schools at least through the 1950s. In both humble and wealthy homes, recitation often played an important role in family and social life. The Uruguayan poet Idea Vilariño in her memoirs (*Diarios de juventud* ["Diaries of Youth"]) often refers to long family evenings when the children would insist that their father recite poems after dinner and would sometimes join him. Modern pedagogy has rejected recitation in general, relating it to the suppression of creativity and the stifling of authentic understanding. Thus recitation has become a kind of collateral damage in an otherwise praiseworthy project.

The broad-based educational movements, not just for the elites but for the general populace, had vast repercussions for literature in Latin America. From the late nineteenth century onward, literacy rates soared, creating an audience for print culture that was expanded even further by technological improvements in printing.[16] The combination of increased literacy along with printing advances introduced a wide range of social classes not just to print but also to illustration (as for the corrido and *lira* forms), and then to color printing and photography. Unlike most publications today, poems and short stories always found a place alongside news and essays at the turn of the century and beyond.

The early twentieth century saw astounding new technologies that lit up cities at night and shortened distances by faster speeds in ships, cars, and, later, airplanes. The telephone shortened distances between human voices, and the radio and movies opened up new geographic panoramas and changes in perception. Film's advantage in representing simultaneous actions or scenes posed a major challenge to writers and was an incentive to find techniques to do this in literature. This can partly explain the avant-garde push to expel the old—and the acceleration and expansion of communication can explain how a young provincial poet like César Vallejo could read works of the international avant-gardes in little magazines while he studied at the University of Trujillo, far from the Peruvian capital of Lima, where the currents of socialism and indigenism were powerful influences.

Social and political turmoil found expression in all genres. In the case of Vallejo's poetry, the turmoil is linguistic as well as social and political. In the same way that he resists Catholicism and protests social injustice, he fights to break down language itself in the poems of *Trilce*.[17] *Trilce* is a challenge for all readers. I have often asked students to translate a poem from *Trilce*, and the results have been stunning. Most students rise to the challenge of altering the English lexicon and syntax, and as they share their creations they see that they also can be radical or vanguard poets, working at the very limits of language. A colleague teaching the vanguards asked students to write their own artistic manifestos, and then to publicly recite them in an open space with a lot of foot traffic.

Altazor, by the Chilean poet Vicente Huidobro, is one of the most ambitious attempts to break with traditional forms. While altogether different from Vallejo's *Trilce*, it also questions the communicative function of language itself. Structured in cantos like early epic poems, *Altazor* ends with the breakdown of language. Octavio Paz in *Convergencias* ("Convergences") makes a compelling case for understanding the Babelian quality of the seventh and final canto as the age-old desire to speak in tongues (glossolalia), to communicate with the sacred without the mediation of language.[18] José Quiroga sees this same canto as an indication of the erasure of indigenous languages and cultures and as a call to understand that this "babbling" is full of meaning now forbidden, disdained, or erased (21).

Avant-garde poets of the early twentieth century often combined image with text and experimented with new types of publication (as today's avant-garde poets, equipped with electronic resources, do now). Jorge Luis Borges cofounded and collaborated in avant-garde magazines in Buenos Aires in the 1920s. The first was *Prisma* ("Prism"), published in the form of large illustrated posters and pasted like murals on city walls. Its intent was to shock the public. Borges at that time even advocated a localized kind of written Spanish that would incorporate Río de la Plata verb forms and altered orthography to reflect local pronunciation. This impulse coincided with literary movements in many other regions, such as Harlem or the Greater Caribbean, to make writing reflect local speech. While Borges later rejected this endeavor, the impetus to bring writing, speech, and thought together had powerful repercussions for literature, both in the social sense, encouraging group or ethnic solidarity, and in the technical sense, giving rise to stream-of-consciousness writing.

The first known calligrams in Spanish, poems arranged graphically to correspond to their content, were composed by José Juan Tablada, of Mexico, who was influenced by Japanese culture and who experimented very early in the twentieth century with radically new forms of poetry. Vicente Huidobro's calligrams and other visual experiments, including collaborations with the painter Juan Gris, are particularly striking because of their number and variety, including painting poetry on glass. The Peruvian poet Carlos Oquendo de Amat in his *5 metros de poemas* (*5 Meters of Poetry*) makes graphic play with words—for example, writing *ascensor* ("elevator") vertically with the letters in reverse order while forming other designs—to disorder a serial reading of his poem. The title itself, which might have led us to expect a rolled or accordion-folded paper measuring five meters when opened, upsets our usual means of measuring. Octavio Paz's calligrams and graphic experiments were influenced strongly by surrealism and by contact in India with non-Western forms of spirituality and philosophy. Paz also dedicated himself to understanding the pre-Columbian cultures of Mexico. His poem *Piedra de sol* (*Sunstone*) is an homage to the Aztec calendar, the icon that now represents Mexico in many parts of the world. His poem has 584 verses, drawn in a circle, to correspond to the 584 days of a solar cycle. Another long poem, *Blanco*, is printed as a scroll, resisting division into pages. *Discos visuales*, produced jointly with the graphic artist Vicente Rojo, is printed on four paper discs.[19]

On reviewing poetic works that contain visual elements, it becomes clear that Paz, Huidobro, and many other poets would have delighted in the possibilities presented by today's technologies for animation of image, text, sound, and movement. Although it is beyond the scope of this essay, Eduardo Ledesma, in *Radical Poetry: Aesthetics, Politics, and Technology in the Ibero-American Avant-Gardes, 1900–2015*, studies poets who work with digital technology. By understanding the avant-garde as a timeless concept, Ledesma is able to trace connections through over a century in experimental poetry and visual material in Spanish and Portuguese.

Women's writing began to flourish after the introduction of broad-based educational movements. With the expansion of education to more social classes and the expansion of publications, women began to enter the professions and to claim space in the literary world. Their heightened presence in literature also reflected the mobilization for women's rights in the first wave of feminism at the turn of the century. Mistral and Storni were widely known in their times, both for their poetry and for their journalistic essays. An earlier example of breaking restrictions can be found in the short life of Delmira Agustini, who was the first woman to be granted a divorce in Uruguay and was subsequently murdered by her ex-husband.[20] Although Agustini largely followed traditional poetic forms, her work's explicit eroticism shocked her contemporaries, and poems like the brief "Nocturno," with its incompletion and fragmentation, signal some of the changes to come.[21] Rosario Castellanos, a defender of women's rights in Mexico who is known as a novelist, poet, and essayist, drew from Greek tragedy, indigenous life, and her experience as a mother. Nancy Morejón brought black female consciousness to the fore with her iconic poem "Mujer negra" ("Black Woman"), which traces the subjection of black women in Cuba from the Middle Passage up to the Cuban Revolution.

Nicanor and Violeta Parra, brother and sister from Chile, constitute an unusual case in poetic history. Brother and sister followed very different poetic routes — Nicanor with satiric and colloquial poetry and Violeta with traditional forms and folkloric narratives — but they both represent important directions in Latin American poetry in the second half of the twentieth century. Born into a family of ten children who struggled to survive, Violeta spoke of singing on the streets as a young teenager to earn enough money to buy food (Andrés Wood). The oldest of the Parra children, Nicanor, went to university in Santiago to study mathematics and physics, and then to the United States and Great Britain. Back in Santiago he was a professor of physics and a prolific poet, with many books and a large audience that appreciated his unorthodox stance toward poetry; his *antipoesía* ("antipoetry") is a form he developed to bring pompous poets down from Mount Olympus ("Manifiesto"). Violeta Parra became a musician, like several of her family members. In contrast to Nicanor's prosaic and often satiric "antipoetry," she recognized the power of traditional and popular music; early in her singing career she began to take her diction, rhythms, and themes from the rural areas where pre-nineteenth-century poetic and musical traditions were still alive. In 1953 she began traveling through the Chilean countryside to document this popular music.[22] The traditional octosyllabic form and full rhyme lent itself to singing, and Violeta accompanied herself on the twenty-five-string *guitarrón*; she is considered to be the impetus for the *nueva canción* ("new song") movement, important politically as well as musically in the 1960s and '70s. Her composition

"Gracias a la vida" ("Thanks to Life") has been sung throughout the world. Also a textile artist, Violeta transformed the traditional *arpillera* (appliqué pictures) into a form uniquely hers, earning an exhibition at the Louvre. By the time of her suicide at thirty-nine years old, her recovery of traditional music, poetry, and art was widely known, and she has influenced several generations in Latin America.[23]

Today we have wonderful access to sound and images through the Internet, vastly increasing our supply of poetic and visual texts and opening new forms of creativity and pedagogy. Using clips of songs and recitations in class or embedding them in texts or assignments helps students construct bridges from oral to textual forms. In addition, exploring the graphic forms of poetry, both traditional and experimental (concrete poetry in Brazil and previously mentioned examples), allows students to find a way from pictorial writing to the visual arts. Perhaps graphic experimentation in poetry best represents how poets try to go beyond the limits of language and cross over into other forms that make meaning; students may then understand how some examples from the visual arts can be read as texts. They should know that there are indeed poems that can be inspiring and beautiful even though we do not fully understand them. By building bridges between the oral and the written, sound and sight, Spanish and indigenous or African languages, the ancient and the contemporary, we can show students how to find the poems they will want to remember and how to understand the place of poetry in our world. Even better, they may find ways to develop their own creativity.

Notes

I am grateful to my colleague Vivaldo Santos, whose knowledge about Brazilian and Spanish American poetry is extraordinary, for his assistance with this essay.

1. For the *sikuri* phenomenon and its move from isolated Andean regions to major urban centers even outside of Latin America, see Thomas Turino and Daniel Castelblanco.

2. The best-known Mapuche urban poet is David Aniñir, who coined the term *mapurbe* to describe his situation as an urban blue-collar worker in the capital. For an interview with him see Andrea Echeverría and Daniel Castelblanco.

3. William Rowe's "Latin American Poetry" and José Quiroga's "Spanish American Poetry" are profound, accessible, and wide-ranging essays on poetry in Latin America. *The Gathering of Voices*, by Mike González and David Treece, offers accessible and engaging essays, and Gordon Brotherston's *Latin American*

Poetry, which focuses on just a few important poets, continues to be a readable and insightful introduction to Latin American poetry.

4. Mary Louise Pratt introduced the term "contact zone" to describe the encounters of languages, ethnicities, and cultures in the same space ("Arts").

5. The recently revised *Princeton Encyclopedia of Poetry and Poetics*, with expanded entries on Latin America in general and on specific countries, provides useful discussion of poetic terms like *corrido*. (Other encyclopedic works, like the *Encyclopedia of Latin American and Caribbean Literature* [Balderston and González], can be helpful for information on writers and literary forms unique to Latin America.) Américo Paredes's work has inspired fascinating research on the corrido as an important social expression that can reveal the tensions and complexities of Mexico's relations with the United States over two centuries.

6. Despite the popularity of the narcocorrido, the extreme violence and carnage produced by the drug trade in Mexico has created a backlash against it because it often glorifies *narcotraficantes* ("drug traffickers") as contemporary Robin Hoods.

7. For a powerful and elegiac reflection on the ways in which poetic forms represent human history and emotions, see Susan Stewart, especially pp. 252–53.

8. Ernesto Livon-Grosman and Cecilia Vicuña's introductions to their *Oxford Book of Latin American Poetry* stress more than most anthologies the *mestizo* nature of Latin American poetry.

9. Josefina Ludmer's "Las tretas del débil" ("Strategies of the Weak") has become a classic essay on Sor Juana's subversions.

10. Vicky Unruh's *Performing Women* offers insight into the different contexts in which Latin American women wrote and acted in the 1920s and '30s.

11. The sonnets in Vallejo's triptych "Nostalgias imperiales" ("Imperial Nostalgias") from *Los heraldos negros* (*Black Heralds*; *Obra poética* 54–56) offer despairing views of the human remnants of the ruined Inca Empire.

12. In 1900 José Enrique Rodó published an essay that claimed the civilized nature of Shakespeare's character Ariel in *The Tempest* for Latin America, characterizing the North as the barbaric Caliban.

13. Some of the earliest *romances* were border ballads arising from the frontiers between Moorish and Christian lands in Iberia. Today many corridos are border ballads about fear and danger along the United States–Mexico border.

14. Martí's compatriot Gertrudis Gómez de Avellaneda had experimented earlier in the nineteenth century with some radically simple verses of one, two, and three syllables (Rodríguez and Szurmuk, [152]).

15. Mexican illustrated corridos are abundantly available on the Internet. Simone Malacchini Soto's *Lira popular* ("Popular Lyre") gives a wonderful overview of the illustrated Chilean *lira* tradition, including the history of this popular form from its Iberian origins in fourteenth- and fifteenth-century *pliegos sueltos* ("broadsheets").

16. See Acree for a revealing case study of Uruguay.

17. After *Trilce* he returns to more accessible language to write some of the most memorable poems in Spanish about social injustice. See Clayton for a comprehensive and revealing study of Vallejo's context and of his poetry.

18. "Speaking in tongues obeys unconscious laws of rhythm not essentially different from those governing the elaboration of poems: meters, accents, pauses, coupling of syllables, explosion of phonemes—in a word, all the variations of verbal rhythm" (Paz, "Speaking in Tongues" 8).

19. Octavio Paz's work encompasses many topics, but in relation to Latin American poetry and poetry in general two essays stand out: *El arco y la lira* (*The Bow and the Lyre*) and *Los hijos del limo* (*The Children of the Mire*).

20. Sylvia Molloy and Cathy Jrade have written insightfully about Agustini.

21. Uruguay has produced an astounding number of important women poets, from the generation of Eugenia Vaz Ferreira and Delmira Agustini to Juana de Ibarbourou (of the same generation as Mistral and Storni) to Amanda Berenguer, Idea Vilariño, Ida Vitale, Marosa DiGiorgio, and Cristina Peri Rossi.

22. See her findings in *Cantos folklóricos chilenos* ("Chilean Folk Songs"), including photos by Sergio Larraín and Sergio Bravo. For additional information on the revival of Andean musical traditions, see Thomas Turino and Daniel Castelblanco.

23. For an excellent and comprehensive study of her poetry see Paula Miranda Herrera.

Eduardo Ledesma

Teaching Experimental Latin American Poetry: Visual, Concrete, Performative, and Digital

This essay explores how experimental Latin American poetry might be included in upper-level undergraduate or graduate courses. By "experimental" I refer to forms of the literary arts that are closely allied with non-literary arts, such as conceptual and abstract art, new media art, performance, photography, and film. A self-reflexive form, experimental poetry expands traditional definitions of poetry and blurs the boundaries between the visual and verbal arts. Teaching experimental poetry to either graduate or undergraduate students represents a challenge. Students often ask questions such as, Does the word *experiment* not connote the sciences? Is literature not a humanities discipline? How does one reconcile the two? My main purpose in these courses, therefore, is to entreat the students to push through from their initial disbelief to an acceptance of the value of experimental poetry, so they might appreciate its long-standing presence in Latin American literature.

Typically I begin a course on the experimental with a historical and cultural overview of three critical avant-garde periods through the twentieth and twenty-first centuries, identifying representative artists from the 1920s, the 1960s, and the 2000s. From the early twentieth century, I introduce well-known avant-garde poets such as Vicente Huidobro, Patrícia

Galvão (Pagu), Manuel Maples Arce, Norah Lange, or Oliverio Girondo. I move to concrete, visual, and conceptual poets from the sixties and seventies such as Décio Pignatari and the Campos brothers, Clemente Padín, Guillermo Deisler, and Raúl Zurita; and I finally include twenty-first-century digital and new media poets such as Eduardo Kac, Arnaldo Antunes, Ana María Uribe, and Gustavo Romano.

Drawing on classroom experience, I would like to touch on several questions that guide the teaching of experimental poetry: How can a single course meaningfully comprise disparate works, created with various media technologies? What interdisciplinary skills will students need in order to interact with poems that engage text, image, sound, and often movement? How might the students' initial resistance (typically phrased, "This is not poetry!") be turned into productive engagement? How might poetry help students make sense of the contradictions of Latin America's interaction with technology? How might it help them examine concepts such as modernity, progress, and rupture, in the context of political turmoil, dictatorship, and neoliberalism?

Despite a certain universal valence to the term *experimental*, each poem comes from a specific context. The students' encounter with poetry should be framed by the historical, cultural, and geographic specificity of the texts and by critical questions regarding the relation between technology and poetry: How does technology change the ways in which we consume poetry? How is poetry itself enriched by technological developments? In addition, the students are asked to consider questions of methodology, such as, How does one read a work of visual, concrete, or digital poetry?

Today, Latin American experimental poetry exists as a multisensorial experience and in that respect connects quite well with a student population increasingly immersed in technologies that augment their sensory perception. Through the range of poetic practices analyzed in a course on experimental poetry, students gain historical insight about past junctures of poetry, media, and technological development—for example by studying the radio poetry of the *estridentistas* or the mail art and poetry of Clemente Padín, Edgardo Vigo, and other neo-avant-gardists. They also learn to engage with the conceptual tools necessary to reflect on the present cross-pollination of established artistic practices and rising media technologies (such as the Internet, cell phones, tablets, virtual reality devices). Perhaps most important, they discover that literary and artistic genres such as poetry are in fact porous, malleable constructs that allow for unlimited variation and hybridity with other art forms.

We might begin by asking, How does one teach poetry in a visual culture-oriented world? Our particular historical moment has great potential, for despite a decreased interest by students in more traditional poetry there is notable interest in newer genres of the poetic, broadly understood to include digital poetry, poetry slams, performance poetry, and an ongoing presence of the lyrical within contemporary music. This suggests that poetry remains, in one form or another, relevant, despite our growing sense that, as Virginia Jackson notes, "poetry is all-important and at the same time already in its afterlife" (183). I would argue that enthusiasm for poetry can still be generated in the classroom and that alternate forms of the poetic are a way to begin to interest students.

And yet, why focus on experimental works? Experimental poetry engages with visuality, with technology, and with the most radical aspects of aesthetic transgression, and it is fully enmeshed with other arts (painting, film, new media), which arguably makes it more relevant for our students by intersecting with their other interests. Quite simply, by teaching poetries that partake of visual culture to students who are immersed in all kinds of new technologies of vision, we open a familiar door through which they enter, eventually leading them to other types of poetry.

But how might students begin to explore and take apart works that are conceptually complex and whose meaning may be difficult to understand, works such as José Juan Tablada's "Impresión de la Habana" (1919; "Impression of Havana"), Mathias Goeritz's *Pocos cocodrilos locos* (1979; "Few Crazy Crocodiles"), or Gustavo Romano's digital *IP Poetry* (2007), to name the three vastly different poems I will use as examples in this essay? They do so by focusing on the close analysis of individual poems, placed within their specific sociohistorical context, understood in terms of the devices and media they employ and the poetic traditions they belong to, echo, or parody. Indeed, readers should begin with a focus on form, and examine how poems function, "before making claims about what they might be saying" (Altieri 259). Of course the study of form needs to be properly contextualized, historicized. Experimental poetry has a way of foregrounding its form, making it quite suitable for close-reading approaches in the classroom. It also tends to be framed by large conceptual theories, which provide many didactic moments.

I have taught the experimental poems of these three distinct periods—the 1920s, the 1950s and '60s, and the 2000s—chronologically, which helps students understand how each period builds on past practices. In addition to the poetry, students engage broadly with other arts, as I teach my courses comparatively. I also bring into the discussion the interplay between texts that are considered canonical and others that are considered avant-garde, even as we question this overly simplified division.

Teaching Historical Avant-Garde Visual Poetry

Let's consider how one might teach José Juan Tablada's visual poems from *"Li-Po" y otros poemas* (*"Li-Po" and Other Poems*), which I included as part of a graduate seminar on Latin American poetry and visual art in the fall of 2014. Tablada's visual poem "Impresión de la Habana" ("Impression of Havana") immediately captures the students' attention because of its highly pictographic component, depicting a coastal landscape and lighthouse (fig. 1), and because it is presented, as Willard Bohn notes, as an "illustrated postcard" (*Modern* 162).

The students' first questions on seeing this work are taxonomic (i.e., What is this?). The work does not fit their prior understanding of poetry. I ask them to go beyond their desire to categorize and to engage with every

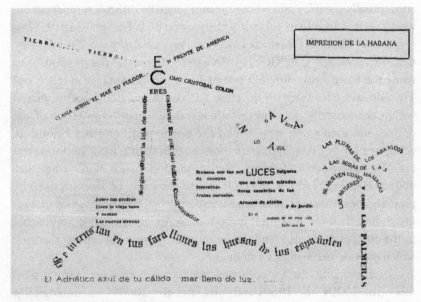

Figure 1. "Impresión de la Habana," by José Juan Tablada.

dimension of the text—with all its visual, verbal, and aural elements—by looking at the image as image, reading the text by following multiple reading paths, and even reciting the words to hear their rhyme and rhythm. Through this multisensorial approach students grasp that all poetry, not just experimental poetry, possesses visual, aural, and performative dimensions.

Of course within any of these perceptual approaches (for instance the appreciation of the visual qualities of the poem) there are other subcategories: the disposition of the individual letters, the overall picture, the different fonts and typographic arrangements, the hierarchy implied by the size and location of letters. Students learn to consider all these elements in order to decode the poem's meaning. As part of an exercise in close reading students work in groups to list the poem's visual and textual elements, using several approaches: viewing the images, reading silently, reading out loud, reading the parts in a different order, examining explicit and implicit letter hierarchies. Only then do we shift the discussion toward understanding the poem's signification, allowing for a variety of potential readings, first in small groups, then as a class.

But form is only one aspect, and readings deepen as historical factors are considered. In this course we discussed the problematic aspects of Latin American avant-gardists, including their belonging to a privileged class, their tendency to exoticize others (for example, the cultures of Asia or Africa, or the pre-Columbian past), their uncritical fetishism of technology, their misogyny and racism. The students were therefore in tune with these shortcomings as they read and interpreted Tablada's poem.

Reading the poem in a postcolonial key, several students observed that Tablada presents an image of Cuba seen through the eyes of the traveler or tourist (but also the colonizer), evoking that other "traveler" who "discovered" the island in 1492 and proceeded to strip it of its riches, exterminating its Taino population. Furthermore, the lighthouse is located atop the Castillo del Morro, a fortress and military prison loaded with oppressive connotations for Cubans. The light rays emanating from the lighthouse read "Tierra! . . . Tierra! . . . / Como Cristobal Colon / clama sobre el mar tu fulgor / en frente de America" 'Land . . . ! Land! . . . / Like Christopher Columbus / your brightness clamors over the sea / in front of America' (my trans.). Working in groups, the students disentangled the meaning of the verses and the image: there is the reference to Columbus's arrival and to the symbolism of the lighthouse as the bringer of the light of "civilization" to a "savage" continent. The lighthouse also stands as the beacon for the seafaring Spanish vessels that decimated the Caribbean. These verses, students typically conclude, reveal Tablada's own position as an elite Creole who identifies with European values and elides the troubling underpinnings of the Encounter. The students become adept at reading against the grain, revealing the darker side of Tablada's poem; they also see how the text and the image can work with and against each other to convey meaning.

The verse forming the lighthouse says, "Surges sobre la isla de amor / Eres / cadáver en pie del fuerte conquistador" 'Surging over the isle of love / You are / cadaver beneath the strong conquistador' (my trans.), further reinforcing the postcolonial interpretation that can now be enhanced with a feminist critique. Here, Cuba is "la isla de amor," a familiar metonymy for America itself, as seen in countless sixteenth-century engravings of America personified as a woman. The verse plays into the stereotype of the hypersexualized native woman that can be traced to Columbus's diary but persists today. Students recognize this stereotype and link it to the sexualized image of Latin American and Latina women in contemporary media. As Bohn argues, in the poem Cuba "is transformed into a vanquished enemy lying dead at his [Columbus's] feet" ("Visual Trajectory" 197). The prone island lies "conquered" at the base of the phallic lighthouse, a symbol of patriarchy and empire. Through attentive analysis, students derive similar feminist and postcolonial readings on their own.

Visual poetry motivates students to think about aesthetic problems involving word and image interaction, ekphrasis, and the blurring between visual and verbal genres. I also use it to challenge students' notions of the correct way to read a work. At first students insist that a Western-oriented, left-to-right, top-to-bottom approach is the natural way to read these works. But nonlinear narratives such as *Rayuela* (Cortázar), collage texts, hypertext, and other experiments with literary form show otherwise. How, I typically ask, does this poem both reaffirm and question our Western approaches to poetry and to telling stories? Most students are quick to point out that, for all its supposed radicality, the poem reasserts left-to-right, top-to-bottom structures, and that even the pictorial image is itself a highly conventional maritime landscape.[1]

Much more could be said about Tablada's poem, but the point is made about both the need for a contextualized close reading of the text and also the importance of using a work's visuality to engage the students' interest and then proceeding to a nuanced analysis.

Teaching Experimental Poetry from the 1960s: Concrete Poetry

Understanding experimental poetry from the 1960s can be challenging for students, since experiments with language during this period are underpinned by complex conceptual frameworks. In the course from which I drew the Tablada example I included experimental formats that emerged soon after World War II, such as concrete poetry in the fifties and performance poetry in the sixties. I teach concrete poetry within the context of Latin American developmentalism (prevalent in countries such as Brazil and Mexico, which underwent rapid industrialization after the Second World War), focusing on the relations between poetry, painting, and architecture.

I begin by showing images of Brasília and then link them to concrete poetry and painting. By comparing the 1958 "Plano piloto para a poesia concreta" ("Pilot Plan for Concrete Poetry") of the Noigandres poets (Augusto and Haroldo de Campos and Décio Pignatari) with the one drafted by architects Lúcio Costa and Oscar Niemeyer for the construction of Brasília, students begin to understand concrete poems as structural works. Concrete poetry revisits some of the aesthetic concerns of the historical avant-garde but provokes a new set of questions for students; as Jill Kuhnheim observes, "Concrete poetry makes meaning visual and textual to loosen conventional reading/viewing practices and, in the process, confronts these, among other, epistemological questions: How can I interpret the world? And what is my role in it?" (*Spanish American Poetry* 49).

To further emphasize the association of concrete poetry with the built environment, I turn to a mural–wall poem by Goeritz, a Mexican architect and poet. The text of *Pocos cocodrilos locos* was cast into a fifty-foot-long U-shaped concrete wall in the Zona Rosa in Mexico City (fig. 2).[2] Goeritz envisioned this poem as a *poema-mural* ("mural-poem"), a work inspired not only by concrete poetry but also by Mexican muralism as well as phonetic poetry and minimalist sculpture; it was, in short, an intermedial work that brought poetry from the page into the built environment, into the street (and therefore facilitated its crossing from one medium into another, from a visual sensory modality to a tactile and proprioceptive one).

To approach Goeritz's work I ask students to research the origins of concretism as well as its aesthetic and political goals. Concretism arose from the rationalist painting of the Dutch neoplasticists (e.g., Piet Mondrian

Figure 2. Photograph of Mathias Goeritz's *Pocos cocodrilos locos*, published on the blog *Unapalabra* (defunct) by the Consejo Nacional para la Cultura y las Artes (Conaculta), 2012.

and Theo van Doesburg) and the Russian constructivists (e.g., Alexander Rodchenko and El Lissitzky), who were close to the building arts. Concrete aesthetics in painting and poetry harmonized with the modernization, urbanization, and industrialization occurring after World War II in formerly agricultural economies such as Russia, Brazil, or Mexico.

The Brazilian poets who sparked interest in concretism throughout Latin America (including Mexico) explored poetry as a material, understanding poems as objects to be manipulated and structured to achieve specific effects. The notion of the poem as object can seem new for students, but it becomes easier to conceptualize when they are given some object poems to manipulate—for instance Octavio Paz and Vicente Rojo's *Discos Visuales* or Augusto de Campos and Julio Plaza's "Poemobiles."[3]

In addition to their materiality, concrete poems draw on sound and are inspired by the music of minimalist composers such as Pierre Boulez, Anton Webern, Karlheinz Stockhausen, and John Cage. Concrete poetry functions as a kind of total poetry that strives to integrate all the senses. As Antonio Bessa observes, concrete poems "display a heightened sense of design that seems to overwhelm other aspects of the text." For Bessa some poems "appear on the page like highly modernistic architecture, while others strike the reader rather like graphic riddles that need to be decoded in order to be read: an operation for the eye," but one in which "sound was submitted to as rigorous a program as the written text" (219).

Once students have this background information they are able to better appreciate the intent of Goeritz's poem. I provide them an adaptation of the text on paper, which reads as follows:

cocodrilos pocos,
pocos cocodrilos locos,
drilos pocos,
pocos cocodrilos locos,
drilos pocos,
pocos cocodrilos locos,
pocos drilos,
pocos locos cocodrilos . . . pocos;
pocos locos,
pocos drilos,
pocos cocodrilos locos.

crocodiles few,
few crocodiles crazy,
diles few,
few crocodiles crazy,
diles few,
few crocodiles crazy,
few diles,
few crazy crocodiles . . . few;
few crazy,
few diles,
few crocodiles crazy. (my trans.)

Here, again, one may encounter resistance from some students at the poem's apparent simplicity or even nonsensicality, reminiscent of a nursery rhyme or a tongue twister. Students may see the work as a word game devoid of real significance. It is useful to have students think of the connection between concrete poetry and something they are familiar with, advertising. Observing the poem's aesthetic similarity to the banner ads they encounter online (succinct, stylized, quirky), students see that concrete poetry works as a kind of parody of advertising.

Another way to overcome student resistance is through a hands-on analysis of the primary elements of the poem (words, verses, rhyme structure, visual patterns). As students begin to take the poem apart they become aware of its reticular nature—the way its grid-like verses seem to have similar numbers of letters and words. This observation yields discussions about how freedom and constraint operate in poetry, where form may regulate meter, rhyme, number of verses, and so on; it can also facilitate a discussion about the relationship between poetry and construction that underpins the project of concrete poetry. As the students begin to see the makeup of Goeritz's work—its visual grid, the repetition of sounds and phonemes, its quasi-mathematical word distribution—and its organizing function, they realize that structure is essential to both poetry and buildings.

As they become attuned to the way it is put together, students also note the work's aural component, observing that the main vowel used is the *o*, which provides the poem with its sonorous dimension, in contrast to the hard sounds of the *p* and *c* consonants. As the students work in groups to analyze the poem collaboratively, they draw on the richness of their different backgrounds. Those trained in music recognize aspects related to sound and rhythm. Those with a science background may see in its experimental nature something similar to the trial-and-error methodology of the scientific method, or in its rationalism they discern the echoes of a kind of mathematization of poetry.

After this first analysis I reveal to the students that the poem was built in the physical world and initiate a conversation about the relationship between poetry, movement, and the corporeal. If a recited version of the poem relies on a temporal flow of words, and the paper version relies on a spatial arrangement of words on a page, the *poema-mural* combines elements of both, transforming them into a three-dimensional, tactile experience, closer to sculpture and architecture. While this built poem is not present in the classroom, I have the students visualize walking around it, experiencing it as object; the surviving photographs aid in this imaginative exercise. Goeritz's intention was that "el lector se enfrentaría a la pieza en cualquier momento y desde distintas perspectivas" 'the reader will confront the piece at any moment and from different perspectives' ("El retorno").

This notion that poetry can be literally built into the physical environment also opens up discussions about other contemporary formats through which poetry has taken to the street, such as spoken word, poetry slams, or rap. Poetry also allies itself with other street art such as graffiti and stencil, forms that are linked to political protest. The realization that poetry can commingle with more popular genres and venues demystifies it for the students, making it more accessible. Moreover, the idea that one can (physically) approach poetry from different perspectives, as one does with Goeritz's poem, reinforces the students' understanding that multiple interpretations are possible. Interpretation, however, begins with the poem's words, and students realize, as Perloff notes, "First, that any serious poem, however disjointed and 'nonsensical,' is meaningful. Second, that the poem's meanings are never quite paraphraseable, never univocal: numbers of alternate readings are possible. And third, that the only way to get at the poem is in fact to read it, word for word, line by line" ("Teaching"). But also, I would add, to experience it as object.

Teaching Contemporary Digital Poetry

When teaching a course about Latin American experimental art and poetry chronologically, I end with a section on the current digital avant-gardes. This provides the students with a vision of continuity (without presupposing a teleology of progress and including ruptures, aporias, and discontinuities), while showing how the avant-gardes rearticulate the poetry of their predecessors. Digital poetry appeared in the last few decades of the twentieth century, stemming from the advances in computing, wireless communication, and Internet technologies. This dynamic poetic form allows for greater intermediality, interactivity, and user participation and is characterized by its embrace of digital technologies (from the now obsolete CD-ROM to tablets to mobile devices) and by its constitutive integration of text, image, and sound. Digital poetry is a subgenre of electronic literature, which the Electronic Literature Organization defines as "work with an important literary aspect that takes advantage of the capabilities and contexts provided by the stand-alone or networked computer" (Hayles).

From a pedagogical standpoint, digital poetry, with its bells and whistles in the form of animated visuals, its sounds and its demand for user input, captures the attention of students. Few have seen poetry designed to be experienced on a computer, so their first encounter can be defamiliarizing. However, given the close relation of electronic literature to other new media arts—including video games—students soon grasp the essential nature of these works: their capacity for interactivity, their degree of openness and lack of resolution, and their dependence on the technological. Once students go beyond the shiny surface of new media poems (the technological component), they also learn to judge the semantic elements (the message). Charlotte Melin notes the advantages of using multimedia in the study of poetry:

> Multi-media capacities have expanded the possibilities for studying poetry beyond bland interaction with a two-dimensional print text. . . .

Students can also experience author readings on-line, experiment with poem-generating software. . . . Far from being dead in the digital age, poetry can be delivered as on-line manuscript, hyperlinked illustrated edition, graphic wallpaper, text-message, or YouTube clip. These modes of delivery invite classroom discussion of how meaning changes as poems are translated into different modalities, and yet they also demand that teachers be critically prepared to use an increasingly complex array of material supports, for each new form or genre potentially requires different interpretive approaches. (354)

To show students that digital poetry requires new ways of interpretation I draw on the Argentine artist Gustavo Romano's *IP Poetry* project.[4] Romano's project explores how humans and machines collaborate to create poetry. The project has had many incarnations, not only as a physical installation piece in art galleries but also as a virtual, Web-based piece, which we work with in class.

This is how *IP Poetry* functions: The program is accessed through its Web site. The online *IP Poetry* program conducts Web searches to obtain text fragments from random Web sites and assembles these linguistic snippets into poems. The poet-user defines the parameters of the search by entering them into a menu with multiple search options, but the final products are poems that are a hybrid of randomly selected sentences lifted from the Web using the search criteria established by the users, combined with lines of verse written specifically by the users. The entire project bears much resemblance to early avant-garde experiments in cut-up poetry; indeed, Romano cites several precursors, from the *I Ching* to Dadaist random poetry created using newspaper cut-up letters, William Burroughs's use of cut-up paper strips for composing poetry, and Oulipo's work on combinatorial poems (*IP Poetry* 46). Once completed, the *IP Poetry* poems are read by four virtual robots displayed as human mouths onscreen, which take turns articulating the verses, one phoneme at a time (fig. 3).

Each virtual robot is represented by prerecorded video images of a human mouth speaking single phonemes, which are stored in the project's memory and serve to generate any word in Spanish. The phonemes are sequentially arranged and spoken by the bots as full verses to match the text of the completed poems. The user determines which lines of poetry will be read by which robot (or mouth), and in what order they will be read. Despite this detailed user input, however, the final product is always a surprise, since the random data mined from the Internet changes each

Figure 3. Screen capture from *The IP Poetry Project,* by Gustavo Romano; ip-poetry.findelmundo.com.ar/localviewer.cgi.

time. There is a balance struck between freedom and constraint, since by choosing certain parameters the user can influence the tone, language, and mood of a poem but can never completely control the outcome. The experience may seem somewhat disjointed at first but powerfully demonstrates the role of randomness in certain kinds of poetry and art. Students also begin to see how the calculating power of digital tools might enhance human creativity. Romano suggests that the project serves as a metareflection on poetry itself:

> The *IP Poetry* project studies the role of poetry and of poets themselves. On the one hand, as far as the construction of the robots is concerned, it highlights the increasing subjectivity of technology, which is endowed with certain artificially enhanced human characteristics (in this case, memory, and the ability to speak and listen). On the other hand, as concerns the resulting poetic structures, it uses the virtual arrangement of the collective human memory found on the Internet to compose poetry that has both mechanical and random elements. (*IP Poetry Project*)

IP Poetry also allows students to create their own random poems. By signing on to the Web site and receiving a password, the students are able to provide their own search parameters and to select the order and way in which the four robot mouths read the generated text; they become, therefore, cocreators and a human part of an otherwise algorithmic process. This experience pushes, once again, against the students' understanding of what constitutes poetry: here it is no longer an activity defined (solely) by authorial intentionality, but one that allows for the random and chance event. It is also not an activity confined to a single author, human or otherwise, but a collaborative experience; in fact complexly so, since the program itself is part of a team that includes computer scientists, humanists, and poets (a team that ought to be acknowledged but sometimes is not).

The notion of collaborative poetry usually finds resonance with today's students, who often think in terms of both group work and interdisciplinarity. Additionally, this project, with its mix of digital and human processes, raises the issue of our becoming posthuman (a preoccupation central to Katherine Hayles, Friedrich Kittler, Mark Hansen, and others), providing an opportunity for discussions about the increasing porosity between the natural and artificial, the human and the technological, in the twenty-first century. Heather Fletcher has explored this concept, arguing that in Romano's project the combination of human and machine is not simply a metaphor but a true interaction within cyberspace. Fletcher insists that the program needs both components, human and technological, in order to function, so that "la hibridación entre ser humano-máquina es el colofón del proyecto *IP Poetry*: la creación de un cyborg literario" 'the hybrid human-machine is the very imprint of the *IP Poetry* project: the creation of a literary cyborg' (48).

No doubt, experiencing *IP Poetry* can lead students to a reflection about what it means to be human—perhaps one of the fundamental questions of poetry since Homer. This is because *IP Poetry* provides an uncanny but fascinating boundary experience, as the virtual cyborgs challenge the notion of human creativity, of who or what can produce poetry. In class, this often leads students into wondering about the potential for artificial intelligence to eventually excel in artistic creation, to go beyond mere calculation.

As with almost any subject, one way to empower students to lose their fear of poetry and even to begin to love it is to place it within their own social and cultural milieu and frame it within their own lived experience. Poetry has taken on a new life on *Twitter*, *Facebook*, and other social media sites. *Twitter* poetry (including Tweet haiku), micropoetry, and other genres defined by their brevity offer new possibilities for both individual and group writing under time and space constraints. Encouraging students to try these and other new tools to create their own work also inspires them to read more poetry, mining it for inspiration. Students begin to connect with even difficult works, since, as Perloff observes, "however scrambled a new 'experimental' poem may be, however non-syntactic, non-linear, or linguistically complex, it is, after all, written in the language of the present, which is to say the language of the students who are reading it" ("Teaching"). Inevitably, once that connection is made, students begin to appreciate poetry contextually, understanding that in Latin America avant-garde poetry has not been imitative but transgressive; not content with following European models, it has been politically, aesthetically, and technologically creative. By the end of the course, many students are converts to poetry.

Notes

1. This critical analysis of the supposed radicality of the avant-garde (and its rootedness in Western canon) is revisited and contrasted with other experiments covered in later parts of the course. Such is the case, for instance, with Octavio Paz's poem *Blanco*, which attempts a rupture with Western thought by linking to both pre-Columbian mythology and circularity, as well as to the tradition of the folding codices of Mesoamerica, but also to Eastern spirituality, the Vedas, and other non-Western texts. In this case the students can physically handle the poem, examine its folding structure, as a visual, aural, and tactile experience.

2. The work was unfortunately destroyed by the 1985 earthquake and was later reconstructed for a 2014 exhibition at the Museo Universitario de Arte Contemporáneo in Mexico City.

3. I found versions of these poems in our library; typically I pass them around so students can experiment with them. An alternative is to have students design their own, an engaging experience in the spirit of 1960s participatory art.

4. The IP stands for Internet Protocol, the communications protocol that enables data packet transfers between hosts, allowing for routing and internetworking between computers, and essentially constitutes the Web.

Bruce Dean Willis

Songs of the *Cenzontle*:
Re-cording Orality in
Contemporary Mexican Lyric Poetry

> *Aquello que dicen las palabras del poeta ya está diciéndolo*
> *el ritmo en que se apoyan esas palabras. Y más:*
> *esas palabras surgen naturalmente del ritmo,*
> *como la flor del tallo.*
>
> —Octavio Paz, *El arco y la lira*

> *That which the poet's words say is already being said*
> *by the rhythm in which the words support themselves. What's more:*
> *those words surge naturally from the rhythm,*
> *like the flower from the stem.*[1]

Mexican schoolchildren of the past five or six decades have often been re-quired to learn by heart—in Spanish, and sometimes also in Nahuatl—the following poem, purported to be a fifteenth-century example of the Nahua genre called *in xochitl in cuicatl*, or flower song, "a metaphor for poetry or a poem" (León-Portilla, *Aztec Thought* 75):

> Nehuatl nictlazotla in centzontototl icuicauh,
> nehuatl nictlazotla in chalchihuitl itlapaliz

ihuan in ahuiacmeh xochtmeh;
zan oc cenca noicniuhtzin in tlacatl,
Nehuatl nictlazotla.

Amo el canto del cenzontle,
pájaro de cuatrocientas voces;
amo el color del jade
y el enervante perfume de las flores.
Pero amo más a mi hermano, el hombre. ("Sobre el poema")

I love the song of the mockingbird,
the bird of four hundred calls.
I love the color of jade
and the flowers' invigorating perfume.
But more than these I love my brother, mankind.

This lyric has become something of a Mexican national touchstone or foundational epigraph—a humanist paean meant to counteract the gory imagery typically evoked when discussing the culture of the Triple Alliance led by the Mexica, more commonly known as the Aztecs. The verses appear in Spanish in tiny lettering on the one-hundred-peso bill that features an imagined likeness of Nezahualcóyotl, the ruler of Texcoco to whom the poem is attributed. Yet, according to one of Mexico's foremost *nahuatlatos* (scholars of Nahuatl), Patrick Johansson, the poem's grammar, syntax, and theme demonstrate that it was written not by Nezahualcóyotl but by a much more recent source (Argüelles). The work's ubiquity and authorial intrigue make it ideal to teach—and to assign for memorization—at the beginning of an undergraduate course in Mexican or Latin American poetry because it encapsulates a wealth of concepts to be explored through poetic examples up to the present day: authorship, voice, imagery, translation, and appropriation. A classroom contextualization of this poetic gem can include viewing an online recitation, such as that of a child reciting the poem in Nahuatl and Spanish at a school assembly in Mexico City ("Amo el canto"). Classroom discussion can revolve around the following questions: What did the flower song encompass exactly (text, music, dance, spoken word), and how does it relate to today's spoken word performance? What is the significance of the number four hundred? Do the flowers evoke the same range of meanings that they might in a European poem? Assuming it was in fact written originally in Nahuatl, who translated this text into Spanish, and what structural decisions did the translator make? Who would have attributed it to Nezahualcóyotl, and why? Finally, why has this become such an important text in modern Mexico? Johansson's works offer expert contextualization of these inquiries, as do works by Miguel León-Portilla and Gary Tomlinson, for example; meanwhile, inviting the students to suggest answers to these questions helps them to think critically about poetry, wordcraft, sound, music, and performance within the repertoire of a people or a nation.

Over the course of their lives, these same Mexican schoolchildren who have learned "Amo el canto del cenzontle"—and probably the first few stanzas of Sor Juana's "Hombres necios" ("Foolish Men") as well—will usually memorize other key stanzas of what can be called a national repertoire of Mexican lyric. But this later memorization, unassigned and without a grade, will occur outside the classroom—at fiestas or concerts, or in bars, taverns, or cantinas, with the midnight arrival of the mariachis. In this way, verses composed by Mexican songwriters like Juan Gabriel ("Probablemente ya, de mí te has olvidado" 'Probably you've already forgotten about me'), José Alfredo Jiménez ("Yo sé bien que estoy afuera" 'I know well that I'm out of the picture'), Agustín Lara ("Solamente una vez" 'Only once'), and Consuelo Velázquez ("Bésamemucho" 'Kiss me a lot') exemplify the communal way in which poetry can become a vocal performance practice that unites a nation with a particularly strong oral culture. In this essay, I will illuminate connections to be traced with undergraduate students that link ancient and colonial Mexican oral practices to contemporary lyric poetry (including a surprising relation between Sor Juana's early sound experiments and contemporary Mexican rock) and examine recent lyric expressions of the Mexican singer-songwriters Julieta Venegas and Rana Santacruz. The four hundred songs of the *cenzontle* ("mockingbird") are recorded (*recordadas*) and re-corded (or revocalized) in ways that can illustrate for our students how the Nahua *in xochitl in cuicatl* flower songs, or the medieval Iberian *romances*, for example, have survived and even thrived in contemporary lyrical production in Mexico.[2]

For students studying Spanish in the United States, the goal is not only to research and write analyses of lyrics but also to be able to sing along with their Mexican peers, so that the act of learning by heart becomes a step toward being able to analyze, and to critique from within, a broadly Mexican worldview and set of cultural practices. If students have knowledge of mariachi music, or of *ranchera* songs, then the next time they are at a restaurant or event with mariachis and have occasion to request a song, they can recall "Si nos dejan" ("If They Leave Us") or "Amanecí en tus brazos" ("I Awoke in Your Arms") or "Golondrina sin nido" ("Swallow without a Nest") and not just "La Bamba" or "Macarena." This kind of background allows them to actively participate in social events where everyone seems to know the words to one song after another. The more students can appreciate the give-and-take, lifeline flow of the language as a very quotidian yet very complex means of expression passed along and modified from generation to generation, the more they can appreciate it as a means of expression that they themselves can also internalize or in which they too can participate. It is a way to see, as Jill S. Kuhnheim points out, "that poetry does not exist just in the classroom or as text (the traditional object of study) but is oral, alive, in transformation, and participatory" ("Cultures" 107). In the context of a literature course, the example of poems as song lyrics can expand students' understanding of how poetry not only "makes language strange" (119) but also helps concretize or fix language when memorized and recited or sung by a vast population. Since lyrics when memorized are literally embodied, they reside within individual people and link them to a shared culture; this linkage can occur even for individuals not born into a given culture but who learn such representative expressions intimately.

Music and verbal language working together have the effect of internalizing the language more deeply in our brains, the rhythm and melody of both more effectively stored in our memories.[3] Perhaps even more importantly, the interaction of music and language in the classroom setting helps overcome students' doubts and anxieties about poetry. In my experience, a majority of students in the United States view poetry with trepidation or boredom. Framing the subject in a way that invites students to consider what kind of exposure to poetry their Mexican peers may have had reduces the students' anxiety levels and more effectively engages their interest. The language-classroom affective filter (cf. Krashen) can be lowered even further by incorporating the practice of listening to poetry as music, with just a few tasks assigned before and during the listening exercise. First I distribute lyrics, often with a few missing words replaced by blank lines, and ask the students to analyze the lyrics as poetry before we hear them sung. We note structural elements such as meter, rhyme, and voice, and content elements including imagery, tone, and theme. We make predictions about how the music might sound (tempo, style, and accompaniment). Then I play a video of the song, with the monitor off, and ask students to listen and fill in the missing words. After we've discussed how our predictions worked out and our thoughts about the musical version, I may play the song again with the monitor on if there are visual aspects of the performance I want the class to observe. (Sometimes musically talented students are motivated to perform in class, which is certainly welcome although never required.)

Music lends some of its universality—its lack of need for translation—to the lyrics as the rhythm, melody, and other musical elements of the composition make the meaning more comprehensible. Octavio Paz's assertion that words arise naturally from their rhythm, even at the level of individual syllables, invites us to consider this relationship as one of the most essential elements of poetry as a temporal art form.

Even in a unit on modern poetry, an emphasis on the ancient oral origins of poetry is essential to help ground students' understanding of contemporary lyric poetry. When I start out by turning the lens around and peering back through the ages, the class objectives are to help students conceptualize the roles of orality in preliterate cultures; to highlight performative aspects along a scale of speaking, declaiming, chanting, and singing (cf. Tomlinson); and to emphasize the indigenous, African, Middle Eastern, and Asian linguistic elements and cultural practices that inform a modern population expressing itself predominantly in a European language outside Europe. Questions that articulate these corresponding objectives, generally informed by performative studies of the kind pioneered by Diana Taylor in *The Archive and the Repertoire*, might include the following: In what ways and for what reasons can poetry be a memory aid in an oral culture? Do these same ways and reasons apply to a contemporary, Information Age population? How does poetry, or language in general, relate to music, dance, and other kinds of temporal art? Does it also relate to the visual arts, such as drawing, painting, or sculpting? How have linguistic or cultural aspects from non-Iberian groups, such as the Nahuatl-speaking peoples of central Mexico, or the Yoruba-speaking peoples of West Africa, influenced poetry in Mexico? What is the range of settings, genres, and languages in which poetry and lyric are encountered in Mexico today?

Culled from a range of these contexts, what follows are three examples of exercises I have found effective for classroom use.

Exploration of a Mesoamerican Carpe Diem

While traditional claims for the origin of "Amo el canto del cenzontle" may be false, there are authentic flower-song compositions in the sixteenth-century collection *Cantares mexicanos* (*Songs of the Aztecs*) that have been attributed to Nezahualcóyotl.[4] Among them figures one of the best-known stanzas of the flower-song aesthetic:

> Annochipa tlalticpac
> çan achica ye nican ohuaye ohuaye

Tel ca chalchihuitl no xamani
no teocuicatl in tlapani oo
quetzalli poztequi yahui ohuaye
annochipa tlalticpac
çan achica ye nican ohuaya etcetera.

No para siempre en la tierra,
sólo un poco aquí.
Aunque sea jade se quiebra,
aunque sea metal precioso se hace pedazos,
la pluma preciosa se rasga.
No para siempre en la tierra,
sólo un poco aquí. (*Cantares* II.1 204–05)

Not always on earth,
only a little here.
Although it be jade it breaks,
although it be precious metal it crumbles,
the precious feather is ripped.
Not always on earth,
only a little here.

These verses, and other extant passages, reveal an understanding of "la vida como tránsito, floración de un día, estancia efímera hacia un más allá insondable" 'life as passage, flowering of one day, ephemeral station on the way to an unknowable beyond' (Ortiz Domínguez 59). As Efrén Ortiz Domínguez goes on to explain, the fact that the Nahua flower-song tradition was almost completely unknown or forgotten for centuries means that the presence of the carpe diem theme in modern Mexican poetry has derived mostly from the European tradition. However, as Kelly S. McDonough points out, the practice of writing alphabetically in Nahuatl has been "continuous yet changeful" since the early sixteenth century, even when clandestine or ignored by official Mexican cultural establishments (4). By showing students that there are contemporary poets who compose, not only in Nahuatl but also within the flower-song tradition, we can demonstrate this continuity.[5] For instance, the Premio Nezahualcóyotl winner Juan Hernández Ramírez's bilingual collection *Chikome xochitl / Siete flor* profiles seven flowers, each with seven brief poems of seven verses each. The fourth poem of his "Sempoalxochitl / Flor de muerto" ("Flower of the Dead") series conveys this same eternal question of the fleeting, dreamlike sense of life:

Tiitstokeya nikanij,
¿kanij tonejnemil techuikas?
¿uelis ipan tonatij iojui?

Tiitstokeya nikanij.
Kostik xochimej tijtlachillaj
iijuiyo tonatitotl tikitaj.

¿Temiktli in yolistli?

Ya estamos aquí,
¿dónde nuestros pasos nos llevarán?
¿acaso por los caminos del sol?

Ya estamos aquí.
Contemplamos las flores amarillas,
miramos el plumaje del pájaro sol.

¿Es la vida sueño? (Hernández Ramírez 99, 106)

Already we are here
where will our steps lead us?
perhaps along the pathways of the sun?

Already we are here.
We contemplate the yellow flowers,
we regard the plumage of the bird-sun.

Is life a dream?

While Hernández Ramírez's example is undoubtedly meant to hew closely to the rediscovered flower-song aesthetic, another contemporary example shows what could perhaps be a mix of Mesoamerican and European thematic influences regarding the fleeting nature of time and the injunction to "seize the day." The Tamaulipan poet-lyricist Anamaría Rabatté y Cervi enjoyed an extensive yet not widely documented influence on the ways in which many Mexicans conceive of lyric poetry today. Several of her spiritual poems were set to music during her lifetime and were circulated informally in mimeographs or photocopies among churches of various denominations within and outside Mexico. (In general, ecclesiastical settings are an often-overlooked modality in which the Mexican lyric is both conserved and renovated).[6] Particularly popular is Rabatté's poem "En vida, hermano, en vida" ("In Life, Brother, in Life"), which begins:

Si quieres hacer feliz
a alguien que quieras mucho . . .
díselo hoy, sé muy bueno
en vida, hermano, en vida . . .

Si deseas dar una flor,
no esperes a que se mueran;

mándala hoy con amor . . .
en vida, hermano, en vida . . .
(Rabatté y Cervi 10)

If you want to make someone happy,
someone you love very much . . .
tell this to him today, be very good
in life, brother, in life . . .

If you wish to give a flower,
don't wait for them to die
send it today with love . . .
in life, brother, in life . . .

This poem and others by Rabatté reinforce the classic theme of carpe diem without abandoning the kind of flower-song refrain attributed to Nezahualcóyotl. In Rabatté's "Todo es prestado . . ." ("Everything is on loan . . .") the following verses convey the same message, although with less imagery, as the verses of "No para siempre en la tierra" from the *Cantares mexicanos*: "Todo en esta vida, hermano, es prestado . . . / Por un corto número de años . . . / Prestada es la vida . . . / la familia . . . los amigos . . ." 'Everything in this life, brother, is on loan . . . / for a short number of years . . . / Life is loaned to us . . . / family . . . friends . . .' (56). It is productive for students to consider and debate the presence of aspects from both European and Mesoamerican traditions (and perhaps others) when analyzing contemporary poetry in Mexican as well as Mexican-American populations, because it can illustrate phenomena of cultural interaction (syncretism, transculturation) and can lead to more careful and fruitful reflection on the malleability of both tradition and innovation in poetry as cultural expression. The following classroom illustrations continue this idea.

Comparison of Mexico City Dialect, Seventeenth and Twentieth Centuries

A surprising example of the persistence of poetic tradition links the Mexican icon Sor Juana Inés de la Cruz to the contemporary rock band Café Tacvba. An inexhaustible talent desirous of new challenges during her most productive years in the middle of the seventeenth century, Sor Juana endeavored to replicate certain languages, dialects, or speech patterns in

different instances of her poetic output, including Latin, Portuguese, Nahuatl, Africanized Spanish, and Mexico City street slang (Trueblood 19).
Among these poetic affectations or approximations of dialect appears a
satirical sonnet about a young woman, Teresilla, who is expecting a child,
and her long-suffering partner Camacho, to whom she is unfaithful. All
of the sonnet's consonant rhymes include the *ch* phoneme (/tʃ/): -*acha*,
-*acho* in the quatrains and -*ucha*, -*echa* in the tercets. Three centuries later,
the Tamaulipan singer-songwriter Jaime López composed the song "Chilanga banda," later popularized by the band Café Tacvba in the 1990s, in
which the same *ch* phoneme is heard with even greater frequency throughout the lyrics, and not just in the rhyming words. The noun or adjective
"chilango," though recently reappropriated with pride, has traditionally
been a somewhat pejorative term for referring to residents of Mexico City.
Without reproducing the entire poems here, a few verses from each show
a productive comparison:

> Aunque eres, Teresilla, tan *muchacha*,
> le das quehacer al pobre de *Camacho*,
> porque dará tu disimulo un *chacho*
> a aquel que se pintare más sin *tacha*. (Trueblood 114)

> Tessie, you may be a slip of a thing
> but you give your poor Camacho quite a whirl:
> the way you cheat on him could make a sire
> of purest driven snow or flawless pearl. (115)

> Mejor yo me echo una chela
> y chance enchufo una chava.
> Chambeando de chafirete,
> me sobra chupe y pachanga. (Retrofutura)

> I'd rather knock back a beer
> and maybe pick up a girl.
> Working as a taxi driver, I've
> got plenty of booze and parties.

The two poems differ in ambience and objective, but, as Jair Cortés
notes, "Entre los siglos que separan a un poema de otro, permanecen vivos
varios elementos que podríamos llamar mexicanos: el tono humorístico y
satírico, así como una musicalidad inherente a nuestra lengua" 'Although
separated by centuries, what remains alive are a few elements we could call

Mexican: the humorous, satirical tone, and the musicality inherent in our language.' Cortés emphasizes that the /tʃ/ or (*ch*) phoneme is common not only in Spanish but also in Nahuatl, "parte medular del español que se habla y escribe en México" 'an essential part of the Spanish that is spoken and written in Mexico,' and that is why it abounds in the Mexico City area to the extent that both Sor Juana and López would choose to utilize it as a region-specific speech characteristic.

I've found this comparison useful in advanced classes, taught in Spanish, in which Sor Juana's poetry receives more than a perfunctory treatment. The students can read and discuss Sor Juana's sonnet, then read and discuss López's lyrics in relation to the sonnet before listening to the musical arrangement by Café Tacvba. After playing the song, I ask the students to imagine a Café Tacvba–style reading of Sor Juana's sonnet and to consider how such an imagined delivery might highlight the humorous intent of her phonemic exaggeration. According to Frederick Luciani, this poem and four others that he identifies as Sor Juana's "burlesque sonnets" were meant to be humorous parodies, "poems of contrived dissonance" (374). Certainly López's lyrics also give a parodic sense of what can sound, especially to non-Mexicans or to Mexicans not living in the nation's capital, like a "contrived dissonance." The comparison enriches students' understanding of the uses, settings, and contexts for parody, as well as their understanding of the persistence of speech patterns over time.

Love, Pain, and the Ballad Tradition

The ballad or *romance* in Mexico is a genre with a long history that includes representation in *ranchera* music as well as the popular corridos and the romantic boleros.[7] In an Introduction to Literature in Spanish undergraduate course, or in a literature survey course whether focused on history or on genre, the students might read examples of *romances* both ancient and modern, drawing from the medieval Spanish *Romancero*, or collection of *romances*, as well as Federico García Lorca's *Romancero gitano* (*Gypsy Ballads*). The musical origin of the medieval *romances*, as songs performed by *juglares* ("minstrels") within a largely illiterate population, is a key element of consideration here, because of aspects of rhyme and rhythm that both facilitate the troubadour's memory and allow him or her to demonstrate flexibility in improvisation. With a basic understanding of this history, including the *romance* structure (eight-syllable lines, assonant rhyme in the even verses) along with some of the most common themes (such as unrequited or jilted love and idealized love), students are prepared to compare structure and content with those of contemporary songs by Agustín Lara or Juan Gabriel.

The appendix to this essay consists of an in-class exercise featuring two lyrics by the contemporary Mexican singer-songwriters Julieta Venegas and Rana Santacruz. "Limón y sal" ("Lime and Salt"), by Venegas, and "Te quiero ver llorar" ("I Want to See You Cry"), by Santacruz, address romantic relationships, whether long-standing or incipient. The activity is designed so that students analyze the lyrics before comparing them and before listening to the songs (without engaging any kind of accompanying video, which would add yet another layer of interpretation). I also ask students to read a brief text by the Mexican-American journalist Alma Guillermoprieto—her description of the end of a Juan Gabriel concert—in order to more fully immerse the Venegas and Santacruz compositions in the tradition of a national, even international, repertoire of Mexican lyric. Guillermoprieto's text, provided in the appendix, concludes the "Mexico City, 1992" entry from her collection of journalistic essays *The Heart That Bleeds: Latin America Now*. Her observations evoke and question pride, pain, and machismo as forces motivating the sense of national unity that Gabriel's music provides.

All four writers mentioned above—Gabriel, Guillermoprieto, Santacruz, and Venegas—have (or had) complex, involved relationships with the United States, spending significant, formative portions of their lives and careers there. This important circumstance adds another aspect to analysis of their works within what Américo Paredes named "Greater Mexico" (Paredes and Bauman xi), and we must ask: to what extent are musical and poetic styles, imagery, and traditions shared across the border? In the works of contemporary singer-songwriters such as Santacruz and Venegas (among others, such as Lila Downs), are there recognizable instances of blending cultural sounds, styles, or references that could be identified as originating in the United States, in Mexico, or in some other region? Students in high school or introductory courses may be encouraged to identify examples of cultural overlap; the same students, and certainly advanced undergraduates and graduates, can develop larger research projects around this kind of cultural studies–based analytical framework.

Ultimately, the *cenzontle* verses falsely attributed to Nezahualcóyotl emphasize precisely the diversity of lyric poetry in Mexico and the Mexican diaspora today. The mockingbird's four hundred voices sing in a wide range of genres, formats, and styles—from flower songs, *romances*, and sonnets to *rancheras*, boleros, corridos, pop rock, and folk. These exercises of tracing influences and making historical comparisons yield a richer understanding not only of poetry's pervasiveness in oral and musical cultures but also of the diversity of traditions given voice by Mexicans in and outside Mexico.

Notes

1. Unless otherwise attributed, English translations are my own.

2. The awarding of the 2016 Nobel Prize in Literature to American singer-songwriter Bob Dylan, while controversial, nonetheless spotlights precisely this musical aspect of the poetic tradition (in any language). The Swedish Academy's permanent secretary, the literary scholar Sara Darius, explained: "If you look back, far back, 2,500 years or so, you discover Homer and Sappho and they wrote poetic texts that were meant to be listened to, that were meant to be performed, often with instruments—and it's the same way with Bob Dylan" (Smith-Spark). Some critics of Dylan as Nobel honoree make arguments similar to one put forward by T. M. Scruggs in a study on protest music: "in many instances it is impossible to explain the power of song without considering the synergy of semantic content and the meaning generated from musical content. While propositional meaning, found at the level of language, is distinct from the level at which music transmits meaning, an examination of both types of communicative vehicles is indispensable for the fullest comprehension of their communicative power" (42–43). In the classroom context, a solution to this conundrum is to analyze the lyrics as text first, then listen to the music to evaluate any changes in interpretation.

3. See Steven Mithen's *The Singing Neanderthals* for an engaging discussion of music and language in parallel modes of evolution.

4. Regarding the attribution of flower-song compositions to Nezahualcóyotl, see Jongsoo Lee's thorough study in which he argues that our images of the famous Texcocan *tlatoani* as poet, patron of the arts, prophet-sage, and rejector of human sacrifice "were invented by a European colonial ideology after the conquest" (1).

5. McDonough's *The Learned Ones* is an excellent source for understanding the continuation of centuries-old Nahua aesthetic and intellectual engagement. Her book-length study imparts "sustained attention to the complex nature of Nahua intellectualism and writing from the colonial period through the present day" (3–4) and highlights writers such as Doña Luz Jiménez and Ildefonso Maya Hernández.

6. In the same vein of understanding ecclesiastical influence in contemporary Mexican lyric, one can consider the much older "Canción de las posadas" ("Christmas Procession Song"), among other religious songs of centuries-old provenance. It begins, "En el nombre del cielo / os pido posada / pues no puede andar / mi esposa amada" 'In the name of heaven / I request shelter of you / since my beloved wife / can go no further.' The song lyrics and other liturgical text for the *posadas* are often distributed in newsprint booklets or downloaded from the Internet (cf. Willis).

7. Andrew Grant Wood discusses the differences between these genres in his excellent biography of Agustín Lara (19). Also see George Torres's historical and musical treatment of the bolero and its relationship to the "canción mexicana" (154–57).

Appendix: Letra mexicana contemporánea (Contemporary Mexican Lyrics)

In this exercise, I ask the students to read the lyrics, provided with some key omissions, of "Limón y sal," by Julieta Venegas, and "Te quiero ver llorar," by Rana Santacruz. I then ask initial questions about the songs' type, rhythm, tone, vocabulary, and theme. I ask them to guess what kind of instrumental accompaniment the songs might feature. Next, we listen to the songs, without watching any video component. While listening, the students attempt to fill in the blanks on the lyric sheets. After listening, in addition to reviewing those missing words, we discuss the students' impressions and whether their expectations about the music had been fulfilled. Finally, the students, in pairs or small groups, answer questions such as the following:

1. En "Limón y sal," ¿cómo se entiende o cómo se describe la felicidad? ¿Cómo se entiende el significado del título de la canción?
2. ¿Cuál es el papel del dolor en "Te quiero ver llorar"? ¿Cuáles aspectos de la canción sirven para dar una impresión hiperbólica del dolor?
3. Contrasta lo que sigue, en la letra de cada canción, después de la frase "Te quiero _____" ¿Qué indica este contraste en cuanto a lo que piden las distintas voces poéticas?
4. Concentrándonos en la letra, ¿la estructura y/o el contenido de estos poemas continúa algunas de las largas tradiciones poéticas que hemos visto en la clase? ¿Cuáles y cómo?
5. Lee el trecho que les doy de un texto por la autora y periodista mexicoamericana Alma Guillermoprieto. Es una descripción del final de un concierto del cantautor Juan Gabriel en un palenque (como un estadio) en Tijuana, México, 1992. Ahora responde: Estas canciones de Santacruz y de Venegas, ¿se acercan a la tradición ranchera del amante rechazado pero orgulloso, o como dice la autora, "the unbending pride of the loser"? ¿Por qué? ¿Tienen que ver con lo que la autora llama "ecstatic pain"? ¿Se aplica el concepto de una "national wound"?

Teresa Longo

Creativity, Interpretation, and the Public Good in Teaching Latin American Poetry

My senior seminar Local-Global Issues and Latin American Poetry begins with the most famous of Neruda's odes and ends with poetry from the Guantánamo Bay detention camp. Between these bookends I include the work of renowned poets and poetry from the Medellín International Poetry Festival. While some of the readings I select for the course vary from year to year, the theoretical constructs that influence the course design remain the same: From Roque Dalton I take the notion that a poet's work is to keep faith with poetry, with beauty. With Martín Espada in mind, I suggest that poetry of the political imagination engenders progressive social change. Relying on Claribel Alegría and Ariel Dorfman, I propose that for some, perhaps many, Latin American poets, hope is an aesthetic principle. Additionally, in the most recent iteration of this course in 2015, I introduced a perspective made explicit by Doris Sommer: that, for scholars and students alike, it is beneficial to pause alongside the artists, which means to consider art as a public good, and to engage in interpretation as creative, relevant, and useful.

Good university-level courses in the humanities often tell stories. They have a narrative arc, seek engagement with an audience, and require creativity on the author-professor's part. Designing this course, I draw on

John Berger's thoughts on storytelling. His metaphor about threading the stars applies to the work we do as teachers:

> Those who first invented and then named the constellations were story-tellers. Tracing an imaginary line between a cluster of stars gave them an image and an identity. The stars threaded on that line were like events threaded on a narrative. Imagining the constellations did not of course change the stars, nor did it change the black emptiness that surrounds them. What it changed was the way people read the night sky. (8)

The storyline I trace connects poets, Espada and Pablo Neruda, to name just two. It connects places and dates, such as Santiago in 1973 and New York in 2001. The course is divided into three case studies: Beauty and Politics; Poetry, Crisis, and the Two September 11ths; and Poetry and the Public Humanities. My syllabus reflects the storyline and the connections (see appendix). When I write about these topics as a scholar, I try to draw the connections tightly, to trace a full story. In the classroom, however, I need to leave some threads untied. As I see it, my task is to show students how to thread the lines themselves and how to move the story forward. I am always hopeful something will change when they do. This course is designed in such way that students delve deeply into each of the three parts, with the understanding that they have the freedom and responsibility to imagine and investigate other similar stories. For professors designing advanced undergraduate seminars, this structure should be understood as a template. The content will vary according to the instructor's particular expertise.

Beauty and Politics: Pablo Neruda on Places and Things

Roque Dalton's statement about keeping faith with beauty comes from a book of essays called *Poetry and Militancy in Latin America (Art on the Line)*. His argument is that poetry disrupts, and that the beautiful nuances of language contain a political relevance. Dalton's poem "Como tú" ("Like You") from *Poemas clandestinos* (*Clandestine Poems*), also speaks to this notion. I read "Como tú" with my students on the first day of the seminar every year. At this point, my intention is simply to suggest that big subjective concepts like beauty will be central to our class discussions; their openness is our invitation to engage. This is an excerpt from Dalton's poem:

> Creo que el mundo es bello,
> que la poesía es como el pan, de todos.

Y que mis venas no terminan en mí
sino en la sangre unánime
de los que luchan por la vida,
el amor,
las cosas,
el paisaje y el pan,
la poesía de todos. (38)

I believe the world is beautiful,
that poetry, like bread, is for everyone.
And that my veins don't end in me
but in the unanimous blood
of those who fight for life,
love,
little things,
landscape and bread,
the poetry of everyone. (39)

From Dalton we move to Neruda, who compares the work poets do to the baking of bread. His 1971 Nobel address, "Hacia la ciudad espléndida" ("Toward the Splendid City"), posits that a poet's work is to create consciousness, to speak unpretentiously about the most valuable goods a community shares: bread, truth, wine, and dreams (23). His "Oda al pan" ("Ode to Bread") likewise calls for the sharing of beauty, love, bread, and the earth. More global than local, Neruda's perspectives serve, as do Dalton's, as the preamble to the conversations I will have with the students throughout the seminar. The metaphor of poetry as bread facilitates, to use Sommer's terms, an initial pause alongside the artists, a first contemplation of poetry's work in the world.

Like other seminars in the College of William and Mary's Hispanic Studies Program, Local-Global Issues requires students to construct portfolios of their written work. In my class, the portfolio entries are responses to questions I pose each week. The questions for the first two weeks typically resemble these: When Dalton says life is beautiful, what else is he saying? How do you know? What do you find beautiful about Neruda's odes? Do they disrupt or reinforce your idea of what beauty is? Are they hierarchical, critical, or contradictory? Do they envision a *locus communis*, a common ground that we as readers share? I start each class session with one or more of these questions, then home in on the textual details: voice, rhythm, image, silence, and structure, for example. I return to and reframe the questions one more time at the end of each class.

This seminar meets just twice a week. In a typical week the class will discuss only five or six poems in depth. So I tend to assign whole collections, asking the students to read all the poems in them and to view each book as a whole. Throughout the week, they work on writing answers to the questions, taking into account what they have read both in and out of class. Their entries need to include a broad engagement with the questions and detailed interpretations of the poetry. The latter doesn't always come easily, though, and students typically rewrite their essays to strengthen this aspect after an initial review by me. By the end of the semester, each portfolio will include at least four strong pieces, with an introduction, a table of contents, and an epilogue. The portfolio as a whole should link the pieces together, telling a story about local-global issues from the student's point of view. At the end of the semester, students produce an additional final project that complements the portfolio.

Students who take Local-Global Issues pursue majors in Hispanic studies or Latin American studies. They often have another major as well, in government, sociology, economics, history, theater, or business. Some have returned from a summer or semester abroad. Others have completed hands-on field research projects or internships. As juniors and seniors, these students have written many interpretive essays already. And, while they still need work in this area, more often than not they are weary of the traditional paper. For this reason, in addition to their interpretations of the assigned readings, I invite them to write poetry of their own, annotate it, and include it in the portfolio. "Oda a mis Red Toms" ("Ode to My Red Toms"), "Oda al ladrillo" ("Ode to the Brick") and "Oda al mapa" ("Ode to the Map") are examples of work produced in the first weeks in 2015. With few exceptions, the students embrace this kind of writing. The creative response seems to come easily to them.

The challenge for the students (and for me) rests in that part of Sommer's call where she asks us to see interpretation as part of art's work in the world. Good examples of this do of course exist: In 2011 Oscar Maturano Zambrano, an artisan from Northern Chile, built a *mega maqueta salitrera* ("big salt block") that depicts life in Chile's salt mining communities in the first half of the twentieth century. It was exhibited on the sixth floor of the Zofri Mall in Iquique. I came across it not in Iquique but as a result of a *YouTube* search for a reading of Neruda's "Oda a las cosas" ("Ode to Things"): Víctor Silva González had produced a short video ("Oda a las cosas") about the *mega maqueta*, with Neruda's poem as the voice-over. His video adds an artistic and interpretive layer to an already interpretive work of art. I tell the students that I can imagine other interpretations as well: a scholarly reading of all three texts—the ode, the *maqueta*, and the video—could indeed lead to a deeper understanding of the transnational politics of mining; it could result in a new and nuanced response to major works assigned in class, such as Eduardo Galeano's *Las venas abiertas de América Latina* (*Open Veins of Latin America*). I ask them to use this kind of thinking as a tool for the next unit in the course and when appropriate, for their other courses as well.

Poetry, Crisis, and the Two September 11ths

Students love Neruda's odes. They are accessible, political, and beautiful. His *Alturas de Macchu Picchu* (*Heights of Macchu Picchu*) inevitably proves difficult for them, though. And yet, to set up the segment of the course on crisis, hope, and the two September 11ths I see this long multi-layered poem as especially useful. To understand it, students first need to know something about Neruda's trajectory, that in his earlier work, the first *Residencia en la tierra* (*Residence on Earth*) in particular, crisis surfaces as a sign of personal anguish; it emerges again in his poetry about the Spanish Civil War, as a sign of a nation's tragedy: "Venid a ver la sangre en las calles" ("Come and see the blood in the streets"), he writes in "Explico algunas cosas" ("I Explain a Few Things). In *Alturas de Macchu Picchu*, crisis is again center stage, both existentially and politically. This poem chronicles Neruda's departure away from personal anguish and toward an engagement with politics and history. It sheds light on the choices poets make. Crisis in this case signifies a turning point, a choice between hope and despair.

The choice holds true for other poets as well. In her "Ars poetica" Claribel Alegría brings to light the Central American landscapes devastated by political and economic injustice and by war. She criticizes the national and international interventions that make such devastation possible. And yet, more often than not, she selects an ideology and an aesthetic built on hope:

> Yo,
> poeta de oficio,
> condenada tantas veces
> a ser cuervo
> jamás me cambiaría

por la Venus de Milo:
mientras reina en el Louvre
y se muere de tedio
y junta polvo
yo descubro el sol
todos los días
y entre valles
volcanes y despojos de guerra
avizoro la tierra prometida. (34)

I,
poet by trade
condemned so many times
to be a crow,
would never change places
with the Venus de Milo:
while she reigns in the Louvre
and dies of boredom
and collects dust
I discover the sun
each morning
and amid valleys
volcanoes
and debris of war
I catch sight of the promised land. (35)

In the essay "The Latin American Aesthetics of Hope," Ariel Dorfman like-wise posits that the late twentieth-century dictatorships in Latin America's Southern Cone put "hope to the test." According to Dorfman, the choice for writers of his generation was to descend into "skepticism and ambiguity" or to search for the foundations of hope, for the beautiful, "durable," parts of humanity that resist terror and repression (*Other Septembers* 169). His "Love Letter to America" in the same collection pursues this line of thought with an emphasis on the post-9/11 United States (11–14).

With crisis and hope now at the fore, in this part of the seminar my students study the two September 11ths, in Chile in 1973 and in the United States in 2001, side by side. The questions that generate both the class conversations and the portfolio are: What role does poetry play in naming crisis and imagining a way out? If poetry doesn't change history, and if the crisis of September 11 is still tragic, what good in the end is poetry? The readings include Espada's *The Republic of Poetry*, the *Human Rights Watch World Reports*, and selections from Dorfman's *Other Septembers*,

Many Americas and the anthology *In Case of Fire in a Foreign Land*. The anthology, a bilingual collection of Dorfman's poetry from the 1970s and '80s, lays bare the knowledge and the fear shared by political prisoners during the Pinochet years. It introduces the pain of those who survived but lost people they loved, and it emphasizes the sorrow of exile. Hope is an absent presence here.

Having read the background information in the *Human Rights Watch World Reports*, students come to Dorfman's poetry knowing, for example, that after the crises of 1973 and 2001 government surveillance of citizens became legal, if not ethical. They know that torture is seen by some as justifiable for reasons of national security. With information such as this in play, they then choose to read, to interpret, and to write either through a lens of hope or a lens of disillusionment, a choice not unlike the one the poets make. Given the amount of reading students do, class conversations tend to be layered with complexity at this point. It is not unusual to spend an entire class on one poem, such as Dorfman's poignantly ironic "Esperanza" ("Hope"): "Cómo puede ser, / eso les pregunto / que la alegría de un / padre, que la felicidad de una / madre, / consista en saber / que a su hijo / lo están / que lo están torturando?" 'How can it be / I ask you / that the joy of a / father / the happiness of a / mother, / consists of knowing / that they are / that they are still torturing / their son?' (*In Case of Fire* 8, 10). While reactions to this poem were mixed in 2015, a few students read it as a reflection of the ideological foreignness of their own land. They found hope not in the poem itself but in the implicit instruction it offers for our time and place, the United States in the second decade of the twenty-first century. Catherine Freund was one of the students who engaged this conversation in class and then developed it in her portfolio. Freund's interpretation begins with a statement about how poetry brings readers in the United States to an awareness of the pain inflicted by our country's politics. Her argument doesn't end there, however, but speaks to the notion that the crisis of the two September 11ths remains and will remain an unresolved betrayal, at least for Ariel Dorfman. The small textual details in his work, from the open questions to the perpetual present, support Freund's conclusion. It is not the poets alone, but our students as well, who will disrupt the status quo.

In this part of the course, the poem "Not Here" from Espada's *The Republic of Poetry* inevitably captures students' imaginations. It is the second poem in a collection about Espada's journey south to Chile in honor of Neruda's centennial. The eponymous poem that precedes it mirrors the joy of a Nerudian ode: it envisions "a train full of poets" rolling

"south in the rain" (3); it celebrates poets, poetry, and things and projects
an image of the dictatorship turned marvelously and justly upside down.
"Not Here," in contrast, opens up the most ominous of questions about
post-9/11 Chile and the post-9/11 United States. In this poem's final
stanza, Espada recalls learning about the first of the two September 11ths,
and he brings the memory up to date:

> I am the one navigating the night without stars.
> On or around the night of September 11, 1973
> at the age of sixteen,
> I was vandalizing a golf course in the rain,
> fishtailing my car through the mud on the ninth hole
> as beer cans rolled under my feet.
> Ten miles away, at the White House,
> the plotters were pleased; the coup
> was a world in miniature they painted by hand,
> a train with real smoke and bells
> circling the track in the basement.
> The rest of us drank too much, drove too fast,
> as the radio told us what happened
> on the other side of the world
> and the windshield wipers said
> not here, not here, not here. (7)

The last line of this poem invites a nuanced interpretation: Does "*not here*"
refer to the disappeared? Is it a reference to the fallacy of exceptionalism
in the United States? Does its provocation rest in the coincidence of the
two? While the ironies of this history are not lost on our students, in 2015
they didn't fill the pages of their portfolios with responses to these particular questions. References to Espada's imagery (the back-and-forth of the
windshield wipers) did surface in classroom discussions in the final weeks
of the semester, though. For me, this is a reminder that interpretation
includes not just what students write but also what they say.

   It includes formal oral and visual communication as well. Chelsea Easter, a Hispanic studies major with a minor in theater, used our class conversations as the starting point for a final project about September 11 and
the legacies of silence. She produced a video in which she performs lines
from Dorfman's *Death and the Maiden*. In this project she enacts the poetic
principles in Dorfman's play, its particular rhythms, repetitions, silences, and
hopes. While Chelsea reads the lines, viewers see images of silenced women,
their mouths covered, but their eyes wide open. The video ends with a

reference to Dorfman's *Manifesto for Another World: Voices from Beyond the Dark*, his notion that the world doesn't have to be the way it is.

Poetry and the Public Humanities

Fernando Rendón and his colleagues founded the Medellín International Poetry Festival in 1990 when Colombia was under siege by drug cartels and by military and paramilitary forces. The founders' response to the terror was to fill the city with people reading poetry, to reimagine Medellín not as the drug capital of the world but as the poetry capital. Today, more than one hundred poets from Asia, Africa, Europe, and the Americas participate in the annual event. While the poets perform their work, another 200,000 people fill the city's parks, subways, and plazas to listen. As one of the most tangible examples of the public humanities, the festival provides a foundation and a forum for engagement with contemporary issues, both local and global. Knowing that direct human engagement is key to the success of this initiative, I had the good fortune of attending with colleagues in 2010. I would love to return with students. In the meantime, the festival's accessible and up-to-date Web site has proven to be an excellent resource for teaching poetry (www.festivaldepoesiademedellin.org). Each year the organizers also publish poetry from the festival in *Revista Prometeo*, a journal available both in print and on the festival's Web site.

Although the political conversations at the heart of the Medellín Festival range from year to year, certain issues—indigenous rights, the well-being of the planet, war and peace—do emerge consistently. The 2015 festival focused on peace and reconciliation in Colombia. For this reason, I asked the 2015 class to read the poems in *Prometeo* and to study the Festival Web site with "peace" in mind, to tease out the multiple meanings of the term, and to identify the issues that support or challenge the pathways to peace in Colombia. I didn't select the poems myself but encouraged the students to consider works by emerging poets. Our readings in 2015 thus included poems by three Colombian writers, Diana Pizarro, Isabel Dunas, and Felipe Posada. By reading these poets' work side by side, students develop a multilayered understanding of peace and war. Writing from a perspective akin to Alegría's "Ars poetica," in "Sueño" ("Dream") Posada envisions the Colombian landscape in idyllic terms:

¡Diles a todos
que los estruendos callaron

ya no hay bombas en la tierra
salen liebres de las trincheras,
y saltamontes brincan fuera de los parapetos!

. . . .

Regresemos al campo
donde las hierbas verdes
los árboles de mango
las exuberantes cascadas de agua

. . . .

nos ayudarán con el sustento diario. (257)

Tell everyone that the blasts have ceased
there are no more bombs on earth
the hares come out of the trenches
and grasshoppers leap out of the parapets!

. . . .

Let's go back to the country
where the green grass
the mango trees
the exuberant waterfalls

. . . .

will help us find daily sustenance. (256)

Dunas, in contrast, writes from the perspective that peace and war, harmony and discord are personal, internal, and existential. In "Acento" ("Accent") she brings to light an unresolved struggle to invent her own identity through language: "Empiezo a leerme / Habito el fantasma de mi interior huida / . . . Colmada de gozosas inarmonías" 'I begin to read myself / Dwell in the ghost of my previous flight / . . . Filled with joyous non-harmonies' (246, 245). In "Las dos fieras que soy" ("The Two Beasts I Am") Pizarro invokes a similar storm within: "Es temporada de tormentas. / Dentro de mí / habitan dos seres / de naturalezas disonantes" 'It's storm season. / Inside me live two beings / of discordant natures" (242, 240). Reading the latter two poems, students deepen their engagement with interpretation: Dunas's and Pizarro's work leaves room to fill in the gaps, to extrapolate, and to interpret with an eye to the unspoken but still palpable political dimensions of the poetry presented in Medellín.

The last book of poetry we study is called *Poems from Guantánamo: The Detainees Speak*. I pair it with the study of the Guantánamo Public Memory Project. The authors of this project document Guantánamo's history, including the United States' presence there and throughout the region from 1898 to 2015. The project's Web site (gitmomemory.org) makes public the testimonies of people with direct experience at the detention center, including employees and their family members. *Poems from Guantánamo* consists of twenty-two poems, written by seventeen of the prisoners held at the detention center from 2002 to 2007. In addition to the poems, the book contains an afterword by Ariel Dorfman and two introductory essays, one by Flagg Miller, a linguist and anthropologist, and another by the editor, Marc Falkoff, who describes how the poems found their way to the public. Before this book could be published, he says, "hundreds of volunteer lawyers, professors, paralegals, law students, and human rights advocates . . . worked tirelessly to restore the rule of law to Guantánamo Bay." The lawyers at the Center for Constitutional Rights who mounted "habeas corpus challenges on behalf of the detainees" are the same lawyers who facilitated the release of the poets' work (ix). Falkoff notes that more poems than those published in this collection exist, but they were not cleared for release: the Pentagon holds that due to its "content and format" poetry presents a "special risk" to national security (4). The clearance that was granted applied only to the English translations, a decision made in order to avoid the "enhanced security risk" the Arabic or Pashto versions might contain (5).

To a person, the students in the 2015 Local-Global Issues seminar found this book captivating. They noted the Dalton-like beauty of the poems. They named the connections between Shaker Abdurraheem Aamer's "They Fight for Peace" (19) and the Colombian poets' work for peace in their country. They identified the links between Ibrahim al Rubaish's "Ode to the Sea" (64) and Neruda's odes. They noted the stylistic similarities between *In Case of Fire in a Foreign Land* and "My Heart was Wounded by the Strangeness" (61) by Abdulla Majid al Noaimi. In our class discussions, they traced these lines skillfully.

In the second-to-last week of class, I invited the students to engage in a task that necessarily combines art and interpretation: I asked for English-to-Spanish translations of *Poems from Guantánamo*, noting that this assignment would be collaborative, informal, and ungraded, that I just wanted to see what they would learn. This is what I believe they learned: An interpretation never quite matches the original, and sometimes there is no "original" to be found. Art's work in the world is a beautiful, moving process. It is also imperfect, since the distance that separates poets and readers, college students and political detainees, is undoubtedly vast. In those last two weeks I learned some things as well: Our students will work creatively and knowledgably to perform art's work in the world. They will do it willingly, hopefully, and joyfully. They won't change the world in every paper or poem they write. I find it nonetheless moving to follow the shifts in how they read the night sky.

APPENDIX: Local-Global Issues and Latin American Poetry (A Short Version of the Syllabus)

This course takes as its point of departure a basic premise articulated by the Salvadoran poet Roque Dalton that poets must keep faith with poetry, with beauty. Alongside Dalton's idea about aesthetics, we consider the work of poetry in the world. This broad premise guides daily class discussions and serves, with the texts referred to in this essay, as the foundation for the following case studies: Beauty and Politics: Pablo Neruda on Places and Things; Poetry, Crisis, and the Two September 11ths; Poetry and the Public Humanities.

Beauty and Politics: Pablo Neruda on Places and Things. What do we mean when we talk about the order of things? How does a place become poetic? How well do beauty and ideology mix?

Introduction and Week 1: Dalton, "Como tú"; Neruda "Oda a los calcetines"

Week 2: Neruda, *Odes to Simple Things*: "Oda a las cosas"; "Oda a la mesa"; "Oda al violín de California"; "Oda al perro"; "Oda a unas flores amarillas"; "Oda al Pan"; Neruda's Nobel address; student odes

Week 3: Neruda, *Alturas de Macchu Picchu*, cantos 1–8; Felstiner, "Translating Neruda"; student translations; scenes from *The Motorcycle Diaries*

Week 4: Neruda, *Alturas de Macchu Picchu*, cantos 9–12; Neruda, *Absence and Presence*; Dorfman, *Other Septembers, Many Americas*: "Saying Goodbye to Pablo"

Poetry, Crisis, and the Two September 11ths. What do we mean when we talk about crisis? What role does poetry play in naming crisis and imagining a way out?

Week 5: Berger, "The Hour of Poetry"; *Human Rights Watch World Report: Chile 1973*; "The National Security Archive Briefing Book No. 8"; Dorfman, *In Case of Fire in a Foreign Land*: "Esperanza"; "Dos más dos"; "Testamento"; "Los demás compañeros de la celda están dormidos"; "Pruebas al canto"; "Correspondencia"; "Habeas corpus"; "Presente"

Week 6: Dorfman, *Other Septembers, Many Americas*; Espada, *The Republic of Poetry*, part 1; student translations

Weeks 7 and 8: Espada, *The Republic of Poetry*, parts 1, 2, and 3; student translations and poems; *Taller*: the portfolio as a whole

Poetry and the Public Good. What do we mean when we talk about the public? Can poetry and the interpretation of poetry engage the public in transformative ways?

Week 9: Sommer, *The Work of Art in the World*: "Welcome Back"; Neruda, *Absence and Presence*; Medellín International Poetry Festival

Weeks 10 and 11: Sommer, *The Work of Art in the World*: "Press Here" and "Art and Accountability"; poems from *Prometeo*

Week 12: The Guantánamo Public Memory Project; Falkoff, *Poems from Guantánamo*; student translations; *Taller* on the research projects.

Week 13 and 14: Portfolio presentations; poetry reading

Charles A. Perrone

Insularity, Invention, and Interfaces: Brazilian Lyric and Contemporary Imperatives

Decades ago, standard approaches to teaching national poetries customarily involved periods of literary history, epochal styles, canonical authors, consecrated texts, and close readings. In the second decade of the twenty-first century, classes founded on such models in Portuguese / Luso-Brazilian programs in North America are not common. As humanistic schools of thought evolve and technology continues to advance, the pedagogy of poetry adopts and adapts. In the case of Brazil, what facilitates inquiry, instruction, and discussion concerning lyric (in the broadest sense of genre) in both conventional and innovative ways are the nation's singular profile and the diverse endeavors of artists of the word. A profitable technique in presenting contemporary Brazilian poetries is to emphasize what makes them distinctive even as one acknowledges commonalities within the Western tradition, the Portuguese heritage, and poetic domains of the Americas. Comparative angles can consider shared interests and sharp contrasts alike, as well as input from the other arts.

Brazil occupies a unique position in the discipline of Latin American literature as the region's largest and most populous nation, and as the lone Portuguese-speaking land. Assessing aesthetic, sociocultural, and historical parallels with and divergences from Spanish American counterparts can be mutually illuminating. There are also hemispheric aspects to weigh, incorporating North American letters. Pedagogical situations and missions affect the form and content of teaching modern Brazilian poetry. One may have the privilege of offering *poesia brasileira* as part of the Luso-Brazilian curriculum in a Spanish and Portuguese department (or similar foreign- or modern-languages unit), conducting class and assigning readings, at the undergraduate or graduate level, in the original language. Elsewhere one may be teaching Brazilian literature in translation, including poetry, for general-education, comparative-literature, or Latin American studies constituencies. In such cases both primary and secondary sources should be English-language versions, optimally with useful annotations and critical apparatus. The topic of lyric in Brazil can comprise a whole semester-long class, whether covering from origins to the present or focusing on the modern and contemporary periods. Alternatively, one might organize a customized module on poetry within a course in Brazilian / Latin American literature or area studies. While any critical or creative item in translation ought to be able to be used by students studying in the original, the reverse is not necessarily true. Thus, an emphasis on materials in English is justified here.

As for disciplinary flexibility, current courses principally about poetry increasingly expand horizons for reading and interpretation. In the early 1980s, the MLA already recognized the intersections of literary criticism with other arts, humanities, and sciences (Barricelli and Gibaldi). In the age of globalization, multiculturalism, and cultural studies, such encounters between letters and other fields of inquiry or creative expression have naturally become more desirable as both writers and teacher-scholars seek more tools to grasp polyfaceted dimensions of expressive culture, in order to bridge separations and to reduce divisions. Perceptions of lyric in Brazil are enriched by reading through the lenses of history, urban anthropology, gender studies, and other disciplines. The strongest cross-connections in Brazilian poetry are with music and visual arts, two truly distinctive alliances.

A fundamental point of departure for a focused course can be the notion of *imperative*. What is to be done? What have influential poets and organized groups held to be essential in the making and understanding of poetry? What are the combinations of cultural objectives, aesthetic orientations, and situational values that have driven poetics since the pivotal decade of the 1920s? To begin one must examine the modernist imperative, that is, the avant-garde and nationalist preoccupations of *modernismo*, Brazilian modernism, from about 1920 to 1945. With the Week of

Modern Art in São Paulo in 1922 and subsequent activity around the country, vanguardism in Brazil stands out qua declared and defined movement as it does nowhere else in the Americas. In the contemporary epoch, an imperative of invention in Brazil necessarily features the Noigandres poets who headed the internationally recognized movement of *poesia concreta* ("concrete poetry"). This category includes other experimental efforts in the 1950s, 1960s, and beyond. With each step, it is instructive to keep in mind the two definitions of *invention*: discovery, as in the sagas of European explorers, and contrivance of something new, as in cutting-edge industry or art. One should also attend to a social imperative that undergirds engaged, politically conscious, and so-called protest poetry across the decades but especially in the early 1960s.

In the mid-1960s, a cohort of extraordinary poet-songwriters and lyricists employed what may rightly be termed an Orphic imperative. The poetry of Brazilian song remained especially strong for some twenty years, and continues to the present in practice and criticism. In conjunction with this musical mode, one can identify an imperative of youth in varied undertakings related to lyric in the 1970s and 1980s, including both so-called marginal poetry (informal free verse) and intersemiotic creation (akin to material poetry). In the 1980s, developments justify postulating an imperative of renewal to approach the late-career production of the Noigandres poets, both creative and critical. Since circa 1990, heterogeneity and multiplicity of proposal have characterized the realm of Brazilian lyric. Several different imperatives of varying scope, some driven by factors of identity, are at work and in play, as poets draw on the achievements of previous decades and seek fresh ways to express themselves. Some have merited close attention and benefit from publications in translation.

With respect to recommended pedagogical materials, a strategy of consolidation has been adopted in this essay. Readers are encouraged to consult *Seven Faces: Brazilian Poetry since Modernism* (Perrone) for extensive lists of primary and secondary sources apt for a given series of classes. For comparative purposes—especially concerning the tropes of insularity, invention, and interface—there is substantial bibliography in *Brazil, Lyric, and the Americas* (Perrone). Two reference works contain useful creative and critical bibliographies regarding the poetry of Brazil up to the present day: *Princeton Encyclopedia of Poetry and Poetics* (Greene) and the humanities volumes of the *Handbook of Latin American Studies*, with online access to volumes since 1990 (lcweb2.loc.gov/hlas). In the latter case, didactic value varies from year to year but there is something to discover in each volume, whether names, titles, issues, or events. In particular, there are registers of books by select individual poets who may not comfortably fit into a working category, recognized trend, declared movement, or imperative, as used here.

A historic happening in the Brazilian arts that still resonates loudly today was the 1922 Semana de Arte Moderna, a series of interrelated sessions with lectures, musical recitals, and displays of painting and sculpture. In poetry, the principal aims of the movement being officially launched during that week were to put an end to the lingering effects of Parnassianism (no nation cultivated this school longer than Brazil), to advocate for the national idiom (New World language), and to validate formal liberty (free verse, open stanzas, etc.). A groundbreaking volume of futurist verse by Mário de Andrade had a musically inspired introduction that laid out a modernist poetics. There is some criticism in English, notably regarding the city as site of enunciation (see Foster), a thread that stretches through twentieth-century lyric in Brazil. Other modernists with urban or, for that matter, rural interests can be read in anthologies prepared since 1970 (Bishop and Brasil, Tapscott, F. Williams, Vicuña and Livon-Grosman), and in individual volumes such as that of Manuel Bandeira (*This Earth That Sky*), the dean of poetry in the first generation of *modernistas*. In the second wave, Cecília Meirelles was a prominent voice.

The name in *modernismo* that has generated most attention in international venues is Oswald de Andrade, a poet-polemicist responsible for a radical new mode of verse-making (or anti-verse-making) and two epoch-making manifestos. His work has resounded without pause in Brazil since its revival in the 1960s and has become "an obligatory genealogical foundation" in postcolonial studies and treatments of hybridity (Jáuregui 22). His *Poesia pau-brasil* or "Brazil-wood Poetry" is a sort of cubist minimalism. The poems are best read in conjunction with the nationalist manifesto and as a sequence, as they are not independent utterances but rather part of an unfolding set in geohistorical frames. One stand-alone combative poem whose linguistic, historical, satirical, and proto-postcolonial traits have provoked a wealth of responses is "Erro de português" ("Portuguese Error"). Oswald's most celebrated work is the "Manifesto antropófago" ("Cannibalist Manifesto"), which is not a statement about poetry (nor is there a corpus of cannibalist verse) but rather a grand metaphor of cultural philosophy with decolonial flavor. *Antropófago* refers to appropriation of foreign sources and critical reformulation in national terms. In Brazil, the light of this modernist platform shines in the poetics of *poesia concreta*, in the revolutionary popular music of Tropicália, across the spectrum of youth poetry of the 1970s, and in the analysis of Arnaldo Antunes, a leading multimedia artist of the 1990s and 2000s (see Santos, *Arnaldo Canibal Antunes*, "Body Language"). Oswald is truly an indispensable reference for contemporary cultural production. His work can comprise a rubric in a university course—possibilities include its reception in North America and comparison to other artistic counterdiscourses in Latin America—or can be the centerpiece of a class on him and those whom he inspired.

The two most important poets of Brazil—Carlos Drummond de Andrade and João Cabral de Melo Neto—bridge modernist and contemporary stages. Much of what Drummond de Andrade wrote in the 1930s (in ironic existential free verse) and 1940s (in increasingly engaged strophes) remains powerful to this day. Two poems should be highlighted for their reception upon first publication and for their lasting impact: "No meio do caminho" ("In the Middle of the Road"; 3) and "Poema de sete faces" ("Seven-Sided Poem"; 11). His more philosophical and formally rigorous pages of the 1950s demonstrate his astounding agility and versatility (see Perrone, "Carlos"), and in the 1960s he also did some linguistic experiments. While Drummond has been available in English since the 1960s, the ability to include him on a syllabus has been greatly enhanced by an anthology by the critic-translator Richard Zenith (C. Andrade). Similarly, Zenith's renderings of the stellar voice of the second half of the twentieth century, João Cabral de Melo Neto, facilitate Cabral's inclusion in comparative courses (Melo Neto). This poet-engineer is noted for his cerebral, desentimentalized metrified verse, but he also incorporated folk poetry into his textual adventures (see Shellhorse, "Explosion"). In addition to the popular-erudite dynamic in both poets, one ought to attend to poems serving as ars poetica.

In the late 1950s several aspects of Brazil's expressive culture intrigued the international imaginary. On a massive scale, people around the world recognized Pelé's team as victors of their first World Cup in soccer, and the sounds of bossa nova began to be heard. On a more modest scale, interested parties remarked on the architecture of the planned capital city of Brasília, and a neo-avant-garde in poetry emerged from the city of São Paulo: *poesia concreta*. More so than any other aspect of lyric, this movement put Brazil on the mappa mundi of the arts. The experimental poetry and explanatory articles of founders Augusto de Campos, Haroldo de Campos, and Décio Pignatari appeared in articulated phases—organic, early steps; an orthodox or high stage; and the years of open invention—but the principal collective accomplishment was the creation of the verbi-vocovisual ideogram. These spatialized ultracondensed word constructions sought to interweave verb, sound, and shape in sui generis structures. The proponents controversially declared a closing of the historical cycle of verse and took graphic space as a prime structural agent, though semiosis remained essential. It is convenient to refer to the products of the apex of Brazilian concrete poetry in the 1950s and 1960s as *poesia concreta* to distinguish it from other forms of concrete poetry worldwide that lean much more toward graphic page art than toward linguistic mastery. In any case, this corps of poets also pursued interarts paths. Their journal *Invenção: revista de arte de vanguarda* ("Invention: Revue of Vanguard Art") included poetry, verbographic pieces, essays, experimental music, visual art, and foreign contributors. Scholarship on such '50s–'60s phenomena can draw from an abundance of statements, declarations, and critical writings by the poets themselves.

As for international criticism, there have been contributions from the United States by such prominent scholars of lyric as Marjorie Perloff, who ponders contexts from modernism to the dominance of technology to develop the notion of arrière-garde ("From Avant-Garde to Digital"), and Charles Bernstein, who reflects on the world-class career of Haroldo de Campos. Bernstein's Penn seminars on poetics often include Brazil (writing .upenn.edu/bernstein). Spanish American scholars have shown keen interest in *poesia concreta* (see Ledesma in this volume) and produced the most comprehensive studies of the movement and the postconcrete work of its principals (Aguilar, *Poesia*). The best single source for *poesia concreta*—with photographic documentation, color reproductions of poems, select essays, and a CD of musical interpretations—is the bilingual catalogue of a massive 2008 exhibition (Bandeira and Barros). Several North American libraries own this volume.

The extremely dense and detail-dependent forms of lyric in concrete and postconcrete repertories make translation even more difficult than with standard measured verse. Some editors prefer vocabular glosses when reproducing the poems (e.g., Brasil and Smith, Tapscott), but there are indeed other solutions to review (see H. Campos, *Novas*; Perrone, "4 x 3 x 2"). Dozens of English versions of nonstandard and visually inflected poems by Augusto de Campos have appeared since the 1960s in journals in North America and the UK. It is fair to dedicate a substantial amount of class time to *poesia concreta*, including the subsequent production of its founders, and its offshoots, because of the numerous novelties, the prominent role of theory, the international impact, and the unending debate surrounding this poetry. If the imperative of invention oriented some remarkable figures in the 1950s and 1960s, one can posit an imperative of renewal in the 1980s, when circumstances prompted updated thought. Haroldo de Campos developed the idea of the "post-utopian poem" to allow for continued inventiveness without the collective agenda of a vanguard (in Bandeira and Barros 116–38). This wide-ranging statement should be read in conjunction with the much-celebrated essay "Da razão antropofágica" ("Anthropophagous Reason"; *Novas* 157–77). Haroldo was consistently interested in transtemporal stylistics, including the neobaroque, which he practiced (see Sefamí in this volume). For his part, Augusto de Campos satirized the ubiquity of the postmodern in "Póstudo" ("Post-everything") and set off a contentious exchange (see Perrone, *Seven Faces*, 159–69). He would go on to craft much visual lyric in the 1990s and 2000s that questioned *poiesis*, the making of poetry, and life in the age of technology, especially electronic media.

There are significant sociopolitical aspects in *poesia concreta* upon which to reflect (see Aguilar, "Some Propositions," and Shellhorse, "Subversions"); the Noigandres poets even declared a "participatory leap" in 1962 (Pignatari 70). Still, the topic of committed or engagé poetry will be primarily informed by more conventional styles. Chapters in González and Treece explain germane *modernista* background well; they also discuss *poesia praxis*, a 1960s endeavor seeking to merge textual novelty and dialectical consciousness. Social imperatives were the foundational principles of *Violão de rua: poemas para a liberdade* ("Street Guitar: Poems for Liberty") a series of pocket anthologies of established and emerging poets in the early 1960s whose aims and popular sympathies are evident in the title and subtitle (see Perrone, *Seven Faces* 67–86). Critiques of capitalism and its ills were often held to be mandatory in such committed work. While so-called political poetry was most evident in Brazil in the immediate wake of the 1959 Cuban Revolution, as in the rest of Latin America, engaged humanistic verse is transtemporal; it can be found in all epochs and permeates, in varying degrees of intensity, the contemporary period. In this thematic web, many would say that the most vibrant name is that of Ferreira Gullar. Among the contemporary poets included in the English section of the most comprehensive Web anthology in Brazil (Miranda), a leading social poet is Thiago de Mello.

The late 1960s witnessed a flourishing of composers and lyricists in *música popular brasileira* ("Brazilian popular music"), or MPB, whose song texts were of literary quality. An oft-cited inspiration for this poetry of song was the modernist poet Vinícius de Morais, who wrote best-selling collections of sonnets in the 1950s before becoming the main bossa nova lyricist in the early 1960s. The two most outstanding musicopoetic artists of the next generation were Chico Buarque de Hollanda and Caetano Veloso, but several other singer-songwriters and numerous authors of lyrics form a generational marvel moved by an Orphic imperative. The 2016 MLA Annual Convention in Austin featured Veloso and enhanced his international reputation. Ascher and Bonvicino note that the poetry of song "constituted a substantial and diverse entity of its own," yet influenced all poets born since 1950 (27). In terms of teaching, courses in Portuguese have a critical point of departure in *Letras e Letras da MPB* ("Lyrics and Lyrics"; Perrone) and no longer have to depend on physical discography to hear compositions in their natural environment, as recordings are available on the Internet. Lyrical prowess is one of the main themes of *Masters of Contemporary Brazilian Song: MPB 1965–1985* (Perrone; see also *Seven Faces* 87–116). These studies examine both how songwriters employ literary sources (varieties of intertextuality) and how popular compositions actually display serial aesthetic complexities. Scholarship on song, in several academic disciplines, has burgeoned in Brazil; some of it connects directly to poetry or to interrelations of literature. There are fertile musicolyrical corpora related to *modernismo*, to social protest, and, above all, to *poesia concreta*. Selecting and presenting remarkable contemporary songs is a class activity proven to engage students of varied provenance. Song (as sound recording or video) can always be approached as a performance phenomenon as well.

All Brazilian arts of the 1970s were marked by the continuing specter of military dictatorship. In new poetry (primarily by authors born after 1950) there emerged an imperative of youth operating in intriguing contrasts in a continuum ranging from so-called marginal poetry, marked by colloquial informality, to what was dubbed *criação intersemiótica* ("intersemiotic creation"), informed experimentalism that also incorporated constructivist verse (see Perrone, *Seven Faces* 117–48). Marginal poetry disturbed literary traditionalists but was a fascinating sociohistorical experience, part of a generational response to challenging times. Dunn writes that this "literary wing of counterculture" helps us understand "emotions, impulses, and commitments among Brazilians who came of age under authoritarian rule" and to witness quotidian interpersonal politics (1–2). In this conjuncture a novel queer imperative emerged (see Butterman in this volume). Forty years after the heyday of this youthful enthusiasm, it is still a point of reference prompting arguments about tradition or its rejection and disputes about the relative importance of intellectual rigor.

Poetry of the 1980s and 1990s, and into the third millennium, has comprised an ever-diversifying field where straightforwardly discursive verse coexists with a constructivist orientation more concerned with the instrument of language. The productive tension of up-to-date awareness and experiential subjectivity can be read in the work of, among others, Paulo Leminski (see Fróes); the prematurely departed Waly Salomão, one of whose books has been translated into English; and Régis Bonvicino, who edits a well-produced Web space, *Sibila*, with English options (sibila.com.br/author/regis). All accounts of lyric since about 1990 recognize the existence of an array of options and plural practices that reflect everything from the inheritance of liberating *modernismo* to the cosmopolitan science of *poesia concreta* (see Corona). The expansive poem *Taxi*, by Adriano Espínola, is a bright container of such multiplicity in transnational contexts; it also adds to a contemporary neo-epical thread grounded in Gullar's *Dirty Poem*. The rationale of lyricism itself is expressed in a widely acclaimed 1996 poem by Antonio Cicero, "Guardar" ("Keeping"), the centerpiece of a cluster of poems under the overarching theme of music and poetry (Perrone, "Seven"). In the early twenty-first century, concern with alterity has grown, as seen below.

At the end of the twentieth century, Lígia Chiappini, a Brazilian scholar with a European vantage point, pondered the state of Brazilian poetry and its critical reception. Her analysis can serve as a springboard to deliberate issues in lyric to the present. In the early 2000s, she perceived both a certain cynicism and clear hope. Her reading of Brazilian opinion of the day contrasts the views of those who believe poetry escaped commendably the negative constraints of the culture industry with those who complain about dilution and arbitrariness in the production of younger generations. What surprised Chiappini in turn-of-the century commentary was the lack of recognition of "new relations between the local, national, and global" (112). Indeed, in the age of the Internet poets from around the country—not just the biggest cities of São Paulo and Rio de Janeiro—have vigorously participated in common virtual enterprises. And, while it may not be a dominant dimension of contemporary lyric, there has been a demonstrable trans-American imperative among a legion of Brazilian poets that has brought makers and readers of poetry of all the Americas closer together. Diverse initiatives and interfaces have linked Brazil, ever conscious of a limiting historical insularity, and North America, as well as Brazil and Spanish America (see Perrone *Brazil* and "Shared," especially the focus on Afro-descendant themes).

Chiappini further points to two creative preoccupations of late-twentieth-century verse that have been recognized by journalistic and academic critics: *poesia feminina* and *poesia negra ou afro-brasileira* (114). Poetry by female writers and by Afro-Brazilian writers provokes confabulation about the role of identity in a range of expressive cultures and arguments about the very questions of canon and criteria of value. As demonstrated by Ricardo Domeneck, female writers are gaining increasing recognition, and English translations are a testimony to this (e.g., Freitas, *Rilke Shake*). In the second decade of the twenty-first century, some would say that the goals of nondiscrimination based on gender and editorial equity have been achieved or are close to achievement in the realm of lyric (see Costa and Perrone, iv–x). Afro-Brazilian writing—already a topic of a late-twentieth-century binational anthology (Alves)—has also propagated in the twenty-first century, with the recognition of such poets as Salgado Maranhão among the nation's best loved and most accomplished. In the 2010s he has made three reading tours of North America in conjunction with the publication of books in translation.

What most concerned Chiappini in her assessment of turn-of-the-century stock-taking in lyric was the limited attention paid to what we might call a "regional imperative." She wanted to direct attention to two areas that have produced a regionally inflected poetry in Brazil: the extreme South, the homeland of the pampas, and the North, dominated by the grand Amazon and all the concomitant factors of nature. Such a chapter is surely warranted, but it would by necessity be principally for courses taught in Portuguese. It bears emphasizing that the region that best lends itself to literary presentation is the Northeast, in poetry as well as in prose fiction. The poetic giant Cabral is fully Northeastern, and there is also northeastern-tinged material—ample in the original and sufficient in translation—in the repertories of Manuel Bandeira (see *Poesia completa e prosa*), Jorge de Lima, Ascenso Ferreira, and others. Popular poets of the interior and the chapbook poetry of *literatura de cordel* ("stories on a string"), including both traditional pieces and verse composed in the contemporary period, can be incorporated into a class on the Northeast as well, especially if joining literature and the other arts (see Perrone "Backland").

In the North and the Northeast, literature and the environment is a lively comparative theme. As Brazil is one of the most prominent green sites on the planet, it makes sense for there to be ecocriticism in all related fields; what is seen and heard reverberates around the hemisphere and the world. A bioaesthetic orientation composes a green imperative in Brazilian lyric that has been the subject of recent scholarship. Odile Cisneros has launched an academic Web site dedicated to ecopoetics in Brazil, and Malcolm McNee has published *The Environmental Imaginary in Brazilian Poetry and Art*. Two of McNee's chapters examine four germane poets active in the contemporary period: Manoel de Barros, Astrid Cabral, Sérgio Medeiros, and Josely Vianna Baptista all display attentiveness to the natural world and appropriate degrees of situated environmental consciousness. Each of them has recently published a volume in English and contributes to the internationalization of ecocritical art and environmentally concerned humanities in North America.

In sum, teaching contemporary Brazilian poetry can follow chronologies, select authors, articulated groups, and chosen thematic or geocultural foci. Consideration of the linguistic contemporaneity and contextualized historicity of the series of imperatives and topics seen above reveals the originality, vast imagination, and diversity of lyric in Latin America's largest, yet still—where literary arts are concerned—most relatively understudied nation. From full-fledged courses to modules of varying length within courses of wider scope, in Portuguese or in English-Spanish translation, all options can take advantage of concepts and suggestions presented in this essay to employ poetry as a sociocultural reflector and, especially, to explore in itself the wealth of contemporary poetry in Brazil.

Jill S. Kuhnheim

Leaning toward Affect:
Teaching Poetry with Performance

I have been known to open a class or unit on poetry with a poem by Nicolás Guillén that begins like this:

> José Ramón Cantaliso,
> ¡canta liso!, canta liso,
> José Ramón.
> Duro espinazo insumiso:
> por eso es que canta liso
> José Ramón Cantaliso,
> José Ramón. (*Cantos* 85)

> José Ramón Cantaliso
> sings simply!, he sings simply
> José Ramón.
> Hard, invulnerable backbone:
> that is why he sings simply
> José Ramón Cantaliso,
> José Ramón. (my trans.)

We start reading it aloud, each student voicing one of the six verses. Then we do some variations: we may alternate lines, male and female voices; we do a choral reading; we read it backwards, from the last line to the beginning. In each case I ask for reactions, observations about what happens to the poem as we change the voicing. Does our understanding of the poem change? Does the rhythm shift? Are there alterations in how the language works? What kinds of information do we get from hearing the poem, from playing with how it is voiced? I do not mention that the poem is from *Cantos para soldados y sones para turistas* ("Songs for Soldiers and Sones for Tourists") by the Cuban Guillén, because I want the students to experience the work as cultural outsiders, to connect to their first readings, not from context or biography, but from sound and language brought to the forefront by different angles that offer them alternative tools for working with the text. But I really mean *playing* with the text, for one of the results of approaching poetry this way is that it gives students an opportunity to fool around with literature, to interact with form and content without a clearly defined goal. It loosens them up as they approach a genre that has often come to them in the classroom weighed down with stylistic and interpretive demands.

Introducing poetry through artful vocalizations also begins to create a different vocabulary for responding to the genre—we are not counting syllables but experiencing the work: listening and rereading, attentive to voice, gesture, and the place or situation in which the reading happens. This is not a private, individual encounter with the text but a collective experience of reading as a participatory activity. Students hear the poem first, observing how punctuation and line breaks may be vocalized, how rhyme creates pauses and reinforces line breaks (or not), how rhythm and meter can be heard. In his article "Why Teaching Poetry Is So Important," Andrew Simmons notes how incorporating poetry into our classes enables us to teach reading, speaking, and listening skills, as well as grammar and literary devices; but Simmons really embraces the genre for its ability to communicate powerful experiences. "Teachers should produce literature lovers as well as keen critics," he asserts. Staging creative first responses in the classroom creates a dialogue, a community, and an opportunity for inventive engagement that one can build on throughout the course.

After this initial ingress through the voice of the poem we begin to speculate about the speaker in the poem. Does he speak for himself or for a group? How do we decide? His name, Cantaliso, is repeated in a kind of rhythmic roll call that also serves as a description of what he does—he is a simple or smooth ("liso") singer—and this opens the conversation to a metapoetic discussion of the relation between singing and reciting or writing poetry. Where does this singing take place? To resituate the work in its historical context, I ask students if there are any clues in the poem about where it comes from. In this case we may get to Cuba or the Caribbean through language — the references to the musical forms of son or bachata draw on students' expertise, their recognition of these popular cultural styles. Adding more detail, we discuss how cultural and historical knowledge alters our understanding and adds additional layers to Guillén's portrayal of a street singer in Cuba. As we expand this information we are re-inserting the work in its "cultural envelope," Derek Attridge's term for the background necessary to be able to see its roles and its originality (41).

So we get to referential and analytical modes of thought through performance, but arrive there by first engaging the sensuous, affective qualities of the poem. This approach positions students to begin connecting with the emotive and qualitative aspects of the poem, which are elements in an "aesthetic reading," according to Louise Rosenblatt, who contrasts this stance with an "efferent reading" that focuses on the factual, analytic, logical, and quantitative features of a text (24–5). It allows students to experience a poem as an event, to participate in this activity, and to communicate about the work's possible impacts, relating these, perhaps, to their own experiences. Interacting with poetry out loud creates mindful listeners and provides information through channels that differ from those of daily life, highlighting the "good strangeness of poetry."[1] When the instructor presents an idea like the following, students have an experiential basis for understanding it: "A poem, although it is composed in the language of information, is not used in the language game of giving information" (Ludwig Wittgenstein, qtd. in Perloff, "Crisis" 673). In their performance of the poem students may come to see what is particular about poetry's way of communicating, what one can do in this genre that differs from what we do with others.

While some readers may quite reasonably consider the visual aspects of poetic texts on the page as performance, I am using the term here to indicate the literal voicing that sometimes includes the embodiment of poetry. Diana Taylor has defined performance as an expressive behavior and an embodied practice, which can include more than voice and can incorporate gesture, movement, live or filmed "presence," as well as information about the context of a performance (xvi). All these aspects add semiotic material, amplifying the written version of a text. The fluidity of the term *performance* makes it an attractive means of approaching poetry from interdisciplinary or multigenre perspectives, opening up the lyric to dialogues among the arts and with other elements of the cultures in which they are produced, as the examples that follow demonstrate.[2]

In addition to asking students to voice poems, I have shown examples of poetry in performance (which are easily found on the Internet now) or asked them to attend a poetry reading or performance. In the case of the latter, I invite them to write a set of observations on the event, and one serendipitous result of this has been that many students find that people (particularly people their age) actually like poetry, that poetry has a community outside of the classroom, that poetry is cool. In the first case, after students have seen a range of examples of poetry in performance—some with music, some with multiple voices, some with visual aspects, and others with voice alone—I ask them to engage the text we are considering in their own ways. This approximation does not sidestep close reading but brings us to reading from a different angle of interpretation. It also reshapes our awareness of the cultural work poetry has done in the past and may do in the future as poets and performers engage an array of venues and technologies to present their work.

I implemented a performance-based approach for the first time by instructing a small group of upper-division undergraduate students to present a selection from Vicente Huidobro's *Altazor*—a section or a canto or more—to the rest of the class. For two weeks they met on their own to make decisions about how to present the poem, what to do with punctuation, breath, tone, accents, intonation, and vocal counterpoint, aspects we had observed in the examples of other performances. They had to craft a relation between the written voice inscribed in the poem and their roles as speakers. In doing so, they compressed the distance between Huidobro's moment and their own.

The work they presented to me was extraordinarily insightful. They had chosen to perform sections from each of the cantos, alternating choral and solo speakers, using movement and sound that reinforced the rhythm of the text and indicated that they had understood what Huidobro was doing on a much deeper level than had been apparent in our class discussions to date. I framed some of my observations in an analytic mode in order to help them realize what they had done at a metacritical level, modeling how they might link their more intuitive creative experience to a systematic or scholarly mode of understanding. When they presented their performance to the class as a whole, their colleagues responded with multimodal perceptions, bringing the discussion of *Altazor* to a new level. The process encouraged innovation and gave students more agency and authority in dealing with the text.[3]

In a recent article my colleague at the University of Kansas, Jonathan Mayhew, speculates about how we might increase our students' capacity to respond to the inherently valuable raw materials of the humanities through strategies that increase their receptivity (158). In one example he reports on a graduate class we cotaught on poetry and performance and finds that the students' conscientiously conceived presentations of the poetry we read demonstrated that "they were capable of thinking about the pragmatic dimension of performance in highly creative ways" (168). These performances occurred fairly late in the semester, and Mayhew observed some difficulty in getting students to translate their active engagement into their scholarship. One way to do this is by inviting students to respond to performances in both affective and analytic modes throughout the semester. Encouraging students as readers and listeners to respond to poetry in new ways that go beyond their previous experiences with the genre may result in their "aesthetic re-education" (Felski 67) and challenge their notions of what may be pertinent to conceptualizing how poetry works.

New multimedial poetic genres and new modes of poetry circulation offer excellent opportunities for students to acquire a deeper understanding of how poetry works and how it interacts with the culture from which it emerges. In *The Uses of Literature* Rita Felski identifies different modes of textual engagement, noting that we have privileged the analytical and not given "equal weight to both cognitive and affective aspects of aesthetic response" (16). Felski delves into what she calls "aesthetic enchantment" (also characterized by terms such as *rapture, wonder, surprise*, and "an open and generous relationship to the world")—she finds its closest theoretical analogue is *jouissance* (60). She also finds that the pleasure of enchantment is linked to Stephen Greenblatt's concept of "resonance," which gives us "a sense of the thickness of the historical and cultural context" of a work (71). Literature's "power of enchantment" has been "extended and accented by the inventiveness of new technologies" according to Felski, and we certainly see this in poetry's multimodal circulation today (61). There have been profound shifts in methods of communication, changing how poetry circulates and necessitating, in turn, new ways of approaching the genre.

In multimedial forms contemporary poetry is returned to its oral roots and combines different artistic practices in new ways. Against the conventional generic boundaries of the arts, contemporary poetry can be considered both a spatial art and a temporal one.[4] It can be read in spatial terms through the presence of words on the page, pointing to the use of blank space, and is highlighted in new media by poetry that takes particular advantage of its visual aspects: concrete or digital poetries that include words in motion, animated texts, electronic formatting, and hypermedia that do new things within the visual realm.[5] Oral performances, in turn, may call attention to the text's unfolding in time and reinforce its associations with sound and music. There is a long tradition of live oral performance of poetry through bards, griots, the often improvised competitions of *payadores* or *decimistas*,[6] and more formal poetry readings; the late twentieth century has extended this through poetry slams, spoken word events, rap, hip-hop, dub poetry, *polipoesía* ("polypoetry"), recorded *acciones de arte* ("art actions"), and myriad means of accessing these. Much of the experience with poetry that our students bring to class comes through their knowledge of it off the page, in formats that may not involve reading. In his consideration of interartistic dialogues or dissonances, Daniel Albright notes, "speech is a game with sounds just as music is a game with sounds" (176). He examines how music has been analyzed in terms of speech, using linguistic terms such as *phrase, theme*, and *subject* (163), while oral performances of poetry often rely on musical terms: *rhythm, timbre, volume, tone, intensity, duration*, and *resonance*. These terms, among others, can be introduced to students to facilitate the shift from the act of listening to the interpretation of what they hear.

Albright's comparative study of the arts offers other terminology that is useful for thinking about how poetry in performance interacts with other genres. Having used the adjective *multimedial* to describe works that "comprise elements of two or more media," he also proposes that a spectator may generate "intermedial" artworks through attention to elements of different media in a particular work or performance (209). This is another way to conceptualize what happens when we consider poetry off the page. Voice, sound, and movement place the poem amidst different media—music, visual arts, drama, film—and appeal to multiple senses and, perhaps, to diverse audiences. Examining different kinds of performances of poetry opens a range of possibilities. Using these ideas to approach canonical poets, for example, teachers and students might consider how the Argentine poet Juan Gelman's recitations of the Nicaraguan Rubén Darío's poetry change our understanding of or reaction to poems (e.g., "A Roosevelt" ["To Roosevelt"]). Does it matter if we first hear Gelman reciting his own work? And how does Gelman's performance of his own work (e.g., "Juan Gelman—Sefiní") differ from that of the actor Dario Grandinetti, who recites the beginning of Gelman's "Sefiní" ("It'sover") in *El lado oscuro del corazón* ("The Heart's Dark Side")? Embedding the poem in a film adds music and visual images to the voicing of the text, makes the poetic speaker a character, and locates the poem as part of a narrative, but Grandinetti does not sound like Gelman; his timing and intonation also change how we hear the poem ("Juan Gelman—Sobre la poesía").

Each of these performances is a positioning of a text. The time and place, who is speaking and why, alter how a poem is understood. Including performances of a poem in our analysis of how they work or what they do demonstrates how there is more than language creating meaning here. The meter we hear in our silent reading may come to the forefront in performance or it may be altered. This is especially true when poetry is accompanied by music. Many poems have been transformed into songs, and sometimes their origin is then forgotten. A well-known example that is useful for teaching about performance history can be found in the poetry of José Martí. The complex history of the adaptation of his *Versos sencillos* ("Simple Lines") as the song "Guantanamera" has been chronicled in a series of articles by María Argelia Vizcaíno. Charting the origins of the melody from the nineteenth century, Vizcaíno finds that Joseíto Fernández adapted and popularized the tune, featuring the refrain "guantanamera, guajira guantanamera" 'girl from Guantánamo, country girl from Guantánamo' on his 1930s radio program. Julián Orbon set the Martí verses to the traditional country music of the *guajira* in the late 1950s, creating a nationalist anthem in Cuba, where Martí is a revered revolutionary hero. Orbon's former pupil Héctor Angulo then introduced the song to Pete Seeger, who recorded it on his 1963 album *We Shall Overcome*. In the context of the Cold War and the Cuban missile crisis, Seeger "transformed" the song into an "international peace anthem," and other artists covered the song during the 1960s and beyond (Cheal). In 1973 the Cuban singer and composer Sara González, part of the Nueva Trova ("New Song") movement, reappropriated *Versos sencillos*, abandoning the well-known tune and choosing a different amalgamation of poems from the *Versos sencillos* collection for her version of "Yo soy un hombre sincero" ("I Am a Sincere Man") on an LP named after the book, thereby reasserting the poem's provenance. David Cheal has observed how more recent adaptations appropriate the tune; it is used in chants by British soccer fans and in recycling ads in Sweden. In these cases the poetry, along with its Cubanicity, has been abandoned and it becomes simply a catchy tune. Poetry, music, world events, and changing cultural foci interact in this chain of re-creations of the Cuban poet's work as elements are cut and pasted by different artists in diverse circumstances for assorted ends.

Albright discusses figures of consonance and dissonance in multimedial works, and these terms can illuminate how diverse performances work as they are put into contact with other modes of communication. Consonance occurs when the distinct media elements in a performance come together to fortify the text. When Orbón adapted Martí's poetry to a popular form of music that allowed it broad circulation, the music and its performance reinforced the text. Seeger's work was consonant with the text to some extent but resituated the song as part of his effort to recognize rather than reject Cuba and what it came to represent in the 1960s in the United States. González perhaps wrote her music against the international popularity of "Guantanamera," reclaiming the *Versos sencillos* for a Cuban audience. Cheal's examples of recent adaptations of the music are illustrative of dissonance, for the new lyrics and contexts for the song create performances that undermine or reconfigure a well-known combination of poetry and music. The concepts of consonant and dissonant elements can be applied to the analysis of many types of multimedia presentations of a poem.

By including aspects of how poetry is performed or practiced in our pedagogy we see how it can enact, embody, or voice various identities and meanings. We also find examples of how poetic voices can merge with political voices and can capture a different audience and validate marginalized speakers and experiences (Perloff, *Differentials* 28). Students can see this in performances of late-twentieth-century poetry such as the video "Santiago Punk."[7] Carmen Berenguer's poem, a critique of the neoliberal economic boom in 1980s Chile, is propelled by a martial beat; it begins: "Punk Punk / War, war. Der Krieg, Der Krieg" (11). The strong rhythm is reinforced through line break and repetition, but in the recording of Berenguer reading it on *SoundCloud*, she works the beat in unexpected ways. She introduces the poem in a moderate, conversational tone of voice but raises the pace and pitch for the reading, her swift speech and flat affect conveying not emotion but a sense of inevitability. If there is a feeling of desperation, it comes from us, not from her performance. The impersonal quality is reinforced by electronic music interlaced with piano that repeats fragmented melodic phrases. The music is punctuated with bells and electronic sounds creating a kind of random counterpoint as Berenguer moves through her text, voicing the numbered parts (1–4) with barely half-breathed pauses. The reading ends with applause (from an audience at the recorded event) followed by an added cacophony of voices and sounds from the accompanying electronics in the piece.

Since a written text is available in this case, one might teach the poem using the text first and then listen and respond to the recorded version using some of the listening exercises included in my appendix. Rather than creating a unified reading or understanding of the poem, approaching it in this way teases out some of the complex references and implications of language, image, meaning, and sound relative to Chilean (and late-twentieth-century global) modernity, politics, and history. How does Berenguer's performance of the poem reinforce or alter our understanding of it? The goal of this combination of reading and listening in my classes is not to master the poem (to *rematarlo* ["finish it off"]) or to paraphrase it in prose, but to come to a collective understanding of the things it does and doesn't do: how it works.

Contemporary performances of poetic texts by Luis Bravo, of Uruguay, or by Rojo Córdova or Rocío Cerón, of Mexico, offer additional rich possibilities for discovery of the ways in which poetry works. The 2009 Medellín International Poetry Festival in Colombia featured a performance by Bravo of his poem "Hipogrifo" ("Hippogriff"), now available on *YouTube* ("Hipogrifo").[8] Although there is a video component to the performance, the mythical beast of the title (likely familiar to listeners from many cultures from its appearance in the *Harry Potter* series) is created more through undulating sound than through visual image. Bravo's resonant voice is full of affect and multiple tonalities as he draws out the phonetics of the poem's words, elongating vowels and using the microphone to emphasize the acoustics. Andean panpipes and minimal electronic hums and echoes combine with a series of natural images to harmonize contemporary and ancient themes. There are shifting dynamics in this video recorded version of Bravo's presentation of the poem: his voice gets louder and accelerates about two-thirds of the way through, with added percussion. Rather than act as an instrument in a mechanized series, as in Berenguer's voicing, Bravo's mellifluous voice calls attention to itself and to the language he uses. The contrast between the performances of the two poets is illuminating; in both cases, the messenger's voice is crafted to fit the message and is consonant with it.

Córdova offers another remarkable style of aural performance that creates a poem vastly different from one that would exist on the page. He activates his poem about the multiplicity of Mexico, "Dos mil Mex" ("Two Mill Mex"), by describing the country's geography in a steady, animated tone, looking at the camera—but after a few lines he accelerates and takes off, picking up speed with the apparently infinite variety he enumerates.[9] Listeners may respond to his verbal prowess with shock, amusement, or consternation, but they will react. Even if we cannot understand all the words or the eminently Mexican references, we respond viscerally to the vocal pace and the determination to pack in as much as possible, so that hearing the poem becomes quite different from reading what would be a long catalogue. The multifaceted allusions to features of national identity in this poem also demonstrate how different audiences are interpellated by a poetic performance; there are no explanatory notes here, so Mexican listeners will hear this with much more detail and a different level of comprehension than will those unfamiliar with its context.

Cerón offers a salient contrast to Córdova in both her style of poetry and her performances of it.[10] Her collection *Diorama* presents poems that are much less narrative than her compatriot Córdoba's and take different shapes on the page to express "un soplo interior" 'an internal gust of wind,' as the epigraph by Hélio Oiticica expresses it.[11] Cerón's translator, Anna Rosenwong, describes the poet's work as "not plainly legible," "stubbornly elusive, and at times outright hallucinatory" (7). It is clear from the outset that we are not going to understand this poetry in a conventional or logical way. How do we respond to these poems? We might begin by gathering information: investigating the title, "Diorama," which may refer to a miniature scene, a museum display, or a spectacular picture—all visual references that have some link to representation. Rosenwong encourages readers to train their ears to the "text's private language," to "surrender to its associative and auditory insights," for she thinks that "sound provides the surest foothold amid the rush of cascading images" (7). A selection from the volume has been made into a video poem with the collaboration of Nómada, a Mexican video artist ("Diorama"). The text that is performed in this segment appears in the section "Sobrevuelo" ("Flyover") and is the third part of "Anotaciones sobre bricolage o lo nacional telúrico" ("DIY Instructions or the National Telluric"). Again, students might ponder what these titles suggest about this performance piece: is it an overview, an aerial view of the terrestrial nation? These poems are bricolages that unite varied referents.

We see this in the first few lines of the poem (quoted here from the text, translated by Rosenwong, which diverges from the video version):

Fritura de callo de hacha y calamares, salsa romana.
Un toque de eneldo.

Sobre el pequeño portavasos un rosé medianamente frío.
Alzo la vista, al frente un tentáculo se extiende: (31)

Fried scallops and squid, salsa romana
a touch of dill.
On the small coaster a cool rosé.
I look up, a tentacle reaches toward me:

Cerón reads the poem in a matter-of-fact tone, conversationally, im-
parting information like the list of ingredients that initiates this performance. The only sound that accompanies her voice is the irregular pluck-
ing of a bass. The aural effect changes as new locations are introduced in
the poem, bringing together the regions of Latin America in a "sinfonía en
castellano que corteja la herida en el oído" 'a Spanish symphony that woos
the wounded ear' (*Diorama* 32). The sonority is in the written line itself,
in the assonance in the emphasized *i*: "sinfonía," "herida," "oído." As the
poem continues, repetitions of the consonant *c* create a musical structure:
"costa del Caribe" 'Caribbean coast'; "carda" 'card'; "cuerpo" 'body';
"coraza" 'armor,' leading to "un continente a pedazos" 'a continent in
tatters' in which "todo el castellano vuelve a ser patria" 'Spanish returns
to its homeland.' The accompanying visual images are of a mouth eating,
a back, a shoulder with arm extended—all surfaces for the play of tex-
tures created by colored light and language. There is a cut to a cityscape:
a bridge, a fence. The last image is a female torso, illuminated by blue
light, that fragments and explodes into bits or stars at the line "como se
temple una nación antes de ser entregada al tirano" 'the way a nation is
warmed up before being handed over to a dictator,' the penultimate line
of the performed poem. The combination of visual images and voice calls
attention to central concepts in the poem: the point of view, how we see,
and the constructed nature of diverse images. The visual elements of this
performance reinforce these ideas in terms of both style and content.

Instructors might encourage students to listen experimentally, noting
what they see and hear over several viewings. Students may discover that
a particular line resonates for them or even unsettles them; yet they must
be permitted to tolerate incomprehension.[12] They may examine the text,
look up any words that they do not know, and think about associations
between images, words, sounds, or ideas in the poem. Instructors might
ask: What adjectives come to mind to describe the experience of reading or
listening to this poem? Where do you think the poem takes place (can you
imagine who would say this, where)? What do you know about the larger

context for this poem or performance? Cerón has said in an interview that *Diorama* is a "listening book; that is to say, a book that is influenced by the voices, images, and truths of a nation, a continent" ("Poking at Memory"). How does this information change your understanding of the poem? We hear the poet's voice in this recorded segment; is it individual or could it represent a collage of voices (another possible layer of the "bricolage" of this section's title)? As a composite work of art, this assemblage of images and voice loosens our hold on meaning and we learn to accept incomprehensibility. Like the other examples here, encouraging students to respond viscerally lets them use their own experiences to come to an understanding of how these elements work together.

My final example of contemporary poets and performers is "¿Lo oíste? Poesía estereo" ("Did You Hear It? Poetry in Stereo"), a spoken word performance by Argentines Sebastián Kirzner and Diego Arbit.[13] These two performers use loud and dramatic intonation, insistent voices, and emphatic gestures in this dialogic reading before the camera. They alternate lines to address their viewer-listeners, at times speaking together:

[KIRZNER.] ¿Oíste?
[ARBIT.] ¿Estás de alumno también?
[KIRZNER.] ¿Vas a clases?
[ARBIT.] ¿Cursas materias?
[KIRZNER.] ¿Entregas a tiempo tus parciales?

[ARBIT.] ¿Oíste acaso el sonido del poema
[KIRZNER.] en un cuarto lleno de gente,
[ARBIT.] en una casa llena de gente,
[KIRZNER.] en un aula,
[ARBIT.] una mugrienta sala llena de gente,
[KIRZNER.] ¿oíste acaso el sonido del poema?
[ARBIT.] ¿Lo oíste?
[BOTH.] Yo lo oí. ("¿Lo oíste?")

Did you hear?
Are you a student too?
Do you go to class?
Study subjects?
Turn your midterms in on time?

Did you by chance hear the sound of the poem
in a room full of people
in a house full of people

did you by chance hear the sound of the poem?
Did you hear it?
I heard it. (my trans.)

"¿Lo oíste?" is an interrogatory, metapoetic poem about listening. Its performance adds a new dimension to the concept of conversational poetry by asking us to interact with it: "¿Y vos?" 'and you?' The fact that the implied listener here is a student makes this an eminently teachable poem about aural comprehension. It is a striking example of how poetry circulates in the twenty-first century: it is recorded in public places or at home; published in blogs, on Web pages, and on *YouTube*, where people can respond to the work and each other; posted on the street, in metro stations, in bookstores, bars, and parks—all situations that have the potential to alter the balance of power between traditional producers and consumers of poetry.

Any of these works (and others that you find) might be incorporated into a range of classes according to topic (the city, gender, the idea of Latin America today, as well as courses that focus on genre), as points of connection between earlier and more recent poetry and performance, or perhaps in an introduction to literature as a sampling of what is being done currently in this realm. The Internet, slams, and oral performances often deconstruct the idea of the book, stimulate interartistic or transcultural dialogues, and return poetry to its oral roots, doing something new with this orality and taking advantage of the technological possibilities that greatly extend the reception of poetry. In the process they shift the emphasis in their reception to collective audiences who may respond in a range of ways to these works. Joining poetry and performance in our teaching also gets students jazzed about a genre that they may previously have seen as too obtuse, antiquated, or academic to enjoy.

Notes

1. The memorable subtitle of one of Alice Fulton's books.

2. This is an argument I make throughout *Beyond the Page*, my book on poetry and performance.

3. For a compelling example of what might happen in a performance of *Altazor*, listen to Juan Angel Italiano's voicing of canto 7 ("Altazor").

4. In *Iconology: Image, Text, Ideology*, W. J. T. Mitchell offers a detailed exploration of historical dialogues on contrasts between literature and the visual arts in Western thinking through the work of Nelson Goodman, Ernst Gombrich, Gotthold Lessing, and Edmund Burke.

5. One recent exploration of this field that circulates as an open-access download is *Poesía y poéticas digitales / electrónicas / tecnos / new-media en America Latina*, edited by Luis Correa-Díaz and Scott Weintraub.

6. *Payadores* are popular singers and composers of verses, who often perform with guitar and compete with one another. *Decimistas* recite or sing *décimas*, or ten-line improvised poems.

7. Carmen Berenguer is associated with the 1980s generation in Chile, who began to publish during Pinochet's dictatorship. She has published twelve books of poetry, some of which have been translated, and has been president of the Sociedad de Escritores de Chile; her work received the Pablo Neruda Ibero-American Poetry Award in 2008.

8. Bravo has published more than eight books of poetry, several smaller works, various recordings and DVDs, and several collections of literary essays and anthologies. Many of his poems have been translated.

9. Rojo Córdova is the performance name of José Guillermo Córdova Mendoza. He is a slam poet who teaches workshops on spoken word throughout Mexico. I present a longer analysis of Córdova's work in *Beyond the Page*, including a written version of the poem in the book's appendix.

10. Cerón has published a variety of books, several of which have been translated. She has performed her visual poetry in multiple venues and exhibited at the Bienal de Poesía Visual three times. She coordinates the Taller Permanente de Poesía in the creative writing program at the Universidad Claustro de Sor Juana in Mexico.

11. All translations of *Diorama* are by Anna Rosenwong.

12. Thanks to Celia Bland of Bard College for some of these ideas that are adapted from her presentation on poetry and pedagogy at the 2016 meeting of the American Comparative Literature Association.

13. Sebastián Kirzner has published three books and numerous online performances. He also edited *2017: Nueva poesía contemporánea* ("New Contemporary Poetry").

APPENDIX: How to Listen to a Performance of a Poem

When you first listen to or view a performance, make a list of what you see and hear.

Where did your understanding begin? What stands out the most or surprises you? What particularly resonates with you or bothers you?

Who is speaking? Describe what the speaker sounds like (vocal tone, quality, and affect; tempo; gender, age, national or racial identifiers, etc.). Does the messenger's voice fit the message?

How does the speaker relate to the text? Is the speaker the author? Does the speaker simply read the poem or set it up? Is the speaker alone? If there are other performances available, contrast these with that of the author. You might speculate about any differences in the way we listen to authors reading their work and the way we listen to performers.

Are there other sounds in the performance? What are they and how do they affect the performance overall? Do you hear the performer's breath? How do these sounds work with or against particular elements of the poem?

Are there visual elements (such as a setting, gestures, costumes, video)? How do these interact with other elements?

What sound devices do you hear in the language itself (rhythm, rhyme, alliteration, repetition, etc.)? Does this performance emphasize or change some of the sonorous qualities?

If you know the textual version of the poem, does the performance tell us something new about the poem? Are there ways that you might think of it as a translation of the written work? Why or why not?

How does the performance organize and control time? Is it different from the text?

Does the poem's visual appearance on the page alter the way we hear it? How does the performer convey or elide punctuation and line breaks?

How does the performance context change our understanding of the poem? For example, what happens when a conventional verse form such as a sonnet is presented in a wildly experimental context, or how might the place where the poem is performed alter the way we hear it?

Thinking about a particular performance, what questions can you add to this list that would help you to listen to this poem?

Part III

Poetic Contexts
and the Idea
of Latin America

Fernando J. Rosenberg

Teaching Poetry and Human Rights

The association between poetry and human rights is sometimes endorsed at poetry festivals, in anthologies, in classes, and in other contexts where poetry is disseminated to a broader public. It is meant to signal a poetic concern with issues of social justice in general, the poetic utterance fleshing out the abstract universality of human rights. Poetry here would be seen as an expression of a poetic persona speaking from the position or on behalf of victims, later presented in a pedagogical setting as an illustration of the political stance of poetry in search of a reader who would be sympathetic to such a plight. Poetry would elicit affective responses in what might appear as an aesthetic of altruism, a sympathetic solidarity at a distance, only to consolidate already established hierarchies of cultural circulation (archetypally, in the academy in the United States, from a Southern site of poetic production amidst injustice to a Northern site of reception, safely immune and dissociated). We can find poetry concerned with social justice in all epochs and poetic traditions, but this convergence of human rights and poetry, albeit somewhat inevitable when bringing poetry to a literature and human rights class or when bringing up human rights in a Latin American literature class, obscures what might be a richer conversation about possible points of intersection between poetic and human rights discourses. It reduces the multiple manifestations of poetry to mimetic expressiveness, and of human rights to a static and objective label that can be transparently applied to a variety of situations, simplifying history, politics, and traditions into a drama of victims and victimizers.

To avoid the pitfall sketched above, teachers need to resituate the idea of human rights, moving beyond a "magisterial" understanding (to use Feisal Mohamed's term) by which human rights officiate as a master language into which the voices of distant suffering others are translated (and often lost in translation) and their situations, abstracted from local and global factors (e.g., cultural specificity, colonial history, etc.), assessed on a scale of human rights attainment.[1] In what follows, I suggest different ways to explore this intersection, which I have tried in human rights and literature classes and in Latin American poetry classes at the college level, and that are adaptable to different levels of instruction starting with advanced high school literature or human rights classes. The conceptual subtleties and their historical implications can be opened up for deeper critical reflection at upper-level and graduate Latin American literature or literature and human rights seminars. In either case, inviting students to examine their own position as readers when approaching a poetic voice expressing or denouncing oppression or suffering is a fundamental exercise pertaining both to the ethics of reading and to the formation of global citizens.

While poetry is nothing if not discourse, the discursive quality of human rights as a historically determined site of utterance is often naturalized. Restoring the rhetorical, discursive matter of human rights is thus basic to truly investigating its synergies with poetic discourse, while foregrounding through these connections the powers of language. Teachers can start complicating the oversimplified approaches sketched above by examining central traits of the discourse of human rights through its most disseminated document, the 1948 Universal Declaration of Human Rights (United Nations). The idea of a declaration, to begin with, points to the central poetic problem of authority, as the word performatively creates the authority of its statement, while the idea of the universal posits this authority as transcending any specific site of utterance (cultural, historical, etc.) and field of applicability. The postulation of humanity in the term *human rights* imagines a possible commonality predicated on an idea of inherent dignity lying beyond insurmountable differences. Such an idea of dignity is legally expressed through a notion of rights, which implies a socially recognizable entitlement paradoxically endowed to all, regardless of social circumstances. In this essay I offer a minimal unpacking of these fundamental notions, which could be further examined in a classroom setting in their fuller historical and philosophical extension, in order to highlight implications that are often taken in toto and at face value. Every one of these notions might be presented in classes at different levels and in more or less abstract, theoretically informed, or concrete ways, in productive dialogue with different poetic texts.

How, one might begin by asking, does a poetic text render universal its particular voice? How does it build its authority, and what kind of authority is it? Is there some inherent dignity in human existence posited by the text, and, if so, how is it articulated? Let us suggest that, while the human rights document starts by declaring its universality and concealing the multitude of voices and historical processes that contributed to its making, poetry encounters the universal only by assuming a radical singularity—the poem being a singular language that might or might not be identifiable as that of a speaking subject—but that it is ultimately the display of a poetic persona. Thus the ethics of human rights would intersect with that of poetry if we agree that "[t]he ontological affirmation always inherent in the 'reading' of a poem is to this effect: Here is a person" (Grossman 309); but, it might be added, "only one who hears the voice of humankind in the poem's solitude can understand what the poem is saying" (Adorno, "On Lyric Poetry" 38).

Even though poetry is a language of singularity, of an "inalienable" subjectivity (to use a key word from the preamble to the Universal Declaration), it doesn't follow that poetic discourse necessarily celebrates the modern reification of the sovereign individual. (A good antidote for this misconception is Nicanor Parra's "Soliloquio del individuo" ["The Individual's Soliloquy"; *Obra gruesa* 48].) Certainly, poetry cannot be reduced to dramatic monologue, as the masks the poet adopts might vary (e.g., voicing other singular or plural subjects, rendering language impersonal, etc.). But, even in those cases in which poetry cannot be easily identified with a personal utterance, poetic language reaches a level of universality by stressing a particular expression, embodying a paradox also recognized in the ethics of human rights. That is, equality, the radically democratic value that is articulated in the preamble and article 1 of the declaration, is only fulfilled in recognition of this nontransferable, unrepeatable uniqueness of every human being. However, while human rights intend to recognize inalienable subjectivity by constituting a person endowed with rights, by exploring the multitude of voices and perspectives implicitly inhabiting a subject socially constituted in language, modern poetry underscores the intimate foreignness of personal expression.

While human rights claims strive for results against which their efficacy should be measured, a strong tradition in aesthetic philosophy suggests that the power of poetry is precisely the power to withdraw from power. That is, poetry makes room for a language that does not concern itself with acting in the world and thus resists being reduced to a means to an end. But this difference is somewhat suspended when we think of poetic and human rights discourses as both conveying a particular kind of performative utterance—which can be, following Susan Stewart, akin to a promise. "I propose that the sound of poetry is heard in the way a promise is heard," she writes (104), interestingly locating the promising aspect of language in sound and on the side of the audience, or perhaps up in the air, so to speak: the linguistic environment itself is the site of a covenant. A promise can be "called on, called to mind, in the unfolding present," continues Stewart, so any poetry (even the most hermetic) entails a "good faith in intelligibility under which language proceeds and by which we recognize each other as speaking persons" (105). This description of poetic language might be directly applied to human rights, noting that inherent dignity is, like the inalienable particularity of poetic diction, realized only when socially recognized. This ethics of human rights is what Hannah Arendt defined as the foundational right to have rights (297), which entails claiming rights, thus assuming a primary right of speech.

This is how we can understand the notion of dignity, which is often accepted as a given with unquestioned enthusiasm as well as criticized for glossing over specific conditions of existence, different cultural traditions, and so on. This concept can acquire exclusionary and profoundly non-egalitarian meaning, as, for example, when the dignity of the "vanquished races" is monumentally celebrated as foundational to a hierarchical ideal of national identity; or when a certain patriarchal idea of virginal, maternal, domestic, sentimental purity is posited as pertaining to women's dignity, and so on. However, beyond the sacralization that this notion might entail, a notion of dignity that is akin to both the ethics of human rights and the ethics of poetic discourse relies on the possibility of speech, and this speech must be heard and accounted for. This is a notion of dignity that also encompasses agency, as it is only realized in tandem with civil, social, and cultural rights, dialogically in tension with a particular historical situation.

In order to address the complexity of these concepts as they might unfold in poetic texts, I will first offer examples that refer to the condition of slavery, central to the plight of human rights as it represents a total commodification of human life, antithetical to human dignity and to freedom and autonomy as principles that form the backbone of modern subjectivity. The case of the black slave and poet from Cuba Juan Francisco Manzano might be introduced in class to exemplify the paradoxical relation of poetry and human rights from the standpoint of a colonial subaltern subject during the international abolitionist movement—a central development in the pre-1948 discourse of human rights. Manzano's body of poetry illustrated to his abolitionist sponsors the potential of a "Negro poet" (79–80), as the author was introduced, erasing his individual name, when the collection was first published, to write despite his condition, and to do so in highbrow neoclassical and Romantic keys, thus exemplifying the free play of the imagination as an achievement of a universal human spirit measured by European standards. The dignity of the slave, to which poetry was supposed to bear witness, is postulated as transcending its social condition of existence, in an operation parallel to the 1948 Universal Declaration's statement that this dignity is inherent—that is, always potential even if not historically realized. A poem by the contemporary Cuban poet of African descent Nancy Morejón, "Amo a mi amo" ("I Love My Master") might be brought into this conversation and presented as running counter to the idea of inherent human dignity understood, as the abolitionists did, transhistorically and as an abstract universal (196–99). In this poem, written from the viewpoint of a slave who is the master's chosen mistress, racial and gender difference is a necessary condition for speaking of common humanity. This humanity is expressed in the midst of injustices in the context of which a blank-slate, abstract version of universal humanity would only be a form of historical denial. Furthermore, for Morejón, the conditions for this inherent dignity to be materialized do not lie, as they did for Manzano, in the possibility of individual freedom and highbrow artistic expression, nor even in the claim for rights particular to her gender, ethnicity, or class. Rather, they lie in a class-based national, anticolonial movement that would be realized, for this poet, in the Cuban Revolution (as stated for example in her poem "Mujer negra" ["Black Woman"; 202–03]). The problems suggested by Manzano's and Morejón's poetry might serve as an introduction through poetic texts to the classical socialist critique (already found in Karl Marx) of the narrative of human rights as ultimately endorsing liberal capitalism.

Following this line of inquiry, instructors might present another poem by Morejón, suitably entitled "Persona," as the speaker is one who searches for a specific version of common humanity, that of the black woman across geographies and throughout history (204–07). A central aspect of the ethics of modern lyric poetry is manifested in this poem, since the personal, the most genuine place of the poet's search for what is common or universal, is both intimate and alien (the modernist alienation famously expressed by Arthur Rimbaud as "Car Je est un autre" ["For I is someone else"; 374–75]). To introduce in class the perils of the authorial fallacy in the context of the lyric genre might be frustrating and prove insufficient, as lyric poetry is overwhelmingly a language of the first person. Instead, we should ask, What does the lyric first person stand for? In this question a central problem of poetic interpretation converges with the political dilemma of who is entitled to speak for whom, and in particular who is speaking when the narrative of human rights is activated. The fact that this first person is often, as in Morejón's poem, a series of masks, a persona, places this first person in perspective, allowing us to read the poetic first person as always being a construction of sorts. This constructed persona, even when speaking of strictly personal experiences, struggles with a language that, far from transparent, is pregnant with history. Rather than the anxiety of a disembodied male-dominated poetic voice reclaiming its authority by selecting, reinventing, and appropriating a lineage, Morejón's re-creation of the slave's poetic voice endows with authority the multiple singularities that had been silenced within her own Afro-Caribbean identity.

An incursion into the Peruvian poet Antonio Cisneros's book *Crónica del niño Jesús de Chilca* ("Chronicle of the Christ Child of Chilca") offers a complementary example. The book bears witness to the desertification brought about by capitalist development of the surrounding territory, to the destruction of communal living based on sustainable fishing and agriculture. The demise of the Chilca community entails the violent erasure of different layers of history and cultural traditions: the Incan past inscribed in the land and the infrastructure of the water canals, the communal system of economic exploitation of the fishery and the salt flats, and the Christian fabric of the town's identity. Poetically countering the epics of colonization and nation-building, the different voices Cisneros creates, all speaking in the first person, invite readers to imagine themselves as other, positioned in the situation of the soon-to-be-displaced inhabitant. No universalistic discourse of rights is to be found in this poetry, but human rights claims themselves always imply a problematic translation. However, while giving voice to subaltern subjects, the titular allusion to the chronicle, the textual genre of the conquest, points to the history of writing and speaking on behalf of the oppressed, which the poet enacts, as itself entangled in a violent appropriation of subaltern traditions.

Poetry can hardly counter the desertification that forced development and displacement have brought about, but as this material destruction is also an erasure of memory, poetry can represent an effort to counterwrite historical violence. This poetry reveals the plight of refugees, a foundational concern for the 1948 reinception of human rights from the European viewpoint, to be a common subaltern position in the postcolonial nation-states, even for those displaced within the jurisdictional confines of these states (a refugee status resulting not from war but from developmental policies). Moreover, by incorporating voices from a period of national history seemingly unrelated to the history of human rights, this poetry brings up rights issues that became apparent in the decades after the 1948 human rights declaration, such as group and cultural rights, indigenous and territorial rights, and the rights of nature, all saturated with colonial histories of violence.

Having opened up, in dialogue with both poetic traditions and Latin American historical predicaments, ideas concerning authority, universality, rights, and inherent dignity, teachers may need to confront more directly the notion of the human in human rights and in poetry. The essence of what is human can't be settled, and this undecidability, mobilized by regimes that deny humanity to certain subjects, is the reason human rights are needed, which is the paradox at the heart of human rights' very existence. Human rights performatively declare humans' worth in situations where this worth is in effect being disputed, thus involving a powerful act of political imagination—a radical hope against all odds. Modern and contemporary poetry take this undecidability at its core, to a degree that the question of who or what speaks in poetry becomes essential, without necessarily resorting to the aspirational humanistic tradition that supports human rights. Meaning in poetry is polysemic; the arbitrariness of the signifier, denied and overlooked by the necessarily instrumental use of the language of the law, carries positive semantic consequences. Poetry assumes in its language both bright and dark sides of the humanistic tradition, and it is this openness at many levels that fuels its political potential beyond any neatly predefined definition of the human.[2]

When studying poetry of an oppositional intent, or when teaching poetic expressions by marginalized and oppressed subjects, it makes sense to ask why, on the one hand, all oppressive regimes intend to silence even the relatively marginal voice of poets, who might not even have an overtly oppositional message; and why, on the other hand, poetry flourishes in unsuspected places, emerging from marginalized subjects, expressing what the subject cannot bear to remain silent about while enduring threats and hardship in the most desperate social contexts. Of course there are no clear-cut answers, but these questions are good entryways into the problem of poetic language in relation not only to overtly authoritarian language, but to any effort to co-opt language, to use it as a cover-up, to silence it, or in extreme cases to destroy its capacity to provoke and reveal opposi-tional views.

What is suspect for power is poetic practice as an activity of uncer-tain intentions, dealing with language in uncontrollable and obscure ways. If there is poetry, it is because something goes unheard, something that doesn't fit the allowed or available social discourses. Questions about this dynamic serve a related purpose, that is, to dispel once more the idea that poetry meets human rights only at the level of meaning: that poetry that does not denounce, bear witness, or testify must be conformist and nonpolitical. As Theodor Adorno has discussed in a seminal article ("On Lyric Poetry and Society"), a withdrawal from the public to the subjective might express a critical perspective regarding the pretense of a common and transparent language alleged by dominant ideologies, their false uni-versals reified as the only possible or desirable world.

However, this version of the poetic as a discourse of resistance also points to an expanded framework for human rights beyond a defense of the individual vis-à-vis sovereign totalitarian power. We might draw a paral-lel between poetry giving expression to what does not find closure—what remains powerless, marginalized, and oppressed, thus furnishing an ethical stance to multiple forms of life and experience—and the proliferation of human rights declarations, treaties, and conventions since the early 1980s (for example, the 1981 Elimination of Discrimination against Women, the 1982 Declaration on the Rights of Indigenous Peoples, or the 1989 Con-vention on the Rights of the Child). In this way, human rights discourses acquire a prospective outlook, informing claims and modes of social en-gagement and political subjectivities in the making. Every expansion of rights comes with a history of pervasive, systematic, overt, or intricate at-tempts to silence the experience of oppression. This is no romantic idealiza-tion of the margins, but rather an attempt to account for both the historical role of human rights as fostering conditions for speech when societal pow-ers constrain these voices to silence, and the nature of poetic utterance as a radical exploration of the possibilities of speech.

To offer one teachable case among many, we might trace a parallel between the rise of gendered and sexual subjectivities making right claims from the late 1980s on, representing a new generation of human rights, and the increasing presence of female and gay poetic voices in the Latin American context. The explosion of poetry written by women during dictatorships and under postdictatorial conditions in Chile and Argentina is an example (e.g., Carmen Berenguer and Diana Bellessi, among many others), not because it is necessarily concerned with particular women's rights issues, but because women's voices acquired a presence, fostering and expressing emerging subjectivities and pointing to unacknowledged forms of public and private oppression. That is, even poetic strategies that are not easily translatable into the language of human rights might be taught in social context of emerging right claims. Neobaroque poetry, for example, a label that acquired relevance through the 1980s into the 1990s, and that was applied to some of these emerging voices, appeals to theatrical excess, transformative masking, and a carnivalesque mixing of different linguistic levels and sociolects—strategies that were parallel to those deployed by an emerging queer public culture (as in the case of Nestor Perlongher). Poets of the neobaroque thus radically decenter the subject to a point not apparently compatible with right claims, while by the same token upsetting authoritarian or patriarchal values inherent in language. Indigenous writers, who have acquired increased visibility since the 1990s, don't need to denounce oppression for their poetry to counter hegemonic languages, values, and identities, thus opening a space for irreducible particularity and universal equality. Moreover, some of their texts (e.g., those by the Mapuche poet Elicura Chihuailaf or the K'iche' Maya poet Humberto Ak'abal) challenge frontiers not only between orality and writing but also between genres such as poetry, testimony, philosophy, and politics. Poetry works here and elsewhere not by fleshing out preconceived political agendas, or by personally expressing something akin to a right claim, but rather by exploring and articulating the border between the thinkable and the unthinkable where new forms of political subjectivity are forged.[3]

I have been suggesting different lines of inquiry for the intersection of poetry and human rights. But the association between these two discourses gained historical momentum as human rights became the ethical and metajuridical ground for the different Latin American transitions (from dictatorships, civil wars, and dirty wars characterized by a state that resorted to torture and disappearance of dissidents) to democratic governance.

Abuses that became the epitome of human rights violations at the peak of the global narrative of human rights in the 1980s and 1990s were built on previously legitimized state machineries of oppression, exclusion, and disappearance. Human rights violations such as illegal detention and confinement, systematic torture, and rape undermine the victim's privacy, self-worth, and dignity; torture and disappearance inflict pain and terror on the entire social body in an effort to disarticulate language itself as the place where the social bonds are forged.

Juan Gelman's poetry offers many pedagogical possibilities here. The poet and journalist has been associated with the human rights movement as an outspoken, left-wing political activist who became a victim and witness of the state of terror in Argentina in the 1970s and 1980s. As an activist and intellectual of a generation that came of age during the Cuban Revolution, he engaged in the political program of the revolutionary left. After the 1976 military coup, Gelman was persecuted and exiled, while his son was kidnapped and disappeared along with his pregnant wife. Gelman participated in human rights efforts by grassroots and civil organizations to uncover the truth and achieve a measure of justice that in Argentina included a truth commission, the prosecution of former members of the military junta, and the relentless search for the offspring of the disappeared by families favorable to the regime. This search led to the recovery of his son's remains and eventually—twenty-four years after the kidnapping—to the identification of the disappeared couple's daughter, Gelman's granddaughter, who had been adopted by a Uruguayan family.

In the classroom, the saga of Gelman's life can provide an opportunity to problematize, rather than take for granted, the association of his vast and varied poetic work with human rights. Indeed, Gelman's poetry works through topics of every one of these political and intellectual stages, his poetic persona articulating the intimate and the political, questioning and reflecting on his personal involvement in these waves of history. But, while Gelman's poetry needs to be read in these Latin American (specifically, Argentine) historical contexts, it can be hardly reduced to them. Another sense of history traverses it and raises the question, unavoidable for contemporary poets, of why one writes poetry at all, and of how to write it in the midst of disaster, after the hopes of social change opened by the revolutionary politics of the 1960s and 1970s spurred a brutal reaction against these changes. This is why many of Gelman's poems rehearse, some more explicitly than others, the ars poetica trope. Far from relying on an artistic grand gesture that animated poets from earlier generations, or on the ideal of revolutionary arts that served as an epochal answer to the question of the value of poetry, the activity of forging a poetic voice seems to be as fundamental as questioning the reason to do so, perhaps like the persistence of the will of survival itself in extreme conditions, based on a faith in human dignity that animates human rights claims.

Some of Gelman's earlier poems might be taught as poetry of solidarity across class and gender lines (such as "Pedro el albañil" ["Pedro the Bricklayer"] or "María la sirvienta" ["María the Servant"] from *Gotán* [*Poesía reunida* 78–79]), akin in tone and ethics to Vallejo's posthumous *Poemas humanos* (*Human Poems*). This solidarity is personal and affective, and thus the expressive sentimentality traditionally associated with lyric poetry flows from romantic love to political ideals. A poem in the same volume dedicated to Fidel Castro ("Fidel"; 86–87) is a case in point, as History as grand narrative is contrasted to more day-to-day history, and poetry is seen as akin to the latter, thus implicitly tempering the epic tone that the Cuban Revolution instilled in the political and sometime the poetic imagination, including that of young Gelman. The poetic persona figures as someone who wants to be heard and understood; he addresses the readers as his fellow humans, putting his thoughts out for their consideration. If there is something constant in this poetry, it is the dialogical ethos communicated in a minor key of simple lyrical address to a lovable and loving other, which, across his more than five decades of literary production, takes up different registers. Gelman's poetry collections written between 1976 and 1980, for example, address in a very intimate manner the drama of seeing many of his friends and fellow activists, as well as his own son, massacred and disappeared, while by the same token these texts pay homage to their commitment to social change.

Reading Gelman might complicate the historical isolation in which both human rights discourses and Latin American poetry are often studied at the college level, thus opening up the former to its often unacknowledged association with radical politics of social change, and the latter to intellectual dialogues with global ramifications, as this poetry is a repository of poetic traditions. It is important to trace Gelman's poetics back not just to other poetic traditions, but primarily to the Romantic impulse of poetic rebellion that animated the avant-garde (including the Latin American vanguards of the 1920s and 1930s) and that many social, artistic, and revolutionary movements of the 1960s and 1970s reactivated politically. The poem "Épocas" ("Ages"), from *Hechos*, traces analogies between Shelley's and Keats's idealism and the activism of the disappeared Argentine writers

Miguel Angel Bustos and Paco Urondo (*Poesía reunida* 369–70). Further-more, Gelman's overt Spanish classical (i.e., mystical Christian, Golden Age–baroque) poetic influence is activated to convey a global and deep historical vision informing an emancipatory and revolutionary aesthetics. For example, "CDLVI" suggests a continuity between the Spanish colo-nization of America and the war in Vietnam (*Cólera buey* 237–38); and "Comidas" ("Meals") from *Relaciones* compares the experience of hunger in the early Americas and in German concentration camps (*Poesía reunida* 337–39). The frequent association of love with political violence, in "Cosas" ("Things") or "Argelia" ("Algeria") in *Cólera buey* (180–81) and "Prob-lemas" ("Problems") in *Hechos* (*Poesía reunida* 373), is perhaps an entry point to analysis of these multilayered connections.

Another entryway into the relation between Latin American poetry and human rights might be to unfold one of the ethical conundrums of twentieth-century art: namely, what are the implications of the poetic fic-tionalization of that which cannot be communicated, the subjective expe-rience of those whom the writer and Holocaust survivor Primo Levi called "the drowned" (those who didn't survive being the only true witnesses to their atrocious conditions of existence [83–84])? We have touched upon the problem of appropriation, complicated here by the resort to proso-popoeia—the poet making the disappeared and death itself speak. In the work of Gelman and Morejón, we see how the position of the speaker does matter. Gelman's poetic task of speaking to and on behalf of the dead is supported by his personal life experience, and yet his poetry never ceases to problematize the degree to which truth speaking is articulated only through rhetorical devices and multiple levels of translation, so there is no unproblematic expression of personal experience, not even directly from the mouth of the victim.

Gelman's work might be contrasted to that of the Chilean poet Raúl Zurita, to give a sense of the broad range of possibilities that the intersec-tion explored here can afford. Zurita also has been inextricably linked to dictatorial rule, specifically to the 1973 coup that inaugurated Augusto Pinochet's seventeen-year-long tyranny in Chile, with its legacy of hu-man rights abuses. Zurita's *Purgatorio* (*Purgatory*), the first book in a Dantean trilogy including *Anteparaíso* (*Anteparadise*) and *La vida nueva* ("The New Life"), builds his poetic persona as an effort to absorb and incorporate into the body of writing the pain, alienation, and marginaliza-tion inflicted on his compatriots. Zurita transcends the expressive lyricism of the post-Romantic age and the ironic distance of the avant-garde poet, both of which permeate contemporary poetics. He does so by seemingly incarnating, in a gesture simultaneously self-effacing and self-aggrandizing, traditional poetic figures—bard, prophet, martyr, Christological figure, demiurge—that seem at odds with contemporary critical aesthetics, as if ideals of secular modernity had been hollowed by dictatorial brutality. Zurita's poems are often organized in series, with a circular, repetitive quality, in which an attention to the design of the poem on the page adds to the reader's sense that words are not just uttered or written but instead are inscribed and registered as central to the effort of recovering a community of shared meaning.

Far from the denunciatory stance of human rights against power abuse, Zurita's confrontation with a world destroyed, with history interrupted, with voices silenced, is a reimagination of the world through a grand act of poetic creation. In *Anteparaíso*, elements of the geography of the South American continent (ocean, seashore, mountains, desert, grasslands, the vast sky, etc.) are isolated and abstracted as recurring symbols, sites of historical reinscription, and are called upon as witnesses, victims, and perpetrators of a historical disaster. History itself is brought to trial in Zurita's poetry (an operation that Hannah Arendt discusses with respect to the Nuremberg trials), as if every existing natural and human component has been tainted by injury and wrong, summoned in a final poetic judgment.

La vida nueva convenes a dissonant chorus of testimonials in which past, present, and future, memories and visionary dreams, converge. But if poetry invokes the testimonial register, it is no longer to accuse and to demand retribution (as Pablo Neruda did in *Canto general*), given that the place of moral and judicial authority is itself vacant. Whole countries and territories appear as tombs buried in unsolvable, unrealized dreams, waiting to be redeemed or condemned; or perhaps ships sailing through the history of another middle passage (275–83). Zurita hints at a history in suspension, no longer aspiring to any sense of continuity or progress, perhaps because continuity itself is a betrayal of those whose rights have never been upheld by the violent foundation of Latin American nation-states. However, claims continue to be made and are inscribed in the book; certain hopes continue to instill a social imagination even after other hopes are debunked, as if this writing testified to an obstinate persistence that is another name for both poetry and human rights.

Of course, we can find powerful denunciation of human rights abuses in every art form. But perhaps the weight of personal accounts of the suffering inflicted by oppressive regimes whose power is based on the continuity of silence—the witnesses' need to speak up against all odds, the victims' need to be heard and to share experiences — points to associations between human rights testimony and certain basic characteristics of the poetic that the instructor might underscore, thus challenging the class to move beyond a superficial and thematic appreciation of these discourses. Using some of the texts suggested in this essay, among others, the instructor might point out how the deeply personal voice is always already social, even at its most opaque; how language is incarnated in the body through diction and the voice; how the weight of silence punctuates in meaningful ways what is expressed; how memorialization and naming are means of social inscription; how words might be a primary means of transcending suffering and death. Poetic production might be an effort to reclaim the human need to speak, to think, to trust, to convey truth when language is mobilized to distort, obscure, and cover up, thus repairing the violence inflicted on language so that it regains not only freedom but also its polysemy.[4] In its dialogue with human rights, poetry should be revealed as being more than a mere personal expression; rather, it is a truth statement about an experience in the world, the space of an ongoing emergence of an ethical subject.[5]

Notes

1. The "magisterial" human rights framework responds to abstract universals that, although capable of working for emancipatory aims, also reinforce a set of established cultural hierarchies of race, gender, class, or geopolitical location (mainly separating the West from the rest).

2. The reason for the expansion and continuous transformation of the agenda of human rights in certain Latin American situations (i.e., departing from a liberal defense of individual integrity and freedom under dictatorships, and becoming a powerful tool in defense of the right to culture, language, and economic and legal agency of indigenous, displaced, landless peoples) needs to be conceptualized in a historical arc in which the advent of human rights unleashes the indelible memory of foundational injustice going back to colonial times and the perpetuation of coloniality (its economic structures, its powerful elites, its racial ideologies, etc.) inscribed at the very center of national institutions and identity.

3. This line of reasoning allows us to explore a contemporary emergence of the rights of nonhuman entities (such as animal rights and the rights of nature) as an attempt to address present and impending ecological crisis and massive biological extinction. The constitutions of Ecuador and Bolivia (2008 and 2009, respectively) include provisions to defend the rights of nature, which intersect with and follow the emergence of indigenous rights — not because indigenous cultures would be more in touch with nature, but because human sovereignty and centrality assumed both in human rights and in modern nation-states is complicit with the Western colonization of nature, with the approach to nature as an immutable yet inexhaustible resource.

4. In her fundamental book about Argentine dictatorial rule, Marguerite Feitlowitz studies the uses of language to impose terror, to silence potential dissidence.

5. Poetry's relation to truth is not circumstantial—it is limited neither to a referential use of language nor to an expressive function—as there is no false poetry, because in poetry signs and their negation or erasure share the same space. Dominique Combe provides a comprehensive historical discussion of different notions of poetic truth.

Juan G. Ramos

Comparative Arts, Coloniality, and Decoloniality: Teaching the Afro-Descendant Poetry of Antonio Preciado, Elcina Valencia, and ChocQuibTown

In this essay I explore the connection between the Ecuadorian poet Antonio Preciado and the Colombian poet Elcina Valencia as two contemporary examples of Afro-descendant poetry[1] from the broadly construed *gran comarca* or *palenques* of the Pacific coasts of Ecuador and Colombia.[2] Part of the relation I seek to establish is a set of poetic affinities linked to the particularities of Afro-Ecuadorians' and Afro-Colombians' historically situated experiences, as well as their affective ties to land, community, language, and customs that emerge from a sense of belonging to Afro-descendant communities in northwestern Ecuador and southwestern Colombia. Such poetic affinities seek to vindicate the oft-silenced perspectives and voices of Afro-descendants in the national imaginary and their seldom-represented perspectives in the arts, while bringing to the fore a set of relations to contemporary Afro-descendant social movements seeking to cast light on the historical and contemporary injustices and struggles that these racialized communities face.

I have designed a course on this subject, taught entirely in Spanish, for very advanced undergraduate students; however, this material can be adapted to suit the needs of students taking survey courses in a Spanish major or expanded into a full course for graduate students. This essay will deal specifically with three perspectives that I use to approach the teaching of Preciado, Valencia, and the contemporary Colombian musical group ChocQuibTown. The first perspective focuses on a reading of some of Preciado's and Valencia's poems that complement each other and connect with theoretical discussions of coloniality and decoloniality. As a second perspective, I discuss poems by the same authors that address questions of history, music, and Afro-diasporic identities. The third perspective establishes a relation with the concept of comparative arts to examine how, in the work of artists like Preciado, Valencia, and ChocQuibTown, Afro-descendants from *la gran comarca del Pacífico* construct intricate self-representations in both poetry and music. These modes of self-representation are informed by a historical and political understanding of how racialized subjection, which I understand as one important aspect of coloniality, can be undone or at least questioned (as part of the ongoing process of decoloniality) through the arts. This undoing or questioning through the arts is what I understand as a decolonial gesture that highlights the long history of subjugation and racialization, while making contemporary audiences aware of such embedded histories and relating them to contemporary struggles and movements such as Alianza Afro, Red de Jóvenes afroecuatorianos, Piel Africana, and Frente Afroecuatoriano PAIS in Ecuador and Movimiento Nacional Cimarrón, Proceso de Comunidades Negras (PCN), or the Red Nacional de Mujeres Afrocolombianas (Kambiri) on the Colombian side.

General Curricular Considerations

Poems that fall outside the purview of the Latin American poetic canon often come with less literary baggage than do works by canonical figures like César Vallejo or Nicolás Guillén. In the case of Vallejo or Guillén, the daunting issues an instructor faces include deciding among available annotated editions, translations, and scholarly studies, and choosing which representative poems to assign in order to give students a good sense of why these poets are often anthologized, cited, and widely discussed. In the case of Preciado or Valencia, the challenges are of a different sort: their poetry collections are not readily available in the United States, there is scant scholarly attention given to this type of contemporary poetry, and one must hunt for secondary sources that provide context for the work. Yet I would argue that it is precisely because of the lack of materials available to teach such poetry that teaching it becomes rewarding. Moving outside the canon also allows the instructor to establish links with other discourses emerging from interdisciplinary scholarship as well as popular culture.

A brief explanation of the type of academic institution where I teach, the way the Spanish major is set up, and how I have elaborated the syllabus for my seminar will help readers understand some of my decisions and demonstrate how they might adapt these strategies to their respective contexts. My home institution is a relatively small liberal arts college exclusively for undergraduates. Many of our majors choose Spanish for a variety of reasons, but often because it is relevant to their second major, and because they see Spanish as a language that might help them with their job prospects. So, while their primary interest may not be literary, when they come to my seminar they will have completed a composition course, a course on textual analysis, and a survey course on Spanish American literature from the colonial period to the twenty-first century. My senior seminar, entitled Topics in Modern Spanish and Spanish American Poetry, is set up to be transatlantic in nature while allowing enough flexibility for the instructor to decide how the course is taught and which poets to include. I have taught the course with iterations focusing on poetry and adaptation to music and film, on love poetry (in the broadest dimensions), and most recently on Spanish American poetry of resistance. This last version of the course, which has three distinct four-week units, will be at the center of the discussion that follows.

The first unit focuses on poetry as a mode of social and political resistance. To this end, I teach a wide selection of Vallejo's poetry from various points in his career. As a more contemporary counterpart, the course transitions to a discussion of Raúl Zurita's *Purgatory* in relation to the dictatorship in Chile. Needless to say, there are many poets who might well fit into this unit as potential examples, such as Ernesto Cardenal, Roque Dalton, Otto René Castillo, and Juan Gelman.

The second unit focuses on poetry as a mode of resisting patriarchy. We read selections by Alfonsina Storni, Juana de Ibarborou, Magda Portal, Violeta Parra, Josefina Plá, Idea Vilariño, and Ana Istarú. The emphasis in this unit is on giving students a sense of how poetic language evolved in its modes of expressing feminist ideas throughout the twentieth century. Certain poets such as Storni or Parra have found new audiences in the twenty-first century through music, film, and online platforms, and that cultural presence makes it easier for students to see these writers' relevance today.

The third and final unit of this course focuses on Afro-descendant poetry of resistance, which will be discussed in detail below.

On Teaching Poetry of Afro-Descendant Resistance and Decoloniality

Our study of Preciado and Valencia arises from examples of Afro-descendant poetry that embrace, and frequently complicate, the historical engagement of the arts in relation to Pan-Africanism, *négritude*, or *negrismo*. We begin by reading poetry by the Afro-Colombian poet Candelario Obeso as a nineteenth-century precursor to modern Afro-descendant poetry. We study poems by Guillén from *Motivos de son* ("Son Motifs") and *West Indies Ltd.* and explore their musical adaptation by Pablo Milanés for his album *Canta a Guillén* ("Songs to Guillén"). Discussing Guillén allows me to trace a particular moment in the poetics of the Americas in which a number of poets coalesce around some of the ideas emerging from the Harlem Renaissance, *négritude*, and Pan-Africanism. My intention in exposing students to Pablo Milanés's adaptation is twofold: to engage students with thinking about poetry through another medium (music) and to illustrate how poetry from a particular point in time—for Guillén, the 1930s—has different racial and political resonances decades later, here in the context of the Cuban Revolution. We also read select poetry from *Tuntún de pasa y grifería* (*Tom-Toms of Kinky Hair and All Things Black*), by Luis Palés Matos. As a counterpart to Guillén, Palés Matos evokes a different discussion on the emergence of *negrismo* and Afro-Antillean poetry while also eliciting questions about alleged ventriloquism or speaking for a racialized group and community to which the poet does not belong. Having this historical-poetic context, and reading additional poetry by Nicomedes Santa Cruz, Nancy Morejón, and the Afro-Ecuadorian poet Luz Argentina Chiriboga, allows the class to trace a certain genealogy of Afro-descendant poetics and to begin to engage with poetry as a means of social, political, and historical critique, particularly as resistance to patriarchy. We spend some time studying these poets because having them as background in reading more contemporary Afro-descendant poetry allows students to trace historical connections (e.g., engagements with re-thinking the role of slavery and emancipation through verse); link thematic continuities and echoes (e.g., finding a distinctive Afro-descendant voice, revalorizing the role and presence of Afro-descendants in the Americas,

and rethinking the role of both female and male agents in a collective reclaiming of land and reaffirmation of politicized identity politics); and underscore recurring preoccupations (e.g., searching for localized expressions
and references to denote Afro-descendant culture, such as dance, music, or
historical figures, and to connect it to the poetic arc of *négritude, negrismo,*
Afro-Antillean poetry, and contemporary Afro-descendant poetics).

Moreover, investigating such a range of Afro-descendant poets exposes,
questions, and seeks to dismantle the *longue durée* of racialized subjection,
and allows the instructor to introduce the theoretical concepts of coloniali-
ity, particularly as it relates to race and being (in ontological terms). To
introduce these rather complex theoretical concepts, I choose to focus on
what might be the most accessible readings in English by Aníbal Quijano
and Agustín Lao-Montes ("Decolonial Moves"). For instance, from the
essay "Coloniality of Power, Eurocentrism, and Latin America" we trace
some of the broad historical connections in which Quijano anchors and
develops his concept of the coloniality of power. By this phrase, as I stress
in class, Quijano means that, having encountered and forcefully taken pos-
session of the lands now known as the Americas, Europeans needed to construct various categories in order to dominate and subjugate indigenous
peoples and African slaves, and thus to justify the supposed inferiority of
these oppressed populations in relation to Europeans. As such, Quijano
argues, racial categories are one of the modes through which Europeans
create a hierarchy of domination of power. This racial logic served Europeans well in their enslavement of Africans and indigenous peoples and their
takeover of others' lands, histories, languages, and values. This is not to
say that indigenous peoples and blacks did not find modes of resistance,
but that official history has not sufficiently focused on moments of black
and indigenous resilience and resistance to European domination. In the
articulation of the concept of coloniality of power presented by Quijano
and others, race is just one axis of domination; the others are religion, capital, language, gender, knowledge, being, and aesthetics.

When students confront a text such as Quijano's, they are often per-
plexed by the theoretical intricacies and the critical language employed, and
by the historical reach of his work. I use examples of the mechanisms of racialization that are still prevalent in almost every Latin American context,
and of the power hierarchies that have become instantiated through the
limited participation of women, indigenous peoples, and Afro-descendants
in contemporary politics, to demonstrate that *coloniality* refers to a set of
structures, practices, and ideas that have their origin in formal political and

geographical colonization but continue beyond the end of such colonization. This is to say that the coloniality of power, as other forms of domination, continues today in plain sight, yet often goes unacknowledged and unproblematized. A specific example from Latin America might be the ongoing racial and political tensions between Haitians and Dominicans on the basis of racial discourse. One could also bring up examples of Barack Obama's race as an ongoing issue throughout his two terms as president of the United States, how the United States is still one of the few major world powers to deny entry to women in major elected leadership positions with an impact on a global scale (i.e., the presidency), or simply the increasing racial tensions stemming from systemic police violence and the collective response of the Black Lives Matter movement. These examples prove that coloniality does not just happen in Latin America or other so-called developing nations (a term students use because they hear it in the media) but operates in different ways in our very own social context.

I introduce Quijano's work by the second week of this unit and return to these concepts as we discuss other Afro-descendant poets. In our discussions of poetry by Nicomedes Santa Cruz and Luz Argentina Chiriboga, for instance, I assign *décimas* because this poetic form has a deep resonance among Afro-descendant communities throughout Spanish America. One version of the *décima* emphasizes the composition of a poem with ten verses, while in parts of South America such as Peru and Ecuador the *décima* employs a quatrain and four ten-verse stanzas. In the context of improvisation, particularly in public and popular performances, our discussion extends to Violeta Parra's autobiography written in *décimas*. As I try to illustrate to students in our close reading of the various themes that appear in the *décimas*, this form lends itself to both popular and more formal articulations, but almost always with an eye toward humor, social, and historical critique, which I link to the embedded histories of coloniality and the modes of resistance emerging from poetic discourse.

It might seem odd to some to include such theoretical discussions in relation to poetry, particularly when recognizing that Quijano's work (as well as Lao-Montes's) is a type of historical sociology informed by world-systems theory. Yet, as I try to underscore, world-systems theory allows us to look at how what takes place in one corner of the world often has a correlation elsewhere, and it introduces a dimension of political-economy to understand why Africans were enslaved and brought to the Americas, and how they became an integral part of the early capitalist economies of the Spanish empire and later in the emerging republics. In class, I also highlight ideas from the work of literary and cultural scholars such as Michael Handelsman or Catherine Walsh in collaboration with Juan García Salazar. These authors illuminate Ecuadorian literary and cultural expressions in relation to recent social movements and struggles seeking recognition of various indigenous and Afro-descendant communities within constitutional and political discussions around plurinational and pluricultural political reforms. The perspectives of these scholars intersect with and echo some of the more sociological or historical academic terms present in Quijano.

Handelsman cites the Afro-Ecuadorian journalist Juan Montaño Escobar's public interventions in printed and electronic media, which have focused on "pluri-culturalism and pluri-nationalism" (243). In response to an Ecuadorian state that has traditionally silenced, ignored, or simply disenfranchised Afro-descendant communities, Walsh and García Salazar argue, "Collective memory and oral tradition find their historical base here. They are grounded in the experiences, practices, and pedagogies of thinking and being that people of African origin have sown and cultivated on lands they were forced to make their own" (253). Walsh and García Salazar also suggest that collective memory, oral tradition, and a variety of affective communal practices have become a repository of historical injustices and modes of disenfranchisement that have only recently begun to be corrected at the level of the state, with the last two constitutional reforms in 1998 and 2008, which finally recognized and gave rights to Afro-Ecuadorian communities. In addition to recognizing Afro-Ecuadorians as a homogeneous group of citizens, "[t]he 2008 document also recognizes ancestral territory and knowledge, makes mature the subject of rights, and identifies racism and the need for reparation, compensation, and affirmative action" (Walsh and García Salazar 254). These examples from secondary sources serve to illustrate the triangulation between theory (coloniality), poetry of resistance (Preciado), and gestures of decoloniality (recent historical events and social movements) as they interface in a transhistorical and transdisciplinary engagement. In the classroom, these discussions require a lot of patience, repetition, and close reading, and I consistently pose both specific and broader questions to which we return again and again, such as, What does coloniality look like in a poem? Or, how might a gesture of decoloniality appear overtly or in a veiled way in a poem or in specific verses? The point is not to find easy solutions, but rather to read a body of Afro-descendant poetry in relational terms not only to other Afro-descendant poetry but also to theoretical and real experiences that might help students understand how poetry can become a mode of resistance to deeply rooted configurations of racism and racialization.

On Comparative Arts: Teaching Poetry and Popular Culture

From a discussion of coloniality in relation to a variety of poets, we move to comparative arts, a term that Daniel Albright began developing in his book *Panaesthetics: On the Unity and Diversity of the Arts*. Albright argues that before the Enlightenment there was not a strict division or separation between the arts. But, after Gotthold Lessing published his categorization of spatial arts (such as sculpture and painting) and temporal arts (such as music and literature) in *Laokoön oder Über die Grenzen der Malerei und Poesie* (*Laocoon: An Essay upon the Limits of Painting and Poetry*), the academy began to treat the arts as being completely divorced or as having little relation to one another. Put differently, the codification of genres encouraged the study of artworks only in relation to other works of their kind. Now students of poetry learn about form, meter, rhyme, poetic and rhetorical devices, but seldom are they asked to pursue connections between poetry and architecture or film. While I introduce my students to Albright's use of comparative arts only at the end of the semester, in fact, we have been engaging with comparative arts throughout the semester, looking at Raúl Zurita's *Purgatory* in relation to Patricio Guzmán's *Nostalgia de la Luz*, reading Violeta Parra's *décimas* in relation to her own music, studying Pablo Milanés's adaptations of Nicolás Guillén's poetry, or exploring Antonio Preciado's invocation of traditional Afro-Ecuadorian musical rhythms and dance styles such as *marimba* or *bomba*. In calling attention to Albright's concept of comparative arts, I extend his ideas and encourage my students to look beyond Albright's examples of how a poem influenced an opera or how a novel invokes a painting. While his construction of comparative arts enriches our conversation about the connections between different art forms and genres, I extend the concept of comparative arts to reveal relation through themes, devices, historical connections, or problems with which works confront audiences. In my understanding of what comparative arts offers as a critical concept, a song can elucidate specific aspects of a poem and vice versa, so that different art forms are not studied hierarchically but are treated with equal importance precisely because they present complementary pieces of information through recourse to the rich language of poetry, song lyric, or the visual language of a music video.

In short, I employ the framework of comparative arts to show students ways to analyze poetry on its own terms (reading poetry as poetry) and in relation to music, for instance. When we read Nicolás Guillén's poetry in relation to Pablo Milanés's musical rendering of Guillén's verses, the mode of comparison is precisely adaptation, considering how a musician renders meaning through the emphasis, elision, or repetition of specific words or phrases coming from the written verse. Rather than merely studying Milanés's work as adaptation (indeed, I aim to move away from this framing), we discover points of commonality when we understand and interpret written poetry and musicalized poetry on equal ground. In the case of Preciado, Valencia, and ChocQuibTown, there is no such connection by way of adaptation. Instead, we treat each artwork in isolation and then look at possible connecting threads between one poem and another, and from poetry to the sound and visual registers present in a music video.

Teaching Preciado, Valencia, and ChocQuibTown

I approach Preciado's work by giving a brief biographical contextualization of this poet who emerged from conditions of extreme poverty in his native province of Esmeraldas to study political science and economics in Quito. He published his first poetry collection, *Jolgorio* ("Revelry"), in 1961; since 2007, following many decades of writing and teaching in his native province, he has taken on political and diplomatic roles while continuing to publish poetry. From 2007 to 2008, Preciado was Ecuador's minister of culture, and from 2008 until 2013 he served as Ecuador's ambassador to Nicaragua. In his recent collection *De lo demás al barrio* ("It All Goes Back to the Neighborhood"), poems such as "La Efigie de Sandino" ("Sandino's Effigy"; 28–30) or "Llueve sobre Managua" ("It Rains over Managua"; 37–39) present impressions of everyday scenes with a Central American historical and political perspective.

As a way to illustrate a musical resonance, I assign students to read a poem entitled "El timbalero" in which the poetic voice takes notice of the musician in an orchestra, the *timbalero* ("timpanist"), who stands alone and will not play his music. This brief poem takes an interesting turn in the following verses: "Mientras sudo por dentro, / maldigo al mandamás que no le apunta, / desoigo lo demás de la música sin él / y escucho con los ojos su silencio. . . ." 'While I am sweating from within, / I curse the overseer who doesn't point to him, / I unhear the rest of the music without him / and listen to his silence with my eyes . . .' (31).[3] It is important to pause and pay attention to the poetic voice's identification with the musician; the speaker almost has a cold sweat as he listens to the music surrounding the percussionist through his eyes. The word *mandamás* (as a boss or as a farm or plantation overseer) has a particular resonance with plantation history that compels the timpanist to strike the instrument with anger, harking back to the centrality of drumming and percussion as a mode of black celebration and codifying corporeal and performative messages of rage, anger, and frustration during enslavement. This one word invokes a historical reverberation through which the poetic voice identifies with the musician and becomes one with his drumming. In our discussion of this poem, I seek to illustrate how this poem can be read from a decolonial perspective as one that seeks to undo and challenge the historical subjugation of racialized beings (Afro-descendants) and how a recourse to music recuperates and brings into the present a historical memory of resistance that informs contemporary struggles for recognition and self-determination in ongoing discussions of land rights and constitutional reforms.

Other poems in this collection, such as "La marimba" ("The Marimba") and "Remberto Escobar, Bailador de Marimba" ("Remberto Escobar, Marimba Dancer"), emphasize the entangled memories and collective affects related to this particular musical style and dance from Esmeraldas. I show students a *YouTube* video called "Los guardianes de la marimba, el Cununo y el Guasá" ("The Guardians of the Marimba from Cununo and Guasá"), which features a triangulation of *marimba* music, improvisational poetry, and the religious celebration of San Martín de Porres as a patron saint of Afro-descendants. In addition to demonstrating the sounds and steps of the *marimba*, this video helps students understand the complexities related to ritual, community, recalling ancestors, historical memory, and opening up celebrations to *la gran comarca del Pacífico*, which encompasses the ecosystem and cultural system of Afro-descendant traditions and memories extending from Panamá to Ecuador.

There are poems in *De lo demás al barrio* that directly invoke figures related to Pan-Africanism and *négritude*. In "Dos fotografías" ("Photographs"), for instance, we see direct references to the exchanges between the poets Léopold Sédar Senghor and Aimé Césaire, as well as references to the intellectual Frantz Fanon, the poet David Diop, and the island of Gorée, where a museum, the Maison des Esclaves ("The House of Slaves"), memorializes the atrocities of the Atlantic slave trade from this area.[4] The poem "En Gorée, Senegal" ("In Gorée, Senegal") makes direct reference to the House of Slaves and to the overwhelming feelings the poetic speaker experiences at this site.

In teaching another of the collection's poems, titled "Yo, 'Alonso de Illescas'" ("I, 'Alonso of Illescas'"), one of the main challenges I face is to help students envision Ecuador, with its geographical and cultural divisions, and particularly what the region of Esmeraldas in the northwest might look like. This poem allows us to talk about the historical reasons why Esmeraldas has been a traditionally black province: this was both the point of entry for slaves and a region where *cimarrones*, or runaways, came together to form their *palenques* and *comarcas*, geocultural spaces where runaway slaves coalesced as community. Even with this brief contextual information, when we read the title "Yo, 'Alonso de Illescas,'" and the poet's footnote that explains the importance of Alonso Illescas as the leader of the first settlement of self-emancipated slaves in the sixteenth century in Esmeraldas, we are confronted with a little-known enunciation of freedom, pride, and political self-determination around a racialized identity in this region. The construction of the poem forces us to try to figure out who declares, in the opening verses of the poem, "Para mí, lo que hoy piso es tierra anticipada / que estaba aquí esperándome" 'For me, that which I step on is anticipated land / that was here awaiting me' (24). The speaker affirms his deeply rooted connection to the land and his various affective responses to his ancestral environment. In the second stanza, we begin to understand that the poetic "I" is one that now claims his own identity by divorcing himself from the yoke of his former enslaver, or colonizer. While this "I" was once forced to assume the name and identity of his master, now, in his self-proclaimed freedom and independence, he reaffirms his own identity and worth by rejecting the weight and importance of his enslaver: "el que vendió mis huesos, el que afligió mis cantos / ya es nadie en mi albedrío / y nunca más alargará mis días / ni acortará mis noches / ya no me vivirá" 'he who sold my bones, who afflicted my singing / is a nobody in my free will / and will no longer lengthen my days / nor shorten my nights / will not determine my living' (25). And, as the poetic voice tells us by the end of the of the second stanza, what matters now is the new meaning behind his name, even if that name has remained the same. What has changed is the freedom to decide whether to retain the name or to adopt a new name. In other words, when the speaker says, "aquí le puse un negro libre al nombre" 'here I put a freed black to the name,' this "here" denotes a place where there exists no relationship between owner and slave. The speaker's conscious decision to retain his former master's name, despite his new freedom, is precisely to subvert the logic of ownership, of slavery, and to serve as a reminder to future generations.

When teaching the third stanza, I highlight the strong image of liberation, freedom, and self-determination that appears in the last few verses: "hasta que ya después no nos trajeron, / sino que nos trajimos, / porque todo fue como adelantar el rastro / y caminar / tiñendo para siempre la comarca" 'until they no longer brought us / but that we brought ourselves / because all there was to it was to advance the trail / and walk / staining forever the *comarca* (extended region)' (26). The poetic voice is drawing our attention to the double function of the land of Esmeraldas as a site to which blacks were brought as slaves ("nos trajeron") but also as a site where Africans enslaved each other and thus "stained" what the *palenques* and *comarcas* stand for, which is none other than a historical memory of liberation and freedom from enslavement ("nos trajimos"). The poet records a collective decision to reappropriate and reclaim these lands as ancestral sites that will always be theirs. This is why in the very last stanza there is such an emphasis on the idea of belonging, of being reborn, of seeing oneself in connection to others, to a community. The last three verses are particularly powerful: "aquí soy, aquí estoy, aquí gobierno" 'here I am being, here I am, here I govern' (26). The place where one lives, where one exists, is also the place where one can attain freedom, self-determination, and the ability to control one's own political, social, and communal life.

I begin the unit on Valencia with her collection *Todos somos culpables* ("All of Us Are Guilty"). What interests me about the opening poem is the ambiguous meaning of "mi tierra," which is already signaled in the title of the poem and the interrogative signs framing it: "¿Esta es mi tierra?" 'This is my land?' Does the phrase refer specifically to Valle del Cauca, a quintessential Afro-Colombian region facing the Pacific Ocean? Colombia's four western (Pacific) regions, namely, Chocó, Valle del Cauca, Cauca, and Nariño, are geographically, culturally, and ancestrally connected to the province of Esmeraldas in northwest Ecuador. Does the title suggest a broader reference to this *gran comarca del Pacífico*? Does it refer to Colombia as a whole? The first verse suggests a double look toward the Pacific Ocean and Colombia's Caribbean, which is also a site of historical importance for the presence and trade of slaves. The most powerful stanza is the second one, in which the speaker anchors herself in an ancestral sense of identity, harking back to those who died as a result of the slave trade on both coasts. This stanza opens with the following verses: "Nací y morí mil veces en éstas tierras / donde aún se ciernen las huellas / del yugo esclavos" 'I was born and died a thousand times in these lands / where the footprints still sift / from the enslaved yoke' (13). I try to show students how these verses suggest that the transition—from an alleged idea of Latin American independence toward freedom in which formal slavery and colonialism are no longer present—rests upon the repetition of the cycles of life under slavery and upon the historical remnants and effects of slavery that have left indelible traces upon this land and its people. This is where the idea of coloniality becomes crucial to understanding how the contemporary world is constricted by mechanisms of power that are linked to capitalism, race, gender, etc. The rest of the poem requires close reading in order to digest the deceptively simple language and the formidable images it evokes of manual labor, of all-pervasive suffering and misery, and of the social costs of a shifting moral compass and value system, including widespread robbery, killing, and fear. In other words, the poem moves from an exploration of Afro-descendant presence in Colombia to a more general discussion of the forces present in contemporary life that compel the poet to wonder whether or not this is really what her land has become. *Todos somos culpables* was published in the early 1990s, during the time of the drug cartels and at the height of widespread violence in Colombia. What we see in the poem, then, is how the poetic voice establishes parallels between past and present; though power has shifted from some hands to others, it always neglects and afflicts the same communities, in this case the Afro-descendant communities. In contrast to the first stanzas, in which the poetic voice clearly anchors herself in an Afro-Colombian identity, by the last stanzas of the poem, there is a marked attempt to transcend racial differences, to work toward a common goal, to make those who control power and money aware of those who suffer and work to allow the rich to enjoy life. In the last verses of the poem, what interests me is precisely the question of what it means to live life fully, to enjoy it, to actually be part of the world, to exist in it, and to contribute to it.

After analyzing this poem, along with Valencia's "Dejemi voz" and "Geografía en versos," students watch a few seconds of the music videos "Oro" and "De donde vengo yo" by ChocQuibTown. I ask students to pay attention not only to the lyrics but also to the visual representation of Afro-Colombian life and to the ways in which the images construct a sense of pride in Afro-Colombian identity and community. Then I ask them to connect "De donde vengo yo" to Elcina Valencia's poem "¿Esta es mi tierra?" The song and the poem express a contemporary sense of identity and pride in being Afro-Colombian, but also acknowledge the social and economic inequities in contemporary Colombian society. Students point out how the song lyrics (e.g., "De donde vengo yo / la cosa no es fácil pero siempre sobrevivimos / vengo yo / De tanto luchar siempre con la nuestra nos salimos / Vengo yo / Y aquí se habla mal pero todo está mucho mejor/ Vengo yo / Tenemos la lluvia, el frío, el calor" 'Where I come from / things are not easy but we always survive / I come / After so much struggle, we always persevere / I come / Language is not spoken well here but everything is much better / I come / We have rain, cold, and heat') encapsulate in a different register intended for everyday audiences a similar message of resilience and pride that we find in the poetry of both Valencia and Preciado.

The song "Oro" is a powerful reminder of how Spaniards forced African slaves to extract gold from the lands of El Cauca (and by extension of Esmeraldas on the Ecuadorian side). As we acknowledge this history we can relate the images in the videos, the lyrics of the songs, and Preciado's and Valencia's poetry to our readings on coloniality and decoloniality. In tracing these associations, we observe how Daniel Albright's concept of comparative arts lends itself to reflecting upon the connections between contemporary popular music and poetry. Given the richness of the music video's visual and sonorous registers as well as its lyrics, I ask students to treat the video on its own but also to reflect on how this visual and musical representation enhances their reading of Valencia's poetry. Often, students begin to see connections and find specific resonances in these works' reclaiming of Afro-Colombian pride as central to any discussions of contemporary Colombia. For instance, when viewing a video such as "Oro," students are able to visualize the type of land and the conditions in which African slaves were forced to work. This in turn mirrors the kind of poetic remembrance and questioning that happens in Valencia's "¿Esta es mi tierra?" and "Geografía en versos" and in Preciado's poems such as "Yo, 'Alonso de Illescas.'" Furthermore, the predominant instrument in this song is the marimba, which the class can now identify as a central reference to the ways in which Afro-descendants have embraced musical instruments, dance styles, and poetic form (the *décima*) in creating an archive of community-based experiences and memories of enslavement and its aftermath for the inhabitants of *palenques* and contemporary geopolitical regions of Ecuador and Colombia.

The practice of connecting music and videos to poetry allows me to show students regions of Latin America that they may not encounter in the media or in other courses. It also enables us as a class to look for and trace historical links between older generations of Afro-descendant poets and to consider how questions of identity in their work, particularly in relation to race, are still important today and find expression in contemporary poetry and music. I also draw attention to these types of connection in order to underscore how poetry and music interface with the ongoing social and political struggles of social movements in Colombia and Ecuador, as two particular case study sites. My point in framing this unit within the concept of comparative arts is to allow students to establish points of comparison and connections between poetic verse, song lyric, and music videos rather than treat each art form as something disconnected or completely divorced from the others. Such comparisons lead to more substantial dialogues that allow us to tackle deeply rooted historical questions dealing with race and other forms of power, such as coloniality. Finally, I ask students to use the Internet to explore contemporary social movements in Ecuador and Colombia, including their specific demands and their presence in the national political sphere. This additional layer of research forms part of the final course paper and adds a multilayered dimension to our discussion of the arts. The goal is for students to reflect upon how contemporary Afro-descendant poetry relates to pressing and timely social and political issues that not only affect Afro-descendant communities in Ecuador and Colombia but ultimately have deeper (and deeply historical) implications for both countries as a whole.

Notes

1. The term *Afro-descendant* is used here instead of *Afro-Hispanic* to connote these artists' politics of self-identification and their relation to larger social movements in the region. While *Afro-Hispanic* has a longstanding usage in the United States, *Afro-descendant* is an alternative that places subjectivity and agency at the front and center of arts, politics, and social movements around questions of race.

2. Terms such as *la gran comarca* or *la gran comarca del Pacífico* denote the historical, cultural, geographical, and ecological systems that run from Darién in Panamá through the Pacific coast of Colombia (el Chocó y el Cauca) and the northwestern region of Ecuador known as Esmeraldas. The word *comarca* as it is used in Spanish denotes a territory with specific geophysical or cultural characteristics. In rearticulating their contemporary movements, Afro-descendants in Ecuador and Colombia are retrieving ancestral memories of belonging to *palenques* as sites where *cimarrones* or, roughly translated, escaped, self-emancipated slaves coalesced into communities of freed black people. For more detailed information on these terms, see Ordóñez Charpentier and Cepeda Bravo.

3. All translations are my own.

4. These poems identify the francophone poet Diop, of Senegalese and Cameroonian descent; the Senegalese poet and intellectual Senghor; and the Martinican poet and intellectual Césaire as three of the main proponents of *négritude*. They also allude to the importance of the Martinican intellectual Fanon, whose writings have been central to liberation and decolonizing movements across the world and who has become a principal figure among decolonial scholars.

María Rosa Olivera-Williams

Teaching Latin American Poetry as a Vulnerable Genre

Some years ago, I was surprised to hear from students who were linguistically prepared to succeed in upper-level courses in Spanish that they were apprehensive about studying poetry. When and how had a genre that fueled children's imaginations become an impenetrable wall for students? I surmised that neither poetry nor the Spanish language was to blame but that instruction focused on on the supposed autonomy of the genre—its literariness—was the culprit.

Teaching Latin American poetry as a cultural practice among a broad range of other cultural practices has changed my students' relation to poetry and enriched my own reading experience. William Rowe, in his now canonical *Poets of Contemporary Latin America*, shows how, by not privileging aesthetic factors over social and historical information, considering "what a poem can do" expands poetry's power of understanding and its possibilities of communication (5). This approach has made it possible to realize the call of the philosopher Martha Nussbaum, who has underscored the importance of "[s]eeing how another group of intelligent beings has cut up the world differently" and declared that "all students" should learn "at least one foreign language well" in order to gain "an essential lesson in cultural humility" (90). Learning the language of the other is indeed opening a space for the other. It is inviting all languages in the widest sense of the word—methodologies, fields of study, technologies, and cultures—to address the problems of our present. Teaching the lyric through the lens of cultural studies is inviting students to embrace "cultural humility" and open themselves to others. In this essay, I describe how this approach has worked in two upper-level seminars in the program of Iberian and Latin American studies at the University of Notre Dame. First, in Modernization and Modernity in the Río de la Plata, I show how the sexual and erotic lyric language of Delmira Agustini gains meaning through a dialogue with tango. The tango, as a language of the harbor slums or *conventillos* that spread quickly to the entire society and to the outside world, enables us to understand how the increased mobility of individuals, peoples, ideas, and mores galvanized Agustini and other writers of her generation. Similarly, Gabriela Mistral and Her World examines the ways in which the women's movements demanding political rights in the first decades of the twentieth century, and the subsequent silencing of women in the Southern Cone, not only inspired Mistral to create different images and voices for the modern woman but also moved her to form a community of women writers. These poets opened themselves to others, and their poetry demands that we recognize its relation to other voices and cultural practices.

Regarding Autonomy

Is rejecting the autonomy of poetry a loss to the genre? In *Aesthetic Theory*, Theodor Adorno uses Immanuel Kant's emphasis on form, G. W. F. Hegel's emphasis on intellectual significance, and Karl Marx's emphasis on art's embeddedness in society as a whole to argue that the autonomy of art is simultaneously necessary and illusory. For Adorno this paradox of modern art's autonomy enables us to understand the social character of modern art and makes art "the social antithesis of society" (8).

For Adorno, authentic modern artwork shows the difficulties and complexities of the concept of autonomy. In *Postmodernism*, Fredric Jameson understood the culture of late capitalism as the result of "the 'death' of the subject itself." According to Jameson, "the end of the autonomous bourgeois monad or ego or individual" brings with it the waning of the concept of autonomy in art and the reign of pastiche (15). Between the necessary and illusory autonomy of modern art in Adorno and the death of art's autonomy in Jameson I place the contributions of the feminist philosopher Judith Butler on the concept of vulnerability as applied to the creative process of poetry and its reception.

In *Precarious Life: The Powers of Mourning and Violence*, Butler conceives of vulnerability as an opening to the needs and claims of others. She points out that we all live with vulnerability relative to others as part of "bodily life" and that this vulnerability "becomes highly exacerbated under certain social and political conditions, especially those in which violence is a way of life and the means of secure self-defense are limited." In such situations, individuals can acknowledge a shared condition of vulnerability and act in solidarity with one another, or they can deny vulnerability through "an institutionalized fantasy of mastery" that makes them believe that their lives and rights are more important than others' (29). Nussbaum's concept of cultural humility and opening ourselves to others intersects with Butler's manifestation of vulnerability. Both philosophers prescribe an a priori ethical relation to the other as a precondition for regaining humanity and, in the sphere of higher education, realizing the power of the humanities in a world dominated by global market flows.

Literature and art characteristically attend to, respond to, and incorporate the call of the outside. Butler suggests in *Giving an Account of Oneself* that "our willingness to become undone in relation to others is our chance of becoming human" (136). The "vulnerability" (29) of a genre that is always nurtured by multiple discourses as well as by advances and changes in technology not only offers poets the "chance of becoming human" through their willingness to become undone in relation to others but also enables them to shift the conventional boundaries of poetry in order to grasp, feel, and think through contemporary issues. This opening of the genre also broadens our expectations as readers. This opening may seem to negate the autonomy of poetry, yet in it one may find its true autonomy.

This idea is certainly not new. At the peak of Romanticism, when the figure of the poet seemed to possess its maximum autonomy and power, John Keats explained in a letter to his friend Richard Woodhouse that "the poetical Character . . . has no self—it is everything and nothing—It has no character—it enjoys light and shade . . . What shocks the virtuous philosopher, delights the camelion [chameleon] Poet . . . A Poet is the most unpoetical of any thing in existence; because he has no Identity—he is continually in for—and filling some other Body" (386).[1] Thus, the chameleon poet as the paradigm of the poet is essentially vulnerable and opened to the outside and to other, diverse voices.

Reading and teaching lyric poetry as a cultural practice may underscore the genre's vulnerability. It also reveals the tensions, according to Rowe, between the "processing of experience, through operations of language" that is history and the individual human experience, which he terms "inner life" (*Poets* 12). The importance of Rowe's work, not only his *Poets of Contemporary Latin America*, but also his *Hacia una poética radical: ensayos de hermenéutica cultural* (*Toward a Radical Poetics: Essays on Cultural Hermeneutics*),[2] lies in opening a space for Latin American poetry in the realm of cultural studies. *Hacia una poética radical* proposes that the cultural field should be enriched and complicated by a dialogue among many semiotic and disciplinary systems, especially poetry. This enrichment of cultural studies at a moment in which the symbolic field has been and is at risk of being occupied by the neoliberal discourse is further complemented by Jill S. Kuhnheim's critical contributions in *Spanish American Poetry at the End of the Twentieth Century* and her more recent book *Beyond the Page: Poetry and Performance in Spanish America*. Kuhnheim's groundbreaking work gives new life to poetry by opening the golden cage of literature, in which poetry used to reign and was also a prisoner, and recognizing the genre's power to perform its voice, words, rhythm, corporal movements, iconology, and imagination. She moves back to the origins of poetry as a spoken art and swings forward to the present, underscoring the variety of possibilities that new technologies, such as the Internet, offer the genre in order to highlight and analyze the cultural work poetry does.

Upper-Level Seminars on Latin American Poetry

My upper-level seminar on modernization, *modernismo*, and modernity in the Río de la Plata, which focuses on the high aesthetic of *modernismo* and the popular culture of tango, reads lyric poetry and tango dialogically, amid other social practices, demonstrating the interdependence between poetic and cultural knowledge. One of the topics of the seminar—the emergence of a modern woman—will illustrate this affiliation.

At the core of the massive changes brought by modernization to Argentina and Uruguay, the process of transit from "tradition" to "modernity," which in Latin America is the replication of economic, social, and political characteristics of the contemporary industrialized western societies (O'Donnell 244), is the emergence of a modern woman who demands a space in the patriarchal culture of her time. Thus, the poetry of the

Uruguayan Delmira Agustini, the only woman who graces the majority of the anthologies on Latin American *modernista* poetry, becomes the focus of our discussion.

At the end of the nineteenth century and the beginning of the twentieth century, the urban landscapes of Montevideo and Buenos Aires were changing, transforming the ways people occupied space in these capital cities. Photographs from this period of Buenos Aires, Montevideo, and New York, the paradigm of the modern city, show students those changes and the apparent synchronism of modernization. The tall and elegant buildings of Buenos Aires and Montevideo were not less impressive than the ones in New York. (Meanwhile, the slums captured by Jacob Riis's camera portrayed a miserable and tragic life in the Río de la Plata *conventillos* near the harbors and slaughterhouses.) Photographs of the three modern cities at the turn of the twentieth century capture the importance of mobility and the presence of technology: amid street lamps, trolleys, cars, and telephone and telegraph wires, people from all walks of life are moving in the streets.

To the Cuban poet and cultural icon José Martí, the modern city seemed to be robbing human beings of their values and humanity. An 1887 photograph of New York shows the city crossed by a tangled mass of telephone wires, like the web a giant spider might spin to catch human beings; Martí's poem "Amor de ciudad grande" ("Love of the Big City") captures their voices: "De gorja son y rapidez los tiempos. / Corre cual luz la voz, en alta aguja /. . . / el hombre como alado, el aire hiende" 'The times are of noise and speed. / The voice runs like light, the needle high / . . . / man, as if winged, cleaves the air.' The dehumanizing effect of technology made people vulnerable to consumerism and its promises of facility and immediacy: "¡Me espanta la ciudad! ¡Toda está llena / de copas por vaciar, o huecas copas" 'The city frightens me! All is full / of wine glasses to empty, or empty glasses.' The modern city seemed to push people into the streets, where women became the prey of men ("¡Jaula es la villa de palomas muertas / y ávidos cazadores!" 'A cage is the village of dead pigeons / and avid hunters') and love became a speedy carnal exchange ("[s]e ama de pie, en las calles, entre el polvo / de los salones y las plazas" 'one loves standing in the streets, in the dust / of the halls and squares') (88).

Martí understood that modernity was in contradiction with traditional mores. The vertiginous rhythm of the age destroyed the ideal of passivity, immobility, and fragility that symbolized that era's "cult" of women as "death-angels" (Gilbert and Gubar 25)—an ideal that for Martí in this poem serves as the reservoir of all that is beautiful in humanity. How did Agustini, the female creator of a sexual and erotic lyric language in Latin American poetry, negotiate with the system of values that Martí felt had been replaced by disreputable modern mores? How did this woman envision love and erotic desires in her work amid the wantonness of modernization?

In order to answer these questions, we study *Los cálices vacíos* (*The Empty Chalices*), published by Agustini just before her untimely death in 1914. The book is a personal anthology, containing *Cantos de la mañana* (*Songs of the Morning*) in its entirety, twenty-nine poems from *El libro blanco* (*Frágil*) (*The White Book* [*Fragile*]), and twenty-two new poems. Having read Martí's representation of problematic urban spaces for women, we note that Agustini opens her volume by constructing a space, assigning Rubén Darío's foreword the title "Pórtico." A portico is the colonnade at the entry to a temple; as a pathway or threshold, it is a space of transit that enables entrance into a sacred place, but at the same time it can serve as a boundary that prevents access to that desired place. Darío's text, which Agustini used to legitimate her work, is a twofold sign. It is simultaneously a passage and a boundary.

Darío wrote: "Sinceridad, encanto y fantasía, he allí las cualidades de esta deliciosa musa" 'Sincerity, charm, and fantasy, those are the qualities of this delicious muse' (*Poesías completas* 223). The qualities that Darío found in Agustini's poetry, especially her sincerity, open her path into the temple of poetry—yet the father of *modernismo* does not refer to Agustini as a poet. She is instead a "delicious muse" or a mystic who wrote in a trance, like Saint Teresa. Darío quotes Shakespeare: "'that is a woman,' pues por ser muy mujer, dice cosas exquisitas que nunca se han dicho" ("'that is a woman,'" because she is a woman, she says exquisite things that have never been said').[3] Agustini's femininity, her "qualities," grant her access to the portico but not to the temple, leaving her in an undetermined zone. For Darío, Agustini's poetry responded to his eternal questions about the enigma of the feminine. Her voice may have realized the erotic desires that appeared in his poems. Thus, she remained for him "a muse," not a poet.

"Pórtico" also places us, as readers of Agustini's poetry, in the indeterminate zone of the threshold, seeing and not seeing the entire creative process and transformation of this woman into a poet at the beginning of the twentieth century. How do we read the contradictions in Agustini's poetic persona as characteristic of the modern woman? Reading a selection of her diary and letters, we discover that Agustini underscored and played with the nickname "la nena" ("baby girl"). As "la nena," she seemed to obey the binding social expectations of her time; yet she followed social mores in order to subvert them. For example, having married Enrique Job Reyes after a long engagement (in accord with bourgeois values and rituals), she divorced him almost immediately (benefiting from new Uruguayan legislation allowing women to file independently for divorce) but maintained a relationship with him as a lover. Agustini needed legitimation and followed societal norms in order to gain a space from which she was able to question the spirit and culture that created those particular norms. Cathy L. Jrade, in *Delmira Agustini, Sexual Seduction, and Vampiric Conquest*, reads Agustini's "vampirization" or literary cannibalism of Darío's poetics and the *modernista* poetic movement as a way to find legitimation for her voice.

Agustini corrected, from a woman's perspective, Darío's swan as the trope of *modernista* poetry, as noted by Sylvia Molloy (17–18). In the poems "Nocturno" ("Nocturne") and "El cisne" ("The Swan"), the swan comes alive with the blood of the poet, resignifying its meaning: "Y en la cristalina página / en el sensitivo espejo / del lago que algunas veces / refleja mi pensamiento, / el cisne asusta de rojo, / y yo de blanca doy miedo" 'And on the crystalline page / on the sensitive mirror / of the lake that sometimes /reflects my thought, / the swan frightens with its redness / and I, with my whiteness, am frightening!' (Agustini 257; my trans.). The poems refer to the room in Agustini's paternal home where she has exchanged domesticity for creativity—the chamber that becomes the laboratory of her fantasies and the bed that serves as "a dark page" on which she imprints her erotic vision: "En la página oscura de mi lecho; / Te inclinabas a mí como al milagro / De una ventana abierta al más allá" 'On the dark page of my bed; / You leaned over me as over the miracle / Of a window open to the hereafter' (237). Yet these achievements are not just the ingenious creations of a woman who made the *modernista* aesthetic her own in a virtual dialogue with its founding father; they are an indication of broader social changes for women.

The concepts of mobility, circulation, and modernity enable us to think of the ways Agustini was able to carve a niche for herself in a foundational movement in Spanish American literature. Mobility as the physical displacement of people from one place to the other (Europe / Latin America; countryside / urban areas; downtown/suburbs; home / public spaces) was central to modernization. The unprecedented immigration of Europeans to Latin America's largest cities and the migration of rural people to its urban centers at the end of the nineteenth century, which resulted in an unparalleled increase in the population of the Río de la Plata countries, caused Horacio Ferrer to write in *El libro del tango* that the Buenos Aires of the 1880s became "la Shangai de la pampa" 'the Shanghai of the pampa' (xxxv). He explains, "Ya los extranjeros son más—y bastante más—en Buenos Aires que los propios porteños. Se diría, casi, que alguien ha sacado a una ciudad que aquí había, y que, en la misma implantación (la que Hernando Báez escoge en 1536 por orden de Pedro de Mendoza) ha puesto otra" 'Already there are more foreigners—and many more—in Buenos Aires than the *porteños* themselves. It seems that someone has taken a city that was here and that, in the same establishment (the one that Hernando Báez chose in 1536 by order of Pedro Mendoza), has put another' (xxxv; my trans.). The growth of the population in the other harbor city, Montevideo, moved the young attorney and politician Luis Alberto de Herrera to write in 1895: "la blasonada capital crece y se expande tierra adentro con la briosa elasticidad característica de esta época de vértigo y sólo concedida a la propia fuerza" 'the emblazoned capital city grows and expands inland with the spirited elasticity characteristic of this epoch of vertigo and only granted to its strength' (72; my trans.). Nevertheless, mobility was not limited to the hundreds of thousands of immigrants and migrants who transformed the rhythm of the modern cities. A new concept of mobility emerged from the advances of technology.

In "Amor de ciudad grande," Martí saw technology in a negative light. The telegraph and telephone were changing the human voice, which traveled through wires. Speed was destroying human values. The appearance of the car also changed the ways people traveled through the city, transforming their conceptions of space and time.[4] Mobility became the goal of the modern individual, especially for women who had been confined by an ideal of female passivity. Modern women dreamed of the freedom to move and projected that dream onto their literary creations. For example, Agustini's muse is not the mute pale princess of Darío's "Sonatina," static in her fragile and virginal beauty, but "cambiante, misteriosa y compleja" 'inconstant, mysterious and complex.' Her muse is imagined as "águila, tigre, paloma en un instante" 'eagle, tiger, pigeon in an instant' (111). Her muse is movement. Mobility for Agustini is represented in the inner subjective space of her creations and fantasies. But she also moved through the modern city—Montevideo or Buenos Aires—protected, as she wrote in her letters to Reyes, by her parents (see Olivera-Williams 165). The car became a metonym of mobility for a certain social class, enabling people to move quickly and differently through the city.[5] This new means of travel provided different experiences and performances. According to Mimi Sheller and John Urry's "new mobilities paradigm," car travel "is experienced through a combination of senses and sensed" (216). This paradigm also invites us to consider "the embodied nature and experience of different modes of travel," including elements such as talking, working, information gathering, and "maintaining a moving presence with others that holds the potential for many different convergences or divergences of physical presence" (214).

If mobility is central to modernization and modernity, equally important is the concept of circulation, understood as the transmission of aesthetic parameters and cultural processes, especially in the context of popular culture. On May 16, 1913, Agustini presented *Los cálices vacíos* in the magazine *Fray Mocho* ("Friar Mocho"). The issue was published with an offprint entitled "Paraísos artificiales" ("Artificial Paradise"), signed by the very young journalist Juan José de Soiza Reilly, about drugs, alienation, and poetic creativity. One of the images showed the other great Uruguayan *modernista* poet, Julio Herrera y Reissig, dosing himself with morphine in his bedroom. The pairing of *Los cálices vacíos* with "Paraísos artificiales" demonstrated the circulation of the aesthetics of modernity with the tastes and mores of the time. Beatriz Colombi wrote in her prologue to *Los cálices vacíos*: "La convivencia (y connivencia) entre artista y bajofondo, entre escritor y locura, entre arte y degradación, está suficientemente *normalizada* como para compartir un mismo espacio de éxtasis y desorden, con un toque sensacionalista" 'The coexistence (and connivance) between artist and the underworld, between writer and madness, between art and degradation, is sufficiently standardized to share the same space of ecstasy and disorder, with a sensational touch' (8). Mobility and circulation blurred boundaries and placed the corporeal body in touch with others, underscoring human vulnerability and abetting mental and physical gender and sexual violence against women who started breaking out of their static condition.

No cultural phenomenon shows better than the tango the new paradigm of mobilities and the "coexistence and connivance" of modern life and art. Tango is mobility, transculturation, hybridity, and cultural mixing. The cultural practice of tango demonstrates the vulnerability of the population that created it. It is an expression of people who felt their marginal status and desired to belong to an affective place that they could call home and homeland. Studying tango and the work of Agustini—which expresses the position of the female writer on the threshold of the temple of modern poetry, where she longs to occupy a central place—enables students to understand the importance of Butler's concept of vulnerability and Nussbaum's concept of cultural humility. Students learn through tango "how the other half" felt, to paraphrase the title of Jacob Riis's 1890 book. They also learn how women like Agustini found in the rhythms and lyrics of tango not only a channel for their sexual and erotic desires but also a space of transit in the maelstrom of modernization. Here students may test Rowe's proposal of history—the history of modernity—as that processing of experience through the languages of two particular cultural practices, tango and *modernismo*.

Tango dance was born in the *arrabales* ("harbor slums") of Buenos Aires as a hybrid of different styles, places, and periods. The so-called Spanish tango adapted certain movements of African dances, especially the control of the body with an erect torso, at the same time that the rural world of the pampas appeared in the city with the *taconeo* ("stomping") of the gauchos' *malambo* dance. But what gives the tango its historical determination, its rubric as cultural fruit of modernization, is the dancers' tight embrace. That embrace represents the vulnerability of the modern individual, who clings desperately to the other in an effort to grasp the vertiginous present, where everything changes.

Tango as dance, music, and poetry permeated the entire range of Río de la Plata societies. By the end of the first decade of the twentieth century it had reached Paris and become a symbol of modernity. Tango became the star in luxurious lounges and nightclubs; it moved from the slums to the city center but never lost its *arrabalero* origin completely. For Ferrer, people did not go to the *arrabal* to live: "el Arrabal se lleva puesto. Es una fuga, un esoterismo y una fatalidad" 'the Arrabal is worn. It is a fugue, an esotericism and a fatality' (xli). In the real and figurative space of the slum, a new voice emerged—not a single voice but a legion, a fugue in which language, morality, identity, and gender together sound the theme of escape. That fugue is seen in the body language of the tango dance, which offered escape first to women of dubious reputation, to working men and thugs, to young upper-class men who went down to the *arrabal* and its bordellos. The *arrabal*'s polyphony of voices gave shape, even when in tension, to the modern identity in fugue of the Río de la Plata. By reading notes on tango that appeared in magazines such as *Caras y caretas* ("Faces and Masks") and *Fray Mocho*—the same magazines that announced the books of Agustini and other *modernista* poets and published their poems, columns, and chronicles—and by listening to early *milongas* and tangos, and studying pictures of couples dancing in Buenos Aires and Montevideo, students come to understand how tango may have influenced the tone of Agustini's sexual and erotic language. "La nena" did not isolate herself in her paternal bourgeois home but lived in the midst of the mobility and circulation characteristic of modernity.

Having analyzed the lyric poetry of *modernismo*, and especially the emergence of Agustini's voice, from a broad cultural perspective, I enter Mistral's poetic and intellectual world through the study of feminist culture. I begin by examining early-twentieth-century women's movements in the Southern Cone and in the rest of Latin America.

The upper-level seminar on Mistral has two goals: to study her poetic work and to consider her role as public intellectual in the first half of the twentieth century. Thus, I invite students to consider how the Nobel laureate's imagination was nurtured by the women's movements in Chile and in the rest of the Southern Cone countries. We discuss the role of the solid Chilean patriarchal system in the political, social, and educative advances of women (see Eltit 17–61) and the ways Mistral negotiated her space in the polis to create a network of women poets and cultural agents such as Alfonsina Storni, Juana de Ibarbourou, Victoria Ocampo, and Cecília Meireles. We read the lectures that Ibarbourou, Storni, and Mistral delivered in a famous conference in Montevideo in 1938. Here Mistral was the only one who proposed a genealogy of women poets: "Me siento como una acumulación de hablas reunidas. Apenas llevo el acento individual, la voz que lleva un nombre solo" 'I feel like an accumulation of collected speeches. I hardly carry the individual accent, the voice that bears a name alone.'[6] Conscious of the multiplicity of discourses that make her own poetic discourse possible, Mistral articulates her poetic imagination in a new language that she makes available for others' use. She creates new ways of representing women.

Two tropes serve us well in the classroom: those of the mother and of the ghost. In the section "Poemas de las madres" ("Poems of Mothers") of *Desolación* (*Despair*), "La hermana" ("Sister"),[7] written in prose, breaks with the stereotypical readings of motherhood. The female speaker who "ve" 'sees,' "acaricia" 'caresses,' and "la ha traído hacia ella" 'brings close to her' a pregnant woman who is working in the fields charges her language with the possibility of erotic desire for that body in bloom. Mistral uses isotopy—that semiotic figure that consists of the repetition of a certain basic characteristic of meaning (such as "caderas," meaning "hips," in this poem)—to suggest the parallel desires of both women. The body of the pregnant woman is like the earth. The pregnant woman and the earth carry in their wombs the seed of life: "Hoy he visto una mujer abriendo un surco. Sus caderas están henchidas, como las mías, por el amor, y hacía su faena curvada sobre el suelo" 'Today I saw a woman opening a furrow. Her hips are swollen, like mine, by love, and she did her work bent over the ground' (130). The speaker's hips may be read as swollen by the pregnancy that grew from heterosexual lovemaking, or by the speaker's caresses as she holds the desired woman close to her body. Her own body not only grows with love but is also capable of offering rich milk to the pregnant woman. Here students discover the second isotopy. The speaker offers milk from her own glass to the other woman, while the latter will offer the milk of her breast to the speaker's son, feeding in this way the fruit of the speaker's love, a child hungry for the milk of the pregnant woman: "Beberá la leche espesa de mi mismo vaso y gozará de la sombra de mis corredores, que va grávida de gravidez de amor. Y si mi seno no es generoso, mi hijo allegará al suyo, ricos sus labios" 'She will drink the thick milk from my own glass and enjoy the shadow of my corridors, since she is pregnant with a pregnancy of love. And if my breast is not generous, my son will come to hers, his lips rich' (130).[8]

This poem may open a new space for lesbian desire through the rhetorical figure of isotopy. Of course, certain readings and understandings depend upon societal and cultural transformations. The reading that we performed in class could not have happened in 1922. Seeing María Elena Wood's documentary film *Locas mujeres* (*Mad Women*) about Mistral's inner world and her love relationship with Doris Dana, and reading Mistral's correspondence with different writers and personalities of her time, gives students a privileged position from which to understand "La hermana." The poem also offers an opportunity to discuss the boundaries between the constructed poetic voice and the poet's biography. Nevertheless, the poem as a "means of active discovery" (Rowe, *Poets* 5) builds bridges that unite the past with the present and the future. Mistral's poetry creates many imaginary possibilities for women, and all of them have in common the mobility of the trope "women," in all its epistemic wealth.

Mistral's panoply of poems about mothers also includes traditional images, yet the ideal patriarchal mother nevertheless becomes destabilized. For example, the joy of a body that is doubling into another body is praised in "La quietud" ("Stillness"). The pregnant speaker, hidden and immobilized by the size of her abdomen, transforms her "stillness" into a celebration of her pregnant body with flowers, music, and honey: "Que estoy tejiendo en este silencio, en esta quietud, un cuerpo, un milagroso cuerpo, con venas, y rostro, y mirada, y depurado corazón" 'That I am knitting in this silence, in this stillness, a body, a miraculous body, with veins, and face, and gaze, and polished heart' (132). This state of feminine celebration contains incessant activity and movement that contradicts the traditional ideas of pregnancy for middle-class women of that time—which Mistral knew differed from the experience of pregnancy for working rural women as she presented it in "La hermana."

If Mistral's early publications reflected the mobility characteristic of the women's movements of the region, her later work confronts the social perversion of 1950s culture, which, as Julieta Kirkwood states, returned Chilean women to a silenced place: the home.[9] Thus, in 1966, in *Poema de Chile*, posthumously published by Dana, the speaker is a ghost. Liberated from the limitations of the female body—or rather from the constraints that culture imposes on the female body—the speaker can return to her motherland, tracing a map of affects and emotions. The ghostly body is the most vulnerable of all, and the speaker's opening to the outside and to others underscores Mistral's experimentation in a song to the fatherland, lacking any patriotism or nationalism.

Over the course of twenty years of living in Brazil and traveling throughout the Americas and Europe as an internationally recognized intellectual, Mistral found in the figure of the ghost a way to return to and affectively repossess her motherland. Here students may discuss the ghost as a mask that enables the poet to speak without the limitations of a historical body, in which gender, sex, race, and age impose constraints on the speaker. The ghost is also a figure that moves freely through the land. The class compares this identity with others used by Mistral, such as that of the old woman, the rural teacher, and the "queer mother" (Licia Fiol-Matta 37) that a nation like Chile needed in the first half of the twentieth century. In this discussion, the advantages of the ghost as a medium to create an affective bridge between the speaker and the land become clear. It is desire—the desire of the speaker and the desire of the poet—that gives birth to the ghost. In "Hallazgo" ("Find"), the speaker says: "Bajé por espacio y aires / y más aires, descendiendo, / sin llamado y con llamada / por la fuerza del deseo," 'I descended through space and air / and more air, while descending, / without a call and with a flame / by the force of desire' (559).

Mary Louise Pratt states that "one of the most conspicuous features" of this collection is "that its author opts entirely out of a long-standing heroic tradition of patriotic poetry" ("Women" 66). Mistral's ghost as a vulnerable image opens herself to the future, to new generations, represented in a small indigenous child with whom she travels through the Chilean landscape, as a mother-child dyad. She teaches the boy about the past, about history, but the little boy also teaches the ghost, "una loca" 'a mad woman' (Mistral 561) who loses her way and wanders with her offspring, naming trees, plants, rivers, deserts, mountains, minerals, and animals. As Pratt observes, "Mistral maintains white authority in a parental relation with an infantilized indigenous protagonist whose enfranchisement is in her hands, not his own" ("Women" 69)—but the boy who is her companion teaches her, as little children do, the art of questioning without fear, encouraging the mother-ghost to find racial justice for the indigenous population. In "A dónde es que tú me llevas" ("Where Are You Taking Me"), the mother replies to her son: "Te voy llevando a un lugar / donde al mirarte la cara / no te digan como nombre / lo de *indio pata rajada* / sino que te den parcela / muy medida y muy contada" 'I am taking you to a place / where looking at your face / they do not call you / *ragged Indian*, / where they give you a piece of land / fully measured and reckoned' (Mistral 669).

Teaching Latin American poetry as a vulnerable genre not only engages students but makes it possible for them to understand how poetry nurtures itself from all the cultures and semiotic systems of a particular society. The trope of the mother in Mistral's poetry, with its powerful potential for social change, responded to the mother trope that had been used in women's movements as an emblem of the fight for civil and political rights. The Southern Cone suffragists proposed the figure of the mother—not necessarily the Republican mother—as their paradigm, arguing that women as mothers deserved full citizenship because they knew well the social ills of their time (alcoholism, sexual diseases, poverty, neglect of children, prostitution, and lack of education, among others), faced them daily, and knew how to solve them. Nevertheless, in the long silence of the 1950s that trope played an important role in pushing women back into the domesticity of the home. It is precisely at this time when Mistral's "ghost" fought against domesticity with the maximum freedom of a poetic persona that opted to remove all the limitations against the female body.

Teaching poetry as a vulnerable genre helps students to gain cultural humility, enabling them to build bridges with other cultures, voices, and times. Thus, we create a community of eager, curious, and active young people who realize, in the sense of discovering and producing, what a poem can do.

Notes

1. I am grateful to Luis Bravo, who invited me to think of Keats's idea of the "chameleon poet."

2. All translations are my own unless otherwise attributed.

3. Here Darío misquotes Prince Hamlet's line, "What a piece of work is a man!" (*Hamlet*, Act 2, scene 2, lines 1397–98). Darío's misquotation is not in changing "man" for "woman" but in changing the spirit of the line. For Hamlet, humans, in spite of appearing like gods, are merely "dust." Nevertheless, Darío quotes Shakespeare in order to have the blessing of the universal poet, affirming his central place in the modern temple of poetry.

4. Marisol Fonseca analyzes the concept of mobility according to a new paradigm proposed by Mimi Sheller and John Urry. For them, "the car reconfigures urban life, with novel ways of dwelling, travelling, and socialising in, and through, an automobilised time-space . . . Automobility impacts not only on local public spaces and opportunities for coming together, but also on the formation of gendered subjectivities, familial and social networks, spatially segregated urban neighborhoods, national images and aspirations to modernity . . ." (209).

5. According to reports by the U.S. Department of Commerce, from 1910 to 1922, there were 13,241 automobiles imported into Uruguay. "More than 80 per cent of the motorcycles used in Uruguay [were] of American make" (430).

6. Regarding this meeting, see Lorena Garrido.

7. "Poemas de las madres" from *Desolación* appears in the Andrés Bello edition of Mistral's *Poesías completas* ("Complete Poems"), which we use in the seminar.

8. The end of the poem is ambiguous and allows, as is typical of Mistral's poetry, a more traditional reading. The future son of the pregnant speaker, if his mother is not able to feed him, could drink from the generous bosom of the peasant woman. In this reading, the female speaker is creating a solidary community of women. Nevertheless, this reading cancels the erotic voice of the speaker, who looks with desire at the pregnant body of the woman working in the fields. The desire for the pregnant woman and for a child materializes in the speaker's pregnant state, a manifestation of the intensity of her feelings rather than a biological reality. Therefore, the speaker cannot breastfeed her child; however, she can satisfy her desire by imagining her baby as the peasant's baby drinking milk from his mother's breast. The two babies merge into one.

9. See Kirkwood's *Ser política en Chile*. In Kirkwood's words, after women achieved the political right to vote, they were forced into "más de 25 años de silencio" 'more than 25 years of silence' (83). During this time, women stopped writing, except for poetry; and even this work, according to the critics, was superfluous, neither creative nor brave, but for the contributions of Mistral.

Bridget V. Franco

Using Community-Based Learning to Teach Poetry in the Spanish Language Classroom

Recent position statements from the American Council on the Teaching of Foreign Languages emphasize the importance of global competence, interpersonal communication, and real-life application of skills in the twenty-first-century world languages curriculum (*Global Competence Position Statement*, *World-Readiness Standards*). These same characteristics are often used to describe community-based learning (CBL), a pedagogical approach that connects academic learning goals with civic engagement outside the traditional classroom. CBL, also known as experiential or service learning, balances theory and praxis through involvement in the students' local community.[1] Civic engagement can be placement-based, occurring through regular service that meets community-identified needs, or project-based, working through research and experience that holds the promise of social or scientific value to the community. In this mutually beneficial process, students gain a deeper understanding of course content by integrating theory with practice, while communities gain access to volunteers, resources, and expertise housed in the participating academic institution. Through CBL, students transform textbook knowledge from the course into action, benefit from the space and time needed to reflect on and question this acquired knowledge, and face complexities and

235

cognitive dissonances that can lead to significant intellectual and personal development. These components are precisely the reasons why CBL has been identified as among the highest-impact educational practices in terms of student engagement and success. Between 1997 and 2006, the American Association for Higher Education produced a series of twenty-one monographs focusing on how service learning can be implemented within particular disciplines. The majority of the publications (fourteen) cover disciplines in the social sciences or the professions. The four humanities areas represented in the AAHE series are philosophy, religious studies, composition, and Spanish. The essays in the volume on Spanish, Construyendo Puentes *(Building Bridges): Concepts and Models for Service-Learning in Spanish*, emphasize the benefits of service learning in Spanish-speaking communities through the lens of second language acquisition and intercultural competency (Hellebrandt and Varona). Only one chapter, "Altruism and Community Service in Hispanic Literature," addresses service learning in the context of teaching of literature (narrative) in Spanish (95–105). More recently, a special-focus issue of *Hispania* on "The Scholarship of Community Engagement" (Hellebrandt and Jorge) examined CBL in relation to second language acquisition, translation projects, teacher education programs, and heritage speakers. While these publications point to some of the ways that community engagement can transform the Spanish language curriculum, there is scant research on how CBL can be successfully integrated into college-level courses on literature, particularly poetry, in Spanish.[2]

My study explores the integration of a CBL project into a traditional, lecture-style introduction to textual analysis taught in Spanish at an undergraduate liberal arts college. The primary course objective was to identify and analyze literary techniques used in prose fiction, poetry, and drama through a selection of short stories, poems, and plays from *Aproximaciones al estudio de la literatura hispánica* ("Approaches to the Study of Hispanic Literature"), edited by Carmelo Virgillo and others. Students were also expected to further develop their critical writing and speaking skills in Spanish. The structure of the in-class coursework followed the pattern of previous years: the fourteen-week semester was divided into three parts, each one dedicated to a particular genre. At the end of each section, students took an exam and wrote a short essay analyzing a text from the corresponding literary genre. For this particular iteration of the course, I included a third course objective: "Experience the ways in which different literary genres connect with the real world through a community-based learning project in the local community." All students were required to take part in a project with their peers and Spanish-speaking members of the local urban community. In small groups, they selected a text (ideally one we had not studied previously) from each genre, analyzed the theme and relevant literary devices, prepared a list of discussion questions, and made photocopies of the reading before each site visit. Each team made a total of three visits (one per month) to the community partner's site to share and discuss their readings. In this essay, I first outline the logistical considerations for implementing a CBL project and then examine the benefits of CBL within the framework of a literature course taught in Spanish. Next, I explore how the CBL aspect affected and enhanced the poetry module of the course. Finally, I share my perspective on the cost-benefit balance in terms of curricular restructuring, give some suggestions for improvement, and outline possible applications for different academic contexts related to poetry.

Logistical Considerations and Benefits

First, I needed to identify off-campus sites where the target language would be Spanish rather than English, where the interactions would be relevant to our academic learning objectives, and where the community partner had identified a need or project. Because the CBL component of the class was mandatory, I also needed to provide more than one option to accommodate my students' schedules. In consultation with my college's CBL administrative staff and my own contacts in the local community, we decided to offer two options: the Third Day reading group, an after-school program run by the Assumption Mission Associates for elementary and middle school (mostly Latino and Latina) children struggling with reading; and the Latino Elders program, run through Centro las Americas, now CENTRO. The program director of the Third Day reading group wanted to provide students in grades 3–6 with exposure to college-age mentors who were excited about literature and could help foster an interest in reading in any language. The program director of the Latino Elders program, viewed the visits as occasions for the elders to share aspects of their culture and speak in Spanish to young people. The logistics of scheduling and transportation off-campus were arranged through our office of community-based learning.

Studies have consistently found that CBL positively impacts areas such as academic learning, student learning outcomes (including cognitive development, critical-thinking skills, and problem solving), interpersonal development, intercultural understanding, and social responsibility.[3] However, it is important to remember that the benefits of CBL are not automatic or guaranteed. There are several practices that should be considered in order to achieve the outcomes outlined above. Among the principles that Jeffrey Howard encourages are the selection of community sites that clearly align with course learning goals; opportunities for critical reflection and analysis of how service learning informs academic content; and a shift in the traditional faculty role of instructional leader to guide and facilitator in order to increase student-led learning and independent critical thinking (Howard and Galura 5–9). These guidelines can challenge or even deter instructors, especially new faculty members who may not have enough contacts in the community to identify a meaningful off-campus site, or who may be wary about sacrificing classroom time for critical reflection sessions. Such were my own concerns when I was asked to teach a Spanish American culture course with a mandatory CBL component during my first year in a tenure-track position. Saying yes to that experience, however, was pedagogically transformative for me, as I saw the powerful ways that CBL engaged my students, pushed them to reflect on difficult questions, and required them to live culture instead of just reading about the concept in a textbook. There is no question that a successful CBL component requires extra preparation time and adjustments to readings and assignments. However, when incorporated with attention to Howard's guidelines, CBL enhances the learning process and affords benefits that are not typically associated with a more traditional classroom dynamic. Within the context of foreign language education, whether the course is focused on literature, culture, conversation, or writing, a CBL component in which students interact with native or heritage speakers provides unique opportunities for linguistic and cognitive growth, affective development, and civic engagement.

My poetry students' observations and the qualitative assessment data from the course confirmed these outcomes. Students consistently and emphatically commented on the ways in which the CBL experience improved their speaking and listening skills in Spanish. One student reflected, "Without a doubt, I am more comfortable with the language as a result of CBL. This kind of learning presents more challenges when conversing and listening to people who have spoken Spanish their whole life."[4] Students tried hard to speak professionally and only in Spanish with their partners; yet, because they were not being observed by a professor or graded for their oral production, they also felt less pressure to craft grammatically perfect statements. By the end of the course, students reported increased confidence and comfort speaking in Spanish that resulted from their interactions with real-world language use and with the rich linguistic diversity of their local community. In the traditional foreign language classroom, students quickly become comfortable with their instructor's accent and cadence, which are usually clearer and slower than speech in nonacademic scenarios. If they are nervous about speaking, students can rehearse their answers before class or defer to their peers. The CBL experience, on the other hand, forces all participants to produce the language without recourse to the safe classroom environment. As another student observed, "In class, the most important thing is to analyze, write, and read, and for this reason sometimes it is acceptable to express your ideas in English if you don't know how to say something in Spanish. In the real world, you cannot do this. You have to struggle to understand and communicate your ideas." The students' lived understanding of language in context and their improved listening and speaking skills are outcomes that no amount of lecturing on or discussion about Pablo Neruda's *Odas elementales* ("Elemental Odes") or Juana de Ibarbourou's "La higuera" ("The Fig Tree") can bring about.

In addition, autonomous and collaborative learning paradigms in the CBL experience demonstrably led to enhanced cognitive development. Students at both sites were expected to select their own poems, create discussion questions, and lead their partners through a reading and analysis. These activities inverted the traditional top-down learning paradigm. In one student's words, "At first, one would think that this would be something simple or easy to plan out. It turns out it isn't, there's a lot of planning to do." Many students reflected that in explaining the course content to others they came to understand and articulate that content better. These observations align with studies that have found significant gains for CBL participants with respect to cognitive development, including increased complexity in problem analysis, a greater resolve to act in the face of acknowledged uncertainty, and improved critical-thinking skills (Batchelder and Root; Eyler and Giles; and Osborne et al.). In his foreword to *Community-Based Learning and the Work of Literature*, Gerald Graff observes that, "When students take their coursework into the community outside the classroom—to the elderly or a class of high school students—they must assume a teaching role themselves, reexplaining, recontextualizing, and thereby remaking what they have learned in a fully active way that is not guaranteed by classroom learning alone" (ix–x). Indeed, the CBL process moves through the four stages or ways of knowing outlined in Marcia Baxter Magolda's epistemological model as absolute, transitional, independent, and contextual. When students must teach course content (in this case, a poem) to someone else, they learn how to formulate their own questions about poetry, moving beyond the basic, cognitive stage of absolute or known answers. Additionally, the presence of peers as co-creators of knowledge creates a bridge to the transitional stage of knowing in which the reliance on professorial authority recedes.[5] Through the CBL experience, my students' understanding of the poems shifted from an external interpretation provided by the professor (often considered absolute by students) through a peer-to-peer process of collaborative knowledge building (transitional), eventually arriving at the contextual knowing stage, characterized by independent thought that also took into account the CBL partners' different opinions and interpretations. Independent exit survey statistics (administered by the office of CBL at my college and not tied to student grades) confirmed the impact CBL had on student learning: ninety-three percent of my students agreed or strongly agreed that "including community-based learning in this course enabled me to learn more deeply than I otherwise would have" (Sterk Barrett).

Poetry in and out of the Classroom

My experience using CBL in an introductory literature course (and in a variety of other Spanish-language courses) has confirmed the aforementioned important outcomes linked to linguistic and cognitive development. But what is singular about the poetry component of the CBL project? How does the CBL experience enhance the more traditional aspects of presenting and teaching Spanish-language poetry in the classroom? First, my students read the introduction to poetry in the anthology selected for the course, define the terms presented there, and practice identifying examples of poetic styles and techniques in the textbook exercises and other handouts. I give presentations about meter and rhyme, rhetorical devices, and tropes. Students learn about synalepha (or elision), diphthong, hiatus, and syneresis while practicing versification using the lyrics from their favorite songs by Spanish American musical artists. They identify different kinds of verses according to consonant and assonant rhyme schemes and syllabic meter. We discuss alliteration, personification, apostrophe, metaphor, simile, antithesis, anaphora, synesthesia, periphrasis, and metonymy while analyzing a selection of sonnets, *rimas, romances,* and free verse poems from

Spanish America and Spain, dating from the sixteenth century through the present day. We review the biographical information about the poets from the very brief "Vida y obra" (Life and Work") sections in the anthology and talk about the ways in which the literary devices help to transmit or reflect the poem's message or theme. Each student gives an oral presentation analyzing a poem's versification and rhyming sequence and identifying and explaining the rhetorical devices used. At the end of the five-week period dedicated to poetry, students write a short essay about a poem we have not studied in class and take a written exam testing their knowledge of poetic devices, definitions of important terms, specific poems studied in class, and versification. While I incorporate interactive activities, pair exercises, and small group discussions, the pedagogical model in the classroom is based on top-down learning, text-based knowledge acquisition, and the prioritization of individual achievement.

In his oft-cited chapter "Traditional vs. Progressive Education" in *Experience and Education*, John Dewey, one of the founding philosophers of experiential education, contrasts the traditional lecture style of teaching with what are now considered the major tenets of service- or community-based learning: learning through experience and the acquisition of skills through hands-on practice in a changing world (5–6). While Dewey opposes traditional and experiential pedagogies, scholars in recent years have come to view these learning processes not as antagonistic but rather as synergistic: "Rather than serving as a parallel or sidebar activity, the students' community service experiences in academic service learning function as a critical learning complement to the academic goals of the course" (Howard 21). How exactly does the CBL poetry project function as a "critical learning complement"? My course incorporated two different off-campus sites, where small groups selected different poems and visited on different days. This heterogeneity created an opportunity to reflect, in postvisit sessions where the students learned from one another's experiences, on why certain poems and activities worked well and for which audiences.

Because my groups were visiting community partner sites that catered to different age groups, they had to make their poetry selections accordingly. This was their first encounter in the class with collective curriculum building. These collaborative and student-centered exercises happened before each site visit and fostered deeper engagement with the course material. The students paired with the youth in the Third Day reading group decided to present Mexican *calaveras*, poems published or recited on the Day of the Dead, because their visit coincided with this holiday. They selected short poems and wrote a series of questions for discussion, focusing on tone, metaphor, and theme in connection with the Day of the Dead. After researching the tradition, they also decided to bring skull coloring pages and sweets for the children. This decision, entirely of the students' making, led to an opportunity for affective engagement and intercultural exchange that would impact their postvisitation, in-class work on poetry.

First, the small groups read their *calavera* poems with the children. During the discussion that followed about the differences between the Day of the Dead and Halloween, many of the children who came from households with Mexican or Central American family members volunteered anecdotes about relatives who had passed away. My students were surprised at how comfortable these young children felt talking about death, a topic that is more taboo in the United States. In the course of being open to the young children who were enthusiastically sharing their memories of deceased relatives, my students had the opportunity to face their own cultural assumptions about death and dying. This exercise illustrates the concept of interculturality as developed by the Language Policy Division in response to the Council of Europe's 2008 white paper on intercultural dialogue: "Interculturality refers to the capacity to experience cultural otherness, and to use this experience to reflect on matters that are usually taken for granted within one's own culture and environment" (10). In this case, poetry was the impetus for bringing a cultural difference to the fore. This awareness could also have been achieved in a traditional classroom through lecture or discussion. However, the dynamic of CBL further decentered my students from their linguistic and cultural comfort zones. They were not simply acknowledging the difference distantly. They had to engage the children in conversation and "come to understand culture not only as information about diverse people and their practices but also, and most importantly, as the contextual framework that people use to exchange meaning in communication with others and through which they understand their social world" (Scarino 324). The intercultural experience came full circle the following day in our class.

As part of our academic curriculum, I introduced a writing exercise that was related to the cultural context of Day of the Dead: *el conjuro*, the conjuring poem. While a Mexican altar or *ofrenda* commemorates and invokes the spirit of a lost loved one through favorite objects, foods, and smells, the conjuring poem lures back memories using words. Verses that describe the departed person's speech and physical attributes summon the individual's spirit, and the magic of the words brings the deceased back to life. Such an activity would have seemed arbitrary and strange in the context of the more canonical poems we had read in class, but I relied on the students who had been at the youth reading group to explain to their classmates the ease with which the children had spoken about their loved ones. I then projected a template to guide the writing process through which my students would experience the cultural otherness of the conjuring poem and its approach to death and loss through a perspective of acceptance, closeness, and celebration. Their poems were powerful, intimate, and honest. Some students asked if they could have more time to finish and edit their work. Other students independently incorporated rhyming and meter schemes into the verses. Many of the poems moved me to tears. The CBL experience the day before had created an intercultural moment that in turn fostered my students' (and my) willingness to take a risk and use poetry to facilitate the expression of deeply personal and vulnerable feelings.

Risk-taking occurs often in CBL. The next two scenarios illustrate the consequences of taking such risks or not. The students who visited the Latino Elders were divided into two groups in order to accommodate their schedules. The groups made two different poetry selections and the results were significant. One group chose a poem that we had not discussed in class, "Los maderos de San Juan" ("The Woodsmen of San Juan"), attributed to Colombian poet José Asunción Silva. The other group made a less risky choice, selecting a poem that we had already covered in class: "Rima LIII" ("Rhyme LIII") by the Spanish poet Gustavo Adolfo Bécquer. While both groups had struggled in the first session to keep their community partners engaged in the narrative reading, the reactions to these poetry selections differed considerably. Here is one student's description of the Latino Elders' reaction to "Los maderos de San Juan":

> After the first stanza of the poem, they paid attention. Almost immediately, many of the Latino Elders began to sing the poem to the melody of a children's song. One woman said to me with a smile, "Thanks for taking me back to my childhood." Before arriving to the site, I didn't know that the poem also existed in the form of a song. . . . I found the song using my cell phone, connected it to the speaker, and we all listened and danced.

This experience with the Latino Elders resonates with Roland Barthes's concept of the reading experience as pleasurable, collaborative and intertextual, as developed in "From Work to Text." No longer was the poem a collection of static, black-and-white words on a page in an anthology that would soon be resold to another student and forgotten. The poetic verses came alive through music, memory, and joy. A poetic text was transformed into a cultural object that created a connection between the past and the present for the elders, and that bridged a generational and linguistic divide between the students and their partners in the community. Poetry in that moment was a lived experience. Indeed, the elders answered one of my students' prepared discussion questions (How does the poem's meter make it seem like a song?) not through words or explanations, but in a more visceral and emotive manner through music and dance. The Latino Elders' performance of the text crossed the boundaries between academia and popular culture and reconfigured for my students the relation between reader and text.

The poem selection, although serendipitous, was critical to achieving a breakthrough moment. Indeed, this particular interaction directly addressed the larger issue that many of the students who worked with the Latino Elders articulated in their first journal entries: "I didn't expect them to be so uninterested in the literature. It's a bit frustrating and embarrassing to ask them to pay attention because we have to read something to them. In the future we could try to find something with themes more applicable to them." The group that chose "Rima LIII" expressed greater frustration with the CBL poetry unit than did their peers who selected "Los maderos de San Juan." However, the struggle to engage their partners led to a critical reflection during our debriefing session about how and why poetry connects with its audience. We discussed questions like, In what ways does the cultural context (of the reader and of the poem) matter? What is my responsibility for finding poems that will engage my community partner rather than reusing a text from class that I already feel comfortable with? How can a poem transport the reader or listener temporally or spatially? How do rhythm and musicality interface with affect? Who defines the literary canon, to whom does that canon matter, and why? How does poetry intersect with popular culture? In the difficult moments that arise from what some might consider a failed CBL site visit, students must think about poetry beyond the constructs of a classroom lecture about rhyme, meter, and rhetorical figures.

Indeed, reflection sessions are essential for critically unpacking both the positive and the more challenging aspects of the CBL experience. Recent research highlights the primary role of critical and self-reflection in

CBL projects.[6] The small-group reflection discussions can be facilitated by a peer group leader, a CBL student intern, or another professor (this is an excellent way to pique interest in CBL among faculty), and students benefit from answering some guiding open-ended questions beforehand (see appendix). The reflection piece of the CBL puzzle serves as a bridge between theory and praxis, between academic content and real-world application, between learners' minds and hearts. Not surprisingly, this is also the piece that is most closely connected to the promise of civic engagement and future commitment to or interest in social justice issues. In their journal entries, students reflected on their partners' struggle with literacy, the barriers to successful bilingual education in the public school system, socioeconomic disparities, the lack of support for different populations in the local community, and their own privileged position within higher education. One student commented: "Perhaps the children don't read Spanish at home . . . or, it's possible that they do read in Spanish at home. It seems like the schools teach the students that Spanish is not a language for school. I hope that the readings show them that Spanish is not only a language for home, and that it can be important in school too." Here my student, himself enrolled in a university-level foreign-language literature course, grapples with the realization that the public school system does not seem to value Spanish as a language for communication in the public sphere. His observation points to one of the many complexities that students will encounter during their CBL experience. By processing the reality that languages other than English are not valued in many public schools in the United States, especially at the elementary level, college students who have invested heavily in foreign language acquisition realize firsthand that their own perspective is just one of many. They are faced with the fact that their passion for Spanish and their belief in the curricular value of speaking another language is embedded in a wider social context that does not easily transfer to their community partners' experience. This awareness is particularly relevant to a CBL project that explores the role of reading and literature in the community. Because the projects were tied to literary genres, my students had to immediately engage with questions about different levels and types of literacy and the relevance of literature to Spanish-speaking communities in the United States—questions that would probably not arise in a traditional poetry classroom. The reflection process provides a space where students can think about questions of privilege and about possibilities for future action. Assessment data for this course showed that eighty-seven percent of the class agreed or strongly agreed that "this course increased my interest in community service or engagement."[7]

As we have seen, in addition to the linguistic and cognitive growth that CBL affords students, increased affective and civic engagement are two other reasons for expanding academic learning into the local community. My students consistently talked about how the experience touched their hearts and opened their eyes:

> Our CBL experiences help me recognize how important some of the works we learn about in class are in Latin American culture. . . . Some of the works we read are just as important to the Latino Elders as works from poets like Robert Frost are to American literature. I learned the importance of understanding the language and culture of other people in the community. Each person has an interesting story to share.

These reflections show how the affective relationships with their community partners deepened my students' engagement with the course material and helped them understand the different ways that individuals in nonacademic settings connect to poetry and literature.

Challenges, Changes, and Applications

Deep, engaged learning does not come without a cost, and inevitably CBL introduces complexity and challenges for the students, the professor, and the community partners. In this last section, I will focus on some of these issues, offer possible modifications, and suggest ways that this pedagogical model might function in other contexts related to Latin American poetry. Many students observed that, because poems are shorter in length than narrative or drama, this module of the CBL experience left more time for discussion with their community partners than did the modules in other genres. In their final reflections, the groups that selected more accessible poems (in the case of the children, *calaveras* that were not overly abstract; in the case of the Latino Elders, a poem that was also a popular song) rated poetry as the genre that worked best for the CBL project. The students who did not experience the same kind of breakthrough or affective moments rated poetry as the most difficult genre for CBL, commenting that metaphors were too difficult for children and poetry required more intellectual attention because it was more abstract than narrative or drama.

Even these perceived drawbacks or disadvantages, however, can be turned into learning moments. A task need not be discarded simply because it is difficult. In fact, the students who rated poetry as the least effective genre for CBL also pointed out that their chosen poem's rhetorical devices, ambiguous language, and variety of possible interpretations forced them to work closely with their partners on analysis. In a traditional classroom, if students are confronted with a difficult, abstract, or complex poem, they have the option to disengage and let their peers do the work. Their lack of participation on a particular day will probably not adversely affect their grade, and they can feel comfortable with someone else's analysis of the poem. With CBL, disengagement and deflection are not possible. My students' comments about the difficulty of teaching poetry to others also reflect to some degree their own discomfort with the genre. Their negative descriptions recall attitudes toward poetry identified by Muriel Rukeyser as common in American society: boredom, indifference, distaste, hatred, and resistance. "This resistance has the quality of fear, it expresses the fear of poetry" (7). For the students who experienced a personal and emotional connection as a result of their community partners' reactions, the resistance to poetry quickly dissolved. No longer was the poem an abstract artifice, only to be studied and analyzed. Instead of trying to answer the question, "What does this mean?" students entered into an affective state with their community partners. For those students who do not have this experience, their peers' testimony and targeted reflection questions about negative perceptions of poetry can lead to a stimulating discussion about why we resist texts that seem at first inaccessible, abstract, or difficult.

Another challenge for CBL is the time commitment. When I teach with a CBL component, I ask students at the beginning of the semester how they feel about undertaking this aspect of the course. The responses include surprise, uncertainty, discomfort, nervousness, lack of enthusiasm, and annoyance. The few students who have prior CBL experience typically report excitement and interest. Only in the end-of-semester evaluations do students claim that they would have liked to spend more time at their off-campus site; rarely do they ask for more frequent visits during the semester. For this particular course, a majority of students reported at the end of the semester that they would have liked the opportunity to visit more than three times.[8] Since my class was required for Spanish majors, but the mandatory CBL component was a pilot program, problems of equity could have arisen if a student needed the class for the Spanish major but could not invest additional time for legitimate academic, work-related, or extracurricular reasons. I decided that a two-hour commitment, once a month, for a total of three visits, would be manageable for everyone. In hindsight, I agree that more visits would have enhanced and deepened the students' and the community partners' experiences; however, expectations regarding this time commitment should be clearly conveyed before students enroll in the class.

Lastly, CBL projects can be modified and adapted in response to a variety of factors: community demographics, course learning objectives, community partner needs, student and faculty time commitment, and project- versus placement-based options. Here is a short list of possible applications for combining CBL with academic content that includes Spanish-language poetry at different levels of the curriculum.

> Explore poetry through songs by Spanish American artists with Spanish-speaking young people or elders in the community. Students conduct weekly visits (one song per visit) in conjunction with an advanced intermediate culture or conversation course.
>
> Students conduct Spanish-language or bilingual poetry workshops at the local library or after-school program. On each visit, students present a poem, lead a discussion about a specific rhetorical device (or meter, rhyme, theme), and help the participants craft their own poems or verses, in conjunction with a course on poetry or creative writing in Spanish.
>
> In urban settings, students attend weekly or monthly hip-hop or spoken word poetry readings by Latino and Latina performers and reflect on how these experiences expand the definition of poetry, as part of an advanced seminar on poetry. As Priya Parmar and Bryonn Bain note, these performances showcase the art of the spoken word, a revival of oral poetry movements dating back to ancient times that utilizes the dynamic range of the voice, engages the nuances of vernacular speech, and often articulates the social marginality that African Americans as well as Latinos and Latinas experience.

While my case study is just one possible model for integrating CBL in a poetry module or course, these examples point to different ways in which the CBL model can be modified for a variety of applications at different levels of the Spanish language curriculum. Rukeyser observes: "A poem invites you to feel. More than that: It invites you to respond. And better than that: A poem invites a total response" (8). By participating in a Spanish-language CBL project, students can enhance their academic experience of poetry through personal affective engagement, deeper intercultural understanding, challenging linguistic encounters, and civic engagement in the local community—indeed, a total response to poetry.

Notes

1. While there has been a notable increase in service-learning publications since the early 2000s, the following are considered core resources for new practitioners: *Introduction to Service-Learning Toolkit* (Campus Compact), *Where's the Learning in Service-Learning?* (Eyler and Giles), *Service-Learning in Higher Education: Concepts and Practices* (Jacoby et al.), and *Successful Service-Learning Programs: New Models of Excellence in Higher Education* (Zlotkowski).

2. Kevin Guerrieri explores the intersections of literature and community engagement in his essay in *Community-Based Learning and the Work of Literature*, proposing that CBL can help mediate the curricular challenges that arise as students move from language to literature courses.

3. See Janet Eyler's *At a Glance: What We Know about the Effects of Service-Learning on College Students, Faculty, Institutions and Communities, 1993–2000.*

4. This and all subsequent quotes from student reflections are reprinted with permission. Special thanks to Nicole Bambara, Tiffany Holland, Jeffrey Ibarra, Meghan Kelly, Sydney Latour, William Olsen, and Charlie Suse.

5. Student reflections such as the following articulated this movement from the absolute stage to the transitional stage of cognition: "There is a great difference between the experience that you obtain in the traditional academic classroom and CBL. In the former, you . . . have the help of the professor, whereas when you teach in the community you are alone with the help of your peers and you are teaching the material."

6. In *A Practitioner's Guide to Reflection in Service-Learning*, Eyler and colleagues summarize the "4 C's" for productive reflection: continuous (throughout the experience), connected (directly related to learning objectives), challenging (demands high-quality effort and instructor feedback that then stimulates further learning), and contextualized (class- and level-appropriate) (16–21).

7. This statistic becomes especially significant in the light of recent debates about the role of higher education and the perceived crisis of the liberal arts in particular. In *A University for the 21st Century*, James J. Duderstadt posits that the founding principle of American colleges and universities is to advance knowledge and to educate students who will in turn apply their knowledge to serve others in society. Hence institutions of higher education are responsible for modeling and transmitting essential civic and democratic values and developing the experience and skills necessary to put them into practice.

8. In a survey of 144 students in twenty-three different courses, J. Beth Mabry found that service learning was more effective when students performed at least fifteen to twenty hours of service and enjoyed frequent contact with their partners in the community.

Appendix: Reflection Questions

After each visit with their community partners, students should write a short reflection in response to the following prompt questions. Instructors are encouraged to dedicate some class time to a discussion based on these reflections. Questions and answers can be written in English or Spanish, depending on instructor's preference.

Preliminary Reflection—Complete prior to first site visit

What was your reaction when you learned that this class had an experiential learning or community-based learning (CBL) component?

What are your expectations for this project?

What expectations do you think your community partner has for you?

What are your objectives for this project? What do you want to accomplish? What do you want to learn? What will you have to do throughout the semester to achieve this?

Poetry Reflection—Complete within one week of poetry site visit

How did you feel before visiting your CBL site?

What has been the most frustrating or difficult part of this experience? Why?

Describe the process of selecting your poem.

How does what you have done in your CBL project relate to this course? What connections can you see between your CBL project and what we are studying in class?

What did you enjoy about discussing poetry with your partner? How has this experience differed from our classroom discussions about poetry?

What kinds of challenges have you encountered during your discussions with your partner?

If applicable: Which genre (narrative/short story or poetry) has been easier to discuss with your partner? Why do you think this is?

Comment on the best aspect of the CBL experience so far.

Mid-Semester Reflection

What problem or issue does your community partner's organization address? What is your role in addressing this issue? How does this make you feel?

In what ways do you think your partner benefits from this experience?

What has been the most positive aspect of your experience? What has been the most rewarding? Why?

What has been most challenging about your experience? Have you ever felt frustrated or confused? Have you ever felt uncomfortable? Why?

How does your CBL project relate to what you are learning in this course? Do you see any of the course objectives at play? Could you make this connection more explicit? How so?

How has this experience been different from or similar to what you anticipated? Has it met your expectations?

What do you want to get out of your CBL experience? What do you want to learn? How can you make this happen for your last site visit this semester?

Final Reflection — Complete within one week of last site visit

Read your first reflection again and compare the way you felt before your first CBL visit to the way you felt about your last visit.

What was the best part of the last visit? What was the most difficult part? Why?

Which literary genre worked best for your CBL project? Why do you think so?

What did you learn from your community partners this semester? What do you think they learned from you?

How has your experience in the community affected your ability to express yourself in Spanish? How does this kind of learning compare with the experience of learning in a traditional academic classroom?

Silvia R. Tandeciarz

On Poet-Scholars:
Un Taller de Poesía

Since 2010 I have been teaching a poetry workshop (*taller de poesía*) in Spanish for intermediate and advanced undergraduate students at the College of William and Mary. Distinct from other courses in our curriculum, the *taller* invites students skilled in cultural criticism and translation to tap into their creative capacity for invention, linguistic exploration, and performance in order to create an original body of work while deepening their understanding of Spanish American poetic traditions and their contexts of creation and expression. We begin with a simple question: why write? And students develop their particular, situated responses to this prompt—why write poetry? why now? why here?—by considering how poets in Spanish America and Latino and Latina poets in the United States engage this question in the contexts of political activism and human rights. While similar prompts could guide a traditional seminar dedicated to the critical study of poetry, by activating the vital creative force within my students I hope to advance a different kind of learning—one derived from practices that, in the words of Brian Massumi, "might not have so much to do with mastery and judgment as with affective connection and abductive participation" (cited in Zournazi 220). I am convinced, moreover, that the risk, self-discipline, collaboration, openness, and sensitivity this work requires can make it transformative. In coming to voice as part of this larger conversation, students not only refine their linguistic competencies and affirm their ways of being in the world; they do so by deepening their cross-cultural awareness, their understanding of the literary form, and their appreciation of the tools for change the public humanities can offer.

The idea for this course grows out of my own experience and practice. As a cultural studies scholar with expertise in post-dictatorship Argentina, I have spent most of my academic career in the United States teaching Spanish American literature and culture to nonnative speakers. Over the years I have found ways to express different facets of my own voice as scholar, poet, and translator in my published work. I also have integrated these various modes of engagement in my pedagogy, primarily through creative assignments in issues-driven, interdisciplinary seminars. My *taller de poesía* builds on these experiences to explore largely uncharted territory. A brief review of curricular offerings in departments of Spanish and Hispanic Cultural Studies suggests that creative writing classes taught in Spanish are few and far between. I believe this represents a missed opportunity to harness the awe-inspiring, revelatory, and critical capacities associated with second language acquisition, including the joys of linguistic discovery and experimentation. While the idea of teaching a poetry workshop in Spanish to nonnative speakers may seem misguided—is there a literary form, after all, that requires greater precision and linguistic mastery?—it attracts me because of the demands poetic language makes of us. Aspirational and exacting, poetry calls us to attention; it turns on a detail and opens up new worlds. Exercises in reading and writing poetry can help sharpen even more the usual focus required of students by the foreign language classroom while simultaneously reactivating deep-seated memories of when students first tried new sounds, discovered speech through a different alphabet, moved from estrangement to recognition and back again. A focus on poetry makes immediately evident the difference an error in conjugation or spelling can make; how choices in punctuation, gender, a pronoun or form of address can impact meaning; and why, while many options could be grammatically correct, poets might choose one over another. But, even more than the language skills students refine with such practice, I am interested in the ways unfamiliarity, the strangeness of a foreign language—as an oblique, disruptive element that introduces a welcome randomness—can serve to enhance creativity, problem solving, and learning.[1] While working through this language filter is only one layer of the experience, it sets the stage for the ways in which we engage the course questions that bring us together.

The discussion that follows draws on Diana Taylor's theorization of the archive and the repertoire to analyze the contents and processes that constitute my *taller*. By organizing my remarks in this way I hope to show the variety of levels on which the course operates, "the live and the scripted" (32) forms of knowledge it facilitates. The archive on which I draw familiarizes students with great works from the Spanish American canon and includes scripted assignments designed to advance their critical, linguistic, and poetic capacities. My approach to the repertoire explores "those acts usually thought of as ephemeral, nonreproducible [forms of] knowledge" (Taylor 20) that correspond to students' embodied memories of the course. While my remarks are limited by my perspective as facilitator and guide, I hope they nevertheless convey some of the ways in which the collaboration, contemplation, and invention students practice might remain with them, encouraging them to seek new creative challenges and shaping how they choose to face them.

An Archive

So why write? And why write poetry? Half of our time in class is focused on how published poets have responded to this question. Assigned readings correspond to the Spanish American literary tradition—in which I include Latino and Latina poets writing in the United States—and foreground the ways in which history and social location shape utterance, in both method and message. Our archive features works by canonical figures like Ernesto Cardenal, Alejandra Pizarnik, and Pablo Neruda, as well as lesser-known poets like Juana Goergen and Andrea Cote. Short texts by John Berger, Carolyn Forché, Martín Espada, Roque Dalton, and Eduardo Galeano provide the theoretical frameworks for approaching our interpretive and creative labor. Specific prompts invite students to identify other works they like or find particularly compelling in the only required textbook, an anthology of Spanish American poetry, and to unpack those poems' appeal. In discussing our choices, we focus on beauty and lyricism, on composition and mechanics, and on how these poems speak to the issues and debates of their time.

A favorite touchpoint in the course is the poetry of Juan Gelman, not only because of the mastery with which Gelman wields his craft, but because his poems lend themselves beautifully to conceptualizing the poetic gesture as a form of activism or *militancia*. Full of idiomatic expressions and neologisms, they can prove challenging for undergraduate students with limited proficiency; yet reading his work offers the class an opportunity to deconstruct it while addressing the histories of repression in the Southern Cone, details of Gelman's own biography, and his response to the defeat of the political project that accompanied the massacre of his generation at the close of the twentieth century. I prepare students for engaging with Gelman's work by asking them to read John Berger's essay "The Hour of Poetry," paying particular attention to the evidence behind Berger's claim that "poetry can repair no loss but it defies the space which separates." Berger's assertions that "[p]oetry addresses language in such a way as to . . . incite a caring" and that its "unceasing labour is to bring together what life has separated or violence has torn apart" (249) guide our analysis of one of Gelman's poems in class. Addressed to the author's disappeared son, "Si dulcemente" ("So Gently") begins with a series of questions:

> si dulcemente por tu cabeza pasaban las olas
> del que se tiró al mar / ¿qué pasa con los hermanitos
> que entierraron? / ¿hojitas les crecen de los
> dedos? / ¿arbolitos / otoños
> que los deshojan como mudos? / en silencio (*Si dulcemente* 79)

> If waves from someone who threw himself into the sea/
> came to mind gently / what about our brothers who were/
> in-earthed? / do leaves sprout from their
> fingers? / saplings / autumns /
> soundlessly losing their leaves? / silently (St. Martin 87)

In our discussion I direct students' attention to the way Gelman's poetic voice conjures through these questions the bodies of the disappeared, their bones, in their final resting places. We note his point of departure—the image of a cadaver at the bottom of the sea, rocked by waves generated by a diver—and how this one death moves the poet to wonder about those other "little brothers" disappeared as a result of state terrorism, those left in *fosas comunes* ("burial pits") and unmarked graves.[2] Unpacking the metaphorical language this reverie evokes helps students see how it operates, how the image of sprouting leaves introduces the natural cycle of life and death, through autumn's decay to the silence of a figurative winter. Then we turn to consider how this opening stanza sets up the rest, breaking that silence to conjure the voices of those gone, to name them, to reconstruct their militancy and their humanity with tenderness, effectively remembering the shared hopes of a shattered collective before closing again with the muteness of bones disintegrating in the summer night.

Reading the poem closely together facilitates a discussion of Gelman's craft—how his expert use of metaphorical language transforms the scene of annihilation into something more, and how he creates pockets of intimacy vital both to the construction of collective memory and to the future work this memory might engender. I spend some time addressing those pockets Gelman opens through language, pausing to consider as an example his use of the word "entierraron" 'in-earthed' in line 3. Students don't always notice the erroneous conjugation in Spanish of "to bury" or understand why Gelman has chosen to retain in the past perfect conjugation of the verb both the word *earth* (*tierra*) and the present tense (*entierran*). Pausing together to consider Gelman's choice helps them recognize how it functions to interrupt the poem's gentle flow of questions. Like a snag or a slap after the caress of the opening lines, it is a deformation that demands the addressee pay attention, revisit what is stated there, in order to grasp the very finitude of death and simultaneously the never-ending and also creative nature of mourning. This understanding leads, in turn, to a discussion of the way Gelman's poetry processes trauma to tap into the liminal, the not-yet-available to culture, and to communicate a deeper truth: the incomprehensible, almost unassimilable reality of a loved one's body buried deep underground, rendered mute in humid darkness, but also in the very medium from which, through recollection, a life-nurturing energy might be harvested. It is as if the metaphor of the tree and the genealogy of resistance it images had sprouted from Gelman's poetic unconscious, a gift that when spoken might also generate community through the intimacy of shared understanding.

If I have chosen to share this classroom exercise in some detail it is because it captures the workshop's general approach to the archive. Studying poems like Gelman's alongside Berger's theory helps students appreciate the sort of purposeful, directed intervention poetic language pursues while at the same time identifying what is distinctive about the forms it takes; it makes visible strategies they may want to borrow and invites them to experiment with form. Appreciating poetry's "continual labour of reassembling what has been scattered" (Berger 249) through metaphor helps students discern the technique and discover some of the reasons poets might use it. Whatever the circumstances that bring new poets to voice, I have found that Berger's formulation of the problem, the call to poetry, proves scalable.

All the readings I select for the workshop speak to the labor of poetry. Each example we discuss in class answers in its own distinct way the central course question; each provides an opportunity to situate poetic utterance in a particular historical moment, social experience, or debate, and to focus on the formal elements that make up that particular poet's toolbox. Brought together as a series of case studies, the readings lay the foundation for our semester-long curriculum. What is more, while the archival elements chosen may vary in different iterations of the course, they are always selected to serve a double function: to familiarize students with a body of work corresponding to Spanish American poetic traditions and to prepare students to make the leap from reception to action as they seek to answer the central course questions for themselves and in their own voice. In other words, students must be given enough historical and contextual information to make sense of the poet's social location; and the study of each work must make visible the range of choices available to the poet, how voice and silence, rhyme and repetition, line breaks and enjambment, imagery and metaphor, linguistic innovation, and even punctuation are used to greatest effect. But equal attention must be addressed to how the live and the scripted might optimally come together to encourage students' development of their own poetic language. The course archive must, for this reason, also include another sort of script, one made up of exercises and assignments designed to maximize other ways of knowing through the affective creative charge of the embodied workshop experience. In practice this means understanding the course as a form of experiential learning and, following Spinoza, understanding affect as a bodily operation aligned less with feeling or emotion and more with transformative potential—the "capacity of *affecting* and being *affected*" (Massumi cited in Zournazi 212), of moving and being moved. If, as Brian Massumi claims, "Affect *is* this passing of a threshold, seen from the point of view of the change in capacity" (Zournazi 212), the repertoires folded into the workshop will prove vital to the learning experience—not because all the students will become published poets, but because what they feel in the course of engaging this medium will stay with them long after the workshop is finished. For this reason, the scene must be primed with assignments and exercises, like those described below, designed to give "the body's movements a kind of depth that stays with it across all transitions—accumulating in memory, in habit, in reflex, in desire, in tendency" (Massumi cited in Zournazi 213).

A Repertoire

So how do "the archive and the repertoire work [together] to constitute and transmit . . . knowledge" (Taylor 33) in the Spanish-language creative

writing workshop? What difference might this approach to engaging poetry make? One way to begin answering these questions is to describe
what students are called upon to do as part of this class, both in terms
of formal assignments and in our face-to-face encounters. The students I
work with are generally very comfortable with the structure of intermediate and advanced Hispanic cultural studies classes that require them to
apply a range of theoretical paradigms to literary analysis and develop close
textual readings. They are also accustomed to detailed grading rubrics that
incorporate objective measures into evaluation criteria, such as adherence
to MLA format, grammatical accuracy, and use of textual evidence. Given
this, I include in our program of study an assignment that is relatively standard in our discipline, a short analysis of a poem or series of poems that
invites students to demonstrate the critical expertise they have developed
in previous courses and helps build their confidence as they venture into
less familiar terrain. But I also incorporate hybrid assignments that require students both to identify and to experiment with techniques expertly
employed by published poets. Working within the relatively safe confines
(formal and linguistic) of a preexisting text helps students make the leap
from the familiar to the unfamiliar and provides them with the scaffolding
necessary for developing their own poetic voice.

    A favorite hybrid assignment is an annotated translation of a poem
originally written in Spanish. I prepare students by discussing with them
published examples, the choices translators are called to make, and how
cultural expertise and historical context necessarily condition these choices.
We analyze together how very challenging works like Vicente Huidobro's
"Golondrina" ("Swallow") have been rendered into English and discuss
my own translation of Juana Goergen's poem "Reconquista" ("Reconquest"), along with the translators' notes.[3] I also ask them to consider
how the creative labor of translation aligns with our central course question: why translate, why make the effort to recreate a particular poem in
another language? Before they select a poem to translate on their own, I
make sure they are primed to consider length, theme, format, difficulty,
and their familiarity with the poet's cultural background, and to create
meaningful annotations and commentary. I also reserve time in class for
guided feedback on first drafts. When all is said and done I find that students tend to select poems for personal and political reasons, to gravitate
toward free verse and toward lesser-known authors, and to fret most over
challenging turns of phrase and idiomatic expressions. In almost every
case, however, the critical and creative attention this effort entails helps

them understand not only the way the text they are translating has been put together and why but how the creative choices they make contribute to the final product expressed as their own poem. The exercise reminds them that writing and translation do not occur in a vacuum, that they are powerful interventions in the public sphere, and that they can be strategically deployed to act in the world, touch a community of readers, and shape our collective imagination.

A second hybrid assignment I have found very effective in the first part of the course focuses on the genre of blackout or found poetry. It entails having students identify a newspaper article or other brief text in prose (manifestos work well, as do short canonical pieces) published in Spanish that they would like to express as a poem. I explain that it is up to them to find the poem within the text by blacking out all the extraneous words and punctuation without changing the order in which the words appear. Their task is to apply what they have learned about poetic language in their selection process in order to distill new meaning from their found text. The blackout poems they generate fall along a continuum reflecting individual combinations of poetic sensibilities, skill, and chance; but they always include lovely surprises, powerful juxtapositions, and metaphorical expressions that are worth exploring further. Some are so beautifully composed that they could certainly be published. A recent memorable example is Lydia Hurtado's "Demandarán regresar" ("They Will Demand to Return"; see appendix). Hurtado takes as her point of departure a story published in the Mexican daily *La Jornada* ("The Day") about a protest organized by the National Immigrant Youth Alliance ("Demandarán"). In her brief introduction, she explains that she chose to focus on this particular subject because of its timeliness and because of her desire, as a first-generation citizen of the United States, to intervene in the conversation about "dreamers," children of undocumented migrants born in the United States. Crossing out most of the words, she begins and ends her poem with the same affirmation, "intentarán" ("they will try"):

Intentarán
reunificar familias
separadas
por la deportación.

Tijuana, México
San Ysidro, California—
parte del movimiento

"Llevarlos a casa."
"Dreamers"
(traídos cuando eran niños
criados y educados en este país)
deportados.

Intentarán.

They will try
to reunite families
separated
by deportation.

Tijuana, Mexico
San Ysidro, California—
part of the movement
"Bring them home."
"Dreamers"
(brought as children,
raised and educated in this country)
deported.

They will try. (my trans.)

Hurtado extracts from the prose description of the organized protest what she wants to make visible, what she believes matters most: the hope and determination the protest underscores. And she uses repetition, one of the poetic tools we discuss, to convey the conviction that underlies the participants' attempt. What is more, she enacts what Carolyn Forché calls a "poetics of witness"—a poetics situated in "the sphere in which claims against the political order are made in the name of justice" (31). Having been introduced to Forché and other writers who make explicit the links between humanistic pursuits and civic responsibility, Hurtado activates her own creative and cultural agency to turn theoretical principles into practice. Her blackout poem not only recognizes how powerful "the work of art in the world" can be; it demonstrates how assignments like these can spark students' imaginations and offer them the ways and means—the words, the mechanism, the tools—to become "judicious citizen artists" (Sommer 9) and agents of change.

While hybrid assignments prime students for coming to voice, most of our energy throughout the semester is focused on the development of an original body of work: a series of poems authored by students in Spanish. In this sense, the exercises that structure our time together in the workshop environment are as important as the kinds of assignments students complete outside of class. I deliberately choreograph every class meeting to balance our critical and creative engagement with poetry. Our very first encounter sets the tone for what will follow. After brief introductions, I ask each person to take two minutes to think about and write down a favorite word or phrase in Spanish. I want the students immediately to reconnect with what drew them to Spanish, the sounds and cadences that sparked their imagination. They come up with all sorts of things, from verses learned in a middle school Spanish language class to words spoken by grandparents and phrases overheard while studying abroad. I share with them my own early fascination with Federico García Lorca's "Romance sonámbulo" ("Dreamwalking Ballad"), particularly the verse "verde que te quiero verde" 'green, how I want you green' (191). But I also introduce songs like "Canción para mi muerte" ("Song for My Death") by the Argentine rock group Sui Generis that captivated me as a teenager, with its haunting opening lines: "Hubo un tiempo que fue hermoso / y fui libre de verdad, / guardaba todos mis sueños / en castillos de cristal" 'There was a time that was beautiful / and I was truly free, / I kept all of my dreams / in crystal castles.' Once everyone has had a chance to weigh in, I explain some of the reasons for the exercise: I want the class to see that poetic language is everywhere and that we often have a visceral connection to its sounds and rhythms. Attending to what provokes this response within us is not only a first step toward figuring out how we might mold words to shape our own poetic expression; it also can transform the way we relate to our everyday. Practicing an openness to what may come is part and parcel of activating the poetic imagination; and welcoming the unexpected can lead, with care and labor, to extraordinary results. I also take this opportunity to underscore how much of the workshop experience hinges on a climate of mutual respect and to establish some ground rules about listening and offering constructive feedback. Having their writing discussed by their peers can make students feel vulnerable and exposed, even under the best of circumstances, so creating a safe space for sharing our creative work must be a top priority. Before ending the class, we review the syllabus, and I give the first writing assignment: a mnemonic exercise wherein students recall in detail their earliest memories of Spanish. I also ask the students to bring to our next class an object for show-and-tell, and to begin noting in their *cuaderno de anotaciones* ("writing journal") those images, words, phrases, questions, dreams, and bits of overheard conversations they encounter in their everyday lives that might find their way into future poems. By the time they return for our second class, I find they are what I call "in it," invested in the work that lies ahead and cognizant that they will demonstrate their mastery of course materials, not in the usual ways, but rather by becoming practitioners of the craft. They will learn by doing—by striving, by failing, by revisiting and revising in pursuit of their own creative vision.

If day one sets the tone, other elements in my toolbox help shape the encounters that follow. I bring to these a set of "oblique strategies" adapted from exercises commonly used in poetry workshops taught in English and from exercises developed for the foreign language classroom.[4] The trick, I've found, is to mix things up, following the principle that disruption, frustration, and unforeseen obstacles can enhance rather than block creativity. My own set of oblique strategies is designed to shift students' attention, to help them relate to the language they are utilizing in a new way, and to reinforce the formal aspects and poetic techniques we are covering. Some of these are scripted while others are improvised. Anne Waldman's "Intriguing Objects" exercise is a good example of the first. Its point of departure is the collection of objects students bring to our second class for show-and-tell. As students take turns sharing the stories of their objects, their classmates take notes. Once everyone has had a chance to present, students are asked to write a poem based on one or more of the objects presented. Pairing this writing exercise with readings from Pablo Neruda's *Odes to Common Things*, like "Oda a los calcetines" ("Ode to Socks") or "Oda al pan" ("Ode to Bread"), further helps students understand how metaphors are constructed, with one thing standing in for the other, and how images and objects can operate in a poem to convey meaning. Students often choose to write about a fellow student's object, adding their own interpretations as gentle offerings. And I borrow each of their first lines for a derivative exercise that asks students to choose an opening verse they like and write a poem to follow.[5] Our "Poetic Snapshots" exercise is structured in a similar way. Inspired by Maggie Anderson's "In a Dark Room: Photography and Revision," it draws on photographs instead of objects. I ask only that students select an image to share that captivates them for some reason, whether it is a personal or family snapshot or a professional photograph by an artist or photojournalist. I then ask that they write three different poems inspired by the image from three different perspectives and with three different audiences in mind. Before doing so, they must think about what is visible within the frame and what has been left out; what is blurry and what is in focus; what details jump out at them and how these relate to the feelings the photograph elicits. This exercise helps students think about the differences between narrative and poetic forms of expression, the evocative power of visual details, and questions of perspective and voice—from where and to whom the poetic voice is addressed. Follow-up exercises like Robin Behn's "Letter Poems"—"Write a poem in which a particular speaker who refers to him or herself as 'I' is addressing a particular 'you'" (70)—help students develop their own poetic voice further, a task once again informed by examples of published works. Together, these activities help students assimilate and synthesize a range of techniques and strategies; and students demonstrate their understanding of how such poetic choices shape outcomes by putting them into practice.

In addition to all the necessary work these scripted poetic encounters accomplish, spontaneous collaborative exercises inspired by the foreign language classroom round out the workshop learning environment. Participants, after all, are language learners, called upon to compose in a less familiar tongue. Approaching the language filter as an asset rather than a hindrance means practicing a form of pedagogical jujitsu, and bringing in an element of play is key to helping students wrestle with the blank page. Given this, I often ask students to work in pairs or in teams and have them respond to prompts under ridiculous time constraints. This formula paradoxically seems to mitigate their stress and maximize their enjoyment. I call on them, for example, to transform idiomatic expressions and *dichos* ("sayings"), or a set of unrelated words generated through a *lluvia de palabras* ("brainstorming"), into a poem in ten minutes; to string together existing lines of verse in new ways that generate new meanings; to write "class poems" in real time by the progressive addition of a single line of verse, often to great comic effect; and to move between English and Spanish, using translation, to help fine-tune their efforts. Peer feedback, opportunities to read original poems out loud and to hear them read by others, and open discussion about what is working, what needs work, and why, round out most of our class sessions. Rather than finding students' imperfect mastery of Spanish to be an obstacle in this creative process, I find it enhances their creativity and willingness to collaborate. Indeed, at its best, this melding of workshop environment and foreign language classroom confirms Brian Eno's observation that "[t]he enemy of creative work is boredom . . . And the friend is alertness . . . what makes you alert is to be faced with a situation that is beyond your control so you have to be watching it very carefully to see how it unfolds, to be able to stay on top of it. That kind of alertness is exciting" (cited in Harford, *Messy* 22). Full of "attention-grabbing challenges" (Harford, *Messy* 22) the foreign language poetry workshop invites students to engage in pleasurable linguistic play, to attempt new formulations, and to share their creations in a climate of mutual support and open discovery. In so doing it fulfills "a special mission by keeping aesthetics in focus" and facilitating "charmed moments of freely felt pleasure that enable fresh perceptions and foster new agreements" (Sommer, 3).

Perhaps the most distinctive aspect of the *taller de poesía* is its insistence on valuing process as much as, if not more than, discrete outcomes or final products. This emphasis is reflected not only in the ways we work together in class but also in course evaluation rubrics that include categories like development and growth. Measuring these means recognizing students' openness to risk and experimentation while insisting on the importance of correction and revision. The course's culminating assignment is a portfolio composed of six to eight original poems the students consider their best work. I make clear that all the work in the portfolio should have been through at least one rewrite following feedback from me or from a peer review. I also ask that students write a short introduction that establishes the parameters through which they would like me to approach their work; that they reflect on the development of their own poetic journey; and that they make explicit where that journey began for them and where it led. This self-reflection, I explain, should function like a position paper in which they develop and defend, given their own experience, newfound expertise, and location, their view of what the work of poetry entails, what poetry can do for those who write it and those who consume it, and what they consider special—or not—about its labor. I regard the workshop as a success to the extent that most students arrive at "a conception of poetry in strong relation to—or as a form of—knowledge-production and knowledge-work . . . that conceives of learning, researching, interpreting, as forms of *poiesis*" (Ronda); and that they leave with a deeper appreciation not only of the beauty of this art form, but of the small and transcendent ways in which the poetic imagination can "reframe experience, offset prejudice, and refresh our perception of what exists so that it seems new and worthy of attention" (Sommer 10). I am convinced, moreover, that the workshop provides excellent training in cultural agency. By following "a model of poetic production as grounded in inquiry, instruction, and labor (rather than, say, the expressivist ideals of natural genius, creative imagination, and emotional spontaneity)" (Ronda), the foreign language creative writing workshop can play a unique role not only in Hispanic studies curricula but more generally in a liberal arts education, broadly conceived. As part of a comprehensive program of study, it can offer students necessary space in which to pause, to listen to one another, to take risks, and to find joy in acts of creation, while simultaneously recalibrating their approach to the academic enterprise and preparing them for public life. And it can help form poet-scholars whose experience of making art will stay with them as a memory of the possible through creative challenges and transformations to come.

Notes

1. I draw here from Tim Harford's TED talk "How Frustration Can Make Us More Creative." Harford expands on these ideas in his recent book, *Messy: The Power of Disorder to Transform Our Lives.*

2. The addressee is most likely Gelman's son, mentioned at the end of the preceding poem, whose body was identified in 1990 in a cement-filled drum found in the San Fernando River. Among the "little brothers" Gelman goes on to name are Paco Urondo, Rodolfo Walsh, and Haroldo Conti, all writers and activists assassinated during the dictatorship. Walsh's and Conti's remains have not been recovered.

3. For the Huidobro translation, I rely on *Thinking Spanish Translation: A Course in Translation*, edited by Sándor G. J. Hervey and others.

4. The "oblique strategies" were developed by Brian Eno and are described in Tim Harford's TED talk ("How" 00:12:35). I rely on Robin Behn and Chase Twichell's *The Practice of Poetry: Writing Exercises from Poets Who Teach* for most of the exercises I use in class.

5. See Michael Waters's "Auction: First Lines (for a Group)" for more on how this exercise works.

APPENDIX: Blackout Poem

Demandarán

regresar

intentarán

reunificar familias separadas por la deportación.

Ysidro, California   parte del movimiento   Tijuana, México   San
Llevarlos a casa

"dreamers"   traídos   cuando eran niños
criados y educados en este país   deportados.

intentarán

John Burns

From Paz to the *Infrarrealistas*: Rethinking the Mexican Canon

Educators and their students can foster original and creative readings by contrasting poetry that is not part of a recognizable canon with poetry that fits into more widely accepted notions of the canon. For example, by taking the poetry of Octavio Paz and the work of the *infrarrealistas*, a rather marginal group of Spanish American poets from Chile, Peru, Argentina, and, in their majority, Mexico, who began writing and collaborating in Mexico City in the mid-1970s and who viewed Paz as their intellectual enemy, students can process texts they can easily contextualize and compare them with texts whose context is far less obvious. Although I will delve into some of the strategies for teaching these poetries to undergraduates at a small, liberal arts institution in the United States, I will also suggest ways in which these circumstances can illuminate broader considerations of the pedagogy of literary studies in a variety of other higher-education contexts and with a variety of other writers.

In a course in which I taught the work of the *infrarrealistas* and Paz, students created wikis on the factors in contemporary Mexican culture and history that informed the poems we read, developed questions to ask surviving members of the *infrarrealista* group, and produced final projects that created a dialogue between the students' own experiences of community, culture, and crisis and representations of those themes in the work of the poets we examined. Studying canonical and less canonical works side by side creates a framework for producing cultural and historical awareness in the face of textual and contextual ambiguity. Students in my class could do so with an intellectual safety net in the form of the abundant critical information on Paz, yet they also ventured beyond the preestablished critical apparatus since there is relatively less work to be found on the *infrarrealistas*. While I will discuss this approach in a very particular context, one could certainly extend it to other literary and artistic forms, from novels to the plastic arts to films, in order to make experimental work more legible to students in the context of more transparent or more traditional forms of writing and representation.

Octavio Paz is a towering figure both inside Mexico and within academic circles in the United States. Biographical descriptions of Paz are often included in introductory-level Spanish textbooks, and his work is frequently anthologized in intermediate language and upper-level textbooks in the United States. Additionally, virtually all upper-level literature textbooks that touch on twentieth-century Spanish-language literature from the region include his work. Without argument, he is a mainstay of Spanish American literature curricula. Most undergraduate Spanish majors will be likely to read, at the very least, *Piedra de sol* (*Sunstone*), his 1957 meditation on the Aztec sun stone, or sections of his 1950 book of essays *El laberinto de la soledad* (*The Labyrinth of Solitude*), in which he discusses topics ranging from Mexican attitudes toward death to Mexican-American culture or the colonial origins of machismo in Mexican society. Having won the Nobel Prize in 1990, he is even read in translation in some English curricula at the high school and college levels by means of anthologies such as *The Norton Anthology of Latino Literature* and *The Norton Anthology of World Literature*.

The overwhelming majority of the *infrarrealistas* are situated, in contrast, squarely outside university studies in the United States. The great exception would be Roberto Bolaño, who, particularly since his death, is perhaps beginning to supplant Gabriel García Márquez as the most recognizable figure of Spanish American narrative fiction in the United States' relatively small literary translation market. While Bolaño's fictionalization of the group as the "real visceralists" in *The Savage Detectives* has garnered attention in the pages of magazines such as *The New Yorker*, where the novel was described as showing the "teeming literary underworld" of Latin American literature (Harvey), the work of the group that inspired this representation has not. The *infrarrealistas* have been historically marginalized in the world of Mexican letters. Take, for example, noted Mexican novelist and public intellectual Jorge Volpi's dismissive characterization of the group and Bolaño's role in it:

> Ahora todos conocemos la prehistoria: cuando era joven y todavía no era Bolaño y vivía exiliado en la Ciudad de México, Roberto o Robertito o Robert o Bobby participó en una pandilla o mafia o turba o banda—por más que ahora sus fanáticos y unos cuantos académicos despistados crean que fue un grupo o un movimiento *literario*—, cuyos miembros tuvieron la ocurrencia de autodenominarse "infrarrealistas". Una pandilla o mafia de jóvenes iracundos, de pelo muy largo e ideas *muy* raras, macerados en alcohol y las infaltables drogas psicodélicas de los setentas, que se dedicó a pergeñar manifiestos y poemas y aforismos y sobre todo a beber y a probar drogas psicodélicas y, de tarde en tarde, a sabotear las presentaciones públicas de los poetas y escritores oficiales del momento, encabezados por ese gurú o mandarín o dueño de las letras mexicanas, el todopoderoso, omnipresente y omnisciente Octavio Paz. (80)

> Now we all know the prehistory: when he was young and wasn't Bolaño yet and he was living exiled in Mexico City, Roberto or Robertito, or Robert or Bobby took part in a gang or mafia or mob or ring—in spite of the fact that now their fans and a few clueless academics believe it was a group or a *literary* movement—, whose members had the notion of calling themselves "infrarealists." A gang or mafia of angry young men, with long hair and *very* strange ideas, steeped in alcohol and not-to-be-missed psychedelic drugs of the seventies, and who dedicated themselves to coughing up manifestos and poems and aphorisms and, above all, to drinking and experimenting with psychedelic drugs and, some afternoons, to sabotaging public presentations of the official poets and writers of that moment, headed up by that guru or Mandarin or boss, the all-powerful, ubiquitous and all-knowing Octavio Paz.[1]

Some in the literary establishment considered the group unworthy of attention and viewed Bolaño's participation in it as an obstacle that the Chilean-born writer overcame rather than part of his formation as one of foremost writers of the region at the end of the twentieth century.

Recently, the *infrarrealistas'* work has become somewhat less marginalized. In 2014, for example, culturally normativizing publications in Mexico such as *Proceso* ("Process") and *Letras libres* ("Free Letters") reviewed the anthology of *infrarrealista* poetry titled *Perros habitados por las voces del desierto* (*Dogs Inhabited by the Voices of the Desert*), edited by

Rubén Medina. These same magazines also covered the controversies the anthology stirred up (critics who shared Volpi's estimation of the group and the academics whom Volpi had attacked as *despistados* ["clueless"] had a few arguments about the anthology[2]). Because of this notable and available coverage, and because of the anthology's innovative scope, I used *Perros* as a textbook for teaching the *infrarrealistas*. Medina includes poems by original members of the group as well as work by poets who were not associated with the movement until later. In other words, the anthology opens the movement up from its historical anchoring in the 1970s, suggests that it has continued on the margins of Mexican literary culture, and shows how the movement appeals to a certain segment of younger poets in Mexico today.

In addition to Bolaño's novels, the poetry of the infrarealist Mario Santiago Papasquiaro has become more visible in recent years. The Mexican novelist and public intellectual Juan Villoro wrote a piece for the newspaper *La Jornada* ("The Day") in 1999 in which he pointed out that Bolaño's character Ulises Lima[3] was inspired by the *infrarrealista* poet:

> Ulises Lima, protagonista absoluto del relato, es el poeta Mario Santiago. Los visceral realistas representan a los infrarrealistas, el grupo que alborotó nuestra república de las letras en los setentas.

> Ulises Lima, absolute protagonist of the story, is the poet Mario Santiago. The visceral realists represent the infrarealists, the group that stirred up our lettered republic in the 1970s.

Though Papasquiaro published only two books in his lifetime, in 2008 Fondo de Culura Económica published the anthology *Jeta de santo* (*Saint's Mug*), and several *cartonera* publishers worked in concert across Latin America to produce another anthology, *Respiración del laberinto* (*Respiration of the Labyrinth*).[4]

In the final analysis, what little mainstream coverage there has been of the *infrarrealistas'* work can be attributed, to some degree, to the posthumous Bolaño publishing phenomenon in Spanish America and beyond.[5] Scholars have documented the real-world figures corresponding to the characters in the novel, with perhaps the most extensive work on the topic being that of Montserrat Madariaga Caro in *Bolaño infra: 1975–1977: Los años que inspiraron* Los detectives salvajes (*Infra Bolaño: 1975–1977: The Years That Inspired* The Savage Detectives), based on interviews with various members of the group. Aside from Bolaño and, to a lesser degree, Papasquiaro, writers associated with the group, such as José Peguero, Pedro

Damián Bautista, Guadalupe Ochoa, Rubén Medina, and Edgar Artaud, have remained marginal.

Beyond these very recent discussions about the limits of the group and its belonging (or not) in the Mexican canon, students have very little criticism to go on, particularly searching in the sources they are trained as undergraduates to use in their information literacy preparation, such as *JSTOR* or the *MLA International Bibliography*. What they can glean from the *infrarrealistas'* work itself is the group's disdain for official, state-sponsored poetics in Mexico and, according to their manifestos, all things associated with Octavio Paz. As Bolaño wrote, the *infrarrealistas* saw themselves as *guerrilleros* (guerrilla fighters):

> El verdadero poeta es el que siempre está abandonándose. Nunca demasiado tiempo en un mismo lugar, como los guerrilleros, como los ovnis, como los ojos blancos de los prisioneros a cadena perpetua. (386)

> The true poet is the one who is always abandoning himself. Never too much time in one same place, like guerrilla fighters, like UFOs, like the white eyes of prisoners serving a life sentence.

The *infrarrealistas*, it seems, were always on the attack. Readers of their work are tasked with reaching beyond what the group was against and deducing and articulating what they were for. Students are faced with a literary movement whose limits and aesthetics have not been digested for them: they must do a greater share than usual of the metaphorical chewing.

There is a claim to be made for this kind of contrast between canonical and far less canonical work that goes well beyond literary studies. As teachers in the humanities navigate the shifting landscape of educational values in the twenty-first century, there is a growing administrative chorus that demands real-life applicability in undergraduate education, as well as the development of so-called soft skills such as adaptability, problem solving, and collaboration. In the face of the growing tide of pro-STEM (science, technology, engineering, and math) rhetoric,[6] one case for the value of studying the documentation of human experience is found in the humanities' propensity to offer a guided encounter with ambiguity and with seemingly contradictory statements. This propensity even carries over to the business world, where, as we are often reminded, there is a demand for tolerance of ambiguity that current undergraduates are perceived as lacking.[7] While few things could be thought of as further afield from the business world than Spanish American poetry, it could easily be argued that our field of study provides a particularly compelling space for exploring uncertainty. Including poetry that has a long critical bibliography attached to it and poetry that has very little in the way of an established critical apparatus opens up a space in the classroom, and in written assignments, that facilitates student inquiry into the underpinnings of aesthetic judgment. Students can evaluate and react to the critical reception of Paz, and, while they can certainly produce their own readings of his work, they are more likely to reproduce professional critical readings when these are available (the surrealist elements, for example, that are so often cited in *Piedra de sol*). When it comes time to produce similar readings of the *infrarrealistas*, students are in a position in which there are no "right answers." In other words, they cannot corroborate their reading of a poem by Mario Santiago Papasquiaro, Ramón Méndez Estrada, or Bruno Montané with an article or book found in the MLA database. However, to ask even advanced undergraduates to produce a critical account of this work (or, for that matter, the work of any writer or group of writers whose work had not received much critical attention) in a literary vacuum would be unreasonable and unproductive. Some students, who are entrenched in the notion of right and wrong answers, experience anxiety in the face of ambiguity; therefore it is highly unlikely they will spontaneously generate a tolerance for it when given a set of decontextualized poems.

So, in order to piece together the literary and historical context of these works, I encouraged my students to focus on what the *infrarrealistas* have to say about Paz. Why do they dislike Paz so much? If Paz's work exemplifies the officialist aesthetic, what does the *infrarrealista* aesthetic look like? What are the main points of difference? Why does the dismissal of their work persist? Why are there some scholars and poets who are committed to preserving their work? In broad strokes, questions such as these guided both in-class and online discussions as we began to study the *infrarrealistas* in the context of Paz-dominated Mexican poetry. Open-ended questions within a specific historical-critical framework helped move us toward open-ended questions within a less specific historical-critical framework. By asking what makes a poem either good or bad from certain perspectives, students ultimately interrogated the underlying assumptions about poetry, and, in the broadest terms, about culture, that make answering that question possible. In classes where I teach poetry, I often point out to my students that, as a general rule, they are far more willing to express their opinions of narrative works, be they films, stories, or novels, than they are to offer judgments of lyric poetry. To some degree, this is the cultural heritage model of literary studies at work. As Mary Macken-Horarik writes, this model is "linked to induction of readers and writers into the great works of the literary canon." She continues:

> The relationship between teacher and student is like that of the incumbent to a cultural insider (or mentor). The pedagogy is often implicit, drawing attention to the sensuous particularities of an image, the rhythmic patterning of a sonnet, the influence of, say, Elizabethan world views on Shakespeare's tragedy, the aesthetic pleasures of the Haiku or, in a contemporary genre, the rap poet. Predictably enough, the specialised practices of the Heritage model are privileged in examinations and, by extension 'privilege' those students who control them. At the heart of this model is the text and this is a key source of epistemological validity. (10)

Poetry, like the plastic arts, is revered as a mysterious and privileged form of cultural production about which students do not feel entitled to offer their opinions because they feel like outsiders who have not been inducted into some sort of secret society.

In the United States, many students are not familiar with poetry in their native language, much less with lyric poetry in the Spanish or Spanish-American traditions. They may or may not have been exposed to poetry at all before entering an upper-level literature class in Spanish; or they may have a working knowledge of the poems of a handful of luminaries, such as Federico García Lorca, José Martí, or Pablo Neruda. Those who were formally educated at some point in Spanish-speaking countries may have heard of the best-known poets of that nation (especially if those poets appear on the print currency, such as Gabriela Mistral on the five-thousand-peso bill in Chile, Sor Juana on the two-hundred-peso bill in Mexico, or César Vallejo on a limited-edition twenty-sol coin in Peru). Yet, in general, students lack confidence in their knowledge of poetry, and, as Daniel Xerri points out, their anxiety can be a self-perpetuating cycle that "has a negative effect on the way they engage with poetry during a lesson" (4). In reading lesser-known poets, students come to understand that there is no clear, existing pathway to authority on these texts, that critical reception is ongoing, and that they are as worthy as any group of readers to construct an informed account of the *infrarrealista* movement.

Other poets or groups of poets could be similarly used to promote students' engagement and confidence and to develop their critical abilities. For example, in a Peruvian context, one could contrast the *infrarrealistas'* slightly older aesthetic siblings, Hora Zero, with the work of Vallejo (whom they revered to the extent that the *infrarrealistas* rejected Paz).[8]

In a Chilean context, one could examine the shadow that Pablo Neruda cast on twentieth-century poetry, leaving poets like Winétt and Pablo de Rokha to peddle their own wares door to door.[9] Or a class could contrast the relatively underappreciated work of Juan Luis Martínez with that of the more politically adept Raúl Zurita (critical work such as Scott Weintraub's *Juan Luis Martínez's Philosophical Poetics* would be indispensable here). Anthologies of younger poets are constantly being published in different national contexts: examples are the Mexican poet Daniel Saldaña París's anthology of Chilean poetry *Doce en punto: Poesía chilena reciente* ("Twelve on the Dot: Recent Chilean Poetry") and *Astronave: Panorámica de poesía mexicana, 1985–1993)* ("Spaceship: Panoramic View of Mexican Poetry, 1985–1993"), which contains work written by poets born in the 1980s and 1990s; selections from these could be contrasted with the work of better-known poets in those same nations. One could also teach an anthology of poetry in indigenous languages and contrast it with more canonical poetry written in Spanish during the same time period. The lack of plentiful and rigorous academic resources on lesser-known anthologized poets can be offset by the context anthologies provide in ordering and distributing the material and in adding biographical notes. Finally, an advantage of teaching poets who are little known in the academy is that many can be interviewed, in person or even by video chat. Face-to-face encounters with living writers can take the edge off students' cultural heritage anxieties and diminish the idea of literature as a foreign, idealized, and distant practice. They also encourage students to be more actively engaged in the construction of their own knowledge.

When working with poetry that falls into my particular research area, I have found it helpful to purposefully increase so-called guide-on-the-side activities as a way to engage students and to resist the temptation to simply lecture about a body of poetry that I know well. In my class on the *infrarrealistas*, since we were studying a group of poets and exploring the notion of collectivity, I emphasized group assignments. We began with an Octavio Paz wiki using the university's learning management software. I set up the wiki with a brief series of entry headings and students then met in small groups to fill in the content of the entries. These included summaries and reactions to selections of *El laberinto de la soledad* (*The Labyrinth of Solitude*) and *Piedra de sol*, as well as a brief biography establishing the prestige and influence of the works and detailing Paz's diplomatic appointments and literary prizes. Alternatively, I might have asked the groups to research this material and present it in class, but creating the wiki outside of class allowed more class time for discussion and prepared students to assess Paz's institutional enfranchisement from the point of view of the disenfranchised young writers of the *infrarrealista* movement.

Once students were able to articulate some of the textual qualities (such as a polished style and an authoritative voice) and contextual factors (such as an association with the state) that marked Paz as a target of the *infrarrealistas*, we moved on to some other texts that would help them situate the term *infrarrealista* with greater specificity. Using the learning management software, I created forums where students were asked to respond to fairly open-ended questions about pertinent texts. I restricted the forum so they could not view other students' reactions until publishing their own; once they had done so I instructed them to comment on at least two other student responses. Contrasting Bolaño's and Mario Santiago's manifestos, students were struck by the disruptive form of writing as much as by the exhortations to create a freer form of art. One student noted that Bolaño "quiere que hagamos algo positivo en vez de aceptar lo que nos pasa" 'wants us to do something positive instead of accepting what happens to us.' Another wrote: "En el manifiesto de Mario Santiago Papasquiaro, él propone que todos pueden y deben hacer arte y que el arte no está en una clase sino que está dentro de cada uno de nosotros" 'In Mario Santiago Papasquiaro's manifesto, he proposes that everyone can and should make art and that art is not in a class but rather inside each one of us.' After beginning with an examination of what the *infrarrealistas* were not, the online discussions slowly got us to the point of identifying what they were.

In an undergraduate setting, continually questioning the status of canonical literature and reading marginal writers might appear to risk destabilizing literary studies as a valuable and distinct discipline. Yet my experience has been to the contrary, for at the end of the semester students seemed more engaged with the liberating possibilities of literature than they were at the beginning. Emphasizing a cultural analysis model rather than a cultural heritage framework helped demystify and desacralize literature. Lifting poetry out of the perceived realm of disinterestedness (undergraduate students, if they have not been exposed to the notion of disinterestedness in Emmanuel Kant, may find it useful to know that it is an idea with a particular history[10]) and tying it to the political may help students understand firsthand the ongoing negotiation of canon formation. If nothing else, the exploration of the canonical in contrast with the noncanonical encouraged them to ask, perhaps for the first time, why they were reading what they were reading. And it helped them answer, to some degree, the following related important questions: Do I like what I am reading? If so, why? If not, why not?

In terms of the literature studied, exploring the relationship between center and periphery illuminated larger social, cultural, and political considerations. The *infrarrealistas* defined themselves against the Mexican state. As Medina put it in the introduction to his anthology, speaking of the figures and concepts the *infrarrealistas* opposed:

> [N]o sólo nos oponíamos a las concepciones imperantes del lenguaje, del poema y la poesía . . . sino que nos oponíamos a sus propias concepciones de la literatura, sus mecanismos de legitimación y sistemas de valor, así como a la práctica tan peculiar del escritor mexicano de depender del Estado mediante nombramientos. (21)

> [N]ot only did we oppose the dominant conceptions of language, poem and poetry . . . but we also opposed their very conceptions of literature, their mechanisms of legitmation and value systems, such as the very peculiar practice of the Mexican writer depending on appointments of the state.

For university students, part of the appeal of this group of poets is their rebellious nature and their youth at the time they were exposed to the oppressive machinations of the Mexican state during the dirty war,[11] in particular the massacre of Tlatelolco in 1968 or the Corpus Christi Massacre (El Halconazo ["Hawk Strike"]) in 1971 in which Mexican students were targeted. Examining conflicting reports on these events from the time and subsequent investigations, we speculated in class about why the *infrarrealistas*, who were so young in the 1970s, seem to hold a particular fascination for young writers and readers of poetry in Mexico today. Students were able to bring the discussion into the present day by looking at how the disappearance of the forty-three students from the Ayotzinapa teachers' college in Guerrero, Mexico, and the violence of the drug war affect Mexican youth today. Additionally, students drew their own conclusions about the dearth of reliable, objective information about Tlaltelolco and Ayotzinapa.

In a comparable fashion, more strictly delimited literary studies became meaningful for the students when they began to feel that understanding poetry was not a chore based on memorizing terms, but a puzzle to be put together. The *infrarrealistas* were voracious readers of twentieth-century experimental writing, and the group's appropriation of earlier literature became more apparent to students when we dedicated a week to in-class presentations on surrealism, dadaism, the Beat generation, *estridentismo*, and Hora Zero. I suggested that the presenters avoid making overt connections to the style and practice of the *infrarrealistas*, leaving that bit of literary sleuthing for in-class discussion following each presentation. At times, students engaged in creative mimicry by trying to write poems in the styles of the literary movements we studied. At others, they wrote short analytical pieces comparing and contrasting *infrarrealista* texts to Beat or surrealist texts to find points of relative similarity and difference.

By contrasting the canonical with the noncanonical students were able to discover (rather than simply be told) that the canon is neither innocent nor impenetrable. They could trace the negotiation involved in canon-making and even see that they are, by virtue of being in an institution of higher learning, in some small measure part of it. Along the way, we explored the complexities of cultural tastes and of power, both literary and political. We desacralized poetry without diminishing it. In fact, some students reported an increased interest in the subject at the end of the semester. One student wrote that she found our conversations about culture were not only applicable to Mexican poetry in the 1970s; "también es aplicable a mi vida" 'it is also applicable to my life.'

Notes

1. Unless otherwise attributed, all translations are mine.

2. For example, Heriberto Yépez wrote of Rubén Medina's introductory essay, "Ese texto es uno de los ensayos más completos que haya escrito un poeta mexicano en los últimos cuarenta años; su combinación de lenguaje urbano y teórico, testimonio y crítica literaria lo pone aparte" 'That text is one the most complete essays that a Mexican poet has written in the last forty years; its combination of urban and theoretical language, testimonial and literary criticism sets it apart' (Yépez 12). David Medina Portillo, a critic writing for *Letras libres*, stated, "El proyecto de un infrarrealismo activo es una posibilidad tentadora. Sin embargo, apenas resiste la prueba de un sentido común mínimo" 'The project of an active infrarealism is a tempting possibility. Nevertheless, it barely stands the test of common sense' (Medina Portillo).

3. In an essay for the critical editon of Papasquiaro's poem *Consejos de 1 discípulo de Marx a 1 fanático de Heidegger* (*Advice from One Disciple of Marx to One Fanatic of Heidegger*), Peruvian poet Tulio Mora points out that the surname Lima was, in part, a nod to the work of the roughly contemporary group of Peruvian neo-avant-garde poets, Hora Zero: "Lima por el gordo Lezama y por la ciudad donde nació HZ" 'Lima after fat Lezama and after the city where Hora Zero was born' (Mora 167).

4. Silvina Friera mentions different editions from Argentina, Bolivia, Brazil, Chile, Mexico, Paraguay, and Peru.

5. The Mandarin Chinese translation of Bolaño's *2666* "sold out immediately" in China when it was released in 2011 (Ziru).

6. For example, in a piece written for National Public Radio, Marcelo Gleiser writes, "We need to unify America around the need for science and STEM education as the only guarantee for prosperity."

7. In 1996, the American Council on Education published *Higher Education and Work Readiness: The View from the Corporation*, stating that employers sought this trait and felt that it was lacking in graduates of institutions in the United States, leaving prospective employees unable to function "effectively in an ambiguous, complex and rapidly changing environment" (8). More recently, in a piece for *Inside Higher Ed*, the president of Goucher College affirms that a high tolerance for ambiguity "is essential for democracy, and it is being used in research on global leadership because it is related to cross-cultural communication and performance in diverse work environments" (Bowen).

8. The largest Hora Zero anthology to date is titled *Los broches mayores del sonido* (*The Greater Brooches of Sound*), which is a verse from "Poema XXVIII" in Vallejo's *Trilce*.

9. As Naín Nómez writes, "[E]l caso de Pablo de Rokha representa uno de los fenómenos literarios en América Latina de mayor marginalidad y exclusión. Resulta asombroso comprobar cómo Pablo de Rokha ha sido borrado en forma sistemática de toda referencia relevante en la historiografía vanguardista latinoamericana y en gran medida también la nacional" 'the case of Pablo de Rokha represents one of the literary phenomena of Latin America of the greatest marginality and exclusion. It turns out to be amazing to verify how Pablo de Rokha has been systematically erased from all relevant reference in Latin American avant-garde historiography as well as at the national level in great measure' (19).

10. A text that could be used for an in-class discussion of the history and apparent contradictions in Kant's theory of disinterestedness is Paul Guyer's "Disinterestedness and Desire in Kant's Aesthetics," in which he writes: "Thus, Kant took it to be a key conclusion of his theory of taste that the only proper objects of aesthetic appreciation are the spatial and temporal forms of things, as opposed to . . . material properties of objects" (449).

11. Sylvia Karl defines the specific characteristics of the Mexican Dirty War of the 1960s and 1970s in this way: "Mexican governments, like other governments all over the world, employed enforced disappearance as a repressive method of state terror against its own population. One reason that this dirty war is less visible than those of other Latin American countries lies surely in the different role that Mexico played within international politics and within Latin America in the 1970s. The country was governed from 1929 to 2000 by the PRI (Party of the Institutionalized Revolution). Internationally it was considered a stable democracy, despite the hegemonic, authoritarian one-party system. This system granted the military a specific role as protector of the Mexican Revolution, the founding myth of the modern Mexican state" (727).

Tiffany D. Creegan Miller

Ri Pach'un Tzij aj Iximulew: Teaching Contemporary Maya Poetries from Guatemala

From 1978 to 1983, the Guatemalan military regime waged a genocidal campaign in the mountainous countryside to counter any form of what they considered subversive behavior. In the years that followed, the Guatemalan government established the Comisión para el Esclarecimiento Histórico (Historical Clarification Commission) and the Catholic Archdiocese of Guatemala developed the Proyecto Interdiociano de Recuperación de la Memoria Histórica (REMHI) to investigate the human rights violations that occurred throughout the Guatemalan armed conflict, from January 1962 until December 1996, the date that marks the signing of the Peace Accords. Although the military targeted both Ladino (similar to a mestizo in the context of Guatemalan race relations) and indigenous people, during the final years of the armed conflict the majority of the victims were Maya.[1]

The anthropologist Edward Fischer has explained that from the ashes of the violence there has emerged "a vibrant social movement working to revitalize Maya cultural forms, to promote Maya ethnic pride, and to create new spaces for Maya peoples in Guatemalan political, economic, and social networks" ("Beyond Victimization" 83). The military and other

279

political leaders viewed the revitalization of Maya culture, such as the recognition of language rights, as a nonpolitical project, equivalent to the study of folklore, and therefore did not consider it a threat (England 734). In this context, Pan-Maya activism has included founding organizations and publishing houses, like the Centro de Documentación e Investigación Maya (CEDIM) and Cholsamaj, that solely address Maya themes. These entities have supported the publication of various Maya authors, such as the poets who will be discussed in this essay: Humberto Ak'abal, Kaqjay Juan Yool Gómez, and Calixta Gabriel Xiquín.

Though there are many Maya authors and artists involved in contemporary Pan-Maya activism in Guatemala, I focus on Ak'abal, Yool Gómez, and Gabriel Xiquín because they represent two of the primary linguistic communities involved in Pan-Maya activism—Kaqchikel and K'iche'—and they are available to varying degrees domestically within Guatemala and internationally. Humberto Ak'abal is perhaps one of the best-known Maya poets today. Ak'abal has written poetry in K'iche' and Spanish, and his verses have been translated for an international audience. He received the Miguel Angel Asturias Literary Prize in 2004 but declined the award for political reasons, "citing a long list of racist acts and abuses that would have made him feel treasonous to his people had he accepted this 'Ladino' award" (Arias, *Taking Their Word* 180). Other Maya authors, such as Yool Gómez and Gabriel Xiquín, have not enjoyed as much visibility as Ak'abal. Unlike Ak'abal, Yool Gómez has worked solely with organizations directly associated with Guatemala's Pan-Maya activism to publish his poetry. The poems by Yool Gómez I discuss in this essay are published in a collection of children's poetry, *Pach'un tzij kichin ak'wala': Poesía infantil en idioma kaqchikel* ("Children's Poetry in the Kaqchikel Language"), which was published in Kaqchikel with Spanish translations through CEDIM/FAFO (Programa Noruego para Pueblos Indígenas). Gabriel Xiquín is both an *ajq'ij* ("spiritual guide") and a poet, and to date she has published a bilingual poetry collection in Spanish and English with the Yax Te' Foundation in California—*Tejiendo los sucesos en el tiempo / Weaving Events in Time*. Publication in the United States has helped this collection gain an international readership, though the volume is also available in Guatemala.

This essay will situate the study of indigenous poetry within Spanish American literary studies before discussing my interdisciplinary approach to teaching the aforementioned contemporary Guatemalan Maya poets. I will address ways to incorporate a multimedia approach to analyzing these poets' works, including digital technology, online recordings, songs, and anthropological case studies. Adopting a cultural studies lens, students work with these sources to understand the primary goals of Pan-Maya activism in Guatemala. Once an understanding of the sociopolitical context is established, students focus on literary techniques deriving from orality in connection to the *Popol Wuj* (the K'iche' Maya sacred text featuring the story of creation and mythological narratives), whose lyricism informs oral traditions in present-day Maya cultures. Although many of these texts are written in a Mayan language, most are also available in Spanish or English translation. Therefore, my approach to teaching these poems could be applied in a variety of courses for students who may not be proficient in these indigenous languages. Finally, in this context of translation, students study other forms of poetry that do not employ the conventional Western alphabet in order to use theoretical concepts associated with writing, textuality, and translation to analyze the poetry. They explore issues of audience and examine what is translated (and what is left untranslated), noting how these features shift our understanding of the poet's work. This introduction to Guatemalan Maya poetries and other forms of indigenous artistic production calls into question students' preconceived ideas about poetry, the politics of translation and cross-cultural communication, and what it means to be Maya in the twenty-first century.

As is the case with other indigenous poetries of Latin America, approaches to many Guatemalan Maya poets in the classroom have historically been the subject of inquiry of anthropologists and linguists rather than cultural and literary critics. In traditional literature departments, survey courses typically incorporate indigenous texts from the period prior to the arrival of Europeans to the Americas. As Rolena Adorno has explained, in Latin American literary anthologies it is common to see texts such as the *Popol Wuj* included in the beginning pages as a pre-Colombian introduction to the literary traditions following the Encounter (3), which, as Paul M. Worley has observed, typically represent the national language, Spanish (2). More recently, however, indigenous studies has emerged as a growing subfield within Latin American literary studies. Although the disciplinary boundaries are changing, Worley also notes that most traditional anthologies of Latin American literature and Latin American literary criticism continue to "cite and/or include indigenous literatures as a pre-Columbian prelude to or influence on literatures composed in the years after 1492" (3). The institutional effects of the marginalization of indigenous cultural and literary production can be seen in the organization of academic departments and their curricula. Working with contemporary indigenous poetry in the classroom, many students have studied pre-Hispanic indigenous texts but are unfamiliar with indigenous authors publishing today. My approach to teaching Maya poetries emphasizes a continuum of sustained artistic engagement to underscore that Maya peoples have written poetry for centuries. I use pre-Hispanic indigenous texts in class to illustrate the historical roots of contemporary Maya cultural and literary production and to explore lasting literary influences.

Class assignments introducing the main ideas of Guatemalan Pan-Maya activism feature a variety of sources and media. For example, pairing a selection by the anthropologist Kay B. Warren with an online recording by Nikte Sis Iboy, an Achi Maya linguist from Guatemala ("Presentation") allows students to work with ideas from the perspective of a Maya intellectual directly involved in Pan-Maya initiatives within Guatemala and from that of an academic based in the United States whose research focus is Latin American indigenous movements. Students observe that both Sis Iboy and Warren emphasize the importance of teaching children to value their heritage if Maya languages and cultures are to continue to exist.

To situate Maya peoples in the present and destabilize the traditional notion that Maya-ness—and, more broadly, indigeneity—is at odds with modernity, it is useful to show examples of songs in which Maya artists work through twenty-first-century musical genres such as hip-hop and rock.[2] For example, I often show the online music video of the song "Grito" by Sobrevivencia/B'itzma, a rock group from San Idelfonso Ixtahuacán, Huehuetenango. Sobrevivencia/B'itzma is comprised of five primary school teachers who write songs in Spanish and Mam (a Maya language spoken by approximately half a million people in Guatemala), at times incorporating Kaqchikel and Achi. Paying particular attention to the lyrics and the images that accompany the song, students reflect on how the songwriters represent Guatemalan Maya peoples as well as Maya cultures and languages in general. During the first few minutes of the video, the lyrics are in Mam, with an abrupt change to Spanish at minute marker 2:45 ("Sobrevivencia"). The first few minutes of the song feature the accompaniment of the traditional marimba; then, for the remainder of the song, the band members play the electric guitar and drums. Students typically respond to the juxtaposition of languages and musical styles with two observations. On the one hand, they are often surprised to see Maya musicians who make rock music instead of limiting themselves to traditional musical forms incorporating the marimba. On the other hand, they feel alienated by their inability to understand the lyrics in the indigenous language, since virtually none are proficient in Mam or any other Maya language from Guatemala. As a result, they are able to identify with the exclusion that Guatemalan monolingual Spanish-speaking audience members experience and to relate meaningfully to some of the politics of language use in this sociopolitical context.

Discussions intended to historically contextualize the marginalization of Guatemalan Maya communities begin with poems that present the idea that the oppression of Maya peoples began with the arrival of the Spanish. Some examples of note are Ak'abal's "500 años" ("500 Years") and Gabriel Xiquín's "Communism, Capitalism, Socialism," which address the suffering and marginalization of indigenous peoples since the Conquest across Abya Yala (a term from the Kuna language in Panama to refer to the Americas in their totality).[3] In the poem by Ak'abal, the speaker underscores the burdens of poverty, indifference, and injustice that indigenous peoples face, explaining that "esto data / de un poco más allá / de 500 años" 'this dates / back to a little more / than 500 years' (7–9).[4] Gabriel Xiquín emphasizes indigenous resistance to oppression, which the speaker connects to the violence of the Conquest: "y desconocen nuestra resistencia por muchos siglos. / A los indios de la América / no nos han 'vencido como pueblos'" 'and our resistance has been ignored for centuries. / The Indians of the Americas / have not been "defeated as a people"' (18–20). Apart from the physical violence associated with the Spanish Conquest and later with the Guatemalan armed conflict, many Maya peoples in this Central American country continue to face institutionalized racism and social inequalities, including but not limited to a lack of access to education and health care. As the speaker in Gabriel Xiquín's poem explains, "Ser indígena es pecado en mi país Guatemala. / En nuestra América, no es respetado ser indio" 'To be Indian is a sin in my country, Guatemala. / In our Americas, being Indian is not respected' (10–11). The juxtaposition of the word "indígena" with the derogatory term *indio* in Spanish emphasizes the marginalization of Guatemalan Maya peoples and reinforces the systemic oppression against them. The structural violence in the cultural and social fabric stemming from the arrival of the Spanish more than five hundred years ago continues to marginalize the indigenous population in Guatemala, and by extension in other regions of Abya Yala.[5]

Ak'abal's poem "El pregonero" ("The Town Crier") provides entrée to discuss the marginalization of Mayan languages in present-day Guatemala. Racism continues to be integral in the dominant discourses and ideology of the Guatemalan state (Casaús Arzú 90), and one of its key manifestations is through the discrimination against indigenous languages. Despite the Peace Accords that promised to raise the status of Mayan languages within Guatemala (Helmberger 80–81), most official discourses of the state—legal, juridical, medical, financial, etc.—are in Spanish.[6] K'iche' and other indigenous languages are seen as antiquated or backward, whereas Spanish is considered inherently more modern (French 59; Maxwell 197). In the poem by Ak'abal, however, the town crier presents public discourses in the indigenous K'iche' Maya language:

> En mi pueblo
> el pregonero
> —cada lunes—
> daba el mandado de la auxiliatura
> en lengua K'iche'. (4–8)[7]

> In my village
> the town crier
> —each Monday—
> gave the orders of the local government
> in the K'iche' language.

These official communications are offered not in Spanish, but rather in the indigenous language, symbolically elevating K'iche' Maya—and by extension the other twenty-one Mayan languages spoken in Guatemala—in status and importance.[8] The circularity of "El pregonero," which begins and concludes with the same expression, underscores the desire to hear such discourses in the indigenous language: "Pido la palabra" 'I ask for the word.'[9] Although the expression stands alone as the first stanza of the poem, in the final verses the poetic voice exclaims, "¡Pido la palabra: / la quiero en mi propia lengua!" 'I ask for the word: / I want it in my own language!' (16–17). The speaker identifies with the language and describes it in terms of ownership; the K'iche' Mayan language is an intrinsic part of his or her identity. By advocating for the use of indigenous languages in public spaces associated with civic life, Ak'abal's poem prompts discussion of the politics of cultural and linguistic identities. For many Maya peoples the revitalization of indigenous languages in professional semantic domains is directly related to a push for an elevated status of these native languages, which hinges on their utility in an official, publicly sanctioned capacity.

Similarly, Yool Gómez advocates for the preservation of his indigenous language, Kaqchikel Maya. The poems of *Pach'un tzij kichin ak'wala': Poesía infantil en idioma kaqchikel* reinforce the crucial role children play in the preservation of Maya cultures by passing on their traditions of language, dress, and respect for the elders in the community. In the poem "Idioma Kaqchikel," Yool Gómez notes the sacred connotations of his native language by claiming, "Nunca te cambiaremos, / nunca te olvidaremos. / Sagrado Kaqchi" 'We will never change you, / we will never forget you. / Sacred Kaqchi' (9–11). Working through anaphora and apostrophe, the speaker directs the verses to this indigenous language by equating the "tú" ("you") of the poem with the Kaqchikel Maya language. Students often note the importance of the first-person plural verb forms in "cambiaremos" and "olvidaremos" and their possible connections to the solidarity of the Maya affiliated with contemporary Pan-Maya activism in Guatemala. In a similar vein, class discussions typically touch on the implications of the future tense of these verbs to underscore the hope and sociopolitical vision that many Maya intellectuals have for the future of this Central American country.

"Idioma Kaqchikel" also provides students with examples of literary techniques deriving from orality. I focus on these poetic devices because they can be traced to the *Popol Wuj*.[10] Some of these are forms of repetition, such as parallelism and anaphora. For example, the verses "Flor de mis labios, / flor de mis oídos" 'Flower of my lips, / flower of my ears' (5–6) exemplify both literary techniques. Apart from the repetition that these devices embody by definition, the juxtaposition of the terms "labios" and "oídos" as complementary concepts highlights the oral characteristics in Maya poetries. Traditionally, the verses were meant to be spoken aloud and appreciated by the ear. Students can be encouraged to analyze the continuum and historical grounding of contemporary poetries in examples of ancient Maya texts. Introducing these literary techniques in the context of contemporary Maya poetries also prompts discussion of their effects in relation to the overarching goals of Pan-Maya activism. Poems such as "Idioma Kaqchikel" serve as a case in point to show students how contemporary Maya peoples affiliated with Pan-Maya activism initiatives have drawn from the historical legacies of their past to create a vision for the future. This approach moves the analysis of these poems away from anthropology to situate them both politically and literarily, recognizing their cultural value alongside canonical texts such as *Hombres de maíz* (*Men of Maize*) by Miguel Ángel Asturias or Otto René Castillo's poetry collection *Tecún Umán*.

Establishing the basic underlying ideas of contemporary Pan-Maya activism prepares students to discuss some of the more abstract concepts informing Maya poetries. For example, by focusing on theoretical issues such as translation, students explore questions of audience and examine how translation shifts our interpretation of the poets' work. In many cases in Ak'abal's poetry, the poetic voice explicitly acts as a translator for readers, providing the Spanish equivalent for the K'iche' in the verses. For example, in the poem "En mi lengua," the speaker provides Spanish translations for a variety of expressions, all of which relate to the concept of poetry in K'iche':

Aqajtzij
(palabramiel).

Je'ltzij
(bellapalabra).

Pach'umtzij
(trenzapalabra). (3–8)

Aqajtzij
(honeyword).

Je'ltzij
(beautifulword).

Pach'umtzij
(wovenword).

As we can see, the poem's verses alternate between the two languages. Working with this didactic poem gives students a window onto the bilingual (and perhaps multilingual) world that many Maya citizens of Guatemala inhabit. Although the dominant language of society is Spanish, many Maya peoples also speak their indigenous language and must become accustomed to code-switching, often negotiating terms and concepts without exact translations.

Given the different cultural and literary approaches to defining poetry in Mayan languages, students must also address conceptualizations of writing and textuality. Indigenous writing is not limited to alphabetic forms, as Walter Mignolo has argued in his analysis of the media Latin American indigenous communities use, such as the picto-ideographic writing systems of Mesoamerican cultures and the quipus in the Andes ("Colonial" 125). In the introduction to her study on Classic Maya ceramic painting, the archaeologist Dorie Reents-Budet acknowledges that in Mayan languages "there is no linguistic or semantic differentiation among the words for painting, drawing and writing; all are referred to by the verb stem *ts'ib.* . . . For the Classic Maya, then, the making of images was born from the brush, be it writing, drawing or painting. Technically and conceptually, all were the same creative activity" (8). The Kaqchikel scholar Irma Otzoy reminds us that "the language codified in Maya weavings 'speaks' of the Maya as a people, of their roots, of their lives, and of their causes" (149). As we have seen in Ak'abal's poem, one of the terms for poetry in K'iche' Maya is *pach'um tzij,* which literally means the weaving of words. Therefore, in addition to conventional forms of writing that have undergone multiple processes of translation, textiles are also a culturally significant medium for Maya authors and artists.

Students work through these textual issues using Kaqchikel poems by Gabriel Xiquín, as her work directly connects to Maya weaving traditions.[11] The title of Gabriel Xiquín's poetry collection, *Tejiendo los sucesos en el tiempo / Weaving Events in Time,* positions the poetic voice in relation to historically female traditions of weaving. In Maya cultures, weaving does not refer only to the use of thread to create textiles. According to Gloria Chacón in her treatment of the relationship between weaving and writing, "[l]as poetisas mayas . . . interpretan el tejer como escritura, sin privilegiar una sobre la otra, ni verlas desde un punto de vista evolutivo como prácticas, o sea, que primero se teje y después se escribe" 'Maya poets . . . interpret weaving as writing, without privileging one over the other, or seeing them from an evolutionary point of view as practices, that is, that first one weaves and later one writes' (99). Similar to the K'iche' expression in Ak'abal's poem "En mi lengua," one of the Kaqchikel Mayan terms for poetry is "pach'un tzij."[12] At the beginning of her poetry collection, Gabriel Xiquín uses the image of weaving to position her locus of enunciation as a Maya woman before she addresses the violence of the armed conflict and some of the social consequences of this historical moment. Specifically with regard to Gabriel Xiquín's "Poem," Alicia Ivonne Estrada has noted that writing poetry and weaving textiles are acknowledged as similar artistic acts (145). In the final verses, the speaker explains that the woman in the poem "weaves the poetry of sorrow" (28). Historical events can also serve as the raw material for weaving, as the Nobel laureate Rigoberta Menchú Tum has explained: "our sacred dream is to say our people are weavers—a people who have woven history with our hunger, sacrifice and blood" (qtd. in Vaughn and Cabrera 91). In *Tejiendo los sucesos en el tiempo*, personal and collective memories of the armed conflict are the threads the Kaqchikel poet uses to weave her verses, blurring the boundaries between poetry and textiles.

In conclusion, by exposing students to Maya poetries responding to contemporary political issues such as the armed conflict and later Pan-Maya activism, instructors can create unique opportunities for reflection on what it means to be Maya in the twentieth and twenty-first centuries. The meaning of the term *Maya* has changed over time—it is a marker of indigenous identity that is constantly in transformation. As the anthropologist Diane Nelson explains, Maya-ness is "part of this practice of *formando*, making or forming this new, pan-indigenous identification" (5). Until the mid-1990s, archaeologists and anthropologists used the term *Maya* almost exclusively to refer to the builders of Tikal who lived several centuries ago. In postwar Guatemala, however, Maya activists have appropriated the term and divorced it from its association with long-forgotten relics of the past. In addition to responding to linguistic concerns, Guatemalan Maya authors and artists have used their cultural production to address other contemporary social issues as part of Pan-Maya activism. For example, the Kaqchikel *ajq'ij* and writer Baldomero Kawoq Cuma has written the poem "Pa Jotöl" ("Up North"), which is available digitally on *SoundCloud* in song form, to represent the effects on indigenous identities of migration to the United States. Focusing on gender inequalities, the K'iche'-Kaqchikel Maya poet and activist Rosa Chávez has written poems—such as "Arde vagina seca" ("Burns Dry Vagina") and "Ut'z baby" ("Good Baby")—to contest and redefine the politics of sexuality as a Maya woman. Indeed, many Maya authors like Cuma and Chávez have engaged other contemporary political issues in addition to cultural and linguistic revitalization, including the role of women and diasporic indigenous identities, underscoring the intersectionality of their social concerns. For students who do not study abroad or travel on their own, classroom discussions of Maya poetries may be their only exposure to contemporary Maya peoples. As educators, it is fundamental that we invite students to question their understanding of the Maya, debunking any potential stereotypes or misapprehensions.

Moreover, studying contemporary Maya poetries as a form of resistance to cultural oppression lends itself to a comparative analysis of other indigenous movements and forms of protest in the Americas. For example,

in recent years in Chile, indigenous activists have fought against the construction of hydroelectric dams and worked to protect the environment
from imperial interests. Mapuche activists have united to defend their
lands—and indigenous traditions connected with the earth—against the
dam in the Biobío river. Cecilia Vicuña is an example of a well-known
Chilean activist who has used her poetry and performance art to denounce
ecological destruction, economic inequalities, and cultural oppression.
Considering other contemporary forms of indigenous social mobilization
and commitment to the earth provokes questions of how cultural and literary production represents and dialogues with these issues. A hemispheric
approach encourages students to compare the distinct goals of the activists
in each sociopolitical context and to explore their relation to the politics of
representation in poetry and other forms of cultural production.

Examples of indigenous mobilization are not limited to Latin America, as evidenced by the recent struggles of the Standing Rock Sioux and
other indigenous communities in North Dakota against the installation of
an oil pipeline on their sovereign lands. This indigenous social movement
in the United States is a productive example connecting the study of other
cultures to a political milieu with which students may be already familiar.
Students analyzing contemporary indigenous poetry from Latin America
may grapple with the racial legacies in their own country as they compare
the distinct sociopolitical contexts of the Standing Rock Sioux and the
Maya of Guatemala. As global citizens, students must constantly process
and negotiate political realities, both in the United States and abroad, in
order to productively discuss the effects of using cultural products like
poetry to resist physical oppression and symbolic marginalization of indigenous cultures. To that end, students need the tools to think critically, not
only about course content focusing on twenty-first-century Guatemalan
Maya poetries, but about connections to other contemporary events and
forms of resistance across Abya Yala.

Notes

This essay's title uses the Kaqchikel phrase "ri pach'un tzij aj Iximulew," which may
be translated as "poetry from Guatemala."

1. The Guatemalan critic Mario Roberto Morales has claimed that "Ladino refers to those who, accepting or not an evident biological and cultural miscegena-
tion, identify with the values of the so-called 'Western culture,' follow their models
and accommodate them to the reality of their countries, usually scorning what they
perceive as autochthonous, indigenous, and different from those models, unless
the differences are viewed as an archaeological trace of a mythic, splendorous past"

(1). Ladinos have an ambivalent relationship with their indigenous past—they emphasize their European heritage, yet they also exalt their pre-Hispanic indigenous ancestry.

2. Drawing from Peruvian theorist Aníbal Quijano's conceptualization of the coloniality of power, I use *modernity* to refer to the global power structured by Eurocentrism since the arrival of Europeans to the Americas, which has largely continued into the present day, in which economic and social relations distinguished the racially dominant subjects of Latin America from their counterparts, classed as inferior, who were primarily indigenous or of African descent. From this relationship between the conquerors and the conquered, a series of dualisms developed: "East-West, primitive-civilized, magic/mythic-scientific, irrational-rational, traditional-modern—Europe and not Europe" (542). Under this lens, the indigenous and other dominated subjects have been seen historically as opposed to projects of modernity.

3. Calixta Gabriel Xiquín defines Abya Yala in the following way: "Nombre original del continente, antes de la invasión española, que comprende desde Alaska hasta la Tierra del Fuego. La denominación Abya Yala se deriva de voces kunas de Panamá" 'the original name of the continent, before the Spanish invasion, which includes from Alaska to the *Tierra del Fuego*. The term Abya Yala is derived from Kuna voices from Panama' (*La cosmovisión maya* 39). In the Kuna language Abya Yala translates as the "land of vital potential, or land in its full maturity" and invokes the American continent as a whole. In recent years, prominent indigenous activists and indigenous studies scholars have adopted this term to broadly refer to the distinct indigenous groups and movements across the Americas as a whole. For example, Arturo Arias, Luis E. Cárcamo Huechante, and Emilio del Valle Escalante have elaborated on this trend in *LASA Forum* (see Arias et al.).

4. All translations are my own unless otherwise attributed.

5. Similarities in tone exist between these twenty-first-century poems by Ak'abal and Gabriel Xiquín and the famous Nahua poem "Después de la derrota" ("After the Defeat"), an account from the perspective of an anonymous Aztec survivor after the Spaniards, under the leadership of Hernán Cortés, decimated the pre-Hispanic city of Tenochtitlán. This poem has been widely anthologized, featured in collections such as the *Oxford Book of Latin American Poetry: A Bilingual Anthology* (Vicuña and Livon-Grosman) and *"Aquí, ninfas del sur, venid ligeras": Voces poéticas virreinales* (*"Here, Southern Nymphs, Come Light": Virreinal Poetic Voices*; Chang-Rodríguez). This is a useful comparison for students as they study the historical trajectory of the oppression of indigenous people in Mesoamerica and their uses of poetry as a form of decolonial resistance.

6. For more information, see Melvyn Paul Lewis and Emily Tummons and colleagues.

7. The *auxiliatura* is a local form of government composed of mayors (*alcaldes*) and other officials.

8. Most scholars agree that there are twenty-two Maya linguistic communities, whereas some argue that there are twenty-three. Although Rabinal Achí and K'iche' are the same linguistically, the Academia de Lenguas Mayas de Guatemala considers them as two separate languages for political reasons.

9. Although the literal translation is, "I ask for the word," a more natural way to translate this is, "I ask permission to speak."

10. For more information about the poetic devices in the *Popol Wuj*, see Tedlock.

11. Another author whose work connects to issues of textuality and weaving is the Q'eq'chi' poet Maya Cu Choc. For example, in her poem "Canción por la vida," the speaker describes life as "enredada en hebras de tu trenza / en hilos de arco iris güipil" 'tangled in threads of your braid / in rainbow-colored huipil strings' (8–9).

12. Apart from the K'iche' and Kaqchikel terms for poetry (*pach'um tzij* and *pach'un tzij* respectively), there are numerous lexical and grammatical similarities between these indigenous languages, given the organization of the linguistic tree of languages deriving from Proto-Mayan.

Clare Sullivan

Teaching Indigenous Poetries through Translation

Indigenous poetries have gone virtually unnoticed in Latin American poetry courses. Though such writing exists in at least sixteen Latin American countries (and there are approximately fifty-six language families in Latin America[1]), indigenous languages are frequently invisible in their countries of origin. Speakers and writers tend to exist apart from the majority language group (in this case, Spanish or Portuguese), both geographically and culturally. In addition, indigenous poets tend not to publish their work or to have access to publishers, prizes, or even readers. As a result, the customs and cosmologies that indigenous poetries portray have not always been appreciated by dominant cultures. This fact is exacerbated by the reality that many of these linguistic traditions cross national boundaries (for the simple reason that they predate borders). The sheer variety and extension of indigenous literatures is what makes them distinctive, but it also makes them difficult to teach.

Another aspect of indigenous poetries that informs their pedagogy is the fact that indigenous poets are, by necessity, self-translators.[2] Their published texts typically exist as both originals and translations since there is no mechanism in place by which indigenous poetries can be translated into Spanish or other languages. The concept of self-translation provides a compelling intellectual framework within which themes of authorship, nationality, and style can be taught. For historical reasons dating back to the European conquest, indigenous poetries do not reside in or represent a single culture but rather inhabit a space—literally as well as theoretically—between two or more languages and cultures. By interacting with indigenous texts (principally in the form of their Spanish version) and by the act of translating them into English, students can experience what it means to exist in this liminal space. By struggling with word choices or with images that may not be readily understood in the target culture, students become aware of the double process by which indigenous poetry comes to be, and begin to grasp its marginalized status in Latin American literature.

The Workshop as a Liminal Space

The translation workshop is a valuable way to introduce indigenous Latin American poetry to an undergraduate or graduate class with a high level of Spanish proficiency. A workshop setting underscores the fact that the translation process is essential to the transmission of all indigenous poetries. Engaging in this process encourages students to critically examine notions of cultural difference and the effects of translation. Active participation in the workshop requires students to read as translators: that is, they must prepare background research, explore textual features, understand content enough to re-express it in another language and, finally, evaluate the translation as text and transmission.[3] Whether pedagogical outcomes constitute publishable translations or simple glosses, students will learn to research and read with much greater skill.

A translation workshop—that is, a translation class based on the model of a creative writing workshop[4]—is an appropriate way to teach students about indigenous poetry because it imitates the liminal space in which the poetry was created. Like the mix of cultures that produces indigenous poetry, a workshop can be community based, multilingual, and predominantly oral. Such a format is common in both undergraduate and graduate classroom settings, and larger classes can be accommodated by group work and online collaboration. Furthermore, a workshop model is consistent with a process-oriented approach to translator training (Gile 149) and requires that students collaborate with each other and with the instructor throughout the course. The workshop model is organized around the group review and discussion of texts produced by the students themselves. These group editing sessions are often complemented by theoretical and literary readings and by writing exercises.[5]

Indigenous poetry could be a point of departure for any literary translation workshop since it situates and interrogates the act of translation so well; it could also be taught as a unit within a Latin American literature class or a class on indigenous cultures. The only requirement is sufficient knowledge of Spanish to read the indigenous poems in translation. After researching the cultural and linguistic context of the poem, students have a chance to engage with the raw materials of imagery and sound to create a new text, one that will not replace the indigenous verses or the culture they emerge from but can give the poetry new life by acknowledging the space of "glocalized hybridity" (Jones 48) where indigenous poetries exist.

Students first enter this intercultural space when they choose a poet to translate and begin to investigate that writer's language, region, and cultural background. The instructor needs to make resources available, providing an anthology of poems, a list of poets, or simply a list of languages depending on the students' readiness for independent research.[6] It is advisable that each individual (or small group of students) work with a few poems by the same poet since, as the astute learner will notice immediately, the boundaries of language, custom, and culture are already constantly shifting for each indigenous poet. For example, Enriqueta Lunez is a Tzotzil poet from a mountain village in Chiapas, Mexico. Her parents taught her Spanish from birth so that she could function in the wider country and the world, but she elected to learn Tzotzil in an effort to better understand the stories and songs of her parents and grandparents. Lunez now writes poetry in Tzotzil and translates her verses into Spanish. She lives in a mountain village in Chiapas with little access to the Internet. Still, she often travels to larger towns in Mexico and has read her poetry as far away as Canada and Spain. Lunez's situation illustrates what is true for many indigenous Latin American poets: their voices must be translated among the different languages and cultures they inhabit. Students may be invited to present their chosen poet to the class for discussion and comparison.

Taking Hold of Imagery

Exploring poetic imagery affords students the opportunity to learn about the physical realities of indigenous life as well as the customs and worldview of particular peoples. For example, Natalia Toledo's poetry contains many references to the regional landscape, cuisine, and traditions of her Zapotec culture in Juchitán, in the state of Oaxaca, Mexico. The careful student can learn details hidden from the casual observer and even unknown to people from nearby language groups. Some of the plants and animals that appear in her poetry are unknown in other regions of Mexico. The translator must wrestle with how to express these images in English. Should the term *tlayuda* (a huge, crispy tortilla from the Oaxacan region) be defined, or should it be left untranslated for the reader to investigate? Should the *bereleele* (a bird whose name imitates the sound it makes and that is said to predict the weather) be given its Spanish or Latin name, or should it be replaced with a comparable species in English? Though these puzzles may have more than one acceptable solution, the struggle to find that solution is what brings the student into the "contact zone" (Pratt, "Arts" 40).

Concentrating on imagery teaches students about indigenous traditions, many of which have been altered by contact with other cultures. Lunez's poem "La jti jbe'svayel kajvaltik" ("I Woke Up God") combines Catholic sacraments with Tzotzil spiritual rites to portray a new experience of the divine. The poetic voice mentions honoring God by burning incense but also by pouring out *aguardiente* ("homemade spirits"). The dove, a familiar Christian symbol, is said to "become" the speaker's "flesh" (*Yi'beltak ch'uleletik* 44, 45). Such images challenge students to see the world and what people hold as sacred from another point of view, but also reveal the complex melding of any worldview.

The challenge of translating imagery from the natural world reveals to students the strong yet precarious tie that binds many indigenous peoples to the earth, precarious because many groups have been geographically displaced and many resources compromised by development. In "Kataa o'u-outaa" ("Living-Dying"), Vito Apüshana from Colombia writes in the Wayuu language:

Mulo'ushii waya, müin aka saa'in wunu'u
süchikanainru'u
tü wapüshi sümaiwajatkalüirua.
Kato'una waya, müin aka saa'in alekerü, süsheke'eru'u
shi'nüin tü weikaa.

Acheküshii waya weinshi sotpa'a tü miaasükaa.

A'lapujaashii waya cha'aya, sainküin Kashikaa je Ka'ikai,
suumainpa'a tü asheyuuwaakalüirua.

Outushii waya müin aka katakai wo'u. (69)

We grow, like trees, in the shelter
of our ancestors' footprint.
We live, like spiders, in the corner
of a motherly web.

Always loving the thirsty seashores.

We dream there, between Kashi and Ka'i, the Moon and the Sun,
on the ancestral lands of the spirits.

Dying as if we were still alive.[7]

In the Wayuu culture, the sun and moon have proper names. As students decide how to translate these names in English, the instructor can facilitate a discussion about how different cultures regard themselves in relation to the natural world.

Toledo reiterates this common ground when she writes: "Dxi guca' nahuiini' guse' ndaani' na' jñaa biida' / sica beeu ndaani' ladxi'do' guibá' " 'At night I slept in my grandmother's arms, / like the moon in the heart of the sky' (14, 15). This poem offers the parallel image of the moon cradled by the sky, mirrored on earth by the child in her grandmother's arms. Such an image sets up a structure in the poem that can be recreated in translation. The act of translating invites students to examine the echoes inherent in the double image: the protective love and physical presence of a mother's mother; the sky that is visible and relevant to human experience. The words can be written in English, but to what degree is the worldview present in the students' universe? Unlike English Romantic poetry, where the moon controls human behavior from above, or modern Anglo-American poetry, where the moon is objectified (Buchloh 142), in this poem and in Lunez's collection *Sk'eoj jme'tik u: Cantos de luna* ("Moon Songs"), the moon and other natural phenomena are regarded as a reflection of human life. Students and instructors would be well advised to read carefully and to question the initial interpretations they might assign to an object or natural phenomenon.

Poetic imagery can also be a point of departure to consider indigenous cultures' fight for survival when confronted with other, more dominant cultures. In spite of the great variety of their poetries, indigenous poets tend to have in common a desire to acknowledge the lifeways of their linguistic group and to preserve them for future generations.[8] For Hugo Jamioy, of Camëntsá, Colombia, borrowed shoes represent a loss of contact with the earth and with his own body, and the imperative of adopting the clothes and words of others (Rocha Vivas, *Palabras mayores* 190–91). In "Atšbe pueblebe juabn" ("My People's History") he writes:

> Atšbe Pueblbe juabna
> endbomn atšbe bëtstaitabe tšabe anán
> tšam tojobenacá endán;
>
> quemauanÿe juabn
> otëjajonán endá
> uantšamen shecuachëtjonëshec
> endán shecuatšec aubiamnay
> chabe canÿoy ndajuachen betšašec
> y chë jabuachán ntsetatšëmb benachëján
> šmontsanchá. (104)

> My people's story
> has my grandfather's clean steps
> moves to its own rhythm
>
> this other story
> moves too fast
> in borrowed shoes,
> goes along writing with its feet
> without its head attached,
> and that haphazard torrent
> carries me away.

An image as quotidian as a pair of shoes can be unpacked to reveal what many indigenous cultures fear losing: a stride in tune with nature that touches and knows the earth, not a careening and desensitized gait that runs toward an uncertain future.

Of course, instructors should remind their students that indigenous poets are not merely representatives of their culture or language group. Like poets of any background, they are also individual writers with their own style and voice. As the Mexican poet and indigenous scholar Elisa Ramírez writes in her review of Lunez's *Cantos de luna*: "Enriqueta doesn't write indigenous poetry, but rather poetry—plain and simple—in an indigenous language and in elegant Spanish." Though it is useful to make observations about peoples and their lifeways through poetry, students must remember that these authors, and the images and concerns they portray, must be carefully considered on their own.

Sound to Guide the Student Translator

A workshop acknowledges the foundations of indigenous poetries in *oraliture* and provides opportunities to actively listen to examples of the original languages and poetry. The term *oraliture* recognizes that indigenous poetry is often created by merging the spoken word and the written word, by melding the words of ancestors and those of contemporary poets with the intention of representing native cultures in a global world.[9] Recordings of many indigenous poets are available via *YouTube* or academic databases.[10] Whenever possible, a student should listen to the poem in question or to an example of the source language. Listening to poetry in an indigenous language underscores linguistic features, such as glottal stops or tonal changes, that surprise the unaccustomed ear. When Toledo reads her Zapotec poetry in Italy or Thailand, or even in her own country, listeners are mesmerized even when they don't understand a word.[11] This is because the language sounds so different from what her audience is accustomed to hearing. Listening to the original language is the best way for students to begin to understand the linguistic features that may differ from their own poetic tradition and language.

Though the students (and even the instructors) may not be linguists, they can learn to identify their poet's language group and some of its basic features. A *Wikipedia* search of the language name (and possibly its variants) will yield a concise description of its sounds and basic sentence structure. The online source *Ethnologue: Languages of the World* contains a detailed description of each language, including where it is spoken and by whom, and provides links to resources such as grammars and dictionaries. *The Archive of the Indigenous Languages of Latin America* is a Web site that provides an overview of the various language families and their sounds and grammars. These resources will allow students to compare their chosen languages in terms of sound variations, sentence structure, region, and culture. Students should also be asked to research the language family to which their poet belongs and to find out where else that tongue is spoken. For example, a student might discover that Wayuu speakers have lived in Colombia and Venezuela since before those nations were divided by a border. Their language belongs to the Arawak family and is also spoken in the Caribbean. In the collection of Mexican indigenous poetry he edits with Víctor Terán, David Shook provides clear yet simple descriptions of the linguistic features of each language. Discovering information such as this allows students a glimpse into the complicated interaction among languages in Latin American history.

As an essential feature that shapes poetry, sound has been used differently in distinct poetic traditions. In order to place contemporary indigenous poets in a literary historical context, students need to be reminded of what they already know about how sound has shaped poetic forms and figures of speech. Students and teacher can collaborate on a review of certain Spanish and English poetic traditions, offering examples of sound-dependent poetic forms or techniques. The sonnet, for example, is a sound-dependent form inherited from Italian and incorporated into both language traditions. Both English and Spanish have also employed assonance and onomatopoeia in their poetry. This study need not be exhaustive but should emphasize how sound contributes to meaning and structure in poetry. It is also important to point out that, while English verses traditionally structure meter in feet, Spanish verses are counted syllabically. Once the class has an idea of how sound operates through examples from more familiar traditions, students will be better equipped to observe how sound shapes the form of indigenous poetry and contributes to specific literary devices in poems.

The poetic elements that meld sound and meaning reiterate the oral underpinnings of most indigenous poetry. For example, part of the beauty of Toledo's poetry lies in the echoes created by words such as *guie'* and *guie* in the verse "Gucaladxe' niza neu' naa lade guie' ne lade guie" (40). Though they sound very similar, *guie'* means "flower" while *guie* means "stone." Here is a solution that partially captures the sound without straying from the original meaning: "I wanted you to walk with me on petals but also over pebbles" (41). While sound is integral to all poetry, since much indigenous poetry has grown out of an oral tradition and is often still sung in performance, the sound of indigenous verses should be emphasized by instructors and considered carefully by students as they translate.

Though sound can never be reproduced completely in translation due to linguistic differences, the student who truly listens to the original language will begin to experience what sound can teach us about the origins and message of indigenous poetry. Most indigenous peoples live in intimate connection with the natural world and struggle to preserve the earth's resources, and indigenous poetry often imitates or suggests sounds from the natural world: as Miguel Rocha Vivas observes, "El camëntsá es fonéticamente una de las lenguas más complejas y hermosas de los Andes en Colombia. Esas *sh* y esas *ts* son con frecuencia el sonido de la naturaleza . . . eran el sonido mismo de la Madre en la lengua de los hombres" 'Camëntsá is phonetically one of the most beautiful and complex languages of the Colombian Andes. The *sh*'s and *ts*'s are often the sound of nature . . . they were the very sound of the Mother in the language of man' (*Palabras mayores* 99). With guidance, an observant student can hear these echoes of nature in the verses of indigenous poetry.

One way to help students pay attention to sound is to have them record their translations. Indigenous language readings as well as student recordings can be collected and stored in a sound library on a course management Web site or other online platform that allows a student translator to hear the poems as they were meant to be presented. Students and teacher can provide links to *YouTube* videos of indigenous poets readings their own verses or to sound samples of the original languages. And students can upload sample voice recordings after they have produced drafts of a few translated poems.[12] As Kelly Washbourne has observed: "By recording their texts, novice translators learn to experience their work more sensorially, and thus through this embodied knowledge have more critical access to it and its emotional impact. At the same time, they are motivated to translate for an audience outside the classroom" (57). Such a sound bank can be used by the class and shared with students or researchers in other places.

Just as sound can be used as a point of departure to compare nonindigenous and indigenous poetic traditions, sound-based techniques can help instructors reveal commonalities among different indigenous poetries. Though many contemporary indigenous poets (like poets in many languages) seem to ignore traditions and write in free verse, sound-based techniques such as rhyme, alliteration, or assonance still appear in their verses. Onomatopoeia can be found in Toledo's and Ak'abal's verses but also in Wayuu poems by Vito Apüshana, of Colombia, and Mapuche poems by Lorenzo Aillapán, of Chile (Rocha Vivas, *Palabras mayores* 169). Toledo has recently begun to compile examples of both traditional and contemporary poems that employ onomatopoeia in Zapotec and to translate them into Spanish. In order to translate these short poems, a reader would need to first understand the context of the traditional onomatopoeia and then pay close attention to sound in the original and the translation. (See the appendix for a sample exercise.)

Beyond the Classroom: Extending the Life of Indigenous Poetry Aloud and in Writing

Indigenous poetry (especially in its early, oral form) has traditionally been considered a common inheritance rather than the property of individual authors (Chikangana 79). Since students exposed to indigenous poetry are joining a minority of people who have read such texts, they might be invited to share their work by performing their poems for the public. A performance is a natural outlet for indigenous poetry and follows a strong Latin American tradition of declaiming poetry in various public venues. If the instructor elects to organize a declamation, such an exercise can be limited to classroom participants or can include other student or community groups. In my experience, students benefit most from presenting poetry when they have memorized the verses. When one memorizes a poem, one must spend time with the verses and internalize the imagery and sound.[13] If at all possible, the instructor should have students recite a portion of the poem in the indigenous language and in Spanish as well. At the very least, students can present a recorded example of the original language to the audience.

Another exercise that extends communal practice involves submitting edited poems for publication. There are many online journals that seek international verse in translation.[14] Students will usually be asked to provide a succinct description of the poet and of their translation process as well. While a student's work may not be published immediately, the experience of perusing these journals and reading other poems in translation is invaluable.[15] This exercise also invites the student to reflect once again on the role of the translator.[16]

Just as self-translation releases indigenous verses from a community of origin in order to share them with a country or region, translation gives the larger world a chance to hear these poems. Even when indigenous poems are rendered completely into English, they are typically published in conjunction with the original version and often include a Spanish translation as well. This highlights translation's role in teaching students and readers in general about the existence of indigenous poetries. In this way translation serves as a vital tool for preserving poetry and the people it represents, even as languages themselves disperse and die out (Sullivan 209–10).

Notes

1. *The Archive of the Indigenous Languages of Latin America* provides descriptive and statistical information about the region's languages.

2. Jan Walsh Hokenson and Marcella Munson were the first to discuss the issue of self-translation and its implications for literature and translation in a book-length work.

3. "The core skills and strategies are textual. Poetry translators need sophisticated source-poem reading skills, to identify not only surface semantics, but also underlying imagery, idiom and allusion, plus the form and function of intrinsic-poetic and stylistic features. They also need expert writing skills in a highly specialist

target genre, plus need the strategic ability to decide how their reading should influence their writing" (Jones 176).

4. Translation professor and literary translator Kelly Washbourne suggests that the workshop format usually employed for creative writing programs can be adapted successfully to teach translation.

5. The volume *Does the Writing Workshop Still Work?* offers critiques of this classroom model and suggestions for further development and evaluation (Donnelly).

6. Monica de la Torre and Michael Wiegers, Alison Hedge Coke, Miguel Rocha Vivas (*Antes el amanecer* and *El sol*), David Shook and Víctor Terán, Ilan Stavans, and Cecilia Vicuña and Ernesto Livon-Grosman have anthologized poetry by indigenous Latin American authors.

7. All translations from the Spanish (via indigenous self-translations) are mine.

8. In her article "La literatura indígena: una mirada desde fuera" ("Indigenous Literature: A Look from the Outside") Gabriela Coronado Suzan describes the social function of indigenous literature in Mexico.

9. As the Colombian indigenous poet Fredy Chikangana explains, the term *oralitura* acknowledges the complexity of indigenous poetry as something that is both word and text, individually authored and communal, culturally specific and diverse (78–80).

10. UNAM (Mexico's public research university in Mexico City) features podcasts of poetry in Spanish and seven different indigenous languages on the Web site *Descarga Cultura* (descargacultura.unam.mx/app1?lang=es#categoriasAPP1).

11. Toledo reads her poetry at www.asymptotejournal.com/poetry/natalia-toledo-the-black-flower-and-other-zapotec-poems.

12. *Voice Thread*, for example, is a fairly popular tool. Student recordings are gathered together in a kind of discussion board where voice (instead of text) serves as the form of communication.

13. In "Teaching Poetry," Elaine Showalter explains why memorization has reemerged as a pedagogical tool (69–70).

14. See Jones for a discussion on the relative merit of print and Internet publications (192–93).

15. The following is a small sample of online translation journals: *Asymptote* (www.asymptotejournal.com), *Exchanges Literary Journal* (exchanges.uiowa.edu), *Three Percent* (www.rochester.edu/College/translation/threepercent), *Latin American Literature Today* (www.latinamericanliteraturetoday.org/en), *Words Without Borders* (wordswithoutborders.org).

16. Reading and commenting on the translations of others can serve as a final activity or a final unit if the class schedule permits. The instructor can show examples of translation reviews and invite students to reflect upon how translation is viewed in the wider society and what expectations we hold as readers.

APPENDIX: Sample Exercise: Highlighting Sound in Translation

After reading and listening to a poem's original text and Spanish translation, students may be asked to analyze

the difference between the original and the translation on the page (format, number of verses, line length, line breaks, etc.);

repetition of sounds, such as alliteration and end rhyme, in the original, and its correspondence or lack thereof in the translation to Spanish; and

words or expressions in the original that present particular challenges for translation (e.g., homonyms; quantities that don't exist in a given region; grammatical differences such as gender of nouns in Spanish).

Students may then be asked to render the poem into English and to present their translation to someone else, explaining their choices and what was gained or lost in comparison to the Spanish translation.

Recommended Texts

"Vobil vayich" / "Delirio" ("Delirium"; 25) or "La'mtabane" / "Anuncio" ("Forewarning"; 27) from *Yi'beltak ch'ulelaletik: Raíces del alma* (*Soul Roots*), by Enriqueta Lunez; "Guendarapa xiiñi'" / "Tener hijos" ("Having Children"; 74, 75), from *The Black Flower and Other Zapotec Poems*, by Natalia Toledo. Recordings of both poets can be heard at descargacultura.unam.mx/app1?lang=es#inicioAPP1.

Steven F. Butterman

The Queerospheric Classroom: Queer Pedagogy and Brazilian Poetry

As a professor of queer studies and Luso-Brazilian literary and cultural studies at the undergraduate and graduate levels, I have come to recognize the importance of not defining "queer" at any point in a course in queer studies.[1] The advantages of maintaining the multivalent ambiguity of the term cannot be overestimated. Since the term is charged and misunderstood, and imbued with political, aesthetic, and philosophical connotations, an integral part of the journey of a queer studies class is students' transit and transition between these multilayered meanings as they construct an understanding of the term both individually and as part of a community of intellectuals. Similarly, confining the artistic genre of poetry within the limitations of language unwittingly reinscribes traditional canonical texts with heteronormative conventions inherent and unquestioned in the educational system, at both the secondary and postsecondary levels.[2] In the mid to late 1980s and early 1990s, as queer theory was challenging heteronormativity in all its sociopolitical manifestations, many contemporary Brazilian poets were already hard at work disrupting and subverting oppressive phallogocentric patterns using language, the most powerful tool at their disposal. I use the term *phallogocentric* to denote not only hegemonic masculinist discourse but that which operates to systematically and definitively erase women's voices from a wide variety of literary genres, whether poetry, essays, novels, short stories, or some fusion thereof. Phallogocentrism is indicative of the conscious and unconscious ways in which words are created and employed to centralize and center heterosexist discourse at the expense of the expression (and often the existence) of marginalized gender and sexual minorities. Many of these poets, such as Ana Cristina César, Leila Míccolis, and Roberto Piva, were writing during the peak of military dictatorship in Brazil (1964–84).[3] Much of Brazilian *poesia marginal*[4] of the 1960s and 1970s employs what Denilson Lopes has called homotextual[5] subversion and ultimately transgression of thematic, stylistic features that had previously been heterostandardized and not critically assessed as heteroconventional and heterocanonical.

For the purposes of this essay, I would like to invoke the poet and cultural activist Glauco Mattoso's paradoxical but succinct definition, featured in *O que é poesia marginal?* ("What Is Marginal Poetry?"), as follows: "A poesia marginal não apresenta qualquer homogeneidade, prática ou teórica . . . Se existem traços comuns à maioria dos autores da década, são eles a desorganização, a desorientação e a desinformação. E mais: a despreocupação com o próprio conceito de poesia e o descompromisso com qualquer diretriz estética" 'Marginal poetry does not reflect any type of practical or theoretical homogeneity . . . If there are any commonalities the majority of the poets of the decade [1970s] share, they would be disorganization, disorientation, and misinformation. But there's more: the lack of concern with the very concept of poetry and the absence of commitment to any aesthetic imperative' (29).[6] In resisting classification, the genre of poetry, much like queer theory itself, remains in motion, shifting in a nonlinear fashion, perhaps boundaryless but not boundless, bouncing in and out of prescribed aesthetic codes, dancing freely, away from any directives that would normalize its very existence. In order to break through (break apart?) the usual straight/gay dichotomies, a queer pedagogy encourages students to examine and unhinge the binary through the concept of transliminality. I imagine transliminality as a creative and productive space in which the reader not only accepts but dwells and revels in uncertainty. Queer readings allow "the gray area" to represent an existing but resisting structure, using the study of poetry as a companion through the unknown while realizing that this very partnership may be conflicted in nature.

Many global literary traditions substantiate connections between poetic process and queer desire. In North America, for example, pairing

Audre Lorde's groundbreaking feminist essay "Poetry Is Not a Luxury" (36–39) with her essay "The Uses of the Erotic: The Erotic as Power" (53–59) provides an excellent opportunity for our students to understand otherwise difficult theoretical conceptualizations, for they show connections between poetry, freedom, overcoming repression, and embracing eroticism. In a specifically Brazilian context, Charles Perrone cites José Carlos Barcellos: "To be effective in the exploration of eroticism or sexuality, to overcome the dichotomy of the vulgar and the hygienic, creative writers must indeed create; and such fabrication, Barcellos stresses, will necessarily be *poetic*" ("Signs of Intercourse" 198). Indeed, as Perrone suggests, this Brazilian poetry is indebted to a "metapoetic interrelation of lyrical and sexual activity" perhaps rooted in Iberian *trovadorismo* ("medieval lyric poetry") and taken up again in *Romantismo* ("Romanticism") (201). In this essay, Perrone confirms that "Since 1950 there have been numerous instigating instances in Brazilian lyric that . . . illustrate novelty in the trajectory of the genre as well as diversity or intentioned positioning in matters of sexuality, be it related primarily to a gender focus or to prospects of alternative conduct" (200–01). Perrone's use of the adjective *alternative* can also evoke *queer* in that the "conduct" to which he is referring is unconventional if not entirely nonheteronormative in nature.

Teaching in the queerospheric classroom affords us the luxury, the challenge, and the ethical responsibility to ask our students to undefine certain terms and concepts to enable a far more productive pedagogical process than giving a name or solution. The pages to come will use examples from contemporary Brazilian poems to consider the following questions: To what extent is poetry inherently a queer literary genre? To what extent is the critical analysis of poetry a naturally queer pedagogical exercise? Why and how is poetry critical to teaching about and around queer theory? This essay will cultivate, queerly, the creative process in flux by striving to attain unformed but informed ideas. As instructors at any level of the curriculum, we work hard to develop a safe space where in high school and college students can think out loud, and we must be actively engaged in subverting the paradigm, "I speak because I have the answer." In this construction and application of queer pedagogy, I assert the importance of generating and degenerating ideas such that they cannot be pinned down or owned. Ultimately, I argue that the strategies and characteristics of what I have come to call "the queerospheric classroom" form a powerful pedagogical tool for teaching poetry, creating a Lordesque freedom of expression and encouraging the consistent and constant cultivation of critical thought (see appendix). As such, though the specific examples I consider in this essay pertain to Brazilian poetry, a queerospheric classroom transcends borders of nationality and rationality. A combination of critical thinking, conscious investment in undefining (and not necessarily redefining), and displacement from product to process, together in creative partnership with wordplay, constitute the ingredients that form the basis for any and all of our literature classes that reach to the ever-changing queerosphere for inspiration.

The brilliant poetic composition "Metáfora" by Gilberto Gil is a pertinent point of departure for reconsidering contemporary Brazilian poetry from a perspective gently but deeply rooted in queer studies. Gil's poem foments a productive tension and simultaneous liberation by embracing infinite and unresolvable ambiguity, challenging students to engage and analyze poetic texts with queer eyes. The lyrics of this highly ludic and philosophical song are far more profound than they may seem at a first reading or hearing. We find an example in these lines near the beginning: "Uma meta existe para ser um alvo / Mas quando o poeta diz: 'Meta' / Pode estar querendo dizer o inatingível" 'A goal exists to be a target. / But when the poet says "Goal," / he may be alluding to the unattainable.' The use of the term *meta* in Brazilian Portuguese has polysemantic connotations and denotations, enriching and complicating our interpretation of the lyrics. As a noun, *meta* refers to "goal" or "outcome." As a prefix, *meta-*, taken from the Greek prefix meaning "after" or "beyond," also parallels the English self-referential and often self-critical assessment, as in the terms *metapoetic* or *metacinematic*, which are utilized to refer to poems or films that reflect on the art of poetry or conventions of filmmaking. As a Portuguese verb, *meter* (in the imperative or command form *meta*) means literally "to put in" but can refer to sticking one's nose where it does not belong, to intervening, to interrogating that which traditionally (or heteronormatively) would hold itself as exempt from any discourse that would question or challenge it. *Metáfora*, in addition to the obvious figure of speech, when separated into its two constituent words (*meta fora*), is the equivalent to the expression "stay out of it" in Brazilian Portuguese. Thus, Gil's brilliantly playful and deceptively facile song is both an invitation and a warning, a way of suggesting that readers of poetry enter at their own risk. And, though the reader is responsible for the interpretation of a poetic work, we must be conscious that a poem is not meant to unwrap itself or unravel per se; it is therefore "incontível" in the sense that it cannot be contained or forced to fit into any prefabricated structure that the reader may construct.

Gil continues: "Mas quando o poeta diz: 'Lata' / Pode estar querendo dizer o incontível" 'But when the poet says: "Can," / he may be wanting to express the uncontainable.' The word "incontível" alternates with "incabível," literally and metaphorically "unfittable." If we separate the pieces of *metaforicamente* ("metaphorically") into three distinct words, we can tease out the following paradoxical reading: "Throw out the mind" (i.e., "meta a mente fora") to accomplish the goal (the *meta*) of enriching (*-rica*) the mind (*-mente*). Is this interpretation too complex, too literal, too nerdy for our students? If so, then *meta fora*. The noun *lata* refers, of course, to a can, tin, or container. However, *lata* can also be the verb *latir*, "to bark." Does a tin can bark? Are we to expect our students to dissect each and every single word in a poem to exploit as many meanings, inferences, allusions, or inflections as linguistically possible? Is that a right-brain or a left-brain process? Is it too literal to be metaphorical? The answer, of course, is "absolutamente," which when used by itself in response to a question in Brazilian Portuguese means "absolutely not" (disagreement) at least as often as it means "absolutely" (reinforcement). How then do we read the "lata absoluta" 'absolute container' at the end of the song? Together, and in dialogue with one another, these readings form examples of a critical yet still ludic interpretation of the poem, further emphasizing that, for this instructor, critical thinking plus wordplay equals queer. Furthermore, the poem offers itself to a queer reading because it allows not only subjectivity of meanings but multiplicity of combinations of meanings in dialogue with one another. An alternative reading, for example, brings lewd to ludic. *Meta* can also be heard as "fuck." Thus, "meta dentro e fora" may be interpreted as "fuck in-and-out," inside and outside, giving renewed meaning to the metaphor of the "absolute can." Maintaining the queerness of multitudinous readings enhances the complexity while resisting normative aesthetic codes that would otherwise hierarchize meanings.

A more recent poem, written by the *gaúcha*[7] poet Angélica Freitas, challenges us, in one devastatingly and liberatingly succinct verse, to entertain the idea that "[t]odas as leituras de poesia são equivocadas" '[a]ll readings of poetry are mistaken' (52). The poetic universe of Freitas is marked by its near-total unmarking: it lacks punctuation of any kind (notably, except for parentheses, question marks, and concluding dashes in the penultimate verses of the poem), evades capital letters, mingles words in foreign languages with Portuguese, and resists any degree of apparent complexity through accessibility of language (see Marra). "A mulher é uma construção" ("Woman Is a Construct"), then, is reminiscent of the heroic phase of Brazilian modernist verse, which mocked and gawked at elitist aspects of content and style that existed in the premodernist phase of Brazilian poetry, principally Parnassianism and Symbolism. The key to Freitas's work is an accessibility of readership that breathes new life (and understanding) into poetry while challenging its sophisticated conventions. In addition, this gesture of unmarking and hence unmasking conventionality provides a liberating space for queer readers, queer readings, and the creative process itself. These literary strategies are certainly not unique to Freitas's poetic universe, especially when we think of Brazilian poets who inscribe feminist resistance to hegemonic masculinity and to patriarchal structures that impose hierarchical (read, phallogocentric) readings in their works. Although Freitas's poetry offers much evidence of modernist aesthetics, it refreshingly subscribes to no prefabricated formulas, to few precedents of literary convention. Her work therefore disregards the rules and regulations of so-called good behavior precisely to mirror the social realities that women in Brazil face in a highly *machista*, or patriarchal, and arguably institutionalized, social misogyny. As such, Freitas's poetry fearlessly questions the rules and roles of poetic convention in a genre in which very few women have been recognized in Brazilian literary historiography.

Written in a quasi-confessional tone with biting satire to provoke and to defend a woman's right to pleasure, "A mulher é uma construção," from the collection *Um útero é do tamamho de um punho* ("A Womb Is the Size of a Fist"), is eminently teachable, refreshingly nondidactic, and a clear example of the poet's courageously critical yet ludic risks. With the words "a mulher é uma construção," the first stanza brings the reader face-to-face with a conventional hegemonic reading of the uses of women in patriarchal contexts. Adopting (and later subverting) a masculinist lens that would objectify women as uniform objects (or even subjects) to be defined, refined, dressed, and undressed by the eyes (and the "I"s) of a *machista* society, the poetic voice quietly and confidently refuses to subscribe to patriarchal convention. As such, the speaker feels neither pride nor shame in admitting to being "a mais mal vestida" 'the worst-dressed' participant in social gatherings, demonstrating both her consciousness of not conforming to the dictates of oppressive norms and her quiet rebellion against them. The personalized line "digo que sou jornalista" 'i say i'm a journalist' plays with the idea of social and professional constructs while ironically conforming to a script that is not necessarily true or real. After all, if woman is a "construct" that will never change, the only agency one may find is in performing one's own autonomy to combat the construction externally imposed by the expectations of others. In this sense, then, the poem is an effective metaphor for queer resistance to established norms that would otherwise confine or restrict a woman's right to freedom. Self-repression and self-denial are part of this construct, but the poetic voice manages to escape an oppressive imaginary of femininity by "suddenly waking up binary and blue" 'e se de repente acorda binária e azul.' This epiphany is formed by a juxtaposition of logic and synesthesia. And what woman would spend the day turning the lights on and off, as the speaker in this poem inquires? The question is hardly a rhetorical one, and readers may interpret this metaphor as recognizing the infantilization of women as part of this societal "construct." We see that employing childlike playfulness is a strategy to recover or uncover adult autonomy. Furthermore, such invisibility in a patriarchal context may indicate that the woman, "binary and blue," becomes a victim of erasure, appearing and disappearing (thus existing merely) as the object of a masculinist gaze. As in Gil's "Metáfora," the critical playfulness of language is a queerly parodic subversion of the authoritarianism of the very language that exists to police its speakers. It is therefore both a Foucauldian and a queer gesture of creative empowerment.

Aesthetically, Freitas's poem seems to be inspired by poets like Oswald de Andrade and Carlos Drummond de Andrade, who composed the *poema piada* ("joke poem") to protest the formalities of poetic convention prior to modernism and to contest the use of language in exclusive, elitist, or repressive modalities with delicious, even *queerlicious*, sarcasm. This feature of Freitas's poem resonates most clearly in the verses, "toda mulher tem um amigo gay / como é bom ter amigos / todos os amigos tem um amigo gay / que tem uma mulher / que o chama de fred astaire" 'every woman has a gay friend / how nice to have friends / every friend has a gay friend / that has a woman who calls him fred astaire.' The lowercasing and limited punctuation throughout the entire piece indicates that the poetic voice is not willing to follow prescribed rules, even of grammar. In a final Machadian pessimistic gesture, the speaker both laments and laughs at the fact that the Freudian psychoanalysts, some of them women, will not be able to change sexist conventions. Her reaction to the sense of permanence is the subversive gesture of laughter, which paradoxically destabilizes essentialist binaries by decoding notions of permanence as masculinist and thus illusory. The poetic voice communicates silently but with knowing glances that this hegemonic construct is as fickle as it is farcical.

Returning now to Mattoso,[8] I would like to highlight in particular poetry whose queerospheric qualities are of inestimable value in undergraduate or graduate classes on Brazilian literature and particularly relevant in studies of the Brazilian countercultural production. Mattoso's strategy of simultaneously degendering and regendering language in his poem makes the work nearly impossible to translate into English, or even into other romance languages, where, as in Portuguese, nouns and adjectives are gendered. We may call this gender-nonconforming surgery that in itself may be read as a queer gesture. "Cera e nata para Desdêmona" ("Wax and Cream for Desdemona"), discussed below, transcends the ambiguity of androgyny and enters into a queer space of transgendered resignification.

A significant part of Mattoso's project involves the subversion not only of gender roles but even of the social constructs of gender at their most basic level. Evidence of this strategy can be found in one of the author's more ludic poems, "Cera e nata para Desdêmona."[9] The words *cera* and *nata*, "wax" and "cream" (perhaps even "the cream of the crop"), when read quickly, merge to form *serenata* ("serenade"), the romantic convention—of chivalry—that this poem attempts to subvert. The traditional image that a serenade evokes is that of an archetypal, unattainable woman, perhaps reminiscent of the construct that Freitas paints and parodies in her poem—for she is the Shakespearean Desdemona—elevated on a pedestal (or a balcony), with the suitor down below on the street, guitar in hand. The words in parentheses in the second line, "p'ra não dizerem que não canto as femeas," can be read in a number of ways: "So that they do not say that I don't sing to [or perhaps 'flirt with' or 'seduce'] females." In Brazilian Portuguese, the traditional serenade known as the *cantada* involves using language to seduce someone into having sex. The object of conquest here, "minha doce amada, / minha goyabada" 'my sweetheart, / my guava,' recalls another allusion to Shakespeare, since *goyabada* is used to make the dessert known as Romeu e Julieta.

In this transsexual poem transformation is taking place at the most basic level of its language, the grammatical gender of nouns. Clearly, three separate subversive processes are occurring. First, Mattoso feminizes neutral and masculine nouns: "anas" is used as the feminine form of *ânus*, and "tua prepucia" inverts *prepucio* ("foreskin") to a feminine feature; conversely, *bunda* ("ass") becomes "bundo." Second, he pluralizes singular body parts, such as "tuas xanas" (the equivalent of "your pussies" in Northeastern Brazilian slang used by some lesbians). Third, the poet may conceal a prefix in order to invert a process by undoing what has already been done and cannot be undone: "cabaçar" instead of *descabaçar* represents a process of revirginizing rather than loss of virginity. "Cabaçar" does not exist but is suggested as an inversion whereby virginity is gained by sexual experience rather than lost. The poem presents an ironic inversion of gender constructs, echoing the language of Freitas's poem analyzed earlier, before such divisions can even be conceptualized; that is, at the anatomical level of human existence, where body parts are almost surrealistically imbued with inverted masculinity or femininity. Regendering takes place on such a ludic, even ludicrous, level that the identity of the object of desire collapses and is rendered genderless, a queer step further than androgynous. Stylistically, the poem demonstrates Mattoso's effective employment of alliteration to enhance musicality as well as to juxtapose ordinarily contradictory elements to form a new ambiguous identity. For example, the consecutive succession of the terms *desdenhosa, divina, demoniaca, diva doidivanas* is a well-rendered play on words that exhibits three distinct aspects of the nature of Desdemona's multifaceted configuration, which is all at once disdainful ("desdenhosa"), godlike ("divina"); diabolical ("demoniaca"); a mad fool or frivolous ("doidivanas"); and, in camp terminology, extraordinarily talented, brash, a prima donna (a "diva"); or all of these.[10]

As we come full circle, completing the Brazilian *roda* ("round") of queerospheric poetry, I corroborate Perrone's observation about the connections between contemporary Brazilian poetry and eroticism: "From the fragmented verse of pre- or proto-concrete poetry, through the high repertory, and subsequent experiments and throwbacks, whatever the codes employed, representations of sexuality transcend constructivist designs to explore the erotic, to expose feminine conditions of disadvantage (to use a non-controversial term), to assert non-conventional practices, to celebrate, in some situations, difference and delight" ("Signs of Intercourse," 213). While we consider Perrone's important contribution, I would like to suggest that the erotic imperatives Perrone highlights in his essay are framed by queer pillars that contribute this "difference and delight" of unconventionality. Embracing desire in and for Brazilian poetry liberates the reader from restrictive codes and formulas that would otherwise challenge the study of poetry as both a ludic exercise and a serious critical endeavor at the same time.

But this connection between homoeroticism and the poetic process, and the rainbow-colored threads that hold the two together, are hardly unique to Brazilian poetry and may be applicable in many contemporary global contexts. The award-winning poet Maureen Seaton notes, "I would say that poetry is not inherently a queer literary genre but that because poetic license exists in the mind of the general population as an accepted possibility, poetry lends itself to a queer literary genre a bit more than the others" (41). As we have seen in the few examples of contemporary Brazilian poetry in this essay, the active experimentation and joyful (perhaps even erotic) manipulation of language opens up our classrooms to a pedagogically queerospheric universe in which richer, more nuanced, and less restrictive spaces of literary criticism are in constant flux and reinflection.

Notes

1. At the University of Miami, the Program in Women's and Gender Studies offers a minor in LGBTQ studies as well as a number of undergraduate and graduate courses in queer studies, including courses in foreign languages and literatures.

2. For a somewhat dated but paradoxically ever-relevant assessment of the perpetuation of heteronormative conventions in literary studies in the United States, see George Haggerty and Bonnie Zimmerman's *Professions of Desire: Lesbian and Gay Studies in Literature* and William Spurlin's *Lesbian and Gay Studies and the Teaching of English.*

3. For a comprehensive though somewhat Rio-centric study of *poetas marginais* ("marginal poets"), see Heloísa Buarque de Hollanda (*26 Poetas Hoje*; *Impressões de Viagem*).

4. *Poesia marginal* is translated in a number of ways in contemporary Brazilian poetry. See Charles Perrone's seminal *Seven Faces: Brazilian Poetry since Modernism* for detailed explanations and examples of *poesia marginal.*

5. "Homotextuality" is a reference to the section "Uma história brasileira" ("A Brazilian Story") in "*O homem que amava rapazes*" *e outros ensaios* ("'The Man Who Loved Boys' and Other Essays"), by the literary and film scholar Denilson Lopes. In this section, Lopes examines homoeroticism in Brazilian literature, casting a wide net to consider not only an author's homosexual identity but also how the text reflects authorial intention or critical reception, which reads a text as homoerotic, or "homoafetivo," regardless of the author's intention. Rudi C. Bleys places the term "homotextuality" into a broader aesthetic and geographic context with his book *Images of Ambiente: Homotextuality and Latin American Art, 1810—Today*, as follows: "I adopt the concept of homotextuality as a heuristic catch-all term, which is diachronic instead of being tied to all-too-reifying notions of 'homosexual' or 'gay' identity. It allows for cross-cultural comparison and avoids the pitfalls of Eurocentric conceptualization. It is inclusive at once of artistic expressions of homoeroticism, as of their perceptions by various audiences. It embraces an image's potential reception as a site of homotextual meaning, even when not intended so by the artist him/herself" (11).

6. Unless otherwise attributed, translations from the Portuguese are my own.

7. The term *gaúcha* refers to a woman from Rio Grande do Sul.

8. See Butterman for an in-depth analysis of Mattoso's vast poetic universe.

9. See also "Soneto travesti [313]" ("*Travesti* Sonnet [313]").

10. In "Deus furioso" ("Furious God"), whose very title is reminiscent of Mattoso's poem analyzed above, Waldo Motta skillfully reconfigures nouns in a joyful literary gender reassignment surgery, courageously affirming and celebrating both his gayness and his Afro-Brazilian heritage.

Appendix: Sample Activity: Queering the Poetic Text

This activity evolved as a direct outcome of trying to teach five hundred years or so of Brazilian poetry in a single semester. A literary critic (including student critics assuming this role) has an ethical and intellectual responsibility to directly engage in the creative process before earning the right to evaluate others. It is my experience that students at any level of the curriculum learn by doing. More specifically, the act and art of composing a good parody involves a deep understanding of the work being parodied. In addition to the traditional critical essays that are written in drafts and resubmitted throughout the semester, I ask students to "sujar as mãos" (dirty their hands) by engaging the creative process through composing (and then queering) their own poetry, in four stages:

1. In the first trimester of the course, when we study colonial poetry, I ask students to produce a parodic imitation or subversion of one of the poems written by Gregório de Matos, Brazil's so-called Boca do Inferno, a baroque poet whose verses are already predominantly satirical in nature. This activity brings out the ironic and ludic qualities of the poet's work, which he used to denounce the hypocrisy and multilayered, institutionalized corruption that plagued colonial Brazilian society. The "intelligent plagiarism" à la Glauco Mattoso involved in this exercise also characterized the work of Matos and his contemporaries (Matos himself paid tribute to Francisco de Quevedo, a renowned satirical poet writing during Spain's Golden Age, by stealing his verses). This first step illustrates both in theory and in practice the uses and abuses of parodic discourse that came to characterize Brazilian poetic convention during the colonial period.
2. In the second stage of this queerly creative process, I ask the students to compose an ultra-Romantic response to the poem they composed in step 1.
3. The third phase occurs much later in the course, when students usually assume that the creative portion of the course requirements has come to a close. After a thorough academic study of Symbolism and Parnassianism in Brazil, I ask students to complete a Parnassian critique of a canonical Romantic poet. For this step, students are encouraged to compose a prose poem that implicitly takes issue with the principles of the movement that preceded Brazilian modernism, so that they get a sense of both historiographic periodicity and literary continuity—as well as rupture between and among literary currents.

4. In tribute to Brazilian concretism, which we study in great detail, I ask students to create a concrete, neoconcrete, or paraconcrete poem of their own. This exercise is accompanied by two further subprojects:

   a. To compose a *chave de leitura* (reading key or map) to guide or even intentionally mislead the reader; and

   b. To assume the voice of literary critic and write a one-page critical analysis of the poem, beginning with, "In the poem, the author attempts to . . ."

The results of this activity are almost always instructive and usually fun, motivating students to engage in much greater depth with the material. Some students choose to glorify their own work, expounding on its merits with all the melodramatic passion and narcissism of the ultra-Romantic style. Others systematically dismantle and intentionally misrepresent their own work in the persona of a misguided (if well-meaning) literary critic. Still others enthusiastically attack their own work, using sophisticated literary tools they have acquired throughout the course. Ultimately, this exercise in critical thinking and wordplay not only leads to queering canonical texts in more nuanced ways but also disrupts and challenges conventional notions of good and bad poetry, encouraging students to critically question who has the authority to make these assessments and evaluations, whence that power derives, and whom it deprives.

Notes on Contributors

John Burns is visiting associate professor of Spanish at Bard College. He has published *Contemporary Hispanic Poets: Cultural Production in the Global, Digital Age* (2015) and, with Rubén Medina, has cotranslated and coedited an anthology of Beat poetry titled *Una tribu de salvajes improvisando a las puertas del infierno* (2012).

Steven F. Butterman is associate professor of Portuguese and director of the Portuguese Language Program at the University of Miami, where, while director of Women's and Gender Studies, he developed the LGBTQ studies minor. Butterman is the author of *Perversions on Parade: Brazilian Literature of Transgression and Postmodern Anti-Aesthetics in Glauco Mattoso* (2005), *(In)visibilidade vigilante: Representações midiáticas da maior parada gay do planeta* (2012), and articles focusing on transnational LGBTQ+ literary studies, gender and queer studies in cultural contexts of a variety of anglophone, hispanophone, and lusophone countries. He is currently completing a book project titled "Brazilian Portugays: LGBT Language and Culture in Contemporary São Paulo and Rio de Janeiro."

Bridget V. Franco is associate professor of Spanish at the College of the Holy Cross in Worcester, Massachusetts. Franco's research interests include memory and resistance in Southern Cone narrative, visual art, and film, and she regularly integrates experiential and community-based learning in her courses. She has published on Argentine and Chilean film and literature from the post-dictatorship periods and is the creator of *Cineglos* (sites.holycross.edu/cineglos/), a Spanish-language digital film glossary, and *Cinegogía* (cinegogia.omeka.net), a digital humanities project devoted to Latin American Film Studies.

Gwen Kirkpatrick has been professor of Spanish at Georgetown University since 2004 and teaches a wide array of courses in Latin American literature and culture. Her publications have centered on Latin American poetry, especially *modernismo* through the twenty-first century, gender studies, and visual arts. Her most recent publications center on Rubén Darío and Marosa diGiorgio.

Jill S. Kuhnheim is professor emerita of the Department of Spanish and Portuguese at the University of Kansas and visiting professor at Brown University. Her books include *Gender, Politics, and Poetry in Twentieth-Century Argentina* (1996), *Cultural Studies in the Curriculum: Teaching Latin America* (with Danny J. Anderson, 2003), *Spanish American Poetry at the End of the Twentieth Century: Textual Disruptions* (2004), and *Beyond the Page: Poetry and Performance in Spanish America* (2014).

Eduardo Ledesma is associate professor of Spanish at the University of Illinois at Urbana-Champaign, where he teaches Latin American literature and culture. He is the author of *Radical Poetry: Aesthetics, Politics, Technology, and the Ibero-American Avant-Gardes, 1900–2015* (2016) and of the forthcoming *Cinemas of Marginality: Experimental, Avant-Garde and Documentary Film in Ibero-America*.

Teresa Longo is professor of Hispanic studies and dean for interdisciplinary studies at the College of William and Mary. She is the author of *Visible Dissent: Latin American Writers, Small U.S. Presses, and Progressive Social Change* (2018).

Jonathan Mayhew is professor of Spanish at the University of Kansas. He is the author of several books on contemporary Spanish poetry and on the literary and cultural legacy of Federico García Lorca, most recently *Lorca's Legacy: Essays in Interpretation* (2018).

Tiffany D. Creegan Miller is assistant professor of Spanish at Clemson University and serves as an adviser to a Guatemala-based medical NGO, Wuqu' Kawoq: Maya Health Alliance. Dr. Miller works on contemporary Latin American cultural studies, focusing on Maya literatures and oral traditions; her research interests include indigenous literatures and social movements, postcolonial and subaltern studies, gender inequalities, and digital humanities.

Melanie Nicholson is professor of Spanish at Bard College. She is the author of *Evil, Madness, and the Occult in Argentine Poetry* (2002) and *Surrealism in Latin American Literature: Searching for Breton's Ghost* (2013). With Mary G. Berg, she translated *A Talisman in the Darkness* (2012), a collection of stories by the Argentine writer Olga Orozco. She is currently working on a book that explores the bestiary and the beast fable in modern literature.

María Rosa Olivera-Williams, professor of Latin American literature at the University of Notre Dame, is the author of *El arte de crear lo femenino: ficción, género e historia del Cono Sur* (2013) and *La poesía gauchesca de Hidalgo a Hernández: respuesta estética y condicionamiento social* (1986), and coeditor with Mabel Moraña of *El salto de Minerva: intelectuales, género y Estado en América Latina* (2005). She is now completing "Tango: Imagining National Roots in the Maelstrom of Modernization and Modernity in Argentina and Uruguay: 1880–1940," a book project that received a J. William Fulbright Research Award.

Charles A. Perrone is professor emeritus of the Department of Spanish and Portuguese Studies at the University of Florida. He is the author of *Seven Faces: Brazilian Poetry since Modernism* (1996) and *Brazil, Lyric, and the Americas* (2010).

Juan G. Ramos is associate professor of Spanish at the College of the Holy Cross in Worcester, Massachusetts, where he teaches a variety of courses at all levels, including Latin American poetry and world literature. He is the author of *Sensing Decolonial Aesthetics in Latin American Arts* (2018) and coeditor of *Decolonial Approaches to Latin American Literatures and Cultures* (2016). He is currently working on a book project on *modernismo* in the Andes and another book project on the relation between world literature and the Andean region.

Justin Read is associate professor and chair of the Department of Romance Languages and Literatures at the University at Buffalo, State University of New York. His research focuses on urbanization, politics, and poetics in twentieth-century Latin America, with particular attention to Argentina and Brazil. He is author of *Modern Poetics and Hemispheric American Cultural Studies* (2009) and is finishing his second book, "Negation Space: Poetic Ecologies of Buenos Aires, 1850–1950."

Fernando J. Rosenberg is professor of romance studies, comparative literature, and film at Brandeis University. He is the author of *The Avant-Garde and Geopolitics in Latin America* (2006) and *After Human Rights: Literature, Visual Arts and Film in Latin America, 1990–2010* (2016).

Jacobo Sefamí is professor of Latin American literature at the University of California, Irvine, and director of the summer School of Spanish at Middlebury College. He has published articles, books, and editions, mostly on Latin American poetry, as well as on Jewish Latin American authors. He is also the author of *Los dolientes* (2004), a novel, which was translated and published in English in 2010.

Clare Sullivan, associate professor of Spanish at the University of Louisville, teaches poetry and translation. She received a 2010 NEA translation grant to translate Natalia Toledo's poetry. The book that resulted, *The Black Flower and Other Zapotec Poems* (2015), was shortlisted for the Best Translated Book Award.

Silvia R. Tandeciarz is professor of modern languages and literatures at the College of William and Mary, where she has worked since 1999. A scholar in the field of Latin American cultural studies, as well as a poet and translator, she has published the monograph *Citizens of Memory: Affect, Representation, and Human Rights in Postdictatorship Argentina* (2017); a book of poetry, *Exorcismos* (2000); and two cotranslations with Alice Nelson of books by Nelly Richard, *The Insubordination of Signs: Political Change, Cultural Transformation, and Poetics of the Crisis* (2004), and *Masculine/Feminine: Practices of Difference(s)* (2004).

Tamara R. Williams is professor of Hispanic studies at Pacific Lutheran University, where she is also executive director of the Wang Center for Global Education. She is the author of several articles on Latin American poetry and was project coordinator of the bilingual edition of Ernesto Cardenal's *El estrecho dudoso / The Doubtful Strait* (1995). Her current research focuses on the resurgence of the long poem in Mexico since the year 2000.

Bruce Dean Willis is professor of Spanish and comparative literature at the University of Tulsa. He has written numerous articles and the books *Aesthetics of Equilibrium: The Vanguard Poetics of Vicente Huidobro and Mário de Andrade* (2006) and *Corporeality in Early Twentieth-Century Latin American Literature: Body Articulations* (2013). His research and teaching interests include contemporary Mexican and Brazilian literature and arts.

Works Cited

"A Roosevelt." *YouTube*, uploaded by Luis Gómez R, 16 Apr. 2011, www.you
tube.com/watch?v=0DhsBRDwSTk.

Aching, Gerard. *The Politics of Spanish American Modernismo: By Exquisite Design.*
Cambridge UP, 1997.

Acree, William G., Jr. *Everyday Reading: Print Culture and Collective Identity in
the Río de la Plata, 1780–1910.* Vanderbilt UP, 2011.

Adorno, Rolena. *Guaman Poma: Writing and Resistance in Colonial Peru.* 2nd ed.,
U of Texas P, 2000.

Adorno, Theodor. *Aesthetic Theory.* Edited by Gretel Adorno and Rolf Tiedemann,
introduction by Robert Hullot-Kentor, Continuum, 2002.

———. "On Lyric Poetry and Society." *Notes on Literature*, vol. 1, Columbia UP,
1991.

Aguilar, Gonzalo. *Poesia concreta brasileira: As vanguardas na encruzilhada modernista.* 2002. Edusp, 2005.

———. "Some Propositions for Reflection on the Relation between Poetry and
Politics." Bandeira and Barros, pp. 176–92.

Agustini, Delmira. *Poesías completas.* Edited by Magdalena García Pinto, Cátedra,
2000. Letras Hispánicas.

Ak'abal, Humberto. "500 años." *Entre patojos.* Compiled by Irene Piedra Santa,
Piedra Santa Editorial, 2002, p. 135.

———. "En mi lengua." *Kamoyoyik.* Cholsamaj, 2002, p. 175. Serie Kaqulja.

———. *Poems I Brought Down from the Mountain.* Translated by Miguel Rivera
and Robert Bly, Nineties Press, 1999.

———. "El pregonero." *Ajkem tzij: Tejedor de palabras.* 4th ed., Cholsamaj, 2001,
p. 238.

Albright, Daniel. *Panaesthetics: On the Unity and Diversity of the Arts.* Yale UP, 2014.

Alegría, Claribel. *Fugues.* Translated by Darwin J. Flakoll, Curbstone, 1993.

"Altazor—canto VII." *YouTube*, uploaded by Juan Angel Italiano, 4 Feb. 2011,
www.youtube.com/watch?v=OzCXE1Op0Kg.

Altieri, Charles. "Taking Lyrics Literally: Teaching Poetry in a Prose Culture."
New Literary History, vol. 32, no. 2, Spring 2001, pp. 259–81.

Alves, Miriam, editor. *Enfim . . . Nós / Finally . . . Us: Contemporary Black Brazilian
Women Writers.* Translated by Carolyn Richardson, Three Continents Press, 1995.

American Council on Education. *Higher Education and Work Readiness: The View
from the Corporation.* Task Force on High Performance Work and Workers:
The Academic Connection, 1996.

"Amo el canto del Zenzontle Poema en náhuatl." *YouTube*, uploaded by teatrob-
lanquito, 24 Mar. 2009, www.youtube.com/watch?v=23dpnByHFOA.

Anderson, Maggie. "In a Dark Room: Photography and Revision." Behn and
Twichell, pp. 231–35.

Andrade, Carlos Drummond de. *Multitudinous Heart: Selected Poems: A Bilingual
Edition.* Translated by Richard Zenith, Farrar, Straus and Giroux, 2015.

Andrade, Mário de. *Hallucinated City.* Translated by Jack Tomlins, Vanderbilt UP, 1969. Translation of *Paulicéia desvairada,* 1922.

Andrade, Oswald de. "Manifiesto antropófago." Schwartz, pp. 173–80.

———. "Manifesto of Pau-Brasil Poetry." 1924. Translated by Stella de Sá Rego, *Latin American Literary Review,* vol. 14, no. 27, 1986, pp. 184–87.

Antin, David. *Radical Coherency: Selected Essays on Art and Literature.* U of Chicago P, 2011.

Apüshana-Malohe, Vito [Miguel Ángel López]. *Shiinalu'uirua shiirua ataa / En las hondonadas maternas de la piel.* Ministerio de Cultura de Colombia, 2010. Biblioteca Básica de los Pueblos Indígenas de Colombia 5.

The Archive of the Indigenous Languages of Latin America. LLILAS Benson Latin American Studies and Collections / Department of Linguistics / Digital Library Services Division of the University Libraries at the University of Texas at Austin, www.ailla.utexas.org.

Arendt, Hannah. *The Origins of Totalitarianism.* Harcourt Brace Jovanovich, 1976.

Argüelles, Juan Domingo. "El falso Nezahualcóyotl." *La Jornada,* 6 Oct. 2013. www.jornada.unam.mx/2013/10/06/sem-juan.html.

Arias, Arturo, et al. "Literaturas de Abya Yala." *LASA Forum,* vol. 43, no. 1, Winter 2012, pp. 7–10.

———. *Taking Their Word: Literature and the Signs of Central America.* U of Minnesota P, 2007.

Ascher, Nelson, and Régis Bonvicino, editors. *Nothing the Sun Could Not Explain: 20 Contemporary Brazilian Poets.* Green Integer, 1997/2003.

Attridge, Derek. *The Singularity of Literature.* Routledge, 2004.

Balderston, Daniel, and Mike González, editors. *Encyclopedia of Latin American and Caribbean Literature, 1900–2003.* Routledge, 2004.

Bandeira, João, and Lenora de Barros, editors. *Poesia concreta: O projeto verbivocovisual.* Artemeios, 2008.

Bandeira, Manuel. *Poesia completa e prosa.* Nova Aguilar, 1986.

———. *This Earth That Sky.* Translated by Candace Slater, U of California P, 1989.

Baptista, Josely Vianna. *On the Shining Screen of the Eyelids.* Translated by Chris Daniels, Manifest Press, 2003.

Barricelli, Jean Pierre, and Joseph Gibaldi, editors. *Interrelations of Literature.* Modern Language Association of America, 1982.

Barros, Manoel de. *Birds for a Demolition.* Translated by Idra Novey, Carnegie Mellon UP, 2010.

Barthes, Roland. "From Work to Text." *Textual Strategies: Perspectives in Poststructuralist Criticism,* edited by Josué V. Harari, Cornell UP, 1979, pp. 73–81.

Batchelder, Thomas H., and Susan Root. "Effects of an Undergraduate Program to Integrate Academic Learning and Service: Cognitive, Prosocial Cognitive, and Identity Outcomes." *Journal of Adolescence,* vol. 17, no. 4, August 1994, pp. 341–55.

Baxter Magolda, Marcia B. *Knowing and Reasoning in College: Gender-Related Patterns in Students' Intellectual Development.* Jossey-Bass, 1992.

Behn, Robin. "Letter Poems." Behn and Twichell, pp. 70–72.

Behn, Robin, and Chase Twichell. *The Practice of Poetry: Writing Exercises from Poets Who Teach.* Harper Collins, 1992.

Bello, Andrés. "Alocución a la poesía." *Obras completas*, Tomo I, Fundación de La Casa de Bello, 1981, pp. 43–64.

———. "Silva a agricultura de la Zona Tórrida." *Obras completas*, Tomo I, Fundación de La Casa de Bello, 1981, p. 65–74.

Benedetti, Mario. "La realidad y la palabra." *Mario Benedetti: Textos preferidos y complementarios del autor y lector*, Anthropos, pp. 125–31.

Berenguer, Carmen. *Las huellas del siglo.* Ediciones Manieristas, 1986.

Berger, John. "The Hour of Poetry." *The Sense of Sight*, Pantheon, 1985, pp. 243–52.

Bernstein, Charles. "Creative Wreading: A Primer." Retallack and Spahr, pp. 275–81.

———. "Haroldo de Campos Thou Art Translated (Knot)." *Pitch of Poetry*, U Chicago P, 2016, pp. 157–61.

Berrett, Dan. "Harvard Mounts Campaign to Bolster Undergraduate Humanities." *Chronicle of Higher Education.* 7 June 2013.

Bessa, Antonio S. "Sound as Subject: Augusto de Campos' *Poetamenos.*" *The Sound of Poetry / The Poetry of Sound*, edited by Marjorie Perloff and Craig Dworkin, U of Chicago P, 2009, pp. 219–36.

Bishop, Elizabeth, and Emanuel Brasil, editors. *An Anthology of Twentieth-Century Brazilian Poetry.* Wesleyan UP, 1972.

Bleys, Rudi C. *Images of Ambiente: Homotextuality and Latin American Art, 1810–Today.* Continuum, 2000.

Bohn, Willard. *Modern Visual Poetry.* U of Delaware P, 2001.

———. "The Visual Trajectory of José Juan Tablada." *Hispanic Review*, vol. 69, no. 2, 2001, pp. 191–208.

Bolaño, Roberto. "Déjenlo todo nuevamente." *Perros habitados por las voces del desierto*, edited by Rubén Medina, Aldus, 2014, pp. 381–87.

Bonvicino, Régis. *Beyond the Wall: New Selected Poems.* Translated by Charles Bernstein, Odile Cisneros, and Thérèse Bachand, Green Integer Press, 2016.

Bowen, José Antonio. "Helping Students Embrace Discomfort." *Inside Higher Ed*, 7 Dec. 2016, www.insidehighered.com/views/2016/12/07/educating-students-ambiguity-and-discomfort-essay.

Bracho, Coral. *Bajo el destello líquido.* Fondo de Cultura Económica, 1988.

Brasil, Emanuel, and William Jay Smith, editors. *Brazilian Poetry, 1950–1980.* Wesleyan UP, 1983.

Breslow, Jason M. "The Staggering Death Toll of Mexico's Drug War." *Frontline*, 27 July, 2015, www.pbs.org/wgbh/frontline/article/the-staggering-death-toll-of-mexicos-drug-war/.

Brooks, Cleanth, and Robert Penn Warren. *Understanding Poetry.* 3rd ed., Holt, Rinehart and Winston, 1960.

Brotherston, Gordon. *Latin American Poetry: Origins and Presence.* Cambridge UP, 1975.

Buarque de Hollanda, Chico. "Cálice." *Chico Buarque*, Phillips, 1978. LP.

Buarque de Hollanda, Heloísa. *Impressões de viagem: CPC, vanguarda e desbunde.* 5th ed., Aeroplano, 2004.

———. *26 Poetas hoje: Antologia.* 6th ed., Aeroplano, 2007.

Buchloh, Paul Gerhard. "The Moon in Modern Anglo-American Poetry." *Literatur in Wissenschaft und Unterricht*, vol. 17, no. 2, 1984, pp. 135–50.

Butler, Judith. *Antígone's Claim: Kinship between Life and Death*. Columbia UP, 2000.

———. *Gender Trouble*. Routledge, 1999.

———. *Giving an Account of Oneself*. Fordham UP, 2005.

———. *El grito de Antígona*. Translated by Esther Oliver. El Roure Editorial, 2001.

———. *Precarious Life: The Powers of Mourning and Violence*. Verso, 2004.

Butterman, Steven F. *Perversions on Parade: Brazilian Literature of Transgression and Postmodern Anti-aesthetics in Glauco Mattoso*. San Diego State UP, 2005.

Cabral, Astrid. *Cage*. Translated by Alexis Levitin, Host, 2008.

Café Tacvba. "Chilanga banda." *Avalancha de éxitos*, Warner Music Mexico, 1996.

Campa, Román de la. *Latinamericanism*. U of Minnesota P, 1999.

Campos, Augusto de, et al. "Plano piloto para a poesia concreta." *Noigandres*, no. 4, 1958, p. 13.

Campos, Augusto de, and Julio Plaza. *Poemobiles*. Self-published, limited edition, 1974.

Campos, Haroldo de. *Galáxias*. Editora Ex-Libris, 1984.

———. *Novas: Selected Writings*. Edited by Sérgio Bessa and Odile Cisneros, Northwestern UP, 2007.

———. "A obra de arte aberta." *Teoria da Poesia Concreta*, by Augusto de Campos et al., 3rd ed., Editora Brasiliense, 1987, pp. 36–39.

Campus Compact. *Introduction to Service-Learning Toolkit*. Brown University, 1999.

Cantares mexicanos. Edited by Miguel León-Portilla, UNAM / Fideicomiso Teixidor, 2011.

Cardenal, Ernesto. *Los ovnis de oro: Poemas indios / Golden UFOs: The Indian Poems*. Translated by Carlos and Monique Altschul, edited by Russell O. Salmon, Indiana UP, 1992.

———. *El secreto de Machu Picchu*. U Alas Peruanas, 2005.

———. *Zero Hour and Other Documentary Poems*. Edited by Donald D. Walsh, introduction by Robert Pring-Mill, translated by Paul W. Borgeson, Jr., et al., New Directions, 1980.

Carranza, María Mercedes. "Patas arriba con la vida." Vicuña and Livon-Grosman, pp. 471–72.

Casaús Arzú, Marta Elena. *La metamorfosis del racismo en Guatemala*. Cholsamaj, 2002.

Castelblanco, Daniel. *Sikuriando melodías de tiempos lejanos: Los sikuris cosmopolitas y la vigencia de "lo andino" en Bogotá, Santiago, y Buenos Aires*. 2017. Georgetown U, PhD dissertation, repository.library.georgetown.edu/handle/10822/1042949.

Cepeda Bravo, Alex Mario Fernando. "Espacio sin ocupantes: estudio sobre el proceso de integración fronteriza colombo-ecuatoriano desarrollado por la Red de Consejos Comunitarios de Pacífico Sur-RECOMPAS-y la Comarca de Afrodescendientes del Norte de Esmeraldas-CANE." 2012. Universidad Nacional de Colombia, MA thesis.

Cerón, Rocío. *Diorama*. U Autónoma de Nuevo León, 2012.

———. *Diorama*. Translated by Anna Rosenwong, Phoneme Media, 2013.

———. "Poking at Memory: A Conversation with Rocío Cerón and Anna Rosenwong." Interview by Paul Holzman, *World Literature Today*, 29 Sept. 2015.

Chacón, Gloria. "Poetizas mayas: Subjetividades contra la corriente." *Cuadernos de Literatura*, vol. 11, no. 22, 2007, pp. 94–106.

Chang-Rodríguez, Raquel, editor. *"Aquí, ninfas del sur, venid ligeras."* Voces poéticas virreinales. Iberoamericana, 2008. Teci: Textos y estudios coloniales y de la Independencia 18.

Cheal, David. "The Life of a Song: 'Guantanamera.'" *Financial Times*, 13 Mar. 2015.

Chester, Eric. *Employing Generation Why: Understanding, Managing, and Motivating Your New Workforce*. Tucker House Books, 2002.

Chiappini, Lígia. "Poesia brasileira pós-João Cabral: perspectivas da(s) modernidade(s)." *Iberoamericana: América Latina-España-Portugal*, vol. 4, no. 14, 2004, pp. 107–26.

Chikangana, Fredy. "Oralitura indígena como un viaje a la memoria." *Palabras de vuelta: Oralidad y escritura. Experiencias desde la literatura indígena*, edited by Luz María Lepe Lira, PRODICI, 2014, pp. 75–97.

ChocQuibTown. "De donde vengo yo—ChocQuibTown (Official Music Video)." *YouTube*, uploaded by Nacional Records, 19 Feb. 2010. www.youtube.com /watch?v=yMS4J6Gp6e4.

———. "Oro—ChocQuibTown (Official Music Video)." *YouTube*, uploaded by Nacional Records, 27 Oct. 2010, www.youtube.com/watch?v=lQZZ_gp8dos.

Cisneros, Antonio. *Crónica del niño Jesús de Chilca. Poesía*, by Cisneros, vol. 3, Peisa and Arango, 2000.

Clayton, Michelle. *Poetry in Pieces: César Vallejo and Lyric Modernity*. U of California P, 2011.

Cobo Borda, Juan Gustavo. Prologue. *Antología de la poesía hispanoamericana*, edited by Cobo Borda, Fondo de Cultura Económica, 1985, pp. 9–54.

Colombi, Beatriz. "Prólogo." *Los cálices vacíos*, by Delmira Agustini, edited by Colombi, Ediciones Simurg, 1999, pp. 7–34.

Combe, Dominique. "La referencia desdoblada. El sujeto lírico entre la ficción y la autobiografía." *Teorías sobre la lírica*, Arcos, 1999, pp. 127–53.

Commerce Report of the United States Department of Commerce. The Bureau of Foreign and Domestic Commerce, 1922.

Córdova, Rojo. "Dos mil Mex—poesía oral x Rojo Córdova." *YouTube*, uploaded by Camilo Molfino, 22 May 2011, www.youtube.com/watch?v=4IIsjKGtYso.

Corona, Ricardo, editor. *Outras praias: 13 poetas brasileiros emergentes / Other Shores: 13 Emerging Brazilian Poets*. Iluminuras, 1998.

Coronado Suzan, Gabriela. "La literatura indígena: una mirada desde fuera." *Situación actual y perspectivas de la literatura en lenguas indígenas*, edited by Carlos Montemayor, Consejo Nacional para la Cultura y las Artes, 1993, pp. 55–76.

Correa-Díaz, Luis, and Scott Weintraub. *Poesía y poéticas digitales / electrónicas / tecnos / new-media en América Latina*. Universidad Central [Bogotá], 2016.

Cortázar, Julio. *Rayuela*. Cátedra, 2008.

Cortés, Jair. "Sor Juana Inés de la Cruz y la 'Chilanga Banda.'" *Granada de Mano*, 28 Mar. 2016. granadademanopoesia.blogspot.com/2016/03/sor-juana-ines -de-la-cruz-y-la-chilanga.html.

Costa, Horácio, and Charles A. Perrone, editors. *Tigertail: A South Florida Poetry Annual* 6. Tigertail Productions, 2008.

Costa, René de. "Del modernismo a las primeras vanguardias." *Huellas de las literaturas hispanoamericanas*, edited by John Garganigo et al., Prentice Hall, 2002, pp. 359–61.

Cu Choc, Maya. "Canción por la vida." *Uk'u'x kaj, uk'u'x ulew: Antología de poesía maya guatemalteca contemporánea*, compiled by Emilio del Valle Escalante, Instituto Internacional de Literatura Iberoamericana, 2010, p. 305. Serie Clásicos de América.

Dalton, Roque. "Como tú." *Poemas Clandestinos*, translated by Margaret Randall, Curbstone, 1990, pp. 38–39.

Damon, Maria, and Ira Livingston. *Poetry and Cultural Studies: A Reader*. U of Illinois P, 2009.

Danielson, Susan, and Ann M. Fallon, editors. *Community-Based Learning and the Work of Literature*. Anker, 2007.

Darío, Rubén. *Poesía*. Edited by Julio Ortega, Galaxia Gutenberg, 2007.

———. *Songs of Life and Hope / Cantos de vida y esperanza*. Duke UP, 2004.

de la Torre, Monica, and Michael Wiegers, editors. *Reversible Monuments: Contemporary Mexican Poetry*. Copper Canyon, 2002.

Deleuze, Gilles, and Félix Guattari. "Rizoma." Translation and notes by Coral Bracho. *Revista de la Universidad de México* vol. 32, no. 2, 1977, Supplement, pp. 1–12.

"Demandarán este lunes 150 inmigrantes deportados regresar a Estados Unidos." *La Jornada*, 9 March 2014, semanal.jornada.com.mx/ultimas/2014/03/09 /demandaran-este-lunes-150-inmigrantes-deportados-regresar-a-estados-uni dos-3776.html.

Dewey, John. *Experience and Education*. Kappa Delta Pi, 1998.

Didi-Huberman, Georges. *Pueblos expuestos, pueblos figurantes*. Translated by Horacio Pons, Manantial, 2014.

"Diorama by Rocío Cerón and Nómada." *YouTube*, uploaded by Eudora Projecto Global, 11 Jan. 2012, www.youtube.com/watch?v=bUnl3cff8KQ.

Domeneck, Ricardo. "Poéticas contemporâneas: a textualidade em algumas poetas brasileiras do século XX e início do XXI." revistamododeusar.blogspot.com .br/2010/04/poeticas-contemporaneas-textualidade-em.html.

Donnelly, Dianne, editor. *Does the Writing Workshop Still Work?* Multilingual Matters, 2010.

Dorfman, Ariel. *In Case of Fire in a Foreign Land*. Translated by Edith Grossman, Duke UP, 2002.

———. *Manifesto for Another World: Voices from Beyond the Dark*. Seven Stories Press, 2004, pp. 22–23.

———. *Other Septembers, Many Americas: Selected Provocations, 1980–2004*. Seven Stories Press, 2004.

Duderstadt, James J. *A University for the 21st Century*. U of Michigan P, 2000.

Dunas, Isabel. "Acento." *Revista Prometeo*, no. 102–103, July 2015, pp. 245–46.

Dunn, Christopher J. *Contracultura: Alternative Arts and Social Transformation in Authoritarian Brazil.* U of North Carolina P, 2016.

Easter, Chelsea. "Selections from Death and the Maiden: Paulina's Story." 9 Dec. 2015. Hispanic Studies 481, College of William and Mary, student paper.

Echeverría, Andrea, and Daniel Castelblanco, "Obrero de la palabra 'mapurbe.'" *El Hablador: Revista virtual*, no. 20, www.elhablador.com/entrevista20_aninir.html.

Eltit, Diamela. *Crónica del sufragio femenino en Chile.* SERNAM, 1994.

England, Nora C. "Mayan Language Revival and Revitalization Politics: Linguists and Linguistic Ideologies." *American Anthropologist*, vol. 105, no. 4, Dec. 2003, pp. 733–43.

Espada, Martín. *The Republic of Poetry.* Norton, 2006.

Espínola, Adriano. *Taxi; or, Poem of Love in Transit.* 1986. Garland, 1992.

Estrada, Alicia Ivonne. "The (Dis)Articulation of Colonial Legacies in Calixta Gabriel Xiquín's *Tejiendo los sucesos en el tiempo / Weaving Events in Time.*" *Romance Notes*, vol. 51, no. 1, 2011, pp. 137–47.

Ethnologue, Languages of the World. 14th ed. SIL International, 2001, www.ethnologue.com.

Eyler, Janet. *At a Glance: What We Know about the Effects of Service-Learning on College Students, Faculty, Institutions and Communities, 1993–2000.* Vanderbilt UP, 2001.

Eyler, Janet, et al. *A Practitioner's Guide to Reflection in Service-Learning: Student Voices and Reflections.* Vanderbilt UP, 1996.

Eyler, Janet, and Dwight E. Giles, Jr. *Where's the Learning in Service-Learning?* Jossey-Bass, 1999.

Fabre, Luis Felipe. *Leyendo agujeros.* Fondo Cultural Tierra Adentro, 2005.

———. *La sodomía en la Nueva España.* Pre-Textos, 2010.

Falkoff, Marc, et al., editors. *Poems from Guantánamo: The Detainees Speak.* U of Iowa P, 2007.

Feitlowitz. Marguerite. *A Lexicon of Terror: Argentina and the Legacies of Torture.* Oxford UP, 1998.

Felski, Rita. *The Uses of Literature.* Wiley-Blackwell, 2008.

Fernández Moreno, César. *Introducción a la poesía.* Fondo de Cultura Económica, 1962.

Ferrer, Horacio. *El libro del tango: Historias e imágenes.* Ediciones Ossorio-Vargas, 1970.

Finch, Jeremy. "What Is Generation Z, and What Does It Want?" www.fastcompany.com/3045317/what-is-generation-z-and-what-does-it-want.

Fiol-Matta, Licia. *A Queer Mother for the Nation: The State and Gabriela Mistral.* U of Minnesota P, 2002.

Fischer, Edward F. "Beyond Victimization: Maya Movements in Post-war Guatemala." *The Struggle for Indigenous Rights in Latin America*, edited by Nancy Grey Postero and Leon Zamosc, Sussex Academic P, 2004, pp. 81–104.

Fischer, Edward F., and R. McKenna Brown, editors. *Maya Cultural Activism in Guatemala.* U of Texas P, 1996.

Fletcher, Heather. "Literatura cibercreativa: ¿Qué lugar tendrán los tecnotextos en el futuro de las Humanidades? (El caso de Gustavo Romano y su proyecto de poesía *IP*)." *Arizona Journal of Hispanic Cultural Studies*, vol. 14, 2010, pp. 335–48.

Forché, Carolyn. Introduction. *Against Forgetting: Twentieth-Century Poetry of Witness*, edited by Forché, Norton, 1993, pp. 29–47.

Foster, David W. "Mário de Andrade: On Being São Paulo-Wise in *Paulicéia desvairada*." *São Paulo: Perspectives on the City and Cultural Production*, UP of Florida, 2011, pp. 13–26.

Franco, Bridget. Syllabus for Introduction to Textual Analysis. Department of Spanish, College of the Holy Cross, Worcester, MA, Fall 2014.

Freitas, Angélica. "A mulher é uma construção." *Um útero é do tamanho de um punho*, by Freitas, Cosac Naify, 2012, pp. 45–46.

———. *Rilke Shake*. Translated by Hillary Kaplan, Phoneme Media, 2014.

French, Brigittine M. "The Maya Movement and Modernity: Local Kaqchikel Linguistic Ideologies and the Problem of Progress." *Proceedings of the Tenth Annual Symposium About Language and Society, 12–14 April 2002*, *Texas Linguistic Forum*, vol. 45, 2002, pp. 58–68.

Freund, Catherine. "Dos días, dos naciones, una voz: Dorfman y la poética de crisis." 4 Oct. 2015. Hispanic Studies 481, College of William and Mary, student paper.

Friera, Silvina. "El homenaje a un autor que escribió en los márgenes." *Página 12*, 1 Dec 2008, www.pagina12.com.ar/diario/suplementos/espectaculos/4-12138-2008-12-01.html.

Fróes, Elson, editor. *P. Leminski Traduzido*. www.elsonfroes.com.br/kamiquase/englishpoems.htm.

Fulton, Alice. *Feeling as a Foreign Language: The Good Strangeness of Poetry*. Graywolf, 1999.

Gabriel Xiquín, Calixta. *La cosmovisión maya y las mujeres: Aportes desde el punto de vista de una ajq'ij (guía spiritual) kaqchikel*. Ministerio de Cultura y Deportes / Editorial Cultura, 2008. Colección Ensayo Serie Luis Cardoza y Aragón 42.

———. *Tejiendo los sucesos en el tiempo / Weaving Events in Time*. Translated by Susan G. Rascón and Suzanne M. Strugalla, Yax Te' Foundation, 2002.

Galeano, Eduardo. *Open Veins of Latin America: Five Centuries of the Pillage of a Continent*. Monthy Review P, 1997.

García Lorca, Federico. "Romance sonámbula." *Poet in Spain*, translated by Sarah Arvio, Knopf, 2017, pp. 191–96.

García Pabón, Leonardo. "Bolivia, Poetry of." *The Princeton Encyclopedia of Poetry and Poetics*, 4th ed., edited by Roland Greene, et al., Princeton UP, 2012, pp. 152–54.

Garrido, Lorena. "Storni, Mistral, Ibarbourou: Encuentros en la creación de una poética feminista." *Revista Electrónica: Documentos Lingüísticos y Literarios UACh*, no. 28, 2005, pp. 34–39, www.humanidades.uach.cl/documentos_lin guisticos/document.php?id=90.{16}

Garza Carvajal, Federico. *Vir: Perceptions of Manliness in Andalucía and Mexico, 1561–1699*. Academisch Proefschrift, 2000.

Gelman, Juan. *Cólera buey*. Seix Barral, 1994.

———. *Poesía reunida*. Seix Barral, 2012.

———. *Si dulcemente*. Lumen, 1980.

————. *Unthinkable Tenderness: Selected Poems.* Edited and translated by Joan Lindgren, U of California P, 1997.

Gil, Gilberto. "Metáfora." *Gil luminoso.* Geléia Geral / Gege Produções Artísticas, 2006.

Gilbert, Sandra, and Susan Gubar. *The Madwoman in the Attic: The Woman Writer and the Nineteenth-Century Literary Imagination,* 2nd ed., Yale UP, 2000.

Gile, Daniel. *Basic Concepts and Models for Interpreter and Translator Training.* John Benjamins, 2009.

Girondo, Oliverio. *Obra completa: Edición crítica.* Galaxia Gutenberg / Círculo de Lectores, 1999.

Gleiser, Marcelo. "The Key to America's Future? Science." *National Public Radio,* 16 Nov. 2016, www.npr.org/sections/13.7/2016/11/16/502270280/the-key-to-americas-future-science.

Global Competence Position Statement. American Council on the Teaching of Foreign Languages, 2014.

Gobat, Michel. "The Invention of Latin America: A Transnational History of Anti-Imperialism, Democracy, and Race." *American Historical Review,* Dec. 2013, pp. 1345–75.

Goeritz, Mathías. *Pocos cocodrilos locos.* Zona Rosa México DF, 1979.

González, Mike, and David Treece. *The Gathering of Voices: The Twentieth-Century Poetry of Latin America.* Verso, 1992.

Gordinier, Jeff. "Review: *The Hatred of Poetry*: Let's Count the Ways." *The New York Times,* 7 July 2016, www.nytimes.com/2016/07/08/books/review-the-hatred-of-poetry-lets-count-the-ways.html.

Gracián, Baltasar. *Agudeza y arte del ingenio.* Castalia, 1969.

Graff, Gerald. Foreword. Danielson and Fallon, pp. ix–x.

Greene, Roland, et al., editors. *Princeton Encyclopedia of Poetry and Poetics.* 4th ed., Princeton UP, 2012.

Grossman, Allen. *The Sighted Singer: Two Works on Poetry for Readers and Writers.* Johns Hopkins UP, 1992.

Gruzinski, Serge. "Las cenizas del deseo: Homosexuales novohispanos a mediados del siglo XVII." *De la santidad a la perversión,* edited by Sergio Ortega. Grijalbo, 1985.

"Los guardianes de la marimba, el Cununo y el Guasá." *YouTube,* uploaded by UNESCO, 2 Dec. 2015, www.youtube.com/watch?v=5xItvN0Rx44.

Guerrieri, Kevin. "Leer y Escribir la Frontera: Language, Literature, and Community Engagement in the San Diego-Tijuana Borderlands." Danielson and Fallon, pp. 154–79.

Guijo, Gregorio Martín de. *Diario: 1648–1664.* Edited by Manuel Romero de Terreros, Porrúa, 1952.

Guillén, Nicolás. *Cantos para soldados y sones para turistas.* Editorial Masas, 1937.

————. "Cuban Poet Nicolás Guillén Reading from His Verse." Archive of Hispanic Literature on Tape, Library of Congress, 1958, www.loc.gov/item/93842839.

————. *Summa poética.* Cátedra, 1990.

Guillermoprieto, Alma. *The Heart that Bleeds: Latin America Now.* Vintage, 1995.

Gullar, Ferreira. *Dirty Poem.* 1975. Translated by Leland Guyer, New Directions, 2015.

————. *Toda poesía.* José Olympio, 2000.

Gullón, Ricardo. *Direcciones del modernismo*. Alianza, 1990.

Guyer, Paul. "Disinterestedness and Desire in Kant's Aesthetics." *The Journal of Aesthetics and Art Criticism*, vol. 36, no. 4, 1978, pp. 449–60.

Haggerty, George E., and Bonnie Zimmerman, editors. *Professions of Desire: Lesbian and Gay Studies in Literature*. Modern Language Association of America, 1995.

Handelsman, Michael. "Afro-centrism as an Intercultural Force in Ecuador." *Race, Colonialism, and Social Transformation in Latin America and the Caribbean*, edited by Jerome Branche, UP of Florida, 2008, pp. 241–56.

Harford, Tim. "How Frustration Can Make Us More Creative." TEDGlobal> London, Sept. 2015, www.ted.com/talks/tim_harford_how_messy_problems_can _inspire_creativity?language=en.

———. *Messy: The Power of Disorder to Transform our Lives*. Penguin, 2017.

Harvey, Giles. "In the Labyrinth: A User's Guide to Bolaño." *The New Yorker*, 18 Jan. 2012. www.newyorker.com/books/page-turner/in-the-labyrinth-a-users-guide -to-bolaño.

Hayles, Katherine. "Electronic Literature: What Is It?" 2 Jan. 2007, eliterature.org /pad/elp.html.

Hedge Coke, Alison, editor. *Sing: Poetry from the Indigenous Americas*. U of Arizona P, 2011.

Hellebrandt, Josef, and Ethel Jorge, editors. *The Scholarship of Community Engagement*. Special issue of *Hispania*, vol. 96, no. 2, 2013.

Hellebrandt, Josef, and Lucia Varona, editors. Construyendo Puentes *(Building Bridges): Concepts and Models for Service-Learning in Spanish*. American Association for Higher Education, 2005.

Helmberger, Janet L. "Language and Ethnicity: Multiple Literacies in Context, Language Education in Guatemala." *Bilingual Research Journal*, vol. 30, no. 1, 2006, pp. 65–86.

Heredia, José María. "En el Teocalli de Cholula." *The Odes of Bello, Olmedo, and Heredia*, G. P. Putnam's Sons, 1920, pp. 85–91.

Hernández, José. *Martín Fierro*. Introduction by Santiago M. Lugones, Alianza Editorial, 2004.

Hernández Ramírez, Juan. *Chikome xochitl / Siete flor*. Conaculta, 2007.

Herrera, Paula Miranda. *La poesía de Violeta Parra*. Cuarto Propio, 2013.

Hervey, Sándor G. J., et al. *Thinking Spanish Translation: A Course in Translation*. Psychology Press, 1995.

Hinostroza, Rodolfo. *Contranatura*. Barral Editores, 1971.

"Hipogrifo (Luis Bravo, Uruguay)." *YouTube*, uploaded by *Revista Prometeo*, 6 Mar. 2011, www.youtube.com/watch?v=l84_CxeOTC8.

Hokenson, Jan Walsh, and Marcella Munson. *The Bilingual Text: History and Theory of Literary Self-Translation*. St. Jerome, 2007.

Hollander, Kurt. "The Tragedy of Tampico, Mexico: A City of Violence, Abandoned to the Trees." *The Guardian*, 2 June 2014. www.theguardian.com/cities/2014 /jun/02/the-tragedy-of-tampico-mexico-a-city-of-violence-abandoned-to -the-trees.

Holloway, Thomas. *A Companion to Latin American History*. Wiley-Blackwell, 2008.

Howard, Jeffrey. "Academic Service Learning: A Counternormative Pedagogy." *Academic Service Learning: A Pedagogy of Action and Reflection*, edited by Jeffrey Howard and Robert A. Rhoads, Jossey-Bass, 1998, pp. 21–29.

Howard, Jeffrey, and Joseph Galura. *Praxis I: A Faculty Casebook on Community Service Learning.* University of Michigan, Office of Community Service Learning, 1993.

Huidobro, Vicente. *Altazor, Temblor del cielo.* Edited by René de Costa, Cátedra, 1989.

———. *Obra poética.* Edited by Cedomil Goic. UNESCO, 2003. Colección Archivos.

Hutcheon, Linda. *A Theory of Parody: The Teachings of Twentieth-Century Art Forms.* U of Illinois P, 2000.

Jackson, Virginia. "Who Reads Poetry?" *PMLA*, vol. 123, no. 1, Jan. 2008, pp. 181–87.

Jacoby, Barbara, et al. *Service-Learning in Higher Education: Concepts and Practices.* Jossey-Bass, 1996.

Jameson, Fredric. *Postmodernism or the Cultural Logic of Late Capitalism.* Duke UP, 1997.

Jamioy Juagibioy, Hugo. *Bínÿbe oboyejuayëng. Danzantes del viento.* Ministerio de Cultura de Colombia, 2010.

Jáuregui, Carlos. "Antropofagia." *Dictionary of Latin American Cultural Studies.* UP of Florida, 2012, pp. 22–28.

Jiménez, José Olivio, editor. *Antología crítica de la poesía modernista hispanoamericana.* Hiperion, 1994.

Johansson K., Patrick. *La palabra, la imagen, y el manuscrito: Lecturas indígenas de un texto pictórico en el siglo XVI.* U Nacional Autónoma de México, 2004.

Jones, Francis R. *Poetry Translating as Expert Action.* John Benjamins, 2011.

Jrade, Cathy L. *Delmira Agustini, Sexual Seduction, and Vampiric Conquest.* Yale UP, 2012.

———. *Modernism, Modernity, and the Development of Spanish American Literature.* U of Texas P, 1998.

"Juan Gelman—Sefiní—*El lado oscuro del corazón* [1992]." *YouTube,* uploaded by Leonel Tupavada, 26 Aug. 2012, www.youtube.com/watch?v=Q9VchdxoI8E.

"Juan Gelman—Sobre la poesía." *YouTube,* uploaded by Ivana Sandez, 8 May 2012, www.youtube.com/watch?v=efUN5fVFbps.

Juana Inés de la Cruz. "Hombres necios." *Obras completas, 1: Lírica Personal,* edited by Antonio Alatorre, Fondo de Cultura Económica, 2012, pp. 320–22.

———. "Primero sueño." *Obra selecta,* edited by Margo Glantz, Biblioteca Ayacucho, pp. 70–119.

Juarroz, Roberto. *Vertical Poetry: Last Poems.* Translated by Mary Crow, White Pine Press, 2011.

Karl, Sylvia. "Rehumanizing the Disappeared: Spaces of Memory in Mexico and the Liminality of Transitional Justice." *American Quarterly,* vol. 66, no. 3, 2014, pp. 727–48.

Keats, John. *The Letters of John Keats,* vol. 1. Edited by Hyder E. Rollins, Harvard UP, 1958.

Kirkpatrick, Gwen. *The Dissonant Legacy of Modernismo: Lugones, Herrera y Reissig, and the Voices of Modern Spanish American Poetry.* U of California P, 1989.

Kirkwood, Julieta. *Ser política en Chile: Los nudos de la sabiduría femenina.* Cuarto Propio, 1990.

Kirzner, Sebastián. *2017: Nueva poesía contemporánea.* Milena Caserola, 2009.

Koch, Kenneth. *Making Your Own Days: The Pleasures of Reading and Writing Poetry.* Scribner, 1998.

Kozer, José. *Bajo este cien*. Fondo de Cultura Económica, 1983.

Krashen, Stephen D. *Principles and Practice in Second Language Acquisition*. Pergamon, 1982.

Kuhnheim, Jill S. *Beyond the Page: Poetry and Performance in Spanish America*. U of Arizona P, 2014.

———. "Cultures of the Lyric and Lyrical Culture: Teaching Poetry and Cultural Studies." *Cultural Studies in the Curriculum: Teaching Latin America*, edited by Danny J. Anderson and Jill S. Kuhnheim, Modern Language Association of America, 2003, pp. 105–22.

———. "The Politics of Form: Three Twentieth-Century Spanish American Poets and the Sonnet." *Hispanic Review*, Autumn 2008, pp. 387–411.

———. *Spanish American Poetry at the End of the Twentieth Century: Textual Disruptions*. U of Texas P, 2004.

Language Policy Division. "Context, Concepts and Theories." *Autobiography of Intercultural Encounters*. Council of Europe, 2009. www.coe.int/t/dg4/auto biography.

Lao-Montes, Agustín. "Decolonial Moves: En-gendering African Diasporas." *Cultural Studies*, vol. 21, nos. 2–3, 2007, pp. 309–38.

Ledesma, Eduardo. *Radical Poetry: Aesthetics, Politics, Technology, and the Ibero-American Avant-Gardes, 1900–2015*. SUNY P, Albany, 2016.

Lee, Jongsoo. *The Allure of Nezahualcoyotl: Pre-Hispanic History, Religion, and Nahua Poetics*. U of New Mexico P, 2008.

León-Portilla, Miguel. *Aztec Thought and Culture: A Study of the Ancient Nahuatl Mind*. Translated by Jack Emory Davis, U of Oklahoma P, 2012.

Levi, Primo. *The Drowned and the Saved*. Summit Books, 1988.

Lewis, Melvyn Paul. *Social Change, Identity Shift and Language Shift in K'iche' of Guatemala*. Georgetown U, PhD dissertation, 1994, UMI 9501841.

Lezama Lima, José. *La expresión americana*. Alianza, 1969.

Livon-Grosman, Ernesto. "A Historical Introduction to Latin American Poetry." Vicuña and Livon-Grosman, pp. xxxiii–xxxviii.

"¿Lo oíste? Poesía stereo." *YouTube*, uploaded by Camilo Molfino, 7 Oct. 2010, www.youtube.com/watch?v=7b_K0WpD-iA.

Lopes, Denilson. *O homem que amava rapazes e outros ensaios*. Aeroplano, 2002.

López, Jaime. *Odio Fonky, tomas de buró*. Opción Sónica, 1995.

Lorde, Audre. *Sister Outsider: Essays and Speeches*. Ten Speed Press, 1984.

Luciani, Frederick. "The Burlesque Sonnets of Sor Juana Inés de la Cruz." *Writers of the Spanish Colonial Period*, edited by David William Foster and Daniel Altamiranda, Garland, 1997, pp. 369–79.

Ludmer, Josefina. "Las tretas del débil." *La sartén por el mango: Encuentro de escritoras latinoamericanas*, edited by Patricia Elena González and Eliana Ortega, Ediciones Huracán, 1984, pp. 47–54.

Lunez, Enriqueta. *Sk'eoj jme'tik u: Cantos de luna*. Pluralia Ediciones, 2012.

———. *Yi'beltak ch'uleletik: Raíces del alma*. Instituto Sonorense de Cultura, 2007.

Mabry, J. Beth. "Pedagogical Variations in Service-Learning and Student Outcomes: How Time, Contact and Reflection Matter." *Michigan Journal of Community Service Learning*, vol. 5, Fall 1998, pp. 32–47.

Macken-Horarik, Mary. "Making Productive Use of Four Models of School English: A Case Study Revisited." *English in Australia*, vol. 49, no. 3, 2014, pp. 7–19.

Madariaga Caro, Montserrat. *Bolaño infra: 1975–1977: Los años que inspiraron Los detectives salvajes*. RIL Editores, 2011.

Malacchini Soto, Simoné. *Lira popular: Identidad gráfica de un medio impreso chileno*. Ocho Libros Editores, 2015.

Manzano, Juan Francisco. *The Life and Poems of a Cuban Slave*. Palgrave Macmillan, 2014.

Maranhão, Salgado. *Blood of the Sun*. Translated by Alexis Levitin, Milkweed Editions, 2013.

Marinetti, Filippo. "Manifiesto futurista" and "Manifiesto técnico de la literatura futurista (1912)." mason.gmu.edu/~rberroa/futurismo.htm.

Marra, Fernanda. "Uma reconstrução pelas palavras de Angélica Freitas: A obra possui um fio condutor: o lugar de onde se fala e de onde se enxerga a figura da mulher contemporânea." *Amálgama*, 17 Oct. 2012.

Martí, José. "Amor de ciudad grande." *Poesía completa: Edición crítica*, edited by Cintio Vitier et al., UNAM, 1998.

———. *Versos sencillos. Ismaelillo; Versos libres; Versos sencillos*, edited by Iván A. Schulman, Cátedra, 1982.

Mattoso, Glauco. "Cera e nata para Desdêmona." *Línguas na papa*, by Mattoso, Pindaiba, 1982.

———. *O que é poesia marginal?* Brasiliense, 1981.

———. "Soneto travesti [313]." *Artes e ofícios da poesia*, edited by Augusto Massi, Secretaria Municipal de Cultura de São Paulo, 1991, p. 172.

Maxwell, Judith. "Prescriptive Grammar and Kaqchikel Revitalization." Fischer and Brown, pp. 195–207.

Mayhew, Jonathan. "What Lorca Knew: Teaching Receptivity." *Hispanic Literatures and the Question of a Liberal Education*, edited by Luis Martín-Estudillo and Nicholas Spadaccini, vol. 8 of *Hispanic Issues On Line*, Fall 2011, pp. 158–69.

McDonough, Kelly S. *The Learned Ones: Nahua Intellectuals in Postconquest Mexico*. U of Arizona P, 2014.

McKenna, Susan M. "Rational Thought and Female Poetics in Sor Juana's 'Primero sueño': The Circumvention of Two Traditions." *Hispanic Review*, vol. 68, no. 1, Winter 2000, pp. 37–52.

McNee, Malcolm. *The Environmental Imaginary in Brazilian Poetry and Art*. Palgrave Macmillan, 2014.

Medeiros, Sérgio. *Vegetal Sex*. Translated by Raymond Bianchi, U of New Orleans P, 2011.

Medina, Rubén. *Perros habitados por las voces del desierto*. Aldus, 2014.

Medina Portillo, David. "Vanguardias de salón." *Letras libres*, 23 Dec. 2014. www.letraslibres.com/mexico/libros/vanguardias-salon.

Medusario: Muestra de poesía latinoamericana. Edited by Roberto Echavarren et al., Fondo de Cultura Económica, 1996.

Melin, Charlotte. "Between the Lines: When Culture, Language and Poetry Meet in the Classroom." *Language Teaching*, vol. 43, 2010, pp. 349–65.

Melo Neto, João Cabral de. *Education by Stone: Selected Poems*. Translated by Richard Zenith, Archipelago, 2005.

Menos días aquí. menosdiasaqui.blogspot.com.

Mesa Gancedo, Daniel. "El poema extenso como institución cultural: Forma poética e identidad americana en Bello, Heredia y Echeverría." *Nueva revista de filología hispánica*, vol. 56, no. 1, 2008, pp. 87–122.

Mignolo, Walter D. "Colonial and Postcolonial Discourse: Cultural Critique or Academic Colonialism." *Latin American Research Review*, vol. 28, no. 3, 1993, pp. 120–34.

———. *The Idea of Latin America*. Blackwell, 2005.

Miranda, Antonio, editor. *Portal da Poesia Iberoamericana*, www.antoniomiranda .com.br/poesia_ingles/brazilian_poetry_index.html.

Mistral, Gabriela. *Poesías completas*. 2nd ed., Editorial Andrés Bello, 2004.

Mitchell, W. J. Thomas. *Iconology: Image, Text, Ideology*. U of Chicago P, 1986.

Mithen, Steven. *The Singing Neanderthals: The Origins of Music, Language, Mind and Body*. Harvard UP, 2006.

Mohamed, Feisal G. "Poignancy as Human Rights Aesthetic." *Journal of Human Rights*, vol. 9, no. 2, 2010, pp. 143–60.

Molloy, Sylvia. "Dos lecturas del cisne." González and Ortega, pp. 14–18.

Mora, Tulio. "Mario Santiago: Un zapatista disfrazado de pachuco." *Consejos de 1 discípulo de Marx a 1 fanático de Heidegger: Edición crítica*, edited by Rubén Medina, Matadero, 2016, pp. 167–76.

Morales, Mario Roberto. "A fuego lento: El dilema identitario de los ladinos." *Siglo veintiuno*, opinion sec., 4 Nov. 2003.

Morejón, Nancy. *Looking Within / Mirar adentro: Selected Poems / Poemas escogidos, 1954–2000*. Wayne State UP, 2003.

Motta, Waldo. *Bundos e outros poemas*. Unicamp, 1996.

Nelson, Diane. *A Finger in the Wound: Body Politics in Quincentennial Guatemala*. U of California P, 1999.

Neruda, Pablo. *Canción de gesta*. Seix Barral, 1983.

———. *Canto general*. Edited by Enrico Mario Santí, Cátedra, 1990.

———. *Estravagario*. Losada, 1971.

———. "Explico algunas cosas." *I Explain a Few Things: Selected Poems*, edited by Ilán Stavans. Farrar, Straus and Giroux, 2007, pp. 28–29.

———. *Heights of Macchu Picchu*. Bilingual edition. Translated by Tomás Q. Morín, Copper Canyon Press, 2014.

———. *Odas elementales*. Edited by Jaime Concha, Cátedra, 1982.

———. *Odes to Common Things*. Selected and illustrated by Ferris Cook, translated by Ken Krabbenhoft, Bulfinch, 1994.

———. *Residencia en la tierra*. 1933, 1937, 1947. Edited by Hernán Loyola, Cátedra, 1987.

———. "Sobre una poesía sin pureza." Schwartz, pp. 522–23.

———. *Toward the Splendid City: Nobel Lecture*. Farrar, Straus, Giroux, 1974.

———. *Veinte poemas de amor y una canción desesperada*. Vintage Español, 2010.

Nómez, Naín. Prologue. *Escrito en Rokha: Antología poética de Pablo de Rokha*. Universidad de Talca, 2013.

Nostalgia de la luz. Directed by Patricio Guzmán, Icarus Films, 2011.

Nussbaum, Martha. *Not for Profit: Why Democracy Needs the Humanities*. Princeton UP, 2010.

"Oda a las cosas." *YouTube*, uploaded by Víctor Silva González, 19 Dec. 2012.

O'Donnell, Guillermo. "Modernización." *Diccionario de Ciencias Sociales*, Instituto de Estudios Sociales, 1976.

Olivera-Williams, María Rosa. "Feminine Voices in Exile." *Engendering the Word: Feminine Essays in Psychosexual Poetics*, edited by Themma F. Berg et al., U of Illinois P, 1989, pp. 151–66.

Olmedo, José Joaquín de. "La victoria de Junín: Canto a Bolívar." *Poesías completas de José Joaquín de Olmedo*, edited by Aurelio Espinosa Pólit, Fondo de Cultura Económica, 1947, pp. 122–52.

Oquendo de Amat, Carlos, et al. *5 metros de poemas*. 1927. *5 Meters of Poems = 5 metros de poemas*. Ugly Duckling Presse, 2010.

Ordoñez Charpentier, Angélica. "El futuro en la tradición: La identidad Afro desde el Consejo Regional de Palenques." *Informe final del concurso: Culturas e identidades en América Latina y el Caribe*, Programa Regional de Becas Clacso, 2001, bibliotecavirtual.clacso.org.ar/ar/libros/becas/2000/ordonez.pdf.

Ortiz Domínguez, Efrén. *La rosa en fuga*. Xalapa, U Veracruzana, 2001.

Osborne, Randall E., et al. "Student Effects of Service-Learning: Tracking Change across a Semester." *Michigan Journal of Community Service Learning*, vol. 5, Fall 1998, pp. 5–13.

Otzoy, Irma. "Maya Clothing and Identity." Fischer and Brown, pp. 141–55.

Palés Matos, Luis. *Tuntún de pasa y grifería*. Sucesión Luis Palés Matos, 1979.

Paredes, Américo, and Richard Bauman. *Folklore and Culture on the Texas-Mexican Border*. CMAS Books / Center for Mexican American Studies, U of Texas at Austin, 1993.

Parmar, Priya, and Bryonn Bain. "Spoken Word and Hip Hop: The Power of Urban Art and Culture." *Teaching City Kids: Understanding and Appreciating Them*, edited by Joe L. Kincheloe and Kecia Hayes, Peter Lang, 2007, pp. 131–56.

Parra, Nicanor. *Antipoems: How to Look Better and Feel Great*. Translated by Liz Werner, New Directions Press, 2004.

———. "Manifiesto." *Obras completas & algo + (1934–1972)*, Círculo de Lectores, 2007, p. 146.

———. *Obra gruesa*. Andrés Bello, 1983.

Paz, Octavio. *El arco y la lira*. Fondo de Cultura Económica, 1986.

———. *Blanco*. Joaquín Mortiz, 1967.

———. *The Bow and the Lyre: The Poem, the Poetic Revelation, Poetry and History*. Translated by Ruth L. Simms, U of Texas P, 1973.

———. *The Collected Poems of Octavio Paz, 1957–1987*. Edited and translated by Eliot Weinberger, New Directions Press, 1987.

———. "Contar y cantar (sobre el poema extenso)." *La otra voz: Poesía y fin de siglo*, by Paz, Seix Barral, 1990, pp. 11–30.

———. *Los hijos del limo: Del romanticismo a la vanguardia*. Seix Barral, 1974.

———. *Sor Juana Inés de la Cruz o las trampas de la fe*. Fondo de Cultura Económica, 1982.

———. "Speaking in Tongues." *Convergences: Essays on Art and Literature*, translated by Helen Lane, Harcourt Brace Jovanovich, 1987, pp. 1–14.

―――. *Sunstone / Piedra de sol.* Translated by Eliot Weinberger. New Directions, 1991.

Paz, Octavio, and Vicente Rojo. *Discos visuales.* Ediciones Era, 1968.

Pérez Firmat, Gustavo. *Life on the Hyphen: The Cuban American Way.* U of Texas P, 1994.

Perloff, Marjorie. "Crisis in the Humanities? Reconfiguring Literary Study for the Twenty-First Century." *Theory's Empire: An Anthology of Dissent,* edited by Daphne Patai and Will H. Corral, Columbia UP, 2005, pp. 668–83.

―――. *Differentials: Poetry, Poetics, Pedagogy.* U of Alabama P, 2004.

―――. "From Avant-Garde to Digital: The Legacy of Brazilian Concrete Poetry." Perloff, *Unoriginal Genius,* pp. 50–75.

―――. "Teaching the 'New' Poetries." marjorieperloff.com/essays/armantrout -poetries.

―――. *Unoriginal Genius: Poetry by Other Means in the New Century.* U of Chicago P, 2010.

Perrone, Charles A. "Backland Bards: From Fine Folk Verse to Lofty Lapidary Lyric." *Review: Literature and Arts of the Americas,* vol. 49, nos. 1–2, 2017, pp. 35–42.

―――. *Brazil, Lyric, and the Americas.* UP of Florida, 2010.

―――. "Brazil, Poetry of." Greene et al., pp. 160–64.

―――. "Carlos Drummond de Andrade." *Cambridge Companion to Latin American Poetry,* Cambridge UP, 2018, 152–62.

―――. "4 × 3 × 2 = Quadrangulating Triangular Pairs: Simultaneous Versions of a Vital Concrete Poem." *Tradução em revista,* no. 6, 2009, pp. 1–17, www .maxwell.lambda.ele.puc-rio.br/trad_em_revista.php?strSecao=input0.

―――. *Letras e Letras da MPB.* 1988. 2nd ed., Booklink, 2008.

―――. *Masters of Contemporary Brazilian Song: MPB 1965–1985.* U of Texas P, 1989.

―――. "Seven Brazilian Poets. Translation and Commentary." *Delos: A Journal of Translation and World Literature,* Third Series, no. 31, 2016, pp. 85–95.

―――. *Seven Faces: Brazilian Poetry since Modernism.* Duke UP, 1996.

―――. "Shared Passages: Spanish American–Brazilian Links in Contemporary Poetry." *Beyond Tordesillas: Critical Essays in Comparative Luso-Hispanic Studies,* edited by Robert Patrick Newcomb and Richard A. Gordon. Ohio State UP, 2017, 162–72.

―――. "Signs of Intercourse: Material Poetry and Erotic Imperatives." *Gragoatá: Revista dos programas de pós-graduação do Instituto de Letras da Universidade Federal Fluminense,* vol. 8, no. 14, 2003, pp. 197–218.

Pianacci, Rómulo E. *Antígona: Una tragedia latinoamericana.* Ediciones Gestos, 2008.

Pignatari, Décio. "Situação atual da poesia no Brasil." *Invenção: Revista de Arte de Vanguarda,* no. 1, 1962, pp. 51–70.

Pizarnik, Alejandra. *Extracting the Stone of Madness: Poems 1962–1972.* Translated by Yvette Siegert, New Directions, 2016.

Pizarro, Diana. "Las dos fieras que soy." *Revista Prometeo,* nos. 102–103, July 2015, pp. 240–42.

Pluecker, John, translator. *Antígona González*. By Sara Uribe, Les Figues, 2016.

Poe, Edgar Allan. "The Poetic Principle." www.bartleby.com/28/14.html.

Posada, Felipe. "Sueño." *Revista Prometeo*, nos. 102–103, July 2015, pp. 255–57.

Pratt, Mary Louise. "Arts of the Contact Zone." *Profession*, 1991, pp. 33–40.

———. "Women, Literature and National Brotherhood." *Women, Culture, and Politics in Latin America*, edited by Emille Bergmann et al., U of California P, 1990, pp. 48–73.

Preciado, Antonio. *De lo demás al barrio*. El Ángel Editor, 2013.

"Presentation on the Kaqchikel Language by Linguist Nikte Sis Iboy, in Achi." *YouTube*, uploaded by Sorosoro, 27 Apr. 2010, www.youtube.com/watch?v =kTByrFmp1IM.

Pring-Mill, Robert. "The Redemption of Reality through Documentary Poetry." Introduction. Cardenal, *Zero Hour*, pp. ix–xxi.

Pullum, Geoffrey. "Nervous Cluelessness." *Language Log*, languagelog.ldc.upenn .edu/nll/?p=1357.

Quijano, Aníbal. "Coloniality of Power, Eurocentrism, and Latin America." *Nepantla: Views from the South*, vol. 1, no. 3, 2000, pp. 533–80.

Quiroga, José. "Spanish American Poetry from 1922 to 1975." *The Cambridge History of Latin American Literature*, edited by R. Echevarría and E. Pupo-Walker, Cambridge UP, 1996, pp. 303–64. doi:10.1017/CHOL978052134 0700.012.

———. "Translating Vowels and the Defeat of Sounds." *Translating Latin America: Culture as Context*, edited by William Luis and Julio Rodríguez, Center for Research in Translation, 1991, pp. 317–23.

Rabatté y Cervi, Anamaría. *En vida, hermano, en vida*. Tres Lunas, 1990.

Ramírez, Elisa. Review of *Sk'eoj jme'tik U / Cantos de Luna* by Enriqueta Lunez. *Latin American Literature Today*, vol. 1, no. 3, Summer 2017, www.latina mericanliteraturetoday.org/en/2017/july/sk'eoj-jme'tik-u-cantos-de-luna-enri queta-lunez.

Reents-Budet, Dorie. *Painting the Maya Universe: Royal Ceramics of the Classic Period*. 2nd ed., Duke U Museum of Art / Duke UP, 1994.

Retallack, Joan, and Juliana Spahr, editors. *Poetry and Pedagogy: The Challenge of the Contemporary*. Palgrave, 2006.

"El retorno de la serpiente: 10 momentos de Mathías Goeritz." *Revista Código: Arte, arquitectura, diseño*, 14 Dec. 2014, www.revistacodigo.com/el-retorno-de -la-serpiente-10-momentos-de-mathias-goeritz/.

Retrofutura. "Chilanga banda / Jaime López (1995)." *Algarabía*, 4 June 2013, algarabia.com/desde-la-redaccion/chilanga-banda-jaime-lopez-1995/.

Rimbaud, Arthur. *Rimbaud: Complete Works, Selected Letters, a Bilingual Edition*. Edited by Jean Nicholas, U of Chicago P, 2005.

Rivera Garza, Cristina. *Los muertos indóciles*. Tusquets, 2013.

Rocha Vivas, Miguel, editor. *Antes el amanecer. Antología de las literaturas indígenas de los Andes y la Sierra Nevada de Santa Marta*. Ministerio de Cultura de Colombia, 2010.

———. *Palabras mayores, palabras vivas: Tradiciones mítico-literarias y escritores indígenas en Colombia*. Taurus, 2012.

————, editor. *El sol babea jugo de piña: antología de las literaturas indígenas del Atlántico, el Pacífico y la Serranía del Perijá.* Ministerio de Cultura de Colombia, 2010.

Rodríguez, Ileana, and Mónica Szurmuk, editors. *The Cambridge History of Latin American Women's Literature.* Cambridge UP, 2015.

Romano, Gustavo. *IP Poetry.* Catalog, Museo Extremeño e Iberoamericano de Arte Contemporáneo, Consejería de Cultura y Turismo, 2008.

————. *The IP Poetry Project.* English version, 2004–2015, ip-poetry.findelmundo .com.ar/index-en.html.

Ronda, Margaret. "'Outside of Knowledge': On the Poet-Scholar." *Jacket 2,* 8 June 2015.

Rosenberg, Fernando. *After Human Rights: Literature, Visual Arts, and Film in Latin America, 1990–2010.* U of Pittsburgh P, 2016.

Rosenblatt, Louise. *The Reader, the Text and the Poem: The Transactional Theory of the Literary Work.* Southern Illinois UP, 1978.

Rowe, William. *Hacia una poética radical: Ensayos de hermenéutica cultural.* Beatriz Viterbo Editora, 1996.

————. "Latin American Poetry." *The Cambridge Companion to Modern Latin American Culture,* edited by John King, Cambridge UP, 2004, pp. 136–70.

————. *Poets of Contemporary Latin America: History and the Inner Life.* Oxford UP, 2000.

Ruíz Pérez, Ignacio. "Contra-escrituras: Delmira Agustini, Alfonsina Storni y la subversión del modernismo." *Revista Hispánica Moderna,* vol. 61, no. 2, Dec. 2008, pp. 183–96.

Rukeyser, Muriel. *The Life of Poetry.* Kraus Reprint, 1968.

Sabat de Rivers, Georgina. *El "sueño" de Sor Juana Inés de la Cruz: Tradiciones literarias y originalidad.* Temesis Books, 1976.

Salomão, Waly. *Algaravias Echo Chamber.* 1996. Translated by Maryam Monalisa Gharavi, Ugly Duckling Presse, 2016.

Santacruz, Rana. "Te quiero ver llorar." *Por ahí,* Chicavasco Music, 2015.

"Santiago Punk. Carmen Berenguer Poeta (Chile). El Baúl de Beats." Beat by Xino Lara. *SoundCloud,* uploaded by El Baúl de Beats, 2012, soundcloud.com /bauldebeats/sntiago-punk-carmen-berenguer.

Santos, Alessandra. *Arnaldo Canibal Antunes.* NVersos, 2013.

Sarduy, Severo. "El barroco y el neobarroco." *América Latina en su literatura.* Edited by César Fernández Moreno, Siglo XXI, 1972, pp. 167–84.

Scarino, Angela. "Assessing Intercultural Capability in Learning Languages: A Renewed Understanding of Language, Culture, Learning, and the Nature of Assessment." *Modern Language Journal* vol. 94, no. 2, Summer 2010, pp. 324–29.

Schopf, Federico. *El desorden de las imágenes: Vicente Huidobro, Pablo Neruda, Nicanor Parra.* Editorial Universitaria, 2010.

Schulman, Iván A. *El modernismo hispanoamericano.* Centro Editor de América Latina, 1969.

Schwartz, Jorge, editor. *Las vanguardias latinoamericanas: Textos programáticos y críticos.* Fondo de Cultura Económica, 2002.

Scruggs, T. M. "Socially Conscious Music Forming the Social Conscience: Nicaraguan *Música Testimonial* and the Creation of a Revolutionary Moment." *From*

Tejano to Tango: Latin American Popular Music, edited by Walter Aaron Clark, Routledge, 2002, pp. 41–69.

Seaton, Maureen. "The Queerosphere: Musings on Queer Studies and Creative Writing Classrooms (*On Poetry, Creativity, and the Fleetingness of Things*)." *Queer Girls in Class: Lesbian Teachers and Students Tell Their Classroom Stories*, edited by Lori Horvitz, Peter Lang, 2011, pp. 39–42.

Sefamí, Jacobo. "Mexico, Poetry of." *The Princeton Encyclopedia of Poetry and Poetics, Fourth Edition*. Edited by Roland Greene, et al. Princeton UP, 2012, pp. 879–83.

Shakespeare, William. *The Globe Illustrated Shakespeare: The Complete Works*. Edited by Howard Staunton, Gramercy Books, 2002.

Sheller, Mimi, and John Urry. "The New Mobilities Paradigm." *Environment and Planning A*, vol. 38, January 2005, pp. 207–26.

Shellhorse, Adam J. "The Explosion of the Letter: The Crisis of the Poetic and Representation in João Cabral de Melo Neto's *Morte e vida severina: Auto de Natal pernambucano*." *Luso-Brazilian Review*, vol. 50, no. 1, 2013, pp. 201–28.

———. "Subversions of the Sensible: The Poetics of *Antropofagia* in Brazilian Concrete Poetry." *Anti-Literature: The Politics and Limits of Representation in Modern Brazil and Argentina*, U Pittsburgh P, 2016, 70–95.

Shook, David, and Víctor Terán, editors. *Like a New Sun: New Indigenous Mexican Poetry*. Phoneme Media, 2015.

Showalter, Elaine. *Teaching Literature*. Blackwell, 2003.

Simmons, Andrew. "Why Teaching Poetry Is So Important." *The Atlantic*, April 8, 2014, www.theatlantic.com/education/archive/2014/04/why-teaching-poetry -is-so-important/360346/.

Slater, Candace. *Stories on a String: The Brazilian Literatura de Cordel*. U of California Press, 1982.

Smith-Spark, Laura. "Bob Dylan Wins 2016 Nobel Prize for Literature." CNN, 13 Oct. 2016, www.cnn.com/2016/10/13/world/nobel-prize-literature/.

"Sobre el poema de Nezahualcóyotl que aparece en los billetes de 100 pesos." 12 June 2014. comoespinademaguey.tumblr.com/post/88614744249/sobre-el -poema-de-nezahualc%C3%B3yotl-que-aparece-en.

"Sobrevivencia—El grito." *YouTube*, uploaded by Elias Itzep, 24 Aug. 2009, www.youtube.com/watch?v=ddtznmd1v-M.

Sommer, Doris. *The Work of Art in the World. Civic Agency and Public Humanities*. Duke UP, 2014.

Spurlin, William, editor. *Lesbian and Gay Studies and the Teaching of English: Positions, Pedagogies, and Cultural Politics*. National Council of Teachers of English, 2000.

Stavans, Ilan, editor. *The FSG Book of Twentieth-Century Latin American Poetry*. Farrar, Straus and Giroux, 2011.

Steiner, George. *Antigones*. Oxford UP, 1982.

Sterk Barrett, Michelle. "CBL Assessment Data." Received by Bridget Franco, 7 Jan. 2015.

Stewart, Susan. *Poetry and the Fate of the Senses*. U of Chicago P, 2002.

St. Martin, Hardie, editor and translator. *Dark Times Filled with Light: The Selected Work of Juan Gelman*. Open Letter P, 2012.

Storni, Alfonsina. "Carta lírica a otra mujer." *Obras completas.* Sociedad Editora Latino Americana, 1976, pp. 196–98.

Strong, Beret. *The Poetic Avant-Garde: The Groups of Borges, Auden, and Breton.* Northwestern UP, 1997.

Sui Generis. "Canción para mi muerte." *Vida,* Microfon, 1972.

Sullivan, Clare. "'I Am Those We Are Here': Multiplying Indigenous Voices through Poetic Translation." *CR: The New Centennial Review,* vol. 16, no. 1, Spring 2016, pp. 195–211.

Tablada, José Juan. "Impresión de la Habana." 1919. *"Li-Po" y otros poemas,* by Tablada, Consejo Nacional para la Cultura y las Artes (Conaculta), 2005.

Tandeciarz, Silvia. "Reconquest." Translation of "Reconquista" by Juana Goergen, *Tameme* vol. 1, no. 3, 2003, pp. 38–43.

———. "Translator's Notes." *Tameme* vol. 1, no. 3, 2003, pp. 216–22.

Tapscott, Stephen, editor. *Twentieth-Century Latin American Poetry: A Bilingual Anthology.* U of Texas P, 1996.

Taylor, Diana. *The Archive and the Repertoire: Performing Cultural Memory in the Americas.* Duke UP, 2003.

Tedlock, Dennis. "Toward a Poetics of Polyphony and Translatability." *Close Listening: Poetry and the Performed Word,* edited by Charles Bernstein, Oxford UP, 1998, pp. 178–99.

Tenorio-Trillo, Mauricio. *Latin America: The Allure and Power of an Idea.* U of Chicago P, 2017.

Toledo, Natalia. *The Black Flower and Other Zapotec Poems.* Translated by Clare Sullivan, Phoneme Media, 2015.

———. "From *The Black Flower and Other Zapotec Poems.*" *Asymptote,* translated by Natalia Toledo and Clare Sullivan, read by Natalia Toledo, www.asymptotejournal.com/poetry/natalia-toledo-the-black-flower-and-other-zapotec-poems.

Tomlinson, Gary. *Singing the New World: Indigenous Voice in the Era of European Contact.* Cambridge UP, 2007.

Torres, George. "The Bolero Romántico: From Cuban Dance to International Popular Song." *From Tejano to Tango: Latin American Popular Music,* edited by Walter Aaron Clark, Routledge, 2002, pp. 151–71.

Trueblood, Alan S., translator. *A Sor Juana Anthology.* Harvard UP, 1988.

Tummons, Emily, et al. "'So that We Don't Lose Words': Reconstructing a Kaqchikel Medical Lexicon." *Proceedings of the First Biennial Symposium on Teaching Indigenous Languages in Latin America,* 14–16 Aug. 2008, edited by Serafín M. Coronel-Molina and John H. McDowell, Indiana UP, 2010, pp. 127–35.

Turino, Thomas. *Moving Away from Silence: Music of the Peruvian Altiplano and the Experience of Urban Migration.* U of Chicago P, 1993.

United Nations. Universal Declaration of Human Rights. 1948, www.un.org/en/universal-declaration-human-rights.

Unruh, Vicky. *Latin American Vanguards: The Art of Contentious Encounters.* U of California P, 1994.

———. *Performing Women and Modern Literary Culture in Latin America: Intervening Acts.* U of Texas P, 2006.

Uribe, Sara. *Antígona González.* Sur+ ediciones, 2012.

Valencia, Elcina. *Todos somos culpables. Poemas y cantos*. Imprenta Departamental del Valle del Cauca, 1993.

Vallejo, César. *The Complete Poetry: A Bilingual Edition*. Edited and translated by Clayton Eshleman. U of California P, 2007.

———. *Obra poética*. Edited by Américo Ferrari, ALLCA XX, 1988.

———. *Obras completas*. Tomo I. *Obra poética*. Edición crítica, prólogo y notas de Ricardo González Vigil, Banco de Crédito de Perú, 1991.

———. *Trilce*. Edited by Julio Ortega, Ediciones Cátedra, 1991.

Vaughn, Lisa M., and Gabriela de Cabrera. "Left Alone, the Widows of the War: Trauma Reframed through Community Empowerment in Guatemala." *Feminist Conversations: Women, Trauma, and Empowerment in Post-Transitional Societies*, edited by Dovile Budryte et al., UP of America, 2009, pp. 91–100.

Venegas, Julieta. "Limón y sal." *Limón y sal*, by Venegas, Sony US Latin, 2006.

Vicuña, Cecilia. *Cloud-Net*. Translated by Rosa Alcalá, Art in General, 1999.

———. "An Introduction to Mestizo Poetics." Vicuña and Livon-Grosman, pp. xix–xxxii.

———. *Spit Temple: The Selected Performances of Cecilia Vicuña*. Edited and translated by Rosa Alcalá, Ugly Duckling Presse, 2012.

———. *Unravelling Words and the Weaving of Water*. Edited and introduction by Eliot Weinberger, translated by Eliot Weinberger and Suzanne Jill Levine, Graywolf Press, 1992.

Vicuña, Cecilia, and Ernesto Livon-Grosman. *The Oxford Book of Latin American Poetry: A Bilingual Anthology*. Oxford UP, 2009.

Villaurrutia, Xavier. "Juana Inés de la Cruz." *Obras*, Fondo de Cultura Económica, 1974, pp. 773–85.

Villoro, Juan. "El copiloto del Impala." *La Jornada Semanal*, 18 July 1999, www.jornada.unam.mx/1999/07/19/sem-villoro.html.

Virgillo, Carmelo, et al., editors. *Aproximaciones al estudio de la literatura hispánica*. 7th ed., McGraw-Hill, 2012.

Vizcaíno, María Argelia. "Aspectos de 'La Guantanamera.'" *La Página de José Martí*, 1998, web.archive.org/web/20060714233125/http://www.josemarti.org/jose_marti/guantanamera/mariaargeliaguan/guantanameraparte1-1.htm.

Volpi, Jorge. "Bolaño, epidemia." *Revista de la Universidad de México*, vol. 49, no. 4, 2008, pp. 77–84.

Waldman, Anne. "Intriguing Objects Exercise / Show and Tell (for a Group)." Behn and Twichell, pp. 35–36.

Walsh, Catherine, and Juan García Salazar. "(W)righting Collective Memory (De)spite State: Decolonial Practices of Existence in Ecuador." *Black Writing, Culture, and the State in Latin America*, edited by Jerome C. Branche, Vanderbilt UP, 2015, pp. 253–66.

Warren, Kay B. *Indigenous Movements and Their Critics: Pan-Maya Activism in Guatemala*. Princeton UP, 1998.

Washbourne, Kelly. "Teaching Literary Translation: Objectives, Epistemologies, and Methods for the Workshop." *Translation Review*, vol. 86, no. 1, 2013, pp. 49–66.

Wasser, Audrey. *The Work of Difference: Modernism, Romanticism, and the Production of Literary Form*. Fordham UP, 2016.

Waters, Michael. "Auction: First Lines (for a Group)." Behn and Twichell, pp. 15–16.

Weinberger, Eliot, translator. *Altazor; or, A Voyage in a Parachute*, by Vicente Huidobro, revised ed., Wesleyan UP, 2003.

Weintraub, Scott. *Juan Luis Martínez's Philosophical Poetics*. Bucknell UP, 2015.

Williams, Frederick G., translator. *Poets of Brazil: A Bilingual Selection*. BYU Studies / EUFBA, 2004.

Williams, Tamara R. "Ernesto Cardenal's *El estrecho dudoso*: Reading/Rewriting History." *Revista Canadiense de Estudios Hispánicos*, vol. 15, no. 1, Fall 1988, pp. 111–12.

———. "La historia como resurrección: Rastros y rostros de Jules Michelet en el *Canto general*." *Anales de la Literatura Chilena*, no. 10, Dec. 2008, pp. 69–82.

———. "Literatura al segundo grado: Literariedad y compromiso social en *El diario que a diario* de Nicolás Guillén." *Nicolás Guillén: hispanidad, vanguardia, y compromiso social*, Ediciones de la U de Castilla–La Mancha, 2002, pp. 471–81.

———. "Queering the *Auto Sacramental*: Anti-heteronormative Parody and the Specter of Silence in Luis Felipe Fabre's *La sodomía en la Nueva España*." *Colonial Itineraries of Contemporary Mexico*, edited by Oswaldo Estrada and Anna M. Nogar, U of Arizona P, 2014, pp. 103–25.

———. "Wounded Nation, Voided State: Sara Uribe's *Antígona González*." *Romance Notes*, vol. 57, no. 1, 2017, pp. 3–14.

Williams, William Carlos. *The Collected Poems of William Carlos Williams. Vol. I: 1909–1939*. Edited by A. Walton Litz and Christopher MacGowan, New Directions, 1986.

Willis, Bruce Dean. "Tradition and Innovation in Mexican Pastorelas and Posadas." *Gestos*, vol. 21, no. 41, April 2006, pp. 41–58.

Wood, Andrés, director. *Violeta se fue a los cielos*. Wood Producciones, 2011.

Wood, Andrew Grant. *Agustín Lara: A Cultural Biography*. Oxford UP, 2014.

Wood, María Elena, director. *Locas mujeres*, Ingeniovisual, Wood Producciones, Televisión Nacional de Chile, 2011.

World-Readiness Standards for Learning Languages. 4th ed., National Standards in Foreign Language Education Project and American Council on the Teaching of Foreign Languages, 2015.

Worley, Paul M. *Telling and Being Told: Storytelling and Cultural Control in Contemporary Yucatec Maya Literatures*. U of Arizona P, 2013.

Xerri, Daniel. "'Poems Look Like a Mathematical Equation': Assessment in Poetry Education." *International Journal of English Studies*, vol. 16, no. 1, 2016, pp. 1–17.

Yépez, Heriberto. "Otro golpe de los infras." *Laberinto*, 11 Oct. 2014, p. 12.

Yool Gómez, Kaqjay Juan. *Pach'un tzij kichin ak'wala': Poesía infantil en idioma kaqchikel*. CEDIM/FAFO, 1996.

Zavala, Oswaldo. "El Chapo, fetiche de la corrupción oficial." *Proceso*, 4 February, 2016, www.proceso.com.mx/428847/la-recaptura-de-el-chapo-y-la-conquista-mediatica-del-estado.

Ziru, Wu. "The Chinese Edition of Bolaño's '2666' Newly Released." *Global Times*, 25 Dec. 2011, www.globaltimes.cn/content/689780.shtml.

Zlotkowski, Edward. *Successful Service-Learning Programs: New Models of Excellence in Higher Education*. Anker, 1998.

Zournazi, Mary. "Navigating Movements: A Conversation with Brian Massumi." *Hope: New Philosophies for Change*, Routledge, 2003, pp. 210–42.

Zurita, Raúl. *Anteparaíso*. Editores Asociados, 1982.

———. *Purgatorio*. Editorial Universitaria, 1979.

———. *Purgatory*. Translated by Anna Deeny, U of California P, 2009.

———. *La vida nueva*. Editorial Universitaria, 1994.